ESSAYS IN QUANTITATIVE
ECONOMIC HISTORY

ESSAYS IN
QUANTITATIVE
ECONOMIC
HISTORY

EDITED, FOR THE ECONOMIC HISTORY SOCIETY,
AND WITH AN INTRODUCTION BY RODERICK FLOUD

CLARENDON PRESS · OXFORD
1974

Oxford University Press, Ely House, London W. 1

GLASGOW NEW YORK TORONTO MELBOURNE WELLINGTON
CAPE TOWN IBADAN NAIROBI DAR ES SALAAM LUSAKA ADDIS ABABA
DELHI BOMBAY CALCUTTA MADRAS KARACHI LAHORE DACCA
KUALA LUMPUR SINGAPORE HONG KONG TOKYO

CASEBOUND ISBN 0 19 877018 9
PAPERBACK ISBN 0 19 877019 7

© OXFORD UNIVERSITY PRESS 1974

TEXT SET IN 11PT. PHOTON TIMES ROMAN, PRINTED BY PHOTOLITHOGRAPHY,
AND BOUND IN GREAT BRITAIN AT THE PITMAN PRESS, BATH

Preface

I am grateful to the Economic History Society and to the past and present Chairmen of its Publications Committee, Professor W. Ashworth and Professor J. R. Harris, both for giving me the opportunity to edit this volume and for the help and advice which I have received during its preparation. Professor D. C. Coleman, Professor P. Mathias, Professor A. Fishlow, Dr. G. Hawke, Dr. M. Walsh, Mr. N. von Tunzelmann, Mr. M. Falkus, and Mr. G. Crossick have read my introduction in draft form, and I am very grateful to them for their many helpful and critical comments. Above all, I am grateful to my wife, who as usual has cheerfully borne a heavy burden of discussion of successive drafts.

I am also happy to thank the authors who have allowed me to reprint their articles, and the editors and publishers of the journals in which they first appeared: Professor R. C. O. Matthews and the Manchester Statistical Society; Professor E. Ames, Professor A. G. Ford and the *Journal of Economic History*; Dr. R. S. Schofield, Mr. J. P. Cooper, Professor L. Soltow, Professor D. K. Adie and the *Economic History Review*; Professor D. Felix, Professor L. G. Sandberg, Professor M. Olson and Mr. C. C. Harris Jr. and the *Quarterly Journal of Economics*; Professor G. Ohlin and Professor H. Rosovsky and John Wiley and Sons Inc. My thanks are also due to the staff of the Clarendon Press for their help and encouragement.

Emmanuel College, Cambridge

RODERICK FLOUD

Contents

R. C. O. Matthews *Drummond Professor of Political Economy,
University of Oxford*

Introduction

ECONOMIC historians have always made use of quantitative evidence, and their articles and books have often contained tables, graphs, and numbers. Until recently, however, the statistical techniques which they used to exploit their evidence were few in number; averages might be calculated, but rarely measures of dispersion such as standard deviations, and even more rarely did economic historians make use of such techniques as correlation and regression analysis, tests of significance or other sampling methods, time series analysis or scaling methods. Recently, however, stimulated by the development of econometrics and quantitative methods in the other social sciences, and by the increasing use of computers, economic historians have turned to the use of such methods to enable them to analyse the huge mass of quantitative data on the economic history of past societies.

Although the use of methods of statistical analysis, combined with the explicit use of models of historical and economic processes and computers, has been a recent phenomenon in the history of the subject, it is already clear that it has contributed a great deal to the discussion of problems of economic history. This is demonstrated both by the articles which are reprinted in this volume and by the work of the 'new' or 'econometric' economic historian in the United States.[1] At the same time, these new methods embody a series of changing techniques, in statistics, economics, and econometrics, and in computing; since the techniques are new and unfamiliar, it has inevitably taken some time for knowledge of them to spread, for scholars to appreciate the potentialities in the application of a particular technique to a particular problem, and for students to be trained to understand the new methods and the results of their use. The difficulty has been particularly acute because the new techniques derive largely from the world of the social and mathematical sciences, but must be applied to a subject in the humanist historical tradition; there has therefore been a delay before the findings of the quantifiers have been successfully integrated with the conclusions of those who have used other methods of historical enquiry. Equally, some of the quantifiers have been slow to understand the pitfalls encountered in working with inadequate or biased historical evidence. Furthermore, for a variety of historical and educational reasons, most students and teachers in the field of economic history in Great Britain have been trained either as social scientists or as historians, not as both; if they are to understand and use in their own work both the approach of the social scientist and the approach of the historian they must therefore make a late, and often difficult, tran-

---

[1] Examples of the latter are R. W. Fogel and S. L. Engerman (1971); R. W. Fogel (1964); A. Fishlow (1965); A. H. Conrad and J. R. Meyer (1965). Footnote references are given to author and date of publication; full details may be found in the Bibliography below.

sition to an understanding of the other tradition. The purpose of this volume, and of this introduction, is therefore to attempt to ease the transition in one direction, towards the increased understanding and use of quantitative methods by historians. It is not implied that this transition poses greater problems than the alternative transition from an expertise in social science methodology towards an understanding of historical problems, but it is believed that economic historians may find it useful to possess a selection of articles which make use of the major methods of statistical inquiry. The articles have, therefore, been chosen with three aims in mind. These are, first, that the article should be concerned with a topic of substantive interest to economic historians; second, that it should be an exemplar of a particular statistical technique, and, third, that it should be concerned primarily with the economic history of Britain, since there exist a number of similar collections of articles relating to the economic history of the United States.[2]

The majority of the articles are concerned, implicitly or explicitly, with the exploration and testing of hypotheses about historical events, hypotheses which have been framed on the basis of established economic theory. In this sense, they fall within what has been called the 'new' economic history, or 'econometric history', and, like many other examples of that type of economic history, they may seem open to the objection that they are divorced from reality, that they consider only a few measurable phenomena, and ignore the complexity of history. This criticism of the 'new' economic history misses the point; the 'new' economic historian concentrates on measurable economic phenomena, and uses economic theory linking those phenomena, specifically because he wishes to cut through the complexity of history and to concentrate on those phenomena which best explain the events he is studying. As an econometrician has put it: 'The purpose of theory [is] to distil from a complicated reality those important elements that explain a large part of the observed phenomena.'[3] It is precisely for this reason that the methods of econometrics, that branch of economics which is concerned with the testing of economic theory by the use of statistical methods, are such powerful tools for the economic historian. These methods, correlation and regression analysis being perhaps the most widely known, permit and force those who use them to state clearly the hypotheses which they wish to test and the assumptions which they are prepared to make about historical phenomena and historical evidence. In choosing his hypotheses the historian naturally picks those pieces of evidence which he feels will help to explain whatever it is that he wishes to explain, recognizing that he will be leaving much out, and that his explanatory hypotheses will be imperfect, but hoping that he will approach sufficiently close to reality and to an explanation to make the effort worthwhile; the methods of econometrics help to tell him how close he has come to a sufficient explanation, and may

[2] For example, Fogel and Engerman (1971); R. L. Andreano (1970); D. K. Rowney and J. Q. Graham (1969).
[3] A. A. Walters (1968), p. 14.

suggest what he has left out. In all these ways, the methods of the econometrician or of the 'new' economic historian differ radically from the methods of the traditional historian interested only in the aquisition of facts (although it is doubtful whether such an historian has ever existed); the econometrician wishes to pick those few facts which will best explain the phenomena he is investigating, and he uses the theories of economics to suggest which those facts will be. Secondarily, he uses the methods of statistics to tell him whether he was right in his choice, and incidentally whether the theory which he has used was appropriate to the particular problem.

In this introduction, the main emphasis is placed on the methods of statistics. This is not because those methods are regarded as more important that the economic theories which they are used to test, but because, particularly to those trained as historians, the methods of statistics are often more complex and more forbidding than the economic theories used by the 'new' economic historians. The difficulty of understanding the formulae acts as a bar to understanding the theory which underlies them. The comments which are made below on the methods used in the reprinted articles are, therefore, designed to clear away some difficulties stemming from the methods and vocabulary of statistics, and thus to enable the reader to concentrate on the historical and economic hypotheses which are the core of the articles, and of the subject of economic history itself.

Apart from the three aims underlying the selection of particular articles which have already been mentioned, one further aim underlies the selection as a whole, and needs some discussion at this point; this is the aim of demonstrating the importance of integrating the methods of statistics and econometrics with other research methods at all stages of historical research. In the past, many historians have tended to regard the methods of statistics as an extra, a special high-powered tool which can be plugged in, perhaps with the aid of an expert statistician as a consultant, at a late stage in the research, to reveal the truths in the data. This approach to statistics and to the use of computers stems from a belief, normally unconscious, that historical research and enquiry follows a 'linear' model. In this model, research is thought of as proceeding along an approximately straight line, beginning with the questions to be discussed, passing through the specification of a model, through the collection and processing of the evidence, and concluding with the analysis of the results and the answering of the original questions. In this model, different aspects of historical and research methodology are kept separate, each appropriate to its particular segment of the inquiry. Thus economic theory is brought in to specify the modal, computing and data processing methods are called in to help in the collection and reworking of the evidence, statistical methods are plugged in for the analysis of the results, while the superior skills of the historian can be reserved to the tasks at each end of the line, posing and answering the substantive historical questions. Computing and statistics, in particular, are often regarded as technical subjects, with which the historian need not bother; he can employ technicians, advisers, friendly graduate students, to undertake the mechanical tasks, thus jumping painlessly and quickly over the tiresome, unfamiliar segments of the linear research process.[4]

Unfortunately, the linear research model bears very little relation to reality, particularly when the research makes use of quantitative materials and methods; the process of research cannot be segmented in the way which the linear model assumes, nor can it be assumed that research begins at one end of the line and proceeds to the other, without any retracing of steps. Thus the specification of the model forces the historian to return to reformulate his original question, and the work of date collection forces a reappraisal both of the model and of the original question. Just as the linear model is unrealistic, so it is unrealistic to imagine that methods such as computing and statistics can be confined to one segment of research, plugged in when they are needed, but otherwise ignored. The use of these methods forces the historian back to an earlier step, perhaps even back to a reformulation of the question, into a form in which computing and statistics can best contribute to a solution. The process of research, therefore, far from being approximated by a linear form, is circular and multidimensioned, with each step affected by, and affecting, each other step. The corollary is that, if maximum benefit is to be gained from the use of statistics and quantitative methods in general, the historian must integrate these techniques within the process of research, understanding them and keeping them firmly under his own control; he cannot relegate them to 'experts' or 'technicians'.

As an example, R. S. Schofield shows (below pp. 80–84)[5] how simple statistical methodology has to be applied at all stages of an enquiry, from the selection of evidence onwards. Having set out the requirements of the statistical tests which were used by Buckatzsch in his article on the distribution of wealth in England, Schofield shows that the tax returns used by Buckatzsch were not independent of each other, as the tests, and historical common sense, require that they should be. Schofield then uses the criterion of independence, together with other statistical criteria, to help him in his search for other sources of evidence on the distribution of wealth, and to allow him to discriminate between such sources. By these means, he is able to extract, from the very large number of tax assessments made in England between 1334 and 1649, those which are best suited to answering the questions which Buckatzsch had raised. Similarly, E. Ames (pp. 38–42) uses a simple test to allow him to decide between two possible explanations of fluctuations in the value of the English currency in the fourteenth century, and as a result can concentrate attention on one set of possible causes of the fluctuations rather than another. Adie, again, uses correlation analysis to aid his choice of a 'proxy' variable; he had no direct evidence of London bank deposits, but correlation analysis suggested that the number of bank offices could be used as a substitute. This last example illustrates the manner in which a combination of statistics and simple economic

---

[4] For discussion of this attitude, see T. K. Rabb (1967); E. Shorter (1971); R. S. Schofield (1972); Rabb (1972).

[5] Articles reprinted below will be referred to by name of author and by page number.

logic can be used to make up for deficiencies in the available historical evidence. This has been the hallmark of much of the 'new' economic history of the United States.

The articles which are reprinted below show, therefore, the importance to the economic historian of integrating the use of statistical and quantitative techniques within the processes of historical research. They also demonstrate the value to the economic historian of those techniques, and the variety of fields and periods to which they may be applied. That these techniques are valuable has sometimes been denied; some historians have argued that the concentration on measurement distorts historical enquiry, and merely produces precise answers to uninteresting questions. This argument, always rather weak, has been refuted by the increasing number of valuable historical studies making use of quantitative methods, and the debate about the value of such methods in historical work is already itself passing into history.[6] It has to be recognized, however, that the methods used in these articles will be unfamiliar to many historians. It is the purpose of this introduction to explain the most important of these methods, and to fit them into the general framework of statistical analysis, which comprises many more techniques than could possibly have been displayed in this volume. In an introduction of this length, it is impossible to discuss fully either statistical methods as a whole, or, in many cases, the particular techniques which are used in the articles; the aim will be to explain some of the concepts of statistical analysis as they have been applied to historical problems, and to refer the reader to other works for detailed descriptions of, and warnings about, the particular techniques.[7]

The role of statistical methods in economic history is twofold, to provide an adequate and comprehensive description of historical evidence, and to provide a basis for inference from that evidence. In practice, the first of these, the descriptive function of statistical methods, has been most widely applied to the problems of economic history, while theories of statistical inference have been applied with more, and sometimes undue, caution, largely because of the difficulty of fitting incomplete historical evidence within the restrictive assumptions of classical statistics. Partly because of this, and partly to redress the balance of most textbooks of statistics, which concentrate attention on concepts of probability and inference, the methods of descriptive statistics, widely conceived, will be considered first; the problems of making inferences from them are logically secondary, and will be considered as such.

SIMPLE DESCRIPTIVE STATISTICS

Most historical problems generate larger amounts of data than can easily be comprehended by the human brain without some form of reduction or

---

[6] Some of the most interesting contributions to this debate are—W. O. Aydelotte (1971); Rowney and Graham (1969); and issues of *Daedalus, History and Theory,* and *Historical Methods Newsletter.*

[7] For introductions to statistics for historians see R. C. Floud (1973); C. M. Dollar and R. J. Jensen (1971); Shorter (1971). R. G. D. Allen (1966) is an excellent introduction, suitable particularly for economic historians. Another is K. A. Yeomans (1968). H. M. Blalock (1960) is also useful.

processing. This can be seen by looking at several examples, reprinted below, of historical data; for one, we can examine Table 1 of Ames (p. 37). If we concentrate on the main body of the table, we can see that we have a series of quotations for the exchange rate of the pound. The data have already been ordered by time, so that we can see at once that they relate to quotations between October 1334 and November 1345, but otherwise the implications of the middle column of the table are difficult to grasp. The value of the pound was clearly fluctuating, and a quick look tells us that it was never less than £9 Florentine, nor more than £11 Florentine, but within those wide bounds the degree of fluctuation is unclear. Similarly, the period of fluctuations is obscure, particularly since the quotations are not given for each month. Although, in looking at the table, we immediately try to pick out its main features in our minds, we would clearly benefit from some method of grouping, to bring out the main features of the data.

Regrouping of data is perhaps the simplest of the tasks of descriptive statistics; the particular method of regrouping is the responsibility of the historian, and is dictated by the points in the data which he wishes to study. Ames, Table 2 (p. 38) shows one such possible regrouping, technically described as a *contingency table*, in which the quotations for the value of the pound have been arranged into four categories, the four upper left-hand cells of the table, according to the date of the quotation and to whether it valued the pound sterling at more or less than £10 Florentine. The contingency table is one of the most valuable of simple descriptive methods, and is also the basis of analysis used in some inductive statistics. Another type of descriptive method, even more common, is that of Ames, Table 13 (p. 49), known as a *frequency distribution*. It is so called because one column of the table, in this case that headed 'number of licences', records the frequency with which a particular event occurred, distributed according to the value of another characteristic of that event, in this case its date. Another type of frequency distribution, in which time does not act as a distributor of the values, given by Soltow (p. 153), in which families are distributed according to their social standing or 'class', on the basis of the estimates of Gregory King.[8]

Although frequency distributions are most often presented in tabular form, they can also be presented in a graphical form, often with a considerable increase in their impact. Soltow, Chart 1 (p. 155), presents in graphical form a particular type of frequency distribution, a *percentage cumulative frequency distribution*. To understand the construction of such a distribution, which, as Soltow shows, is particularly useful in the analysis of inequality of income, we can take a small section of Gregory King's data; Table 1 shows the construction of a cumulative percentage frequency distribution.

It would also be possible to chart data such as those from Gregory King in the familiar form of a *bar-chart* or *histogram*. Another possible graphical

---

[8] For contingency tables and frequency distributions see Floud (1973), ch. 4; Allen (1966), ch. 5; Blalock (1960), chs. 3, 4; Yeomans (1968), vol. i, ch. 2.

TABLE 1. *A Specimen Percentage Cumulative Frequency Distribution.*

Class	No. of families in class	Cumulative no.	Cumulative percentage
Temporal lords	160	4,586	100.0
Spiritual lords	26	4,426	96.5
Baronets	800	4,400	95.9
Knights	600	3,600	78.5
Esquires	3,000	3,000	65.4

Source: Soltow, p. 49.

representation of data from a frequency distribution relating to geographical area is illustrated by Schofield (p. 99). Although in this case the frequency distribution is not explicitly given, it can be constructed from Table 2 of Schofield (p. 97). Om maps 1–4 the first nine countries, ranked in order of their wealth, are shown as black, and counties ranked in groups 10–19, 20–9 and 30–8 are shown with different cross-hatchings.

Types of data

Numerous other types of frequency distributions, and of charts, graphs, and maps based on them, can be found in textbooks of statistics and will be familiar to most readers. What these techniques have in common is that they set out to rearrange the raw data in forms which will help the reader to comprehend them, to capture some feature of the data which was obscured simply by its bulk. The choice of method depends partially on the type of data which is to be rearranged and described, and later analysed; different types of data demand different methods of analysis.[8] The distinction between types of data is crucial in the choice of a number of statistical techniques; it can most easily be illustrated by considering data of the type used by Soltow. Colquhoun in 1801–3 (Soltow, pp. 154–5) counted the number of families falling into different groups within the population, finding for example that there were in England and Wales 40 lunatic keepers, 2,500 lunatics, and 50,000 innkeepers. These data simply tell us the number of people within each group, just as if, on the basis of an agricultural census, we had counted the number of pigs, ploughs and tithe barns. We have given a generic name to each group and counted the number of times each occurred. Data of this kind are known therefore as *nominal data*; they tell us nothing more than the number within each group. Now let us imagine that, in addition, we have some information that tells us that, in general, lunatic keepers were richer than innkeepers, who in turn were richer than lunatics. This is an important piece of information, since it tells us an order or rank into which we can arrange the data; we could use such information to produce an order of groups, a rank order of occupations in terms of their incomes. Data with this capacity for ranking are known as *ordinal data*. Ordinal data are superior to nominal data in a number of ways, because we are able to rank the data, but an important piece of information is still missing. With ordinal data, we do not know, for example, how much richer a lunatic keeper is than an innkeeper, nor even whether the gap in income between these two groups is greater or less than the gap between the income of an innkeeper and a lunatic. We gain this information when we are able to assign an income, measurable in a defined unit like £ sterling, to each group, and can thus measure the interval between groups or individuals. Data with such a property are known as *interval data*.

The importance of the distinction between nominal, ordinal and interval data is that, as we know more about ordinal and interval data, so we can analyse and describe the data in a more detailed way. For example, with nominal data, we can say only that there were more innkeepers than lunatics and lunatic keepers. With ordinal data we can also say that lunatic keepers, in spite of, or perhaps because of, their small numbers, were relatively wealthy men. Finally, with interval data, we can say that lunatic keepers were about five times as wealthy as innkeepers, and nearly seventeen times as wealthy as the lunatics they kept, but that, because of their small numbers, the total income of lunatic keepers, at £20,000, was insignificant compared to the total income of inn keepers, at about £5,000,000.[9]

AVERAGES

The data type places a restriction on the statistical method which may be used. For example, let us suppose that we wish to summarize the incomes of groups in the population, in terms of some *central tendency* or *average*. For the sake of variety, we can take Gregory King's five highest income groups (Soltow, p. 153). If we have nominal data, we know only that there were more Esquires than any other class, and therefore that the income of esquires will appear more often in a list of all the people in Gregory King's first five groups than will any other income; this, the most frequently occurring in a set of values, is known as the *mode* or *modal value*. It is some help to us in summarizing our data, and is the best we can do with nominal data. If we have ordinal data, however, we know the order of the four groups according to their income. One measure of central tendency would be to find that group which had as many groups with higher incomes above it as below it; in this case baronets would be this central group, with two groups above it in income, and two below, and we would call baronets the *median* group. Finally, with interval data, we can make use of the more exact characteristics of data of that type, finding the *arithmetic mean* by summing the incomes of the groups and dividing by the number of groups, and finding the mean income of the groups to be £1,100 per annum.[10]

---

[9] It may be objected that Colquhoun's data are so vague that we should treat them as ordinal, distrusting the assignments of income so much that we do not use them. This seems over-cautious, but it is quite clear that there must be large errors in Colquhoun's income estimates.

[10] This result has been rounded to three significant figures, since the original data are similarly rounded. It is important to note that we have been concerned, in this paragraph, with finding the 'central' group; had we been concerned with the 'central' individual the result would, naturally, have been different.

MEASURES OF DEVIATION

Although the averages which have been described are useful in summarizing data, and thus in reducing them to a comprehensible form, they do not provide a complete summary.[11] They are measures of the central tendency of the data, and thus do not provide any indication of the dispersion of the data values around that central tendency. To overcome this difficulty, it is normal to associate with the averages other measures, known as measures of deviation, which describe the amount of dispersion. Each average, with the exception of the mode, has one or more associated measures of dispersion, and the choice of measure depends on the characteristics of the data and on the particular features which are to be studied. The dispersion of ordinal data, for example, can be described by such measures as the *semi-interquartile range*, which is based upon the distance between the upper and lower *quartiles*, two measures which divide the data into quarters, as the median divides them into two halves. More familiar, however, and more often used, when the data are of interval type, are the *standard deviation* and its associated measures, which describe the amount of dispersion of the data around their mean value. These measures are used in Adie (p. 169) to describe the fluctuations in the volume of Bank of England notes and deposits. Having obtained, for example, a series for deposits from which the influence of long-term changes has been removed,[12] Adie has calculated the mean of the series. He has then subtracted that mean value for the series from each data value, to give an indication of the year-by-year fluctuation. In order to provide a description of the fluctuation over the whole series, these year-by-year fluctuations are squared (to avoid the difficulty that the simple fluctuations around the mean will by definition sum to zero), summed, and divided by the number of years to give an average fluctuation. The square root is then taken to return the result to the original units. Finally, Adie has expressed the result, the standard deviation, as a percentage of the mean of the series.[13] This gives him a measure of the relative amount of fluctuation in a number of different series.

The concept of measures of dispersion is extremely important to the historian when he is dealing, as he usually is, with inadequate and patchy, or estimated, evidence. In such cases, the average or mean value is certainly the 'best guess' which the historian can make, and he should not be deterred from making it by the patchy nature of the data; on the other hand, he should always be aware of the fact that dispersion around the average may have a serious effect on the accuracy of his guess. For example, Cooper (pp. 113–14)

[11] Floud (1973), ch. 5; Dollar and Jensen (1971), ch. 2; Allen (1966), chs. 4, 5; Blalock (1960), ch. 5; Yeomans (1968), vol. i, ch. 3.

[12] For a discussion of this procedure, see pp. 21–23.

[13] For a series of data $X_1, X_2, X_3, \ldots X_N$, the mean of the N values of X is calculated as $\Sigma X/N$, and written as $\bar{X}$ (pronounced X bar.) ΣX denotes the sum (total) of the X values; for an explanation of *summation notation* of this type see Blalock (1960), appendix 1; Floud (1973), ch. 3; Dollar and Jensen (1971), p. 55. The individual deviation of one data item from the mean is $(X_i - \bar{X})$ where i has any value up to N. The standard deviation is then $\sqrt{\{[\Sigma(X_i - \bar{X})^2]/N\}}$, normally referred to as s, and the *coefficient of variation*, as the percentage variation around the mean is called, is $(s/X)\,100$. See Floud (1973), ch. 5; Dollar and Jensen (1971), ch 2; Blalock (1960), ch. 6; Allen (1966), ch. 5.

was concerned to estimate the total landholdings of 'substantial' yeomen at the beginning of the seventeenth century, and made use, as he says, on a 'totally inadequate basis' of estimates ranging from 30 to 120 acres, of a guess of an average holding of 70–80 acres. This is certainly the best guess, but one should also be conscious of the difference which might be made to the estimates of the total landholding if the guess as to average acreage were wrong. One method of gaining some impression of the possible range of difference is to calculate the standard deviation of the acreage estimates, which is about 25 acres.[14] On the basis of the logic of sampling theory, discussed later, one could argue that a safe 'upper-bound' estimate for average acreage would be equal to the mean acreage plus one standard deviation, or $(70 + 25) = 95$ acres, and a safe 'lower-bound' the mean minus one standard deviation, or $(70 - 25) = 45$ acres. Multiplying by 80,000 yeomen in each case would give an upper-bound estimate for total acreage of 8·4 million, and a lower-bound estimate of 3·6 million. The range is clearly huge, about 15 per cent of the cultivated acreage at this time. This is not to argue that Cooper should not have used the mean estimate, which remains the best guess from inadequate evidence; it is merely a statistical demonstration of a point made by Cooper throughout his article, that averages must be treated with grave suspicion. The calculation of, or even a rough guess at, the value of the standard deviation for a set of data is often a corrective to hasty acceptance of an 'average' or 'typical' figure.

A further demonstration of the dangers of making use of averages, when there is wide dispersion in the underlying data, is provided by Felix in his discussion of the Hamilton profit inflation thesis. Felix discusses the indices of prices and wages in England, 1500–1702, compiled by Wiebe on the basis of information about the prices of 79 commodities and the wages paid to 8 groups of workers. The first step in the compilation of such indices is the calculation of *price* and *wage relatives*.[15] If we take salt as an example, it was necessary to obtain quotations for the price of a unit of salt, at as many dates as possible between 1451 and 1500. These were then grouped decennially by taking the mean of quotations for that decade. Wiebe then took the decennial averages for 1451–1500, and found their mean. Using that mean as his base value, set at 100, he then divided all the other price quotations by that base value, thus calculating a series varying around 100; this is a series of price relatives, that is a series of prices relative to the price in a base year. Series for other prices and wages were computed similarly. Finally, Wiebe calculated his price index by taking the mean of the 79 price relatives for each decade, and his wage index by taking the mean of the 8 wage relatives.

The calculation of each index thus involved four averaging processes, at each of which dispersion around the mean was ignored. Felix concentrates attention on the possible dangers in one of these processes, the last stage in the

[14] Based on the estimates, quoted by Cooper, of acreages of 50, 30, 80, 80, 100, 120, 50, 60, 60. Use of these figures, since many of them are themselves upper or lower bounds, has probably inflated the size of the standard deviation, but not necessarily by very much. Ideally, these average acreages should be weighted by the number of farms possessing each acreage.

[15] See Allen (1966), ch. 6, Yeomans (1968), vol. i, ch. 4.

formation of the index. As he shows, Wiebe's index cannot properly be used as Hamilton tried to use it, to demonstrate industrial profit inflation. Felix shows that the Wiebe price index was greatly affected by the inclusion of agricultural prices, which were rising sharply over the period, and that if the prices of manufactured goods were considered by themselves their price index, again computed as a mean, showed a much smaller rate of increase. The gap between prices and wages, for manufactured goods, was therefore less than Hamilton supposed, and was also, Felix suggests, offset by prices for raw materials, which rose faster than prices for finished manufactured goods.

Felix has thus concentrated on the dangers involved in taking the average of two disparate groups of products. A further danger in the procedure used by Wiebe is that his indices were *unweighted means* of the price and wage relatives. It is normal, in compiling indices, to weight the component price or wage relatives according to their importance; in the case of an index of the cost of living of the working classes, for example, prices of bread and potatoes would be given much greater weight in the index than would prices of luxury goods seldom purchased by the working classes. In a general price index, such as Wiebe's, it would be normal to weight each commodity by its share in the total output of the economy. Wiebe did not do this, and it is in fact probably impossible to weight commodities accurately at this period, since we have very little information on total output.[16] Had he been able to do so, the price index would have shown an even steeper rise, since 'unprocessed agricultural products' formed a far larger part in total output than is implied in the simple unweighted average used by Wiebe. It should also be said that, in the absence of accurate weighting, the index of industrial prices, calculated by Felix and used in his attack on Hamilton, is similarly flawed. Whether the 'true' index, if it could be computed, would show a faster or a slower growth is difficult to tell, though it is interesting that the price for slates for building, an important sector in a pre-industrial economy, shows a faster than average growth; if they were given more weight, the index as a whole would rise faster, and Felix's conclusions be correspondingly weakened.

A further problem, which frequently arises in the construction of indices, is that of changes in the quality of the goods whose price is being compared; a change in price may be the result of price inflation, but it may be that the goods are of better quality. Similarly, a fall in price may be the result of technical change which leaves the profit margin unchanged. In the construction of indices, as in other uses of averages, the average may conceal as much as it reveals, and the historian should never accept it uncritically. The article by Matthews, which relies heavily on indices of different types, has been included in this selection because it demonstrates many of the problems of their use; it also demonstrates, elegantly, the great possibilities for insight into historical processes which their use can bring.

In spite of the deficiencies of averages, they and the other methods which we

[16] Matthews, pp. 238–9, is an example of the type of procedure which can be followed when more evidence is available.

have described are of enormous use in describing data, and in reducing bulky sets of data to a manageable and comprehensible form, as can be seen in the varied uses made of them in the articles reprinted below. At the same time, these methods, which will be generally familiar to most historians, represent only a small proportion of available statistical methods. A second group of methods are designed to help in the description not of a single set of data, but rather of the association or relationship between different sets of data; these methods are the techniques of *correlation* and *regression*.[17]

MEASURES OF ASSOCIATION

Measures of association and relationship are employed in several of the articles reprinted below, and they are some of the most useful descriptive and exploratory tools available to economic historians. Adie uses them to describe the relationship between the issue of Bank of England notes and deposits, Schofield to explore the geographical distribution of wealth, Ford to discuss the determinants of British investment in Argentina, and Olson and Harris to describe the causes of declining wheat acreage. Measures of association are particularly useful because they can be considered in some circumstances to support or refute hypothesized causal connections between two or more sets of data, and thus between two or more sets of historical events.

There are a large number of statistical measures of association and relationships, but they share certain features and concepts in common. The most important of these is, paradoxically, the concept of *independence*, the absence of association. We can say that two sets of data are independent of each other when we believe that knowledge of the characteristics of one set of data will not help us in any way to discover the characteristics of the other set. Any departure from this independence, any feature or pattern in one set which will help us in some way to discover something about the other set, indicates that there may be some association between the two sets of data, however slight. In this sense, two (or more, but two for simplicity) sets of data, or sets of events, or characteristics of some people, are either independent, or they are associated. The first task, therefore, of a measure of association must be to discriminate between these two possibilities. Secondly, the association between two sets of data may be very strong, so that knowledge of one set gives us a very good idea of the characteristics of the other set, or it may be very weak, hardly different from independence. The second task, therefore, of a measure of association is to describe the strength of the relationship. Finally, the association between two sets of data can have a number of different forms; the two sets may be inversely related, so that an upward movement of one is associated with a downward movement of the other, or positively related, in which case the two sets move in the same direction. The association may also be of the form such that a change in one set is associated with an equal change in the

---

[17] Allen (1966), ch. 7; Blalock (1960), chs. 14–20; Floud, (1973), ch. 7; Dollar and Jensen (1971), ch. 3; Yeomans (1968), vol. i, ch. 5.

other, or one may change more or less than the other. Thirdly, therefore, a measure of association or relationship must be able to describe the exact nature of the relationship between the two sets of data.

The various measures of association and relationship are designed to meet these requirements, and to fit the characteristics of particular types of data. In general, however, they are designed so that, implicitly or explicitly, they contrast the actual data sets on which the historian is working with hypothetical data sets, constructed on the basis of independence between the data sets. A simple example, using nominal data, will help to clarify the logic of this method. Ames (p. 38) gives a contingency table classifying sterling quotations by date and by reference to whether they were above or below £10 Florentine per £1 sterling. This is given in Table 2.

TABLE 2. *Number of Transactions by Price of Pound Sterling*

Period	At least £10 Florentine	Below £10 Florentine	Total
Jan. 1337–June 1339	6	22	28
Other	54	3	57
Total	60	25	85

Source: Ames, p. 498.

Ames wished to know whether there was any association between the date of a quotation and its value. The table tells us that there were 60 quotations of at least £10 Florentine. If the date of a quotation had no influence on (was independent of) its value, we would expect that such quotations would be distributed, over the months and years, in roughly the same proportions as all the quotations, irrespective of their value, were distributed. We know that 28 of the quotations came from the period January 1337 to June 1339, out of 85 in total, a proportion of about 1/3 or 33 per cent. We might therefore expect that about 33 per cent of quotations over £10 Florentine would come from that period, and the other 67 per cent from the rest of the period. Applying these proportions to the 60 high (over £10 Florentine) quotations, we would expect that about 20 would have fallen into the January 1337 to June 1339 period, and about 40 into the rest of the period; this would be on the, hypothetical, basis that the date of a quotation and its value (high or low) were unconnected. If we use a similar logic on the 25 low quotations, we would expect that about 8 would have come from the January 1337 to June 1339 period, and the remaining 17 from the remainder of the period. Thus, on the assumption that the proportions of high and of low quotations, and of quotations inside and outside the 1337 to 1339 period, remained unchanged, but that no connection existed between the value of a quotation and its date, we have constructed an alternative, hypothetical, independent contingency table, which is given as Table 3. Such a table is known as the table of 'expected' (under the assumption of independence) values, as opposed to the 'observed' data values.

TABLE 3. *Number of Transactions by Price of Pound Sterling, Based on a Hypothesis of Independence*

Period	At least £10 Florentine	Below £10 Florentine	Total
Jan. 1337–June 1339	20	8	28
Other	40	17	57
Total	60	25	85

Source: Table of approximate 'expected' values calculated from Table 2.

We can immediately see that the expected values differ considerably from the original observed values. If we look at the 1337–9 period, we would have expected roughly 20 high quotations, while there were in fact only 6; we would have expected only 8 low quotations, but there were in fact 22. It seems clear, therefore, that the hypothesis of independence has produced results very unlike those that actually occurred, and that it can therefore be concluded that there was some association between the date of a quotation and whether it was 'high' or 'low'. Specifically, it seems that low quotations were associated with the period January 1337 to June 1339. It must be stressed, however, that we have not discussed either the strength of this association or its cause; the two factors, date and value, may not be very strongly associated, and the association may have been coincidental, or determined by any number of other factors which we have not discussed. All that can be said, at this stage of analysis, is that the data are not consistent with the hypothesis, often known as the *'null hypothesis'*, that there was no association between the two factors which we have considered.

This example has been studied in some detail because, as we have said, the logic of most tests of association is that the observed data values are contrasted with hypothetical values constructed under an hypothesis of independence. The particular method which we have used, suitable for nominal data, is the basis of a number of measures using the *chi-square statistic*, which measure the degree to which expected values differ from observed values.[18]

Similar methods, however, underlie other measures suitable for nominal data, and also measures which are designed for ordinal and interval data. Another similarity between these various measures is that they are normally designed so that a measured value of zero indicates no association, or independence between the variables, while a non-zero value indicates some degree of association. In addition, a number of these measures are designed so that perfect association, a one-for-one correspondence between two data sets, produces a measured value of 1; it is important to note, however, that not all measures have this property.[19]

[18] Chi-square is written as χ^2 and pronounced 'Ky square'. Blalock (1960), ch. 15; Floud (1973), ch. 7a; Dollar and Jensen (1971), pp. 79–81.

[19] For example, the contingency coefficient, used as a measure of association for nominal data, has a value of 0·707 for perfect association in a two-by-two cell contingency table. S. Siegel (1956), pp. 196–202; this book is an invaluable reference manual.

CORRELATION ANALYSIS

The procedures for the calculation of measures of association with ordinal data can best be illustrated by Schofield's work (pp. 94f.). As he says, the particular measure which he uses. *Spearman's rank correlation coefficient, R_s,* (the more usual symbol for this statistic)

measures how far two assessments agree in the order in which they rank the counties according to wealth. This coefficient is so designed that when the two assessments produce identical rankings of the counties, R_s has the value + 1; and when the two rankings are as greatly in disagreement as possible, that is when one ranking is exactly the reverse of the other, R_s has the value − 1.

In addition, lack of association between the rankings, either positive or inverse, will produce an R_s value of zero. If we rank two sets of data, as Schofield has done with the county tax assessments for 1334 and 1515 (for example columns 2 and 4 of Table 2, p. 97), R is computed from the formula

$$R_s = 1 - \frac{6 \, \Sigma \, d_i^2}{N^3 - N}$$

where N is the number of items in each data set, in this case 38, and each d_i is the difference between a county's ranking on the 1334 assessment and its ranking on the 1515 assessment. Thus

$$d_{\text{Beds.}} = 4 - 13 = - 9,$$

$$d_{\text{Berks.}} = 5 - 10 = - 5,$$

and so on. It can be seen immediately that if there had been no change between 1334 and 1515 in the order in which tax assessments ranked counties, each d_i would equal zero, so that the term

$$\frac{6 \, \Sigma \, d_i^2}{N^3 - N}$$

would equal zero, and R_s would have the value of $(1 - 0) = 1$, showing perfect positive association.[20]

This property of R_s and similar measures, that they range between defined values, indicating independence or perfect association (positive or inverse), can be used to help us to describe the strength of the association at some point between these extremes. For example, we can say that a R_s of + 0·643 shows a less than perfect positive relationship, and also that the relationship is less strong than one producing a R_s of + 0·892. It was on just such a statement that Schofield based his view that there was a greater change in the distribution of wealth between 1334 and 1515 ($R_s = + 0·643$) than between 1515 and 1636/49 ($R_s = + 0·892$), and therefore reversed Buckatzsch's picture of stability in the geographical distribution of wealth in the later Middle Ages,

[20] For this and other measures of association suitable for ordinal data, see Siegel (1956), pp. 202–38; Dollar and Jensen (1971), pp. 82–7; Blalock (1960), ch. 18; Yeomans (1968), vol. ii, ch. 6.

followed by greater redistribution in the sixteenth century. With ordinal, as with nominal, data our measure of the strength of an association is based on the contrast between the actual data and data constructed on the basis of a hypothesis of independence.

Although measures of association for nominal and ordinal data have been widely used, the most familiar measure of association, *the product-moment correlation coefficient, R,* (sometimes known as Pearson's *R*), is suitable only for interval data.[21] *R* is the main measure of association for interval data, and it is used, for example, by Olson and Harris.[22] They wished to describe the association between the price of wheat in a given harvest year and the amount of new wheat planted during the next year, arguing that there should be some relationship between these two sets of data. (The data are set out in Olson and Harris, Table 1, p. 199). Since they have interval data, they use the correlation coefficient, *R*, as their measure of the degree of association. The logic of the measure is that, if there were perfect association between two sets of data we would expect to find that a high value in one set of data would be accompanied by a high value in the other set. In this example, we would expect that a very high price of wheat would stimulate farmers to plant more wheat, and thus that acreage would be very high. Similarly, a low value in one set should be accompanied by a low value in the other. By contrast, if there was no association, then a high value in one set of data might be accompanied by a high, low, or medium value in the other set. *R* therefore measures the degree to which the data correspond to one or other of these contrasting possibilities.

In order to do this, we must be able to define high and low, and, as is common in statistics, we do this by reference to the mean value. Thus a high value is any value greater than the mean; subtracting the mean from that high value will produce a positive number. *R* is then defined as

$$R = \frac{\Sigma (X - \bar{X})(Y - \bar{Y})}{\sqrt{[\Sigma (X - \bar{X})^2][\Sigma (Y - \bar{Y})^2]}} \qquad (23)$$

It can be shown that, like R_s, *R* will have a value of zero when there is no association, and of $+1$ and -1 for perfect positive and negative association. Applying the formula to the data, where the *Y*s are values for acres of wheat, and the *X*s the

[21] We shall use '*R*' as the symbol for the correlation coefficient with population, or non-sample, data, and '*r*' as the symbol for the correlation coefficient with sample data. For the correlation coefficient see Allen (1966), ch. 7; Blalock (1960), ch. 17; Floud (1973), ch. 7; Dollar and Jensen (1971), pp. 61–5; Yeomans (1968) vol. i, ch. 5.

[22] Schofield uses both R_s and *R* as measures of association for his data. This action appears illogical; if the data are ordinal, then R_s is appropriate, if they are interval, then *R* is appropriate. However, Schofield is not sure of the data type; in particular, he is not sure whether the tax assessments were accurate to the nearest £1, so that the *R* correlation coefficient, which takes account of such small variations and therefore assumes their accuracy, may be too fine a tool for the job. It is therefore a sensible precaution to use the ordinal measure as well, since it seems likely that at least the order of counties is accurate. The reader can select whichever measure he feels is most appropriate, and it is comforting that, in this case, they both produce much the same result. Schofield's problem of deciding the data type is very common in historical statistics.

[23] More convenient computing formulae for *R* can be found in the references listed above, note 21.

prices in the preceding years, Olson and Harris found that $R = + 0.89$, suggesting, as they said, a strong association between the two sets of data. It should be noted, however, that they distrust this result, not in statistical but in historical terms, we shall return to discuss why they are right to do so slightly later in this introduction. At the moment, however, it is sufficient to indicate the logic and methods of the computation of R.

At this point, it is convenient to describe another measure of association, used by Soltow in his discussion of income distribution, which is constructed differently from the correlation coefficient, R, but which is confusingly given the name R by Soltow; this is *Gini's coefficient of inequality* (or *concentration*).[24] Soltow's problem is to compare the amount of inequality in the distribution of income in Great Britain at different periods; this is a common, and important, problem in economics, and it is normally approached through the method of *Lorenz curves*. Lorenz curves are graphical representations of inequality in the distribution of some commodity or possession; they are normally applied to the distribution of income or capital but can be more widely used. To construct Lorenz curves we start with a frequency distribution, such as that compiled by Gregory King, listing numbers of families in particular classes, together with their average incomes. We then transform the two series, numbers of families and total incomes of each class, into percentage cumulative frequency distributions, as shown in Table 4; this gives us the information, for example, that the top 8 per cent of families gained 39·3 per cent of total income. These distributions are then plotted against each other on a graph such as Soltow, Chart 1 (p. 155); the curve formed by joining together the points on the graph is known as a Lorenz curve.

If the two distributions were exactly the same, so that, for example, 80 per cent of the population gained 80 per cent of the income, 70 per cent held 70 per cent, and so on down the scale, the points of the Lorenz curve would fall diagonally on the graph, and we would say that incomes were equally distributed. The extent to which the Lorenz curve representing a particular historical distribution diverges from that diagonal is therefore a measure of how far the distribution differs from perfect equality. We can, therefore, obtain a good impression of changes in income inequality by comparing various distributions as Lorenz curves.

It is, however, desirable to have a more exact measure of inequality, since, as can be seen from Soltow's Chart 1, it is possible for Lorenz curves to cross each other; this makes it difficult to know, from inspection of the graph, which signifies greater inequality. The more exact measure which we use is Gini's coefficient of inequality; it is designed to have a value of 0 when there is perfect correspondence between the two distributions, in other words perfect equality. The Gini coefficient in fact takes the total area under the diagonal as 1, and expresses the area above a Lorenz curve as a proportion of that area. In Chart 1, for example, the area between the curve marked '1688', based on Gregory King's data, and the diagonal is 0·551 of the area (1·00) between the diagonal and the bottom and rightward axes; the Gini coefficient is therefore 0·551. The Gini

---

[24] Dollar and Jensen (1971), pp. 121–6.

TABLE 4

Class	No. of families	Mean income £	Total income £	Percentage of number	Percentage of income	Cumulative percentage of number	Cumulative percentage of income
Temporal lords	160	3200	512,000	0·1	3·7	100·0	100·0
Spiritual lords	26	1300	33,800				
Baronets	800	880	704,000				
Knights	600	650	390,000				
Esquires	3000	450	1,350,000	0·2	3·0	99·9	96·2
Eminent merchants	2000	400	800,000	0·2	1·8	99·7	93·3
Gentlemen	12,000	280	3,360,000	0·9	7·5	99·5	91·5
Greater offices	5000	240	1,200,000	0·4	2·7	98·6	84·0
Lesser merchants	8000	198	1,584,000	0·6	3·5	98·2	81·3
Lawyers	10,000	154	1,540,000	0·7	3·4	97·6	77·8
Lesser offices	5000	120	600,000	0·4	1·3	96·9	74·4
Freeholders 1	40,000	91	3,640,000	3·0	8·1	96·5	73·1
Naval officers	5000	80	400,000	0·4	0·9	93·5	65·0
Eminent clergy	2000	72	144,000	0·1	0·3	93·1	64·1
Liberal arts	15,000	60	900,000	1·4	2·6	93·0	63·8
Military officers	4000	60	240,000				
Freeholders 2	120,000	55	6,600,000	8·9	14·7	91·6	61·2
Lesser clergy	8000	50	400,000	0·6	0·9	82·7	46·5
Shopkeepers	50,000	45	2,250,000	3·7	5·0	82·1	45·6
Farmers	150,000	42·5	6,375,000	11·1	14·2	78·4	40·6
Artisans	60,000	38	2,280,000	4·4	5·1	67·3	26·4
Seamen	50,000	20	1,000,000	3·7	2·2	62·9	21·3
Labourers	364,000	15	5,460,000	27·0	12·2	59·2	19·1
Soldiers	35,000	14	490,000	2·6	1·1	32·2	6·9
Cottagers	400,000	6·5	2,600,000	29·6	5·8	29·6	5·8
	1,349,586		44,852,800	100·0	100·0		

Note. King's last category, of 30,000 vagrants etc., has been omitted; it is insignificant both in numbers and in income.
Source. Soltow, pp. 17–18.

coefficients for the other distributions are given by Soltow in the top left-hand corner of Chart 1, and are the basis for the remarks he makes about changing income distribution on pp. 153–6.[25]

The measures of association which have so far been discussed tell us something about the amount of association between two sets of data, and, in the case of ordinal and interval data, something about the direction of that association. They do not, however, tell us anything directly about the form of the relationship. Yet the form of the relationship between two sets of data may be much more interesting to the economic historian than the demonstration that an association exists. For example, as Olson and Harris say, 'some of the most venerable assumptions of economics' connect the price of wheat with the farmer's decision to plant more or less, and the demonstration that the connection exists in practice is, therefore, not of great interest. In such cases, we are much more interested in the form of the relationship, in answering such questions as, by how much did price have to fall before farmers reduced wheat acreage by a given amount? Similarly, Ford (p. 217) could assume that there was some relationship between Argentine new issues on the London Stock Exchange and the profitability of investment in Argentina; what he wanted to know was the exact nature of that relationship.

REGRESSION ANALYSIS

It is to answer such questions that we make use of regression analysis, one of the most powerful tools of statistical analysis.[26] As with most of the subjects being covered in this introduction, regression analysis deserves far more space than we shall be able to give it; we shall concentrate, again, on an explanation of its logic rather than on the details and complications of its use. As an example, we shall take again the relationship between wheat acreage and price of wheat. We shall use as our measure of price, the data headed X_4 in Olson and Harris, Table 1, and plot as Graph 1 the values for Y, the acreage planted, against X_4 on the particular type of graph known as a *scatter diagram*. Graph 1 shows a scatter of points, each representing a harvest year described by the acreage planted in that year and the average price of the seven previous years; these points fall, roughly, in a straight line cutting diagonally across the graph from the bottom left-hand to the top right-hand corner. If we draw in, arbitrarily, a straight line, such as the line AA on the graph, we see that some of the data points lie above and some below the line, and that some are further away from the line than are others. In other words, the data values are dispersed around the line, in much the same way as the values of a frequency distribution

[25] Details of the methods used by Soltow for incomplete distributions, using Pareto curves, can be found on p. 70.

[26] Allen (1966), ch. 7; Blalock (1960), chs. 17–18; Floud (1973), ch. 7c; Dollar and Jensen (1971), pp. 87–90; Yeomans (1968), vol. i, ch. 5, vol. ii, ch. 4. Regression analysis is one of the central techniques of econometrics, and is therefore discussed at length in many textbooks. The reader must choose that book most suited to his mathematical knowledge—one of the best for those without much mathematics is A. A. Walters (1968). Another, slightly more advanced, is J. Johnston (1963).

are dispersed around some average value or central point. This suggests that we might be able to find a straight line which would represent the average of the points on the graph, and thus, in this case, the average relationship between price and acreage. Each of the data points represents, as we have said, one such relationship for a particular year; the line would represent the average relationship over all years. It is clear that we cannot arbitrarily draw in any line, as we have done with the line AA, but must find that particular line which best fits the data. If we could find a line that passed through each data point, then clearly that would be the best line to choose, but no such straight line exists; we therefore choose that line which passes closest to the data points. This is equivalent to finding the line which has the smallest possible distance in total between itself and each data point; it can be shown that the best line for this purpose is the *least squares line*, (so called because it is the line which minimizes the sum of squares of vertical distances between the line and the data points). The least squares line for the wheat price and acreage data is shown as line BB on Graph 1.

Although we have stated the principle of using a line to represent the average relationship between price of wheat and acreage, or between any two other variables, we have still to discuss how such a line can help us to answer a question such as 'what increase in wheat acreage was associated with a particular increase in wheat price?' The line BB has two obvious characteristics, firstly, it cuts the vertical (Y) axis, and secondly, it slopes upwards in relation to the horizontal (X) axis. The combination of these two characteristics completely, and uniquely, describes the line. As can be seen from Graph 1, the line BB cuts the Y axis at the point, known as the *intercept*, where Y has a value of about 0·2. Secondly, it slopes upwards at a rate which can roughly be approximated by saying that for each movement of 100 units along the X axis, the line rises by about 0·5 units measured along the Y axis. Putting these two characteristics together, we can say that the line is described roughly by the equation

$$Y = 0\cdot2 + 0\cdot005X$$

That is, when X is zero, Y has the value 0·2. When X is 100,

$$\begin{aligned} Y &= 0\cdot2 + 0\cdot005\,(100) \\ &= 0\cdot2 + 0\cdot5 \\ &= 0\cdot7 \end{aligned}$$

This equation has been found by rough inspection. In practice, we find the equation for a particular least squares line by applying two formulae, to find the values of the constants a and b in the equation, known as the general equation for a straight line

$$Y = a + bX$$

The most convenient formulae for the calculation of a and b are

$$b = \frac{N\Sigma XY - (\Sigma X)(\Sigma Y)}{N\Sigma X^2 - (\Sigma X)^2}$$

$$a = \frac{\Sigma Y - b\Sigma X}{N}$$

and by applying these formulae to the data on wheat prices and acreages, Olson and Harris calculated that the least squares line had the value

$$Y = 0\cdot 19 + 0\cdot 0047 X_4$$

This straight line is known as the linear regression line of Y on X_4. Its historical interpretation is that, on average over the period 1873–1914, a change of 1 shilling in the price of wheat was accompanied by a change in the same direction of $0\cdot 0047$ million acres in the acreage of wheat planted.

Regression analysis therefore provides a method by which we can describe the form of an association between two sets of data. We have treated the two sets of data, price of wheat and acreage of wheat, as separate, linked only by the fact that they relate to the same period; in reality, however, simple economic theory suggests that price and quantity supplied are not separate, but rather that quantity supplied is dependent upon price, that there is, in this sense, a causal link between price and quantity. On the basis of that theory, we can give to the regression equation a second meaning, an economic meaning opposed to the statistical meaning of describing the form of the association, and say that our equation $Y = 0\cdot 19 + 0\cdot 0047 X_4$ describes the average effect which a change in price will have on the quantity supplied. It describes, in other words, the way in which Y, which is normally called the *dependent variable*, is dependent on the *independent variable*, X_4.

It is important to remember that the regression equation is only an average measure of the relationship between the two variables. Like all averages, therefore, it may be a good or bad representation of the data, depending on the amount of dispersion around it. It is therefore necessary to associate with the regression line some measure of the dispersion of the data. One such measure is the correlation coefficient, R. If all the data points in a scatter diagram such as Graph 1 lay exactly on a straight line such as BB, then it would follow that a very high value of Y would be accompanied by a very high value on X_4, a low value by a low value, and so on. This is, it will be recalled, the definition which we used in describing the perfect relation between two sets of data which would produce $R = + 1$. Therefore, if there is no dispersion of the data points around a regression line, which is sloped upwards to the right as in Graph 1, R will be $+1$; if the data points fall exactly on a line sloping downwards to the right, R will be -1, high values of X_4 being accompanied by low values of Y, showing a perfect inverse association.

There is, however, a better measure of dispersion around the regression line, which we can associate more closely to the causal interpretation which our theory often allows us to give to the regression line. Let us imagine that we do not know the regression equation, and wish to estimate the most likely acreage which will be planted in a particular year. In the absence of any other informa-tion our best guess of the acreage to be sown in a particular year will be the mean acreage sown in all years. A guess based on the mean acreage will sometimes be too high, sometimes too low, but because of the definition of the mean, the dispersion will cancel out over the whole period. Graph 1 shows the mean acreage (2.23 acres), the best guess, as a straight line CC parallel to the X_4 axis. In practice, however, we do not have to rely on the mean acreage as our best guess, since we have some more information, the regression equation, about the way in which price determines the acreage sown. As we can see, the regression line BB passes much closer to the data points than does the mean acreage line, CC; in other words, the regression line helps us to improve our guess or estimate of the acreage corresponding to a particular price. It does not make our estimate entirely accurate, since there is still dispersion around the regression line, but the estimate has been improved. One measure of the

GRAPH 1

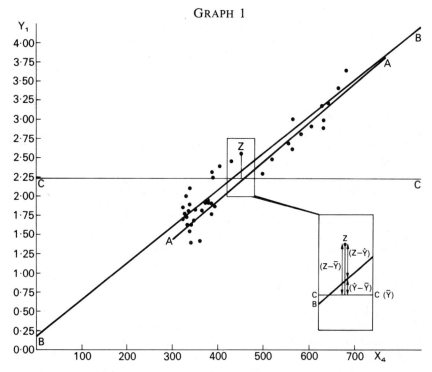

usefulness of the regression line in approximating the data (and therefore of the dispersion of the data around the regression line) is therefore the amount by which knowledge of the regression line helps us to improve our estimate of the acreage for a given price. For an individual data point, such as the point marked Z on the graph, our initial guess, using the mean acreage, was deficient by the vertical distance $(Z - \bar{Y})$. Knowledge of the regression line has helped us to get closer to Z by the vertical distance $(\hat{Y} - \bar{Y})$, where $\hat{Y}$ is the value of the regression line at a particular point. Knowledge of the regression line has therefore helped us to improve our estimate by the proportion

$$\frac{(\hat{Y} - \bar{Y})}{(Z - \bar{Y})}$$

for a particular point, and therefore by the proportion

$$\frac{\Sigma(\hat{Y} - \bar{Y})}{\Sigma(Z - \bar{Y})}$$

for the data as a whole. This can be given an economic meaning by saying that it represents the proportion by which changes in price (as measured by the regression line) affected changes in acreage sown; the corresponding proportion

$$\frac{\Sigma(Z - \hat{Y})}{\Sigma(Z - \bar{Y})}$$

is the proportion of change in acreage affected by change in factors other than price. In other words,

$$\frac{\Sigma(\hat{Y} - \bar{Y})}{\Sigma(Z - \bar{Y})}$$

represents the proportion of change in acreage which is explained by change in price; it is therefore known as the *explained variation* in Y.

It would be possible, though cumbersome, to calculate the proportion directly from the data. In practice, however, we can make use of an identity, that the proportion

$$\frac{\Sigma(\hat{Y} - \bar{Y})}{\Sigma(Z - \bar{Y})} = R^2,$$

the square of the correlation coefficient. R^2 (sometimes called the *coefficient of determination*) should normally be quoted, in preference to R, because it has this important property of describing the proportion of variation in the dependent variable explained by the independent variable, and thus of being directly related to the causal interpretation which we often give to the regression equation. It is for this reason that Adie makes use of the R^2 static, for example on p. 169; he finds that the correlation between bank notes and deposits is (for 1815–21, detrended) 0·60; R^2 is therefore 0·36. This can then be expressed in percentage terms, as the percentage of variation in deposits explained by variation in notes; as Adie says, 36 per cent is rather small, and gives 'little support for the proposition that fluctuations in notes closely controlled fluctuations in deposits'.

MULTIPLE REGRESSION ANALYSIS

We have so far considered regression analysis as a technique by which we may establish and analyse the relationship between two variables or sets of data, one of which can be regarded as dependent on the other. In some circumstances, however, it is more realistic to regard the dependent variable as the product of the influence of more than one other factor. Ford, for example, began his analysis (p. 218) by hypothesizing that Argentine new issues (A_t) were dependent on expectations of profitability (represented by P_{t-1}, the profit rate in the previous year). He estimated the values of the constants in the simple linear regression equation $A = a + bP_{t-1}$ (equation 1*a*) and in similar equations (2*a*, 1*b*, 2*b*), and calculated R^2 as a measure of the explanatory power of the independent variable, the profit rate. Although the R^2 for equation 2*b* suggests that profit rate explains about 65 per cent of the course of new issues, it is clear that other variables must have been influential, and Ford therefore introduces into the discussion new non-Argentine issues. It would have been possible to have estimated the simple linear regression of Argentine issues (A_t) on non-Argentine issues (F_t), but Ford was anxious to explore the effects of the profit rate and non-Argentine issues together, and thus to have two independent variables in the regression equation. Such an equation, with the general form

$$Y = a + b_1 X_1 + b_2 X_2$$

is known as a *multiple regression equation* with two independent variables; it is possible to have more independent variables, as Ford does (p. 221) in equations 5*a*, 5*b*, 6*a*, 6*b*.[27]

In multiple regression analysis, the value of R^2 represents the proportion of the variation in the dependent variable explained by the joint and separate effects of the independent variables. Thus, comparing Ford's equations 2*b* and 4*b*, we see that the addition of F_t as an independent variable has increased the R^2 from 0.650 to 0.788. As Ford says, the effect on equations 3*a* and 4*a* is even more striking. The change in the value of R^2 is thus one way in which we can judge whether the addition of a further independent variable to our analysis helps us to obtain a more accurate explanation. It is important to note, however, that adding another independent variable will normally produce some increase in R^2;[28] if the increase in R^2 is very small, we should place correspondingly little faith in the explanatory power of the new variable. Thus Ford shows, by comparing the R^2 values for equations 5*a* and 6*a*, that the addition of the variable I_t, net home investment in the U.K., hardly helps at all to explain Argentine new issues. Similarly, Olson and Harris find, (p. 204) that the simple regression of Y on X_4 explains almost as much of the variation in Y, $(R^2 = 0.94^2 = 0.884)$ as the multiple regression of Y on X_4 and X_5 $(R^2 = 0.95^2 = 0.903)$, and therefore discard X_5 from their analysis.

[27] Walters (1968), ch. 5; Johnston (1963), chs. 2–4; Blalock (1960), ch. 19; Yeomans (1968), vol. ii, ch. 4.
[28] With the exception of the case, unlikely in practice, where the correlation coefficient between the dependent variable and the new independent variable is actually zero.

The R^2 statistic in multiple regression is therefore a measure of the explanatory power of the variables taken together. The exact form of the relationship between the variables is given, however, by the values of the b coefficients in the regression equation, in multiple as in simple regression. (The value of a in multiple regression represents, as it does in simple regression, the intercept; in simple regression, it is the point at which the regression line cuts the Y axis, while in a multiple regression with two independent variables it is the point at which a regression plane cuts the Y axis). The b coefficients in the multiple regression equation $Y = a + b_1X_1 + b_2X_2 \ldots b_NX_N$ tell us the effect that a change in each X will have on Y, assuming that all other Xs are held constant. For example, Ford's estimated regression 4a, (p. 220) is

$$A_t = -10 \cdot 890 + 1 \cdot 987P_{t-2} + 0 \cdot 129F_t.$$

We can tell from this that, other things being equal, a change of one unit in F will, on average, produce a change of $0 \cdot 129$ units in A. We can also tell, since the sign of b_2 is positive ($b_2 = +0 \cdot 129$), that the change will be in the same direction, that is that A and F are positively related, which confirms Ford's hypothesis that 'The success of an issue—indeed, its placing, would depend on the climate of opinion in Britain towards overseas investment'. Similarly, the negative sign for the coefficients of I in equations 5a, 5b, 6a, 6b confirm the hypothesis of an inverse relationship between home and overseas investment. Inspection of the signs of the coefficients in an estimated regression equation can thus provide a quick initial test of a hypothesis, although it should always be remembered that both the values of the coefficients and their signs may change as independent variables are added to or removed from the regression equation.

CHANGE OVER TIME

Regression analysis has, so far, been presented as a straightforward statistical technique, relatively simple both conceptually and in application. In reality, it is far from simple, and there are a large number of possible sources of error in its use. The principal cause of many of these difficulties, and of difficulties in other statistical methods, is the dimension of time. Time, and the changes in economic variables which accompany the passing of time, is a complicating factor in statistical analysis, but one from which the economic historian, in the nature of his subject, can never escape. When we speak, for example, about 'changes over time' in the economic variables which we are considering, we intend to describe the total effect of many different influences; the weather, for example, may produce seasonal fluctuations, the business cycle will produce changes over a seven- or ten-year period, population pressure on resources may produce an increase in food prices over decades or centuries. In practice, we often need to be able to distinguish between these, and other, possible influences. If, for example, we are interested in the long-term movements of

British investment in Argentina, as Ford was, we may wish to avoid complicating our analysis by considering the short-term effects of business cycles.
If, like Adie, we wish to consider the relationships between short-term fluctuations in notes and in deposits, we need to analyse movements in these
variables uncomplicated by long-term tendencies for both to increase.

Statistical methods of *time series analysis* are therefore concerned with the
identification and description of the components of a time series, the name
which we give to a set of data which is chronologically ordered.[29] The underlying hypothesis of time series analysis is that a time series is the sum or
product of the joint influence of a number of factors each exhibiting a different
time pattern. It is customary to identify four such factors, the *trend, seasonal
fluctuation, cyclical fluctuation,* and *random or irregular fluctuation.* The first
of these, the trend, represents in a sense the average movement of the data over
the time period which is being considered, while the remaining factors represent
different forms of fluctuation or deviation around that average.

The problem of describing the average course of data over time is closely
akin to the problem which we considered earlier, of describing the average
relationship between two sets of data, such as wheat price and wheat acreage.
We now wish to discover, not the average relationship between two sets of
data, but rather the average relationship between one of them and time. In
other words, we wish to estimate, for example, the average effect which the
passage of a certain amount of time will have on the acreage of wheat planted;
we do not assert, of course, that time alone is causing changing wheat acreage,
but rather that the passage of time sums up a number of factors causing such
changes in acreage.

Since the problem is similar, it is natural to make use of the same solution,
that is to estimate the linear regression of acreage, the dependent variable, on
time, the independent variable. This process is known as determining the *linear
trend* in a time series. We measure time in units, in this case years, from zero,
and estimate the values of the constants a and b in the linear regression equation. For the data on wheat acreages shown in Graph 2, the linear trend equation is $Y = 3 \cdot 08 - 0 \cdot 04 X_t$ and the trend line is plotted as line *BB* on Graph 2.

Once we have identified the linear trend in the data, we can calculate trend
values for each year, and subtract those values from the original data values.
We do this to give us the deviations or fluctuations from the average value, in
much the same way as we subtract the mean from data values to give us the
value of deviations from the mean. By doing this, we can argue that we have
removed the influence of long-term changes over time, and are left with shorter-
term fluctuations, which we can then analyse.[30] This is the procedure adopted

---

[29] Allen (1966), ch. 8; Floud (1973), ch. 6; Yeomans (1968), vol. i, ch. 6; vol. ii, ch. 5; Dollar and Jensen
(1971), pp. 126–36.

[30] It is also possible, and often necessary, to distinguish between different types of short-term fluctuations.
Methods by which this can be done are not discussed here; they are described in detail in the references listed
under note 29. Another method of treating time series data, that of smoothing by the use of moving averages,
is undeservedly popular with economic historians; its disadvantages are similarly discussed in those
references, but are not mentioned in detail here since none of the reprinted articles makes use of it.

by Adie (p. 168); since he was mainly interested in the relationship between fluctuations in bank notes and in deposits, he removed the trend from the data, and, for example in Table 2, columns headed $r^2.T$ and $r.T$, analysed the correlation between the resultant *detrended series*.

The procedure of removing the linear trend from the data, before correlating the two series, is justified by Adie's desire to examine the relationship between fluctuations, rather than between the long-term movements over time in his data. This is a historical reason for the procedure, but it is complemented by an equally important statistical reason. We can best approach this by examining further the article by Olson and Harris, (in particular pp. 200–3). If we look at their Figure 1, it can be seen that the long-term movements of wheat acreage and wheat price are very similar. If we described that long-term movement by estimating the linear trends in each series, we would therefore expect that the linear trends would be similar; both would slope downwards from left to right. The corollary of this is that the two linear trends would be closely associated to each other in statistical terms, as measured by the correlation coefficient; calculation of R for two linear trends sloping in the same direction will in fact give an R of $+1$, showing perfect association. This will be clear from the intuitive definition of perfect correlation which we gave earlier, that an upward (or downward) change in one set of data is always accompanied by an upward (or downward) change in the other set of data. Now, it is clear from Figure 1

GRAPH 2

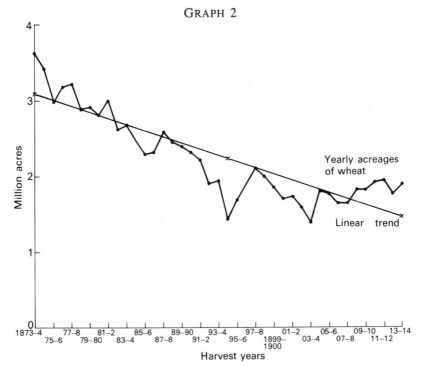

that neither the price nor the acreage series follow exactly a linear trend, and it is also clear that there were some time periods in which the series moved in different directions; some examples are 1879/80 to 1880/1, 1894/5 to 1895/6, 1909/10 to 1910/11. One would not therefore expect that the two series, when correlated, would exhibit a perfect correlation, but on the other hand we would expect the very similar long-term movements over time in the data to influence the correlation in the direction of perfection. In fact, Olson and Harris found that the correlation, in their notation r_{Y_1}, was 0·89 for the period 1873–1914.

Olson and Harris were, of course, aware that the similarity of the two time series over the long term would affect the value of R, and they therefore decided to remove the effect of that long-term trend. They did so not by calculating the linear trend, for a reason which we shall discuss shortly, but rather by 'taking the correlation of the first differences of the harvest year prices and acreage'. The *first differences* of a set of data are calculated by subtracting the data value for one period from the data value for the next period, thus arriving at the change from one period to the next. Correlating the first differences of two yearly series will thus compare changes from year to year. In a series such as those for wheat price and acreage, which have considerable upward and downward fluctuation around a trend, taking first differences will emphasize those fluctuations, and correspondingly reduce the importance of the trend. It should be noted, however, that it does not remove the influence of the trend entirely; it is clear, to take an extreme example, that the correlation between the first differences of two linear trends will still be perfect. Taking first differences, therefore, does not remove the trend, but merely blankets its influence.

As Olson and Harris show, the effect of taking first differences before correlating their two series is to reduce the size of the correlation to 0·22, 'so small as to be trivial'. The previous 0·89 correlation was largely the result of the very similar time trends in the data; it should therefore not be used as evidence for the hypothesis that changes in price were the main determinants of changes in acreage. To test that hypothesis, we need to use a different method, by which the influence of time is removed. The choice is made by the historian; he must be clear as to which hypothesis is to be tested, so that the appropriate statistical method can be used. In some circumstances, as when Adie considers the correspondence over time between notes and deposits, it is appropriate to use the original series, although with care; in others, as when he looks at short-term fluctuations, it is not, and it is necessary to use a series transformed to remove the effects of the time trend.

The need for care when using untransformed series arises because of an important assumption underlying regression analysis. That assumption is that the individual items in a series of data are drawn independently of each other. That is, it is assumed that, from a very large set of data, we have drawn data items at random, and used those items in our analysis; the random drawing of items ensures that the chance of one item being drawn is not affected by (is independent of) the fact that another item has been drawn. Clearly, this assumption is violated with time series data; the data item for one year is closely connected with that for the next. In some circumstances, this will affect the accuracy of our regression analysis, and it is therefore always important to test to see whether the existence of *serial correlation,* as it is called, is serious enough for us to worry about. The most popular test is that used by Ford, and referred to by Olson and Harris, known as the *Durbin–Watson d test,* which allows us to examine the *residuals,* or deviations from, the regression line connecting two or more variables, any or all of which are suspected to be serially correlated. If they are, they are said to be *autocorrelated.* If the Durbin–Watson test, or common sense, shows the existence of autocorrelation, then the variables have to be transformed in some way to mitigate or remove the serial correlation.[31]

We have already considered two methods by which variables can be transformed, the removal of the linear trend and the method of taking first differences. Unfortunately, the removal of the linear trend is not always an appropriate method; it is inappropriate particularly when the data do not exhibit a linear pattern. This can be seen by an examination of Graph 2. Although wheat acreage fell roughly in a straight line to about 1895, thereafter it rose gradually, so that the data have the shape of a curve rather than a straight line over the whole period. In these circumstances, it is clearly inappropriate to represent the trend over time as a straight line; it can also be shown that to remove a linear trend from non-linear data can actually produce serial correlation in the transformed series, and therefore lead to the problem of autocorrelation. Unfortunately, few historical time series exhibit a perfect linear pattern, so that the historian is constantly faced, if he wishes to remove the trend from his data, with the problem of how to do so in a manner appropriate to the data.

In practice economic historians have adopted one of two solutions to this problem. The first solution is the method of first differences which has already been referred to; this method is frequently adopted to avoid the problem of serial correlation, and it provides one way round the problem of non-linearity of the data. It has the disadvantage, however, that it may not meet historical requirements, for the historian may not wish to concentrate on changes from one year to the next. The second solution, which does not suffer from this disadvantage, is to transform the data in such a way that they appear to be approximately linear.[32] There are a large number of methods of achieving this, but the most popular is that used by Adie (p. 169). The series which Adie uses exhibit *exponential growth*; that is, they seem to be changing by a constant proportion each year. If such a series is plotted on normal graph paper, it will appear as a non-linear, curved line. If, on the other hand, such a series is plotted on semi-logarithmic graph paper, it will have the form of a straight line. Taking logarithms, therefore, transforms the series into a linear form, so that it can be approximated by a linear regression equation. When we wish to es-

[31] For a discussion of autocorrelation, see Johnston (1963), pp. 177–200. The Durbin–Watson *d* test is discussed on p. 192. Tables relating to the test can be found in J. Durbin and G. S. Watson (1950 and 1951). The *d* statistic is normally computed by 'package' regression computer programs.

[32] Linear transformations are discussed by Yeomans (1968), vol. ii, ch. 5; Johnston (1963), pp. 44–52; Walters (1968), pp. 98–103.

timate the trend over time in such data, it is therefore appropriate to estimate the linear trend in the logarithms of the dependent variable, so that the regression equation has the form

$$\log Y = a + bT$$

This is the form used by Adie; for notes issued, his equation, as he says, is $\log N = \gamma + \beta T$, where N is notes issued, T is time, and γ and β are constants. An additional advantage of this particular *linear transformation*, as the method is called, is that the percentage rate of growth can be derived directly from the b coefficient; this advantage accounts for the very common use of this method.[33]

Many non-linear series may be transformed into a linear form by such methods.[34] There remain, however, a number of series which cannot be transformed into a linear form by such means; the most common examples of such series are those which have a change in trend, for example the series for wheat prices and acreages, which show a downward trend in one part of the series, and an upward trend in another part. It is sometimes possible to approximate such series by *non-linear trend lines*, or to make use of *non-linear regression* methods, but such methods are well outside the scope of this introduction.[35]

Regression analysis is thus a complicated subject, particularly when applied to the time series which form the bulk of quantitative historical material. At the same time, the analytical power of the method and the availability of computer programs which will perform regression analyses combine to make it certain that the method will be more and more widely used. As this happens, economic historians who apply regression analysis, and those who read results based upon it, have a responsibility to make sure that they understand what they are doing, and so do not misuse a powerful tool.

INFERENCE AND SAMPLES

Although the statistical methods which have so far been discussed appear diverse, they are alike in that they seek to describe, as exactly and effectively as possible, data sets which are assumed to be complete. Thus Olson and Harris assume that they possess all the relevant information on wheat prices and acreages, and set out to describe and analyse that information. In many cases, however, the data cannot be assumed to be complete, and the historian is faced

---

[33] In the semi-log transformation, $\log Y = a + bT$, where T is time measured in years, the average annual percentage rate of growth of Y is strictly not, as Adie implies, the value of b. b is the logarithm of $(1 +$ the proportional rate of growth). For example, the percentage rate of growth of 0.49 for notes, 1845–6, is equivalent to a proportional rate of growth of 0.0049 (i.e. $0.49/100$), b is then $\log 1.0049 = 0.0021$.

[34] The method used by Soltow (pp. 159 f.) with his incomplete income data, is another. He fits a line $X = aL_X^{-b}$, which is a linear equation in the logarithms of both variables, i.e. $\log X = \log a - b \log L_X$.

[35] Some discussion of them can be found in Yeomans (1968), vol. ii, ch. 5. Non-linear trend curves have been used in an interesting article on the British economy of the late nineteenth century: J. R. T. Hughes (1968). Some of the difficulties involved are discussed in E. Ames (1959).

with the problem of making inferences from inadequate evidence. Thus Ames possessed information about only a small number of exchange transactions, many fewer than those which, we imagine, must have taken place; Ames had therefore not only to describe the evidence which he possessed, but also to make inferences from it about the complete set of exchange transactions, most of them unknown to us. Similarly, Ohlin discussed Russell's attempts to make inferences about medieval population change from evidence relating to a very small number of people.

As Ohlin says (p. 60) 'the classical problem of statistics is that of making valid inferences from observations that are known to be poor.' The problem can arise in two ways; firstly, it can arise because the evidence which has survived is poor. Secondly, it can arise because we choose that it should, by using *sample data* rather than working with all the evidence that is available; that evidence may be too bulky, or it may be scattered about the country, or inaccessible in some other way. We shall consider initially the case where sample data are to be used deliberately; although this is less common in practice, it is conceptually simpler.[36]

If we take a sample, we know that the data items which form the sample are an inadequate representation of the complete data set; they are so by definition, since we are not making use of all the data, but are, in a sense, 'throwing away information'. We must, therefore, choose our sample in such a way that, although it is inadequate, it still gives us almost as good information about the characteristics of the complete data set as if we had studied that complete data set. It is, moreover, desirable that we should know by what margin results calculated from the sample data might differ from results calculated from the complete data sets; we need to know, for example, how good is the mean of sample data as a representation of the mean of the complete (or *population*) data set, or how good a regression line calculated from sample data is as a representation of the population regression. The theory of *probability sampling* gives us this information; provided that our sample method is consistent with some requirements, which will be discused shortly, we can, for example, say that the mean of a sample will have a very good chance of falling within a specified distance above or below the mean of the population from which the sample has been drawn. We can, in fact, be more precise, and say that there is a 99 per cent chance that it will be within a specified distance, a 95 per cent chance that it will be within another (smaller) specified distance, and so on. What the distances are will depend upon the size of the sample and its standard deviation, but they can be easily calculated once that information is known.

Let us now imagine that we take two samples separately from the same population, and calculate the mean of each. Since we know, on the basis of sampling theory, that each mean has a 99 per cent chance of falling within a specified distance from the population mean, it follows that the two sample

---

[36] Sampling methods and the statistical procedures based on them form the basis of most textbooks of statistics. They are discussed, for example, in Blalock (1960), chs. 8–13, 18, 19, 22; Yeomans (1968), vol. ii, chs. 1–3; Allen (1966), ch. 9; Floud (1973), ch. 8; Schofield (1972).

means have a 99 per cent chance of falling within a specified (but different) distance of each other. Now let us assume that, instead of taking two samples from the same population, we take one sample from each of two populations. If the two populations have the same mean, they are, so far as their mean value is concerned, the same, and we can therefore use the sampling theory which we have just stated to say that the means of the samples will be within a certain distance of each other. If, on the other hand, the population means were considerably different from each other, then we would expect that the sample means would be much further from each other. The sampling theorem therefore provides us with a simple test of whether the population means are the same or different; if they are the same, then the sample means are likely to be close to each other, while if they are not, then the sample means are likely to be further from each other. The exact boundary, at which we conclude that the sample means are so far apart that the population means are very likely to be different, is dependent on the sample sizes and on their standard deviations, and also on what we choose to mean by 'very likely'; if we wish to be conservative, demanding a 99 per cent likelihood, then the boundary will fall when the sample means are further apart than if we are content with a 95 per cent likelihood.

It is this logic which is used when we say that we are testing whether a particular difference between two samples is *significant*. If, for example, we find that two sample means are so far apart that there is a 99 per cent likelihood that the means of the two populations from which they are drawn are different, we say that the 'difference between the two sample means is *significant at the 99 per cent level*'. The procedure which we have outlined is known therefore as *testing the significance* of the difference between sample means, and there are similar procedures for testing the significance of other sample characteristics, such as proportions, regression coefficients, or correlation coefficients. Significance tests of various kinds are used by Olson and Harris (p. 205), by Ames (pp. 38 f.) who also discusses significance tests for contingency tables in general, by Ford (pp. 218 f.) and Soltow (pp. 161–2) who test the significance of regression coefficients, and by Ohlin (pp. 62 f.).[37]

As an example, Ohlin uses a widely used method, the chi-square test, in his study of Russell's estimates of expectations of life in medieval Britain. Ohlin was concerned to discover how far the incidence of plague in the mid-fourteenth century might have affected these estimates, by producing abnormal changes in mortality. He therefore studies two groups of men, those born between 1276 and 1300, and those born between 1348 and 1375. He shows, in Table 2 (p. 63), that the mortality rates for these two groups differ, the differences being given as col. 4 of that table. Since these data are derived from a very small number of people, rather than from the whole population of medieval England, Ohlin must try to discover whether the observed differences between the mortality rates of the two groups are a good guide to the true

---

[37] Tests of significance applied to correlation and regression estimates are discussed in the references cited above, note 36, and in Walters (1968), ch. 6; Johnston (1963), ch. 4.

differences in mortality for the whole population, or whether they have been produced by the accidents of the selection of the data. That is, as he says,

> The age-specific mortality rates for the different generations can also be subjected to chi-square tests to decide whether they are actually significantly different. The chi-square test in this case posits hypothetically that the true death rates of the different generations were identical and aims to decide how likely it is that samples of the sizes actually drawn would show the observed discrepancies merely as the result of chance.

In other words, taking the age-group 15–19 as an example, Ohlin tests to see how likely it is that a difference of 84 could have appeared as the result of the selection of data, if the real mortality rate for the two groups of all people born 1276–1300 and 1348–1375 had actually been identical. His method is to calculate the chi-square value, shown in Table 2, and then to refer to tables of the chi-square distribution to see how likely it is that such a value could have occurred as a result of the chances of data selection. As he says, when each group is taken individually, the chi-square values suggest that 'the variations . . . could easily be due to chance in most cases', but when the data are regrouped into three groups, those who died before 25, between 25 and 50, and over 50, a different pattern emerges. As can be seen from Table 2, the age-specific mortality rates for ages below 25 were much higher for the second (1348–75) group, than for the first (1276–1300) group, and the chi-square test suggests that there was a less than 2 per cent chance that this observed difference was due to sampling errors. (This statement can be rephrased to read 'there was a greater than 98 per cent chance that this observed difference was not due to sampling errors'; which formulation is used is a matter of individual choice.) Similarly, the difference between the two groups for ages over 50 is also significant.

Ohlin has therefore established that the observed differences are *statistically significant,* and that it is therefore unlikely that the populations born in those two groups of years had identical life-table mortality rates. This statement, in itself, has no historical significance; it is simply a statement about the likelihood of a sample result being due to the chances of data selection. Historical significance is given to that statement only when Ohlin points out that 'The plague hit different generations in different portions of their life span. . . . The generation of 1348–75 was exposed to great hazards in its early years, and that of 1276–1300 only when its youngest members were close to 50'; he suggests that the observed differences in mortality thus relate to differential exposure to the plague, giving a historical explanation for a statistical difference. What must be emphasized is that it is the difference which is 'significant', in this special statistical meaning of the word, not the explanation. Ohlin has not tested the hypothesis that it was the plague that caused the difference, merely the hypothesis that there was a difference. It may seem mere pedantry to emphasize this distinction, but it is extremely important to remember that statistical significance does not in any way imply historical significance; in many instances, as in Ohlin's study, a statistically significant result can lead to, or help to confirm, a historically significant finding, but in other instances the two do not go together. The correlation coefficient between wheat acreage and wheat price, including time, for example, is certainly highly significant statistically, but unimportant historically.

The historian must therefore always take care in reaching conclusions on the basis of tests of significance. In addition, he must remember that the results of the tests will be accurate only if his data and methods meet certain restrictive assumptions which underlie the logic of the tests. For example, many significance tests are based on the assumption that the sampling method is that know as *independent random sampling*. Several of the tests, though not, for example, the *non-parametric tests* used by Ames and Ohlin, are based on theories incorporating further, and more restrictive, assumptions.[38] It follows that, where the data or methods used by the historian do not comply with these restrictions, the tests of significance based on them are of doubtful use and, indeed, may be meaningless. In particular, their validity is very questionable when it is known that the data have not been selected by independent random sampling methods.

Unfortunately, most historical data have not been selected by such methods. The requirements for independent random sampling are rigorous; for example, each piece of evidence in the population must have an equal chance of appearing in the sample, and the inclusion of one piece of evidence must not affect the chance of another piece being included. Further, if two samples are being considered, they must have been chosen independently of each other. Most historical data, on the other hand, have survived through the chances of history, which are anything but random. Thus, for example, the basic series used by Ames (p. 36) consists of 'the transactions recorded by the Peruzzi', and excludes not only all other exchange dealings of that period, but also some Peruzzi dealings; the sample is therefore entirely non-random.

It is very difficult to judge in practice whether it matters that a sample is demonstrably non-random. In many cases, even though it can be shown that data have not been gathered by independent random sampling, it can be assumed that the processes of historical selection have had much the same effect; as Ohlin points out, Russell has used a sample which is clearly non-random, but there is no reason to suppose that it is biased in a way which would affect estimates of mortality made from it, except in the sense that it relates only to the propertied classes. Russell's sample may therefore be regarded as a reasonably good sample of the landowners of medieval England, if not of the population as a whole. In such circumstances, however, it is difficult to justify the use of significance tests, since one of their basic assumptions is violated, except as a very rough guide, as Ohlin uses the test which has been described above. Even if significance tests are inappropriate, however, the data may well not be valueless; just as a 'significant' result may be historically

[38] Very broadly, the difference between the parametric and non-parametric statistical tests lies in the assumptions which underlie the statistical model. For example, parametric tests may normally be used only when the data is of interval type, while non-parametric tests can be applied to data of other types. The assumptions of the two types of tests are set out most clearly in Siegel (1956), ch. 3.

valueless, so a 'non-significant' result or a result from a non-random sample may be historically valuable.

This warning also applies to the use of significance tests with data which are not the result of any form of sampling procedure. At first sight, to use a test in such circumstances seems a waste of effort, and in many cases it is; if we know that our evidence relates to the population, it makes little sense to use a test to see whether it does so. Thus significance tests are of little use in the analysis of the aggregate data which are often used by economic historians, and their use may produce misleading results. With some micro-economic data, their use may be more justifiable, although it is difficult to lay down any general rule, except that the historian should know what he is doing, and therefore not mislead himself or others.[39]

It is appropriate to end this introduction with this warning, since there is no doubt that the methods of quantitative economic history need care, historical understanding, and common sense as well as an awareness of statistical theory. The articles which follow have been selected to illustrate these qualities. It has not been possible, in this introduction, to discuss them all, nor all the statistical methods used in them, but the most popular methods have been discussed, and attention has been drawn to the most useful additional reading. The introduction has also been supplemented by the notes appended at the beginning of each article, and by the bibliography and index to statistical methods. Taking all these together with the most important aid to understanding, the articles themselves, this volume is intended as a contribution to the appreciation by economic historians of the changing technology of our subject.

[39] It has only been possible to touch on a vexed subject in statistical methodology, the 'significance test controversy'. For more optimistic statements of the value of significance tests, see the references listed under notes 36 and 37. For an even more pessimistic view, see J. Galtung (1967), Part II, ch. 4, particularly pp. 358–89. This book is an immensely stimulating treatment of many statistical methods. There is also a short discussion of missing data problems in Floud (1973), ch. 8.

1

The Sterling Crisis of 1337–1339*

E. AMES

Editor's note. This article was first published in *Jour. Econ. Hist.*, 25 (1965), 496–552.
The methods of contingency table analysis are discussed in the Introduction, above, pp. 13–14. Significance tests and related sampling problems are described above, pp. 32–35. For further reading see footnotes on those pages, and: Dollar and Jensen (1971); Schofield (1972).

THE sterling crisis of 1337–9 is interesting for two reasons. First, it seems to be the earliest such crisis for which detailed analysis is possible. Second, the details of this crisis, when compared to those pertaining to the 1340s, offer what might be called a 'textbook example' of the differences between non-convertible and convertible foreign exchange systems.

The basic series to be analysed is given in Table 1.[1] It consists of a chronological arrangement of the transactions recorded by the Peruzzi.[2] Most of these are taken from statements of the form 'x pounds sterling were paid by (or to) so-and-so, and the account was charged y pounds Florentine'. The transactions represented by these quotations mainly represent expenses incurred by the main office of the firm in Florence and by its customers. They are not transactions of the London office of the firm. Most Peruzzi dealings in sterling were presumably transactions of the London office, which was both a lender to the English king and the papal fiscal representative in England. The London office accounts are missing, and the transactions by the Florence office are mainly for relatively small sums. Many are for what we should now call 'expense accounts' by members of the firm travelling in northern Europe for periods of months, or even fiscal years (which seemed to begin 1 July). It has been

* This research was in part supported by a grant from the Rockefeller Foundation.

Notes to Table 1

[1] Most transactions are over intervals centring in given month.
[2] One transaction at 10/15/0, one at 10/10/0.
[3] Two transactions at this rate.
[4] One transaction at 9/5/0, one at 9/0/0.
[5] One transaction at 10/5/0, one at 9/0/0.
[6] One transaction at 10/0/0, one at 9/10/0.
[7] Two transactions at 10/10/0, one at 10/4/0, one at 9/10/0, three at 9/5/0.
[8] One transaction at 10/16/3, one at 10/10/0.
[9] One transaction at 10/10/0, one at 10/5/0.
[10] For the year ending 30 June 1340, which centres between these two dates, rates are quoted as follows: 10/10/0, three; 10/5/0, ten; 10/4/0, one (pp. 91–2, 122, 124, 127, 128, 134, 140–4, 269, 360, 365, 370).
[11] In addition, for the year ending 30 June 1341, centring at this month, quotations of 11/2/0 (p. 370), 10/10/0 (p. 144), 10/4/0 (p. 269), 10/0/0 (p. 140).
[12] Two transactions at 10/10/0, one at 10/5/0.
[13] Two transactions at 11/10/0; one at 10/10/0.

TABLE 1. *The Exchange Rate of the Pound, as Recorded in the Peruzzi Accounts, 1334–1345*

(price of one pound Sterling, in Florentine silver currency)*

Date[1]	Quotation	Page reference
Oct. 1334	10/10/0	58
July 1335	10/12/6[2]	7, 223
Jan. 1336	9/10/0	352
May 1336	10/10/0	223
Aug. 1336	10/10/0	158
Oct. 1336	10/ 8/0	194
Nov. 1336	10/ 0/0	150–2
Jan. 1337	9/10/0[3]	85, 91–2, 136, 346
Feb. 1337	9/ 0/0	57
May 1337	9/ 4/0	195
June 1337	9/ 0/0	255
Nov. 1337	9/ 5/0	124, 134
Jan. 1338	9/ 2/6[4]	91–2, 370
Mar. 1338	9/12/6[5]	136, 352
May 1338	9/ 4/8	365
June 1338	9/10/0	128
Aug. 1338	9/15/0[6]	150, 158
Jan. 1339	10/ 0/0[7]	62, 80, 91–2, 124, 134, 365, 370
Feb. 1339	9/10/0	261
Mar. 1339	10/14/0	113
Apr. 1339	9/10/0	93
June 1339	9/10/0	151
July 1339	10/13/2[8]	62, 261
Sept. 1339	10/10/0	129
Oct. 1339	10/ 7/6[9]	131, 359
Nov. 1339	10/ 5/0[10]	93
Feb. 1340	10/ 5/0[10]	123
July 1340	10/ 5/0	62, 80
Sept. 1340	10/ 0/0	269
Jan. 1341	10/ 5/0[11]	122, 124, 128, 140, 142, 143, 360
Feb. 1341	10/ 5/0	269
Mar. 1341	10/ 8/4[12]	93, 107, 137
Sept. 1341	11/ 3/4[13]	124, 140, 143, 269, 360
Nov. 1345	10/17/4	156

* Throughout this paper, we shall write x/y/z for £x ys. zd. and y/z for ys. zd. All currencies were of the Carolingian type, although the names for 'libra', 'solidus', and 'denarius' varied from country to country.

assumed that on a transaction described as covering expenses between two given times the reported exchange rate was that which prevailed at the mid-point of the interval. Where more than one transaction took place (or centred in) a given month, the quotations were averaged, equal weights being assigned to each transaction regardless of the size of the individual transactions.[3]

The price of sterling ranged from 9 to over 11 pounds Florentine. It is a familiar assertion that if two countries are on metallic coinage, the exchange rates will vary within the limits governed by the cost of shipping and insurance. It is natural to inquire whether fluctuations of this magnitude are apt to have exceeded these 'silver points'.

For the six years 1330–5 the price of wine in England averaged 54 *d.* per dozen gallons, according to Thorold Rogers.[4] Thus, it was possible to make and transport French wine to England at a delivered price of about 0·45*d.* per pound avoirdupois. Transportation alone would therefore have been less than 0·45*d.* per pound avdp. One Tower pound of silver at this time could be made into £1. 3*d.* of coin, so that one pound avdp. of silver would have made £1. 6*s.* 3*d.* If the cost of transporting (and especially insuring) silver[5] were ten times as great as that on wine, it would have amounted to roughly 1·4 per cent of the value of the shipment. If the par value of sterling was of the order of £10 Florentine, the silver import and export points would have been in the order of 3 shillings Florentine above and below par. The actual fluctuations are far in excess of this range.

Table 1 suggests that the exchange rate of sterling, in terms of Florentine currency, was lower between January 1337 and June 1339 than at other periods. Table 2 presents the evidence pertaining to the generalization: The

TABLE 2. *Number of Transactions by Price of Pound Sterling*

Period	At least £10 Florentine	Below £10 Florentine	Total
Jan. 1337–June 1339	6	22	28
Other	54	3	57
Total	60	25	85

price of sterling was below 10/0/0 from January 1337 to June 1339, and above 10/0/0 the rest of the time. This table suggests that there was a significant difference in the probability that a Peruzzi sterling transaction would occur at a lower rate in this period of 1337–9 than at other periods in the interval observed.

Statements of this sort are dealt with in the theory of contingency tables. They are typically of the form: Is event *A* more likely to occur in samples of Type I than in samples of Type II? That is, are the two samples likely to have been drawn from the same population? The theory permits of formulating significance tests[6] which state how likely it is that differences in the proportion of occurrence of event A would be as great as those actually observed, in pairs of samples drawn from a single population at random. If the Peruzzi data may be considered as random drawings from a single population, there is less than one chance in 100 that results as different as these would have been obtained for the two periods.

This sort of test, used with economic data, is apt to be over-optimistic, in the sense that too many hypotheses will be retained and too few rejected.[7] Significance test criteria in this paper eliminate the least acceptable hypotheses. A conclusion which passes a test is considered acceptable, pending the development of more relevant tests.[8]

The data in Table 1 might reflect either (1) a low point in English exchange rates in 1337–9 or (2) a high point in Florentine rates in that period. If the first possibility is correct, the pattern shown in Table 2 would not be repeated if exchange rates were computed between Florentine currency and other north

TABLE 3. *The Exchange Rate of Flanders-Brabant Currency in Transactions Recorded in Peruzzi Accounts, 1329–1339*

(price of one pound Flanders–Brabant currency, in pounds of Florentine silver currency)

	Quotations on Flemish[1]		
Date[2]	Silver currency	Gold currency	Page reference
Mar. 1329	26/15/10		164, 275
July 1335	30/ 0/ 0		7
Jan. 1338	29/15/ 0		86
Mar. 1338	29/13/ 4		269
Nov. 1338	31/ 0/ 0		86
Jan. 1339	30/ 0/ 0	2/ 2/ 3[3]	106, 114, 121, 359, 366
Feb. 1339	30/ 0/ 0	2/ 2/ 0	106
Apr. 1339	[28/10/ 0]	2/ 4/ 0	93
May 1339	30/ 0/ 0		131
June 1339	29/11/ 8		134
July 1339	26/16/ 3	1/18/ 0	260
Aug. 1339	[28/ 7/ 6][4]	1/18/10	135, 137
Oct. 1339	[26/18/10][5]	1/18/ 0[5]	113, 135, 359
Jan. 1340	[26/ 9/ 5][6]	1/17/ 6	106, 107, 140, 269
Feb. 1340	[25/15/ 0]	1/17/ 0	123
Sept. 1340	[23/15/ 0][7]	1/17/ 0	107, 140, 141, 269, 366
July 1341	[23/ 4/ 0]	1/17/ 0	145

[1] Quotations in brackets are derived from gold currency quotations, at rates of conversion given in the source.

[2] Virtually all transactions are on intervals centring on given month.

[3] One transaction at 2/2/6 and one at 2/2/0.

[4] One transaction at 26/15/0 silver and 1/17/11 gold; one transaction at 30/0/0 silver (no gold price listed).

[5] One transaction at 26/16/3 silver and 1/18/0 gold; one transaction at 27/11/4 silver (no gold price listed). In connection with the latter, it was observed that 'good' *gros tournois* were worth 30/0/0 a *fior.*

[6] In addition, for the year ending 30 June 1340, centring on this month, rates of 26/16/10 (p. 141), 26/4/8 (pp. 141, 365) were quoted.

[7] One transaction at 24/9/3 (p. 107); one at 23/9/3 (pp. 140, 269); one at 23/1/9 (pp. 141, 366).

European currencies. If the latter is correct, the 1337–9 dip should be found for other north European currencies.[9]

Tables 3–5 summarize Peruzzi transactions in the Low Countries (actually Bruges and Ghent) and in France (Paris) over this period. In both cases, the transactions involved both gold and silver coin, so that separate calculations are needed. The Peruzzi recorded transactions in Paris and in Avignon. The

TABLE 4. *Exchange Rates for Gold Currency in Paris*

(price of French currency, a *fior*)

Date	Quotation	Page reference
Mar. 1335	1/10/3	29, 111, 192
July 1335	1/ 9/0	109
Aug. 1335	1/10/6	110
July 1337	1/ 9/7	30
Aug. 1337	1/10/6	323
Sept. 1337	1/10/8	120
Jan. 1338	1/10/6	123
Apr. 1338	1/10/9	151
July 1338	,1/11/0	151
Aug. 1338	1/11/0	151
Mar. 1339	1/10/0	123

TABLE 5. *The Price of French Silver Currency in Paris*

(in Florentine silver currency)

Date	Quotation	Description of French coin	Page reference
Jan. 1330	2/ 7/8	good *gros tournois*	30
Feb. 1331	2/ 5/0	good *gros tournois*	30
Mar. 1335	2/19/4	*parisis*	29, 111
	2/10/1	good *tournois*	192
Apr. 1335	2/16/10	good *tournois parisis*	191–2
Sept. 1335	2/12/1	good *tournois parisis*	7, 192
June 1337	2/17/6	*parisis*	30
May 1338	2/11/7	current *parisis*	151
	2/ 9/2	good *parisis*	151
July 1338	2/12/0	current *parisis*	151
	2/ 9/7	good *tournois*	151
Aug. 1338	2/12/0	*parists*	153
	2/ 9/7	current *parisis*	151

latter is disregarded, as being a part of the Mediterranean rather than of the northern economy. The French silver coinage was of two types, *tournois* and *parisis*. In addition, the French coinage was being depreciated over the period, so that the adjectives *good* and *current* appear in the Peruzzi books. It would appear that the *tournois* quotations could be treated as constant about 2/10/0 over 1335–8, while the *parisis* transactions were stable at about 2/16/0 until mid-1337 and then dropped to about 2/10/0 in 1338.

Table 6 presents contingency tables for French and Flemish exchange rates which are comparable to Table 2. Flemish currency tended to be *higher* in

TABLE 6. *Distribution of Monthly Flemish and French Quotations in January 1337–June 1339 as Compared to Other Periods*

	Number of transactions in which price of Flemish silver coin, in terms of Florentine silver currency, was:		
	At least 29/0/0	Below 29/0/0	Total
Jan. 1337–June 1339	5	4	9
Other	3	18	21
Total	8	22	30
	Flemish gold coin, in terms of Florentine silver currency, was:		
	At least 2/0/0	Below 2/0/0	Total
Jan. 1337–June 1339	4	0	4
Other	0	7	7
Total	4	7	11
	French silver coin, in terms of Florentine silver currency, was:		
	At least 2/11/0	Below 2/11/0	Total
Jan. 1337–June 1339	1	3	4
Other	3	2	5
Total	4	5	9
	French gold coin, in terms of Florentine silver currency, was:		
	At least 1/10/6	Below 1/10/6	Total
Jan. 1337–June 1339	6	2	8
Other	1	2	3
Total	7	4	11

1337–9 than at other times. This result is not significant in the case of silver coin, but it is significant at the 0·01 level for gold coin. Neither silver nor gold French coin was significantly different in 1337–9 than at other periods.

Given only the sterling transactions, we would be unable to decide whether sterling fell or Florentine currency rose in 1337. Given sterling and Flemish quotations, we could conclude that sterling fell relative to Florentine currency, and that Florentine currency fell relative to Flemish. But the observation that there was no significant change in Florentine currency relative to Flemish silver, to French gold, or to French silver currency suggests that Florentine currency was stable in this period.

These results are a sort of paradox. During the entire period 1335–45, the metal content of both English and Florentine silver coin was unchanged,[10] yet the exchange rates of these currencies fluctuated outside the silver import and export points. The metal content of French silver and gold coin was steadily reduced.[11] The French exchange rates recorded by the Peruzzi, however, show stability.

Half of the apparent paradox may be resolved simply. The Peruzzi accounts are careful to specify the kinds of French coin purchased. Indeed, in France a variety of coins circulated side by side, so that anyone equipped with a scale was able to reduce the coinage to some common denominator of weight.

The remainder of the paradox will occupy the rest of this paper. It would appear that during the 1330s, at least, sterling had a fluctuating exchange rate. It is natural to inquire whether there is any independent evidence to support this assertion. Table 7, therefore, presents a number of sterling quotations for

TABLE 7. *Price of One Pound Sterling, in (Gold) Papal Florins, Miscellaneous Dates 1342–1429*

Date	Price	Page reference	Implied price of Sterling in Florentine silver	
Apr. 1342	7·2	616	10/ 8/9[1]	10/ 1/7[2]
June 1343	7·5	1	10/17/4	10/10/0
Aug. 1344	7·2	14	10/ 8/9	10/ 1/7
Dec. 1344	7·2	13	10/ 8/9	10/ 1/7
June 1345	7·4	18	10/14/7	10/ 8/7
June 1346	7·5	26	10/17/4	10/10/0
Mar. 1347	7·5	31	10/17/4	10/10/0
Sept. 1348	7·2	38	10/ 8/9	10/ 1/7
May 1356	7·5	634	10/17/4	10/10/0
July 1356	6·7	620	9/14/3	9/ 5/10
Jan. 1357	6·5	634	9/ 8/6	9/ 2/0
(no month) 1357	6·7	624–5	9/14/3	9/ 5/10
Sept. 1359	7·2	633	10/ 8/9	10/ 1/7
Mar. 1380	6·1	262	8/16/10	8/ 9/5
Feb. 1392	5·6	281	8/ 2/5	7/16/10
Mar. 1392	6·4	282	9/ 5/7	9/ 0/7
Dec. 1392	6·7	451	9/14/3	9/ 5/10
Mar. 1414	6·0	134	8/14/0	8/ 8/0
Sept. 1421	6·0	193	8/14/0	8/ 8/0
Oct. 1428	6·0	50	8/14/0	8/ 8/0
Dec. 1429	6·0	171	8/14/0	8/ 8/0

[1] This column was calculated on the assumption that the mean of the rates quoted for June 1345 and June 1346 in this table (7·45) corresponds to the rate quoted for Nov. 1345 in Table 1 (10/17/4).

[2] This column was calculated on the assumption that the rates of 7·5 quoted in this table correspond to a 'normal prewar' rate of 10/10/0 found in Table 1.

Source: Calendar of Entries in the Papal Registers Relating to Great Britain and Ireland (London, 1897).

the period 1342–9. From this table, one would conclude that over much of the fourteenth century sterling was a fluctuating currency. This conclusion does not depend on the existence of a downward trend, since this would be consistent with the increases in the English mint prices of silver which are known to have occurred. Rather it depends upon short-term ups and downs in the quotations.[12]

Is it reasonable to speak of 1337–9 as a crisis? Table 7, taken in conjunction with Table 1, suggests that it is. During the 1340s, it would appear that sterling quotation varied over the range 7·2 to 7·5, or less than 5 per cent.[13] By this standard, the year 1337 was marked by an unusual drop in sterling. Was this drop so great as to suggest that the 'crisis' occurred only in the Peruzzi accounting division? Table 8 shows that a decline of 14 per cent in sterling rates occurred from May 1356 to January 1357, and that a 20 per cent increase in sterling took place in 1392. We conclude that in 1337 a crisis occurred but that this crisis is not unparalleled in magnitude in the fourteenth century.[14]

The crisis of 1337–9 obviously had something to do with the beginning of the Hundred Years War, the abortive campaign in Flanders, and the various schemes by which the King sought to pay for the war by operations in the wool market. We shall consider how these various political and fiscal factors entered into the balance of payments.

A number of statements can be made with some assurance. These will be based on contingency tables, and accompanied by parenthetical numbers to denote the significance of the statement. For any such statement, the reader will be able to construct, from the tables presented, contingency tables of the following form:

	The number of years in which series X was:	
In the period	*Above mean value*[15]	*Below mean value*
1333–6		
(or 1330–6)	4 (or 7)	0
1337–43	1 (or 2)	6 (or 5)

If these tables have the frequencies indicated, or if there is a zero in the lower left box, the statements may be taken as significant. Given two significant statements, we prefer those which relate to four rather than seven prewar years, on the grounds that (1) the test is sharper; and (2) it covers a smaller variety of possible peacetime conditions and thus more closely approximates to 'prewar'. Where we make negative statements, we have in mind that there is not a significant difference between prewar and wartime conditions.

For instance, if we consider the balance of trade, our problem is to compare the import of wine with the export of wool. It is stated in the literature that these are the most important items of trade. Import data (Table 8) are incomplete. However, wartime imports, while a little higher during the war than before (3,634 tons compared to 3,452 for alien imports; 113 ships compared to 91 ships for non-London denizens), are not significantly different. Price data

TABLE 8. *English Wine Prices and Imports, 1333–1343*

Year, ending Michaelmas	Price of wine[1]	Imports of wine	
		By aliens[2]	By non-London denizens[3]
1333	48	1,586	
1334	54˙	6,166	126
1335	51	3,190	77
1336	57		94
1337		2,146	43
1338	54		
1339		4,648[4]	83
1340		2,022	235
1341		4,258	114
1342		3,411	106
1343		3,829	101

[1] Pence per dozen gallons. Thorold Rogers. (His figures are universally criticized, but seldom improved upon.)

[2] In tons. M. K. James, 'The Fluctuations of the Anglo–Gascon Wine Trade during the Fourteenth Century', *Econ. Hist. Rev.*, 2 d ser., iv (1951).

[3] Ships from which the King's prise was taken; ibid.

[4] February to Michaelmas rate.

TABLE 9. *English Wool Prices and Exports, 1333–1343*

(fiscal year ending Michaelmas)

Year, ending Michaelmas	English wool prices		Wool export[3] (thousand sacks)	Value of exported wool	
	Domestic prices	Domestic price plus duty[2]		At farm[4]	At frontier[5]
	(Pence per clove)			(1333–43 mean = 100)	
1333	24·0	26·0	28·3	159	127
1334	17·5	19·5	34·6	142	116
1335	21·2	19·5	34·1	170	115
1336	25·0	28·0	21·8	127	105
1337	24·8	27·8	4·3	20	20
1338	17·8	23·8	19·5	81	81
1339	20·2	26·2	41·8	99	189
1340	18·0	24·0	20·3	43	84
1341	18·0	26·0	19·6	71	88
1342	22·0	28·0	21·8	112	105
1343	19·5	25·5	15·8	72	70

[1] Rogers.

[2] Duties may be somewhat unsatisfactorily estimated from data in Sir James H. Ramsay, *The Genesis of Lancaster* (Oxford, 1913), i. 182; ii. 88–90; and from the papers by F. R. Barnes and by G. Unwin in *Finance and Trade under Edward III*, ed. G. Unwin (Manchester, 1918).

[3] E. M. Carus-Wilson and Olive Coleman, *England's Export Trade, 1275–1547* (Oxford, 1963). It has been necessary to adjust data for some parts to place them on a twelve-month basis.

[4] An index of the products of columns (1) and (3).

[5] An index of the products of columns (2) and (3).

are incomplete. For this period, prices were not increasing; at some later date they doubled, but it is not possible to say now when this increase took place. So we conclude that the value of imports did not change much.

The value of exports, however, fell (Table 9). Domestic prices averaged a little less during the war years than before, but not significantly. Despite a considerable increase in export duties (customs and subsidy) the estimated sum (Table 9, col. 2) of domestic prices plus export duties rose insignificantly during the war years. The volume of exports was significantly lower during the war (0·005). Consequently, the value of exports at the farm (col. 4) dropped significantly (0·05). The drop in foreign exchange earnings (col. 6) is not significant for the war years as a whole. But the very sharp drop in earnings in 1337 coincides with the decline in sterling in Table 1; and the sharp increase in 1339 coincides with the rise in sterling in Table 1. The details of the wool trade during the period are complicated and need not detain us here. We may generalize about the war period as a whole only if we can say that the large exports of 1339 represent a working off of stocks accumulated in England but not exported during the period of the monopoly.[16] We then would obtain (by averaging 1337–9) a significant (0·05) decline in exports. We are reluctant to juggle numbers to obtain a statistically significant table, but we find some force in the argument.

The data on commodity trade therefore associate the crisis of 1337–9 with the decline in wool exports and consequently with the political and economic manoeuvres involving royal trading in wool.

Data on government revenue and spending for this period have never been disentangled. However, it is possible to give average monthly data for ten sub-periods of the period 1329–44 (Table 10) for the Wardrobe, which was the most important single source of spending. A large part of the revenue of the Exchequer (the Receipt) was at this time turned over to the Wardrobe. In particular, the Wardrobe carried out most of the spending in which the King was personally interested, such as wars, the wool schemes, and so forth. Wardrobe began to increase its expenditures some time before the beginning of the Flemish campaign; and the period of greatest Wardrobe spending began late in 1338 (that is, about the time sterling began to rise). The timing of changes in Wardrobe spending do not, therefore, coincide with the changes in sterling reported in Table 1.

In modern times, the outbreak of a major war is apt to lead to increases in the price level because (to oversimplify) governments never raise enough taxes to cover military expenses, and they increase the supply of money at a time when (owing to military procurements) they are reducing the supply of consumer goods. Modern readers will be interested in the significant (0·01) drop in prices following the beginning of the Hundred Years War (Table 11). There is again an oversimplified explanation of this drop. Comparatively speaking, the fourteenth-century army was labour-intensive, and the modern army is capital-intensive. A fourteenth-century army fighting on foreign soil (as the English army was in the Hundred Years War) cost money mainly because it had to buy

TABLE 10. Wardrobe Accounts, Monthly Rates

	Receipts				Expenditures				
	Exchequer of								
	Receipt	Account	Other	Total	Household	Other	Total	Expenses	Advances
Sept. 29, 1329–Oct. 15, 1331	1,101		371	1,473	845	757	1,603	1,519	84
Oct. 16, 1331–Sept. 29, 1332	640		181	821	746	228	974		
Sept. 29, 1332–Sept. 29, 1333	1,856		198	2,053	769	1,156	1,924	1,874	50
Sept. 29, 1333–July 30, 1334	786		490	1,276	824	571	1,395	1,323	72
July 31, 1334–Aug. 31, 1337	3,290	137	130	3,557	886	2,754	3,640	3,562	78
Aug. 31, 1337–July 11, 1338	2,049	111	464	2,624	858	2,396	3,253	2,952	301
July 12, 1338–May 27, 1340	5,842	983	6,902	13,728	1,060	13,988	15,048	9,828	5,221
May 27, 1340–Nov. 25, 1341	1,232	208	948	2,388	793	2,759	3,552	2,897	655
Nov. 25, 1341–Apr. 11, 1344	2,130		274	2,404	897	2,180	3,077	3,039	38
Apr. 11, 1344–Nov. 24, 1347	5,168		194	5,362	1,071	4,695	5,766	5,441	325

Source: T. F. Tout, *Chapters in the Administrative History of Medieval England* (Manchester, 1920), vi. Appendix II. (Details may not add to total because of rounding.)

food and fodder it could not plunder. Such military expenses were a direct reduction of the domestic money supply, since paper money could not yet be used. In contrast, preparations for war (raising troops at home) should not have monetary repercussions, since the taxpayers' money was transferred to the troops, who spent it for food and fodder. Except for imports of horses or armour no foreign repercussions need occur.

TABLE 11. *The 'Price of Composite Unit of Consumables', 1329–1343*
(1451–75 = 100)

1329	119
1330	120
1331	134
1332	131
1333	111
1334	99
1335	96
1336	106
1337	85
1338	79
1339	96
1340	86
1341	85
1342	84
1343	97

Source: E. H. Phelps Brown and Sheila V. Hopkins, 'Seven Centuries of the Price of Consumables, Compared with Builders' Wage-Rates', *Economica,* 23 (1956).

We have not found the date at which English troops began to land on the Continent; but when the king arrived in Flanders in late 1337, he found his army there. The year 1338 was marked by the peak in English military force in Flanders (so far as we can tell), and everyone seems to have gone home in 1339, when exports began to pick up again. The chronology of the military operation (expensive, although abortive) coincides roughly, therefore, with the sterling crisis under discussion.

The data on travel between England and the Continent serve to cast some better light upon the probable timing of military expenditures, since there is probably a connection between the size of the English military establishment on the Continent and the movement of government officials to the Continent.

Movement of people in and out of England was controlled at least as early as the 1230s. Travellers to the Continent were usually required to leave through the Cinque Ports, and were sometimes restricted to Dover. Several categories of traveller were recognized: pilgrims, members of religious orders in England with headquarters on the Continent, merchants, persons travelling on the king's business, and so on.

It would be most interesting, of course, to obtain data on the travel of merchants, although such data are difficult to evaluate, since documents sometimes pertain to entire firms and sometimes to individuals; moreover, it sometimes seems to be the case that some members of a given firm are considered residents of England, while other members are considered aliens because they work in foreign (Florentine or Flemish) main offices. But travel restrictions do provide information which gives clues about foreign spending by English. As early as 1258, exit permits distinguish between persons allowed to take coin out of the country and persons not allowed to.[17] Beginning in the 1290s it is possible to obtain fairly continuous series which separate exit permits into those permitting, and those prohibiting, the carrying of travel expenses, in coin, out of the country (Table 12).

TABLE 12. *Permits to Leave England through Dover, 1294–1326*[1]

Calendar year	Taking silver or coin for expenses	Taking no silver or coin	Page references
1294	1		367
1296	2		511
1299	3[2]	1	265, 328, *CCW*, 103
1300	3[2]	2	349, 355, 369, 379, 416, 445
1301		1	465
1302		2	550
1303	1	4	137, 513, 539, 550, 566
1304		2	69, 169, 209
1305	1	1	236[3]
1306		2	375, 473
1307	8		482, 483, 505, 508, 510, 8, 9, 12
1308	2		24, 122
1309	2		165, 185
1310	2		203, 277
1311	6		310, 316, 451, 372, 430
1313	1		69
1317	4		43, 564
1321		1	499
1326	1		554

[1] Years in which no permits were reported have been omitted from this table.
[2] In these years, one person was given permit to depart without search.
[3] See also *Records of the Parliament Holden at Westminster on the twenty-eighth Day of February in the thirty-third Year of the Reign of King Edward the First (A.D. 1305)*, ed. F. M. Maitland, (London, 1893), p. 95.

Source: CCR, except as noted. This table was prepared using the index to the *Calendar*. To the extent that permissions or prohibitions were issued but not addressed to officials of Dover or to Wardens of the Cinque Ports, or that the index is incomplete, this table is in error.

Permits of this sort are not an exact count of the number of persons travelling, for the permit includes attendants accompanying a person of rank. But permits will be an indicator of the amount of travel.

It is natural for an economist to inquire whether these permits and prohibitions reflect economic and political conditions, or whether they depend solely on the nature and rank of the individual seeking to travel. In the first case, there would be few years in which permits and prohibitions on the export of coin would be simultaneously issued. Actually, the combinations logically possible[18] occur almost exactly as if there were independent probabilities of 0·42 that at least one permit would be issued and of 0·27 that at least one prohibition would be issued. For the period covered by Table 12, there is therefore no evidence of a 'travel-permit policy' in this sense, but we shall later relate these permits to the system of foreign exchange controls.

Beginning in 1324, the *Close Rolls* data come to refer solely to the members of monastic orders and occasionally to other clergy. They use the formula: '*X* may take with him expense money [either a stated sum or a "reasonable amount"] but no *apportum*.' The *apportum* was a contribution by an English order to its foreign headquarters.[19]

The period 1324–49 is covered in Table 13. In each of five years during the first half (1324–36), six or more travel permits were issued; in no year of the second half (1337–49) were more than five permits issued. The number of monks

TABLE 13. *Licences for Members of the Clergy to Leave England Through Dover (or the Cinque Ports) Carrying Expense Money but no* Apportum, *1324–1349*[1]

Calendar year	Number of licences	Page reference[2]
1324	1	211
1327	9	108, 198, 207, 210, 217, 224
1328	1	400
1329	9	494, 564–67, 571
1330	1	145
1331	11	319, 323, 331, 332, 333, 335, 419
1332	4	547, 580, 586, 597
1333	3	119, 121–22
1334	5	246, 294, 305, 324, 330
1335	10	483–84, 488, 506, 518–21, 523, 525
1336	10	555, 648–49, 657, 666, 671, 676, 698, 731
1337	1	118
1338	1	414
1341	2	124, 276
1343[3]	1	118
1344[3]	5	293, 361, 453, 465, 477
1345[3]	5	554, 557, 561, 567, 581
1346[3]	1	143
1348[3]	1	523
1349[3]	3	148, 75, 90

[1] This table was attained through the use of the indexes to the several volumes. It may be in error where the indexes are incomplete. Years in which no licenses were reported have been omitted from this table.
[2] All page references refer to appropriate volumes of the *CCR*.
[3] With two exceptions in 1345 and one in 1349, the licences specify that only gold coin is to be exported.

allowed to take their expenses out of the country was thus significantly less (0·025) during the Hundred Years War than it had been before.

Two varying interpretations of this difference may be made. The monks may have wished to stay in England because of wartime disturbances. Or the king may have kept them from leaving, either because he did not wish them to take information abroad, or because he did not wish them to take money abroad. We may observe (1) that the permits issued began to drop in 1337, when the price of sterling had begun to fall but before hostilities became important; and (2) that when travel revived slightly in the 1340s, the permits specified that only gold coins might be taken out of England. This latter restriction was in accord with monetary policy generally, and we shall return to it later. There is therefore some basis for believing that the restrictions on monastic travel had something to do with foreign exchange policy.

Persons not travelling for monastic orders frequently obtained 'protections' from the king, as well as powers of attorney for persons representing them in their absence. These documents were issued to people travelling to Wales, Scotland, and Ireland as well as 'beyond the seas', but it is specified what their destination may be. It is also specified whether their travel is 'on the king's business' or their own. Persons travelling 'on the king's service' were civilian rather than military.[20] Table 14 tabulates the number of travellers 'beyond the seas'. In this table, travel to Gascony and Aquitaine is listed separately, because such travel presumably did not have the same foreign exchange consequences.[21]

The number of pilgrims going abroad dropped significantly (0·02) in wartime. For other non-officials there was no such drop, but the years 1337–40 were unusually low. This low period either may reflect a genuine drop in travel during the period of the sterling crisis, or it may be the beginning of a true wartime decline which is concealed by an increasing tendency of merchants going to Flanders in 1341–3 to obtain protections. We suspect the later possibility may be the case.

The greatest numerical variations in the number of persons leaving England take place in the category 'on the king's service'. These were highest in consequence of the (presumably diplomatic) missions of 1331–2 or of the king's expedition to Flanders in 1337. It is possible to associate such journeys at least roughly with foreign expenditures on official accounts, as they would be called in modern usage, since they correspond in the first instance to official expenditures on the acquisition of allies or in the second to actual military expenses abroad.

The crisis of 1337–9 was followed by a period in which the price of sterling was at prewar levels, coincident with the recovery in wool exports in 1339. But in 1343–4 there was a new crisis, in the course of which sterling was devalued[22] and gold coinage introduced for the first time since 1279. This second crisis has provoked more discussion in the literature than has the one we have discussed, probably because bimetallism has long interested economists. Some comparison of the two crises is instructive.

TABLE 14. *Protections and Powers of Attorney Issued by Letters Patent for Persons Going 'Beyond the Seas', 1330–1345*

Calendar year	Not on King's Service				On King's service			
					Going abroad		Staying abroad	
	On pilgrimages	Going abroad	Staying abroad	Gascony and Aquitaine	G + A	Other	G + A	Other
1330	10	21	14		19	17	2	1
1331	23	21	40	2	50	104	4	2
1332	23	32	13	1	2	121	2	3
1333	8	13	9		5	27	3	3
1334	5	15	19	1	4	37		
1335	3	15	6		9	23	5	2
1336		17	9	6		31		
1337	1	10	7	15	3	334		4
1338		14	7	11		38	1	24
1339		1	1	2		3		2
1340	1	1	2			8		
1341		16	7		5	6		
1342		27	5			2		
1343	14	19	4			5		
1344	3	9	2			10		1
1345	3		1			1		

Source: CPR. Unlike Table 13, this represents a count taken page by page. It is probably subject to some double counting. Persons receiving protections usually obtained at the same time power of attorney for their representatives in England; where the two documents were obtained at different dates, single individuals may have been counted twice.

There was a 30 per cent drop in wool exports in 1343, with no evidence of a decline in the import of wine. There was an increase in private travel reported, but some of this increase may be illusory (in that merchants seem to have been more inclined than formerly to obtain royal protection). Official foreign travel was low, and of course the Crecy campaign had not yet begun. An explanation in short-run terms would stress the decline in exports in 1343. In longer-run terms, it would be stated that the level of exports had been low for the entire period since 1336, while imports had not fallen.

Table 1, unfortunately, gives no impression of the period 1342–4. It merely indicates that in 1345 the price of sterling was at the prewar level—which might seem odd, since its metal content had been reduced 10 per cent. Table 8 indicates that the range between high and low prices of sterling was about 4 per cent of par value. This range is notably less than the 15 per cent variation in the preceding crisis. The general assessment of the literature, however, is that the second crisis was the more severe, or at least the more interesting, of the two.

Why did sterling fluctuate more widely in 1337–9 than in 1342–5? The simple-minded explanation would be this: in 1343 wool exports declined, but in 1337 they declined more than in 1343; also, there were important royal expenditures abroad in connection with the campaign in Flanders. Therefore, we should expect sterling to have declined more in 1337–9 than in 1343. However, this explanation raises a difficulty: if the crisis of 1337–9 was really the more serious of the two, why did devaluation occur in 1343–4, the 'lesser' of the two crises?

The answer to this question is to be found in the foreign exchange controls of the period. Table 15 gives a history of the regulations governing the export of precious metals from 1279 to 1346. The early part of the period is not under discussion, but it serves to establish basic policies and certain long-run tendencies. The regulations are ordinarily quite explicit; and where no specification is made, it is reasonable to conclude that no restriction existed on exports. In some cases exports are specifically allowed, and these cases have been so designated in the table. Table 16 shows a gradual extension of foreign exchange controls after 1279. At first only silver coin could not be exported, but after 1299 silver and gold bullion were also restricted. In 1324, restrictions on silver coin were briefly eased, but apparently[23] there was a complete prohibition on the export of precious metals until 1333. The 1324 regulation was apparently the occasion for the licences recorded in Table 13. At any rate, during 1333–5 there was a brief relaxation in controls over the export of gold bullion. Licensing of gold bullion exports was in force from 1335 to 1343 but was then lifted. Export of foreign gold coin was allowed in 1342. The following year, when English gold coin was minted, the export of English gold coin (but not bullion) without licence was authorized. Throughout this period, the export of silver in any form was either licensed or prohibited.

It is a commonplace of foreign exchange theory that foreign exchange rates will fluctuate if there is no convertibility. The textbook example usually given is that of countries on an inconvertible paper standard. The theory would equally

TABLE 15. *Regulations on the Export of Precious Metals from England,*
1279–1346[1]

Calendar year	Silver		Gold		Source
	Coin	Bullion	Coin	Bullion	
1279	F	n.s.[2]	n.s.[2]	n.s.[2]	Red Book of the Exchequer, pp. 181–2
1299	L	L	N	n.s.[2]	Ruffhead, pp. 137–8
1300	L	L	N	L	CCR 18 Edw. I, p. 390
1307	L	L	N	L	CCR 35 Edw. I, p. 522; 1 Edw. II, p. 44
1324	r.e.[3]	F	N	F	CCR 17 Edw. II, p. 156
1326	F	F	F[4]	F	Ruding, i. p. 209
1331	F	F	N	F	CFR 5 Edw. III, pp. 251–2
1333	L	L	N	n.s.[2]	CFR 7 Edw. III, p. 347
1335	L[5]	L	N[5]	L	Ruffhead, pp. 215–17
1342	F[6]	F	N[6]	F	CCR 16 Edw. III, p. 685
1343	F	F[7]	N	n.s.[2]	Rotuli, ii. 137–8
1344	L[8]	L	P	L	CCR 17 Edw. III, p. 263
1345	L	L	P	L	CCR 19 Edw. III, p. 587
1346	L	L	P	L	CCR 20 Edw. III, pp. 144, 150

[1] P = permitted; I = licence required; F = forbidden; N = no English gold coin at this date.
[2] Not specified.
[3] 'Reasonable expenses' were allowed travellers.
[4] Ruding's discussion seems questionable to me on this point.
[5] Coin for export was to be bought at the Tables of Exchange in Dover and elsewhere. CCR 9 Edw. III, pp. 514, 529.
[6] The coin of other countries, gold or silver, could be exported without licence.
[7] Nobility was allowed to take out vessels of silver.
[8] Licences were issued for new coin only. CCR 18 Edw. III, p. 457.

well apply to countries which were on a metallic-coin standard internally, but which did not allow the import or export of precious metals. If controls are imperfectly enforced, or if some licences are issued, movements of exchange rates will be smaller than if controls are complete.

Consequently, if we observe that the movement of gold out of England was permitted after 1343, we should predict what actually happened: that fluctuations in the sterling exchange rate would occur with smaller range than they had in the 1337–9 crisis when the export of all precious metals was licensed.

The defence of this hypothesis requires evidence on the movement, legal or illegal, of precious metals in crisis and non-crisis years. The first source of information is the *Calendar of Fine Rolls,* which contains royal injunctions to local officials that they should take appropriate action against currency violators.[24] There is a record of such royal actions over the period 1333–48.[25] In only one year of the period 1333–6 were royal actions taken, and in only one year of the period 1337–48 was no action taken. The king was more likely (0·03) to be concerned about foreign exchange violations in wartime than in peacetime, in the sense of telling his officials to stop them. The only wartime year he took no action was 1340, which by our records was a relatively good year for wool exports.

In every crisis year (1337–9 and 1343–5) at least two royal actions were taken, while in six of the ten non-crisis years fewer than two actions were taken. Thus, the king was more likely to take two or more actions in crisis years than in non-crisis years (0·05).[26]

Unfortunately, the *Calendar of Fine Rolls* entries all tell officials to stop both illegal exports and illegal imports of coin. If there were any entries which enjoined only one illegal action, we could be sure that only one illegal action was taking place. If all entries enjoin both, we cannot be sure that the document is not using a conventional legal expression.

To investigate this question, we present Table 16, which lists the reports of exchange control violations other than those reported in the *Calendar of Fine Rolls.* According to these records, illegal imports of false coin were not more likely to occur in years when there were illegal exports of sterling than in other years. If we take the entries from the *Calendar of Fine Rolls* as evidence of the simultaneous violation of both export and import regulations, and alter Table 16 accordingly, we will conclude that the two violations are more likely to occur together than separately (0·01). I believe that the discrepancies betwen the *Calendar of Fine Rolls* and the other records point to the formula used in the *Calendar* having been a mere legalism.[27]

Table 16 shows that there is a tendency for one or the other of the two offences to prevail in certain periods. Thus, in 1310–20 imports of false money predominated; from 1334 to 1342 illegal exports of sterling predominated; from 1345 to 1348 imports of false money predominated. In only three years of the fifty did the two offences occur simultaneously, and two of these three years were in the crisis period: 1343 and 1344.

If it is profitable to perform an action illegally, it should also be profitable to perform it legally, with the king's licence.[28] Consequently, we would predict that if the records on foreign exchange licensing could be tabulated, they would reveal outflow of sterling until 1342, and an inflow of silver beginning in 1345.

The output of the English mints[29] gives us some clues about the flow of silver. In years when imports of false coin were occurring, mint output was likely to be larger (specifically, over £2,000) than in other years (0·05). Such a

TABLE 16. *Data on Violations of Foreign Exchange Regulations from Sources Other than the Calendar of Fine Rolls, 1300–1349*[1]

Calendar year	False money imports	Illegal sterling exports	Source
1300	X		*CLB-C*, p. 83; *CPR*, pp. 412, 509; *CCW*, p. 113
1301		X	*CLB-C*, p. 89; *CCR*, p. 480
1305	X	X	*CPR*, p. 341; *CCR*, pp. 328, 471
1307		X	*CCR*, p. 522
1310	X		*CCR*, p. 329
1311	X		*CFR*, p. 79
1315	X		*CCR*, p. 228
1317	X		*CCR*, p. 448
1319	X		*CCR*, pp. 123–4
1320	X		*CCR*, p. 198; *CPR*, p. 500; *CCW*, p. 512
1323		X	*CCR*, p. 701
1327	X		*CCR*, p. 140
1334		X	*Rotuli*, ii. 377
1335	X		*CPR*, p. 153
1337		X	*CCR*, p. 76
1341		X	Ruding, i. 213
1342		X	Ruding, i. 214
1343	X	X	*Rotuli*, ii. 137, 141; *CPR*, pp. 81, 100, 170
1344	X	X	*Rotuli*, ii. 149, 155; *CPR*, pp. 392, 430; *CCR*, p. 351
1345	X		*CPR*, p. 587
1346	X		*Rotuli*, ii. 160
1347	X		*Rotuli*, ii. 167; *CPR*, p. 303; *CCR*, p. 284
1348	X		*CCR*, p. 492

[1] Years in which no violations were reported are omitted from this table.

statement cannot be made with respect to years in which there were illegal exports of coin. We can thus support (though not prove) the following argument: England in the long run imported all its silver. We can associate years of illegal imports with years of high mint output; and we can, therefore, surmise an association between illegal and legal imports of silver. If we could associate years of illegal coin exports with years of high mint output, we could associate illegal exports with reduced English demand for cash balances. Since we cannot, we must look to balance-of-payments situations for an explanation of the illegal exports. Owing to the lack of data on wool exports (the customs were farmed) and imports alike in the 1340s, we cannot be as sure about trade at that time as in the preceding decade.

We may make one final observation. Comparing Tables 12 and 16, we may say that in years in which there were illegal exports of coin, the king was more likely to issue two or more licences to export coin (for travel expenses) than in years in which there were no such illegal exports. This statement might merely mean that both legal and illegal export of coin increased in years when there was more foreign travel. It might also mean something more interesting. Suppose that travellers had an option of buying a letter of exchange or of applying for a licence to take out coin. Then in years when the sterling exchange rate was low, applications for licences would be relatively large, while in years when the sterling rate was high, travellers would use the letters.

The second possibility seems to be ruled out by a comparison of Tables 13 and 16. For we know that sterling declined in 1337, and we should expect that the monastic orders would have applied for more, rather than fewer, licences in 1337–9 than formerly.[30] But if the king used these licences as an instrument of foreign exchange control (as he would today), then the drop in licences would be explained by a desire of the king to reduce the outflow of coin rather than by any failure of the monastic orders to realize the desirability of using coin rather than letters of exchange.

The evidence we have discussed suggests that the appearance of illegal imports of false coin in 1343 can be explained by the devaluation of silver. They point to an excess demand for silver beginning at that time. Excess demand is a sign that prices are below equilibrium levels. Walras has shown, of course, that the sum of excess demands and supplies in an economic system must be zero. The excess demand for silver, then, would have to be accompanied by an excess supply of goods and/or gold. Our data on commodity trade suggest a trade deficit rather than a surplus, and we can conclude there must have been an excess supply of gold in the mid 1340s. That is, gold was leaving the country, because the price of gold in England was above equilibrium levels.

This view has been expressed before,[31] in connection with the conclusion that the price of English gold coin should have been lowered so as to keep gold coin in circulation. We suggest that the monetary policy aimed precisely at having the gold used to cover a balance-of-payments deficit without a corresponding reduction in the (silver) domestic money supply. (We are certainly not expressing the policy in fourteenth-century terminology.) In support of the view we cite (1) the permission to export gold coin, after 1342; (2) the provision, in 1343, that merchant importers should be paid in gold coin;[32] (3) the provision, in 1342, that wool exporters should accept payment in Flemish silver;[33] (4) the provision that wool exporters should sell imported bullion to the Exchange in proportion to their exports;[34] and (5) the general interest in Parliament (on which all sources agree) in trying to confine the use of gold to mercantile transactions in international trade. The consequence of this policy was, of course, that exchange rates in the 1340s fluctuated much less than in

1337–9, and we suggest that such a reduction may have been one of the objectives of monetary policy.

In time, of course, gold came to be part of the English monetary system, but in the 1340s it may well have been considered as merely a useful means of stabilizing exchange rates without reductions in the money (silver) supply, or even as a means of increasing the money (silver) supply in a period of deflation—as we should now call it.

NOTES

[1] Unless otherwise specified, all exchange rate quotations are taken from A. Sapori (ed.), *I Libri di Commercio dei Peruzzi* (Milan, Publicazioni . . . 'Studi medievali', vol. i, 1934). Other medieval account books edited by Sapori (e.g. the Alberti and Gianfigliazzi accounts) or by De Roover (e.g. the Guillaume Ruyelle accounts) do not have much information on exchange rates.

[2] The table omits several transactions (pp. 131, 134–6, 359, 365) in which the Florence office credited the London branch for purchases of Flemish currency with sterling. These allowed the London office to reduce slightly its debts on the Continent. As 'capital transactions' they were not important, and as exchange rate quotations they were complicated.

[3] An attempt was made to determine whether the market was 'thin', by investigating whether large transactions were conducted at rates differing from those on small transactions. There seems to have been no systematic difference between the two.

[4] *A History of Agriculture and Prices*, 7 vols. (Oxford, 1866–1902). This wine was presumably of relatively low quality, since (as James has shown) the King's butler paid substantially higher prices than this.

[5] Presumably most of the insurance was self-insurance, but shippers would have to cover the risk somehow.

[6] We used *Tables for Testing Significance in a 2 × 2 Contingency Table*, compiled by D. J. Finney, R. Latscha, B. M. Bennett, and P. Hsu (Cambridge, 1963).

[7] Correlations performed on randomly selected economic time series are, on the average, higher than those to be expected on the basis of ordinary significance tests. See Ames and Reiter, 'Empirical Distributions of Correlation and Autocorrelation Coefficients in Economic Time Series', *Jour. Amer. Stat. Assn.*, 56 (1961).

[8] The main reason for caution in the use of statistical significance tests involving time series data is that economic data change only gradually. Consequently the successive observations in a time series are not independent of each other in the manner assumed by significance tests.

[9] The restriction to northern Europe made in the preceding paragraph seems to be important. At the time under study, the Florentines were the principal Mediterranean power to trade in northern Europe; but the economic affairs of northern Europe were largely independent of those of Mediterranean Europe, because of the difficulties in communication. Our conclusion will be that Florentine currency was a 'key currency', or roughly the equivalent of 'gold and dollars'; and we assume that the market for this currency in northern Europe was largely independent of the market for this currency in the south.

[10] Sir John Craig, *The Mint: A History of the London Mint from A.D. 287 to 1948* (Cambridge 1953); W. A. Shaw, *The History of Currency, 1252 to 1894* (London, n.d. [1895?]).

[11] Shaw lists the following French mint buying prices for one mark of silver: Feb. 1336, 3/12/6; Nov. 1338, 4/12/0; Jan. 1339, 5/0/0; Aug. 1340, 7/0/0; Dec. 1340, 7/10/0; Jan. 1341, 9/4/0; June 1342, 12/10/0. For gold, the buying price, per mark, was: Jan. 1331, 39/0/0; Feb. 1336, 50/0/0; Nov. 1338, 58/0/0; May 1339, 61/10/0; Aug. 1339, 69/0/0.

[12] *The Calendar of Entries in the Papal Registers* lists 54 different months over the period 1372–1489 in which one Florentine gold florin was worth 12 silver *gros tournois*. Thus not all exchange rates in the *Calendar* fluctuate, and not all are stable. This fact lends credence to the assertion that the quotations in the calendars represent rates which may actually have existed in the markets, rather than in book-keeping conventions or aberrations.

[13] Compare this range with the range of about 3 per cent suggested by the calculations of silver import and export points given above.

[14] The long-run changes in sterling rates implied by Table 7 are roughly what one would expect from the changes in the metal content of sterling coin. In 1342 one Tower pound of silver made 243d. of coin and in 1412–65 it made 360d. In 1344 one Tower pound of gold made 15/0/0 in coin, and after 1412 it made 16/13/4. If the (apparently fixed) sterling rate of 6·0 prevailing after 1412 is computed backward we would therefore estimate the silver rate at 8·00 and the gold rate at 6·67 in 1344; these bracket the actual quotations for the 1340s.

[15] Means are calculated for the entire period 1333–43 (or 1330–43).

[16] It is known, of course, that the King had great difficulties in actually laying his hands on wool while the monopoly existed.

[17] *Calendar of Close Rolls*, 12 Hen. III, pp. 31, 317; 43 Hen. III, p. 351. Thus Feaveryear is incorrect in stating that the Statute of Stepney in 1299 is the first prohibition on the export of coin (*The Pound Sterling* (Oxford, 1931), p. 3). See also *CCR*, 7 Edw. I (1280), p. 519.

The following abbreviations are used in citations in the remainder of this paper: *CCR—Calendar of Close Rolls; CCW—Calendar of Chancery Warrants, 1244–1326; CFR—Calendar of Fine Rolls; CLB—Calendar of Letter Books Preserved among the Archives of the Corporation of the City of London* (the letter following '*CLB*' designates the book cited, e.g. *CLB*-C is Book C); *CMI—Calendar of Inquisitions, Miscellaneous*. (All these series are publications of the Historical Manuscripts Commission.) *Rotuli—Rotuli Parliamentorum, ut et Petitiones et Placita in Parliamento, Anno 6 Edward I–Anno 19 Henry VII* (London, 1832); *Ruding—Rogers Ruding, Annals of the Coinage of Great Britain and Its Dependencies* (3rd ed., London, 1840); *Ruffhead—The Statutes at Large, from Magna Charta to the Twenty-Fifth Year of the Reign of King George the Third, Inclusive*, ed., Owen Ruffhead (London, 1786).

[18] Permits only; prohibitions only; both; neither.

[19] In 1304–7, the monasteries were required to make such payments in coin, in contrast to the papal nuncios, who were required to transfer money to Rome by letter of exchange (*CPR*, 35 Edw. I. 514; *Rotuli*, i. 222. and ii. 217; Ruffhead, i. 161). Evidently some change was later made, for the Peruzzi made payments which were evidently *apportum* (Sapori, p. 195, gives an example).

[20] One may compare the 334 persons who travelled abroad in 1337 on the king's service, and mostly 'with the king' in Flanders, with the over 1,200 persons pardoned for crimes from murder on up as reward for military service overseas in 1338–9. Moreover, presumably not all the troops were felons.

[21] Moreover, the large number of protections going to non-officials travelling in Gascony and Aquitaine in 1337–8 seems to have been associated with naval convoys of ships going in those years (and only in those years) to these destinations.

[22] That is, the number of pennies made from a Tower pound of silver was increased from 243 to 270—about 10 per cent.

[23] The word 'apparently' is used advisedly. In other years the qualification 'except by licence' appears in the calendars, and, as Table 13 shows, licences to take coin abroad for travel expenses were certainly issued. Either the phrase escaped the notice of the editors of the Calendars, or else it was taken for granted by royal officials.

[24] The violations include illegal exports of precious metals and also failures to deliver 'false' and clipped coin to the Exchange for minting. (False coin was non-English coin which resembled the penny but contained less silver. In the 1340s it was described as Lussheborne—Luxemburg—and at other dates it had other designations.)

[25] The page references for given years are: 1333; p. 347; 1337, pp. 6, 56, 60, 61; 1338, pp. 81–2; 1339, pp. 113, 135; 1341, pp. 216, 252; 1342, p. 309; 1343, pp. 318–19; 1344, pp. 357, 365; 1345, pp. 415, 443, 448; 1346, pp. 467, 474, 485; 1347, pp. 17, 18, 29, 30; 1348, pp. 67, 68.

[26] 'Two actions' means 'action on two occasions', for a single action often involved instructions to several local officials.

[27] There is no inherent absurdity in the proposition that the two offences might occur simultaneously. In the twenty years since 1945, there have been many occasions when a traveller from the United States could go to Canada with one silver dollar, purchase eleven Canadian dimes with it, and return to the United States to purchase $1·10 in U.S. goods with them. The twentieth-century traveller would have committed no crime, while the fourteenth century traveller would have placed his body and goods at the King's pleasure. The transaction described would have been profitable whether or not Canada was adding to its reserves of gold and dollars at the time.

[28] The converse is not true. It may be profitable to do something if one has a licence but not profitable to take the risk of capture and punishment if the act is illegal.

[29] Harry A. Miskimin, *Money, Prices and Foreign Exchange in Fourteenth Century France* (New Haven, Conn. 1963), Appendix B.

[30] The only reference to the prohibition on the use of letters of exchange by the alien priories relates, as noted in an earlier footnote, to 1304–7; by the 1330s they seem to have been using letters.

[31] Craig, pp. 66–9; Ruding, i. 217–19; Ramsay (cited in Table 9), i. 339; Hughes, Crump, and Johnson, 'The Debasement of the Coinage under Edward III', *Econ. Jour.* vii. (1897), 197.

[32] *Rotuli*, ii. 138.

[33] *CCR*, 16 Edw. III, p. 415.

[34] Ruding, i. 213, states that in 1340 two marks of silver were to be imported per sack of wool exported. I have not found any other source for this statement. In 1343, silver imports were to be one third of the value of exports (*Rotuli*, ii. 138). This provision, in some form, lasted until 1348, when the Flemish instituted a similar regulation, thereby forcing the English to abandon it.

2

No Safety in Numbers:
Some Pitfalls
of Historical Statistics

G. OHLIN

Editor's note. This article was first published in Rosovsky, H. (ed.), *Industrialisation in Two Systems: Essays in Honor of Alexander Gerschenkron* (New York, 1966), 68–90. © 1966 by John Wiley & Sons, Inc.

Sampling methods and the chi-square test are discussed above, pp. 29–33, with particular reference to this article on pp. 31–32. For further reading see footnotes on those pages, and: Dollar and Jensen (1971); Schofield (1972). Some terms used in demographic analysis may be unfamiliar; they are explained in Wrigley (1966) and in an extremely useful glossary of terms and methods, Bradley (1971).

Il est plus d'hommes qui savent calculer que raisonner. Moheau, Recherches et considérations sur la population de la France (1778).

Nur in Ermanglung der Gewissheit gebrauchen wir die Wahrscheinlichkeit. Wenn wir zwar eine Tatsache nicht vollkommen kennen, wohl aber *etwas* über ihre Form wissen. Wittgenstein, Tractatus logico–philosophicus.

IN 1864, Quetelet published a paper 'Sur les Indiens O-Jib-Be-Wa's et les proportions de leur corps' in which he concluded that their bodily proportions were almost exactly the same as those of Europeans.[1] This paper, one finds, was based on the study of a party of twelve Indians visiting Brussels, who had generously allowed themselves to be measured by him. A slender basis for inference, but social historians attempting to reconstruct the prestatistical past must, like Quetelet, squeeze information out of whatever evidence comes their way.

Fortunately, the processes of government and economic activity slough off a prodigious amount of material that can be used for statistical purposes, and many of the classical contributions to economic history have been based precisely on the compilation of statistics from institutional records, tax lists, and the like. As some innovators in the field of historical statistics have remarked, the enormous effort required to deal with data on a large scale has kept many such sources—and precisely the richest ones—from being used.[2] Here, as in so many other fields, the new technology of electronic data processing has opened up a new era.

There is not always, however, an abundance of data awaiting their interpreter. Especially in pre-industrial times, the problem facing the historical statistician is more likely to be that his samples are small, far from random, and perhaps only remotely related to what he is really interested in. The pseudo-statistics compiled for purposes of primitive administration he can use only at his peril; the enumerations are deficient, errors of copying, reporting, and arithmetic abound, and we may not even know what was being enumerated, as in the case of rolls of 'adults'.

Those who distrust historical statistics are right in doing so, but they would be wrong in rejecting them. In fact, any understanding of statistical information is founded on distrust, and the classical problem of statistics is that of making valid inferences from observations that are known to be poor. To abandon the scraps of quantitative insight into the past merely on the grounds of general suspicion would be as foolish as to regard them as wholly accurate.

The question at all times must be how great the uncertainty is and how seriously it affects the conclusions at stake. In the statistical, as in any empirical study of the world, 'a reasonable probability is the only certainty'. This is the problem to which the theory of statistical inference addresses itself; it can provide procedures for estimation and for the testing of hypotheses. Sometimes the application of such standard procedures to historical statistics serves little purpose, since the principal sources of error are not likely to be random and cancel out obligingly. Apart from that problem, however, these procedures do not in themselves tell us what constitutes a 'reasonable probability'. The modern theory of statistical decision-making attempts to provide a rational criterion by assuming that the acceptance or rejection of a hypothesis leads to actions of consequence. Statistical inferences should then be made in a way that takes into account the gain from being right and the loss from being wrong.

Such rational action is not always easy, least of all in historical statistical work. One naturally wishes to be as accurate as possible, to come close to the truth, but what are the consequences of being wrong? As long as one is inclined to regard it as a gain to have a statistical picture of the past at all, the dangers of being wrong seem small. Thus, little attention is usually paid in historical statistics to what the data themselves suggest about degrees of uncertainty, ranges of confidence, and levels of significance.

When systematic error is likely to be very great, classical statistical tests do not suffice. The tests of historical statistics must then be tests of consistency, compatibility, and common sense, with all the knowledge available brought into play. Population history furnishes many illustrations. For instance, enumerations, always incomplete, may really give more accurate clues about age structure and social composition than about total population; growth or decline indicated by a series of censuses may be subject to internal checks which can be surmised if the censuses provide a breakdown by age, for the survival of different age groups over, for example, a decade could not be entirely random. (Due account must of course be taken of known migration and other external factors.)

The more fragmentary the evidence itself, the more important the role of outside knowledge brought to bear on the problem. Thus, to take an example, the information on ages at death on Roman tombstones may constitute a fairly sizeable sample, but it is evidently and for obvious reasons not representative even of the social groups that rated such honours; infants and children are absent or under-represented. Only by analysing this material against the background of what is known about mortality as a function of age in a great variety of human populations is it possible to put this evidence into proper perspective and draw any conclusions from it.[3]

In the following some other contributions to statistical population history will be scrutinized, partly as an attempt to revise them, partly to demonstrate some of the problems of uncertainty and plausibility in historical statistics.

J. C. RUSSELL'S MEDIEVAL DEMOGRAPHY

The Life Tables

Josiah Cox Russell's *British Medieval Population* (1948), which represented an ambitious inventory of English demographic conditions between 1086 and 1545, was based on a wide range of materials, many previously unused for such purposes. Among other things, Russell submitted detailed life tables purporting to represent the course of mortality in England between the thirteenth and fifteenth centuries. Historians, innocent of technical demography, were bound to seize on these calculations with pleasure and relief, and Russell's figures have been widely cited.[4] Precisely for this reason it is necessary to point out that they are not only afflicted with the uncertainties that beset all statistics but actually contain such curious elements of speculation and guesswork that they must regretfully be dismissed altogether.

However, a second reason to reconsider Russell's work is that his sources for the study of English mortality are of undisputable interest. The inquisitions post-mortem on which this part of his work was based state the date of death for owners of property as well as the age of the heir. They do not give the *age* at death, which can only be ascertained by the combination of two inquests, the first giving the date and the age of the heir, the second the subsequent date of his (or her) death.

The major difficulty lies in combining the documents properly. The permanent surname was not yet established, and spelling vacillated among English, Norman, and arbitrary variants. The large material that emerged from Russell's painstaking labour is so far unique in its kind. It is of course drawn from propertied classes, although not so limited as are the records of the peerage. The class limitation alone suggests that one should approach it with caution, but there is some other evidence to suggest that the mortality of adults in the Middle Ages was not strongly affected by economic or social status. In any case, Russell's data should give an indication of minimum levels of mortality.

With the data derived from the inquisitions post-mortem one could in principle proceed in two different directions. The first would be simply to note how many years an heir survived after his appearance in the records. This would provide direct observation of remaining life and thus of life expectation at the age when the heir was first recorded. As a matter of statistical procedure, however, it is advisable to take another path and compare the number of heirs known to have survived to a certain age with the numbers who died within a subsequent period of time, such as five years. In this way Russell calculated age-specific risks of mortality from which a life table could be constructed. From the inquests we learn nothing about infant and child mortality, but it is possible to estimate the expectation of life at some later age. Russell guessed at infant mortality and then completed generational life tables for eight different groups of English male heirs (Table 1).

TABLE 1. *Life Expectation for English Male Heirs at Birth and at 15, According to Russell*

	Expectation of life at:	
Generation born	Birth	Age 15
Before 1276	35·3 years	32·7 years
1276–1300	31·3	28·6
1301–1325	29·8	26·8
1326–1348	30·2	25·1
1348–1375	17·3	25·2
1376–1400	20·5	22·9
1401–1425	23·8	29·4
1426–1450	32·8	30·9

Source: British Medieval Population p. 186. To take account of the plague, a dividing line was drawn at 1348 rather than at the end of 1350.

The smallest group contains 343, the largest, 532 deaths; since all cases entered the samples only at the time of inheritance, there are rather few observations in young and old age brackets, and the sampling error is likely to be substantial. The standard deviations for the life expectancies at age 15 in Table 1 can be computed on the basis of Russell's material and turn out to be of the magnitude of 1·2–1·3 years, which is enough to deprive the minor variations of statistical significance. However, the broad contours of the table are not likely to be due to sampling error but—as we expected—to the plague.[5]

The age-specific mortality rates for the different generations can also be subjected to chi-square tests to decide whether they are actually significantly different. The chi-square test in this case posits hypothetically that the true death rates of the different generations were identical and aims to decide how likely it is that samples of the sizes actually drawn would show the observed discrepancies merely as the result of chance. It then appears that the variations for individual age groups could easily be due to chance in most cases, but the patterns as a whole seem to vary in a significant way. The plague hit different generations in different portions of their life span, as shown in a comparison of the generations born in 1276–1300 and 1348–75 (Table 2). The generation of 1348–75 was exposed to great hazards in its early years, and that of 1276–1300 only when its youngest members were close to 50. Thus, the change in sign in Table 2. For ages below 25 and over 50, chi-square suggests that the differences are significant, but that between 25 and 50, when neither generation was exposed to the worst of the plague, the differences are too small to be taken seriously. There would be a greater than even chance for sampling errors alone to produce the small discrepancies in those age groups.[6]

TABLE 2. *Life-Table Mortality Rates for Males born in 1276–1300 and 1348–1375*

(per thousand)

Age	Born 1276–1300	Born 1348–1375	Difference	Chi-square
5– 9	44	130	86	1·26
10–14	47	184	137	4·61
15–19	57	141	84	3·90
20–24	126	158	32	0·58
25–29	137	167	30	0·65
30–34	110	114	4	0·16
35–39	127	174	47	1·91
40–44	184	192	8	0·04
45–49	167	224	57	1·82
50–54	250	185	−65	1·78
55–59	257	147	−90	2·95
60–64	439	227	−212	9·85
65–69	394	371	−23	0·08
70–74	450	523	73	0·45
75–79	696	476	−220	2·27
80–84	714	636	−78	0·12
85–89	1,000	750	−250	0·60
				33·63

To distinguish the mortality in the period known to have been most plague-ridden from that before and after, one may reorganize the material. Instead of generational life tables one wishes to have tables that measure the mortality in a given period. From the generation born in 1301–25, we might thus take the deaths of those between 50 and 55 which occurred in the years 1351–79 when the plague struck repeatedly. However, the assignment of the age groups to the plague is not always obvious or precise. Out of the same generation, for instance, those who died between 30 and 35 died in the period 1331–59, the first half of which was free from plague whereas the second includes the Black Death itself. If the material were more extensive, the groups with such mixed experiences could have been left out of account, but in the circumstances it seems best to assign the age groups from the various generations to three different periods depending on whether the majority of the deaths fell in the period 1348–1400, or earlier, or later.[7]

The result is shown in Table 3. For age groups under 15, the rates are erratic, and even the rates for 15–19 look suspicious, but between 25 and 50 where the samples are largest, the excess mortality of the second half of the fourteenth century is very marked. A chi-square test shows that the differences from the patterns of the other two periods (for age groups 15–19 and above) are significant on the 0·1 and 1 per cent levels respectively. The same test also

TABLE 3. *Life-Table Mortality Rates (5^{q}x) for 1250–1348, 1348–1400, and 1401–1500*

(per thousand)

Age	1250–1348	1348–1400	1401–1500	Middle group drawn from generations born
5– 9	21	96	13	1348–1400
10–14	29	134	111	1326–1400
15–19	39	113	129	1326–1375
20–24	100	161	150	,,
25–29	128	181	137	,,
30–34	95	133	110	,,
35–39	140	190	143	1301–1375
40–44	163	192	141	1301–1348
45–49	153	216	183	,,
50–54	240	247	181	,,
55–59	284	252	247	,,
60–64	337	356	273	1276–1348
65–69	420	406	354	1276–1325
70–74	493	443	455	,,
75–79	514	645	576	,,
80–84	647	625	643	,,

indicates that the pre-plague and post-plague patterns are significantly different. As the table shows, mortality after the plague seems to have been higher than before the plague for age groups up to 30, and lower for those over 50, whereas the rates criss-cross in the middle range. It would be rash to infer that this pattern has a meaning, but it is at least compatible with the assumption that mortality was rising in the fourteenth century before the plague—since this would raise the pre-plague curve in the higher age brackets—and declined only gradually in the fifteenth century. This would

TABLE 4. *Life Expectation at 15 and 25*

Approximate period	At 15	At 25
1250–1348	30·3 years	24·5 years
1348–1400	24·3	20·9
1401–1500	27·2	24·6

produce a lingering effect of the kind we have tried to eliminate by constructing non-generational life tables.

Life expectation at 15 was several years lower in the plague periods than in the others (Table 4), and it also seems to have been lower in the fifteenth century than before the plague. Since we know that the plague did not vanish, this is in line with expectations. The standard deviations for these life expectancies are of the order of 0·7 years, from which we may assume that there is only a fairly small chance that the difference between 27·2 years (1401–1500) and 30·3 years (1250–1348) is due to sampling error. On the other hand, inspection of the rates in Table 3 shows that the drop is due almost entirely to the excess mortality in the groups between 15 and 24, and the pre-plague rates for the age group 15–19 look spurious. In fact, life expectancy at 25 was about the same for both periods, and we cannot really say, then, that the material demonstrates that the fifteenth century was unhealthier than the thirteenth and early fourteenth.

Infant Mortality and Life Expectation at Birth

Russell made up hypothetical schedules for mortality in the first year of life, and betwen the ages of 1 and 4.[8] 'Remembering the good economic conditions of thirteenth-century England,' he said, 'it would seem that for the period before 1276 a mortality rate somewhat better than that of either China or India might be assumed.'[9] He thought infant mortality might have increased gradually, reaching a peak with the Black Death, and then subsided, as in the following schedule:

Before 1276	140	1348–1375	300
1276–1300	150	1376–1400	260
1301–1325	160	1401–1425	200
1326–1348	170	1426–1450	140

The first thing to be said about this is that it is sheer speculation, and the next that it is also bad speculation. It is only necessary to consider infant mortality rates at various times and places to realize how unlikely it is that infant mortality could have been as low as 140 in the thirteenth and fifteenth centuries, even among fairly privileged groups. This would be even lower than the 165 computed for the English royal family between the eleventh and sixteenth centuries. As late as the last decade of the nineteenth century, Norway, Sweden, Scotland, and Denmark were the only European countries that had reached such a level; in Western Europe infant mortality rates were generally between 150 and 200, and in Eastern Europe and Russia they were closer to 250.

A vague impression of social conditions is no help here. It is tempting, however, to explore the hypothesis that infancy and childhood mortality are sufficiently well correlated with mortality in higher age groups to make possible a statement about the former on the basis of the latter. This is the assumption underlying the United Nations model life tables, which were used by Durand to estimate Roman life expectancy in the study cited earlier. The life expectations at 15 in Table 4 would actually then imply that infant mortality rates were already above 300 per thousand in the pre-plague period, and the model life-tables would suggest the following expectations at birth:

Approx.	1250–1348	21 years
	1348–1400	14
	1401–1500	17

These expected lives are as short as those Durand thought were indicated for the Roman Empire, but since he used essentially the same procedure this only means that adult mortality seems to have been much the same according to Roman tombstones and to English inquests in the Middle Ages.

The unpleasant fact, however, is that the correlation between infant and adult mortality is quite weak. In recorded demographic history it is easy to find instances of different societies with comparable mortality rates for adults but with infant mortality rates differing anywhere between a range of, for example, 150–350. Such a range corresponds to a difference of more than ten years in the life expectancy at birth, even if life expectancy at 15 is identical.

This is a range of uncertainty amounting to virtual ignorance. Infant mortality in British royal families and among the children of English ducal families studied by Hollingsworth was actually a good deal lower in relation to their adult mortality rates than predicted by the United Nations life tables, which are based on modern evidence from high-mortality societies. Their life expectancy at 15 was of the same magnitude as that of Russell's heirs, and the life expectancy at birth of sons of dukes in the generation 1330–1479 was 24·0. Violent death, however, took a savage toll in the feudality, and, if it is disregarded, their expected lives were all of 31·0 years.[10]

In their adult years, the subjects in Russell's samples seem to have lived rather longer than the sons of dukes, but their infant and childhood mortality is unlikely to have been so low; the same must hold *a fortiori* for the population at large.

In the end, then, we cannot say much about the actual length of life in medieval England on the basis of the Russell material. If infant mortality was somewhere around 250, except in the most disturbed plague period, life expectation at birth would have been in the neighbourhood of 25 years. Yet we cannot with any confidence say more than that it is likely to have fallen within the range of perhaps 22–8 years, and it might well have been lower.

The Black Death

Even if there is very little to be said about the absolute level of mortality, it may be possible to draw some pertinent conclusions about the excess mortality caused by the plague. In the absence of direct information about the losses of English population in the Black Death and the following epidemics, evidence on mortality assumes a special interest.

As we have seen, the expectation of life in the second half of the fourteenth century may have been some five or six years shorter than previously. This suggests something about the magnitudes involved, for it implies that the average death rate in that period was 7–16 points higher. If we disregard the problems of a changing age composition and assume that there was no change in the average birth rate over the period, the population shows a decline of 30–55 per cent by the end of the century.

Actually, the plague did not raise mortality gradually. It is true that it became endemic towards the end of the century, especially in the towns where it lingered for centuries. In *Piers Plowman* it was compared to the steady drizzle of the rain coming in through a leaky roof, and it must have contributed to mortality in the early fifteenth century—before 1450, Parliament was adjourned or moved four times for fear of it.[11] Yet, as we have seen in the preceding section, judging from Russell's material, this effect was slight. Demographically, it seems to have been the explosive outbursts of the plague in the fourteenth century that really mattered. Russell was able to present some extremely interesting evidence on the fatalities among property-holding heirs in the four most important attacks.

The Black Death of 1348–9 was followed by a 'second pestilence' in 1360–1, and then by a third and fourth in 1369 and 1375. For each of these, Russell analysed the impact on different age groups, and he also tried to estimate their combined impact, a project that is well worth doing, although his procedure was curious and at times clearly erroneous. To describe it briefly, he ascertained the rates of mortality in plague years; these rates were then applied to a life-table population in order to take approximate account of age distribution. 'Normal' death rates were subtracted from the result, and the remainder was assumed to represent the plague loss.[12]

The deaths among the young were very few and the sampling error enormous. These groups, however, loom large in the age distributions, and the rates Russell assumed to be 'corrected' were therefore only made more precarious. For the period 1348–50, for instance, his cases include three heirs presumed to have been between one and five. Of these one died, indicating a risk of mortality of 0·33. This was taken as a measure of the force of mortality in the plague for the entire age group 0–4, in spite of the fact that it was hardly more than the average infant mortality rate Russell estimated for the entire generation born in 1348–75.[13] The resulting death rate was 23·6 per cent, which Russell cites as evidence of the need for this kind of correction, since the crude rate from all his cases, regardless of age, was 27·3 per cent. If two rather than one of his young children in the 1–5 group had died, the rate of mortality for that age group would have been 0·67, and the corrected death rate would have jumped to 28·6 per cent. A procedure so vulnerable to chance is obviously not satisfactory.

It is not only in the case of the young that Russell's operations are dubious. He concluded from his mortality rates that the plague fell more heavily in older men than on the young and relied on this in his interpretation. But old age is always hazardous, and before we can say anything about the impact of the plague we must take more adequate account of the mortality that would ordinarily have occurred.

The refined procedures usually necessary to isolate the contribution to mortality of a single cause of death are not necessary in this case, for the plagues were sudden whirlwinds. Russell included in his plague mortalities for 1348–50 and 1360–1 all deaths in these periods and did the same for the single years 1369 and 1375.[14] To illustrate: of the 58 heirs between 46 and 50 exposed to the plague in 1348–50, 17 died. Normally, however, we should have expected four or five of them to die in the course of slightly more than two years.

A primitive but in this case adequate way of separating plague fatality from ordinary mortality is simply to subtract, for each age group, the 'normal' rate from that observed in the plague, remembering that the normal rate should be doubled for the two first epidemics. As 'normal' rates we could use those estimated earlier for the century before 1348, but if those rates are plotted in a graph they show a most disorderly curve which cannot reflect a normal state of nature. The statistical impulse is to smooth it. This could be done in many ways; the simplest and most reasonable is to adopt the most appropriate of the United Nations model life tables. Table 5 shows the plague fatality rates arrived at by this method. (Age groups under 15 for which the evidence is too sparse have been left out.) The residual plague fatality rates in the table show

T A B L E 5. *Age-Specific Plague Fatality Rates*

(per thousand)

Age	Normal death rate per year	Death rate in plague years				Plague fatality			
		1348–1350	1360–1361	1369	1375	1348–1350	1360–1361	1369	1375
	(1)	(2)	(3)	(4)	(5)	(6)	(7)	(8)	(9)
15–19	12	200	171	140	110	177	148	128	98
20–24	15	197	225	30	160	167	195	15	145
25–29	18	188	220	140	160	153	185	122	142
30–34	21	283	134	20	60	241	92	0	39
35–39	25	333	233	150	130	283	183	125	105
40–44	31	210	225	210	70	148	163	179	39
45–49	39	294	333	120	30	216	255	81	—
50–54	47	344	182	140	120	250	88	93	73
55–59	58	456	413	50	150	340	297	—	92
60–	103	390	354	250	435	184	148	125	332
					Average:	216	177	96	118

Source: Col. 1 Age-specific death rates corresponding to a life expectation at birth of 25 in the model life tables, United Nations, *Methods for Population Projections by Sex and Age* (1956), p. 72. Cols. 2–5. *British Medieval Population*, pp. 216–18. Cols. 6–9 are reached by subtracting the rates of col. 1 for 1369 and 1375, and twice those rates for 1348 and 1360–1.

no convincing tendency at all to vary with age. They are erratic, as might be expected with samples ranging from 21 to 72, but especially in the first two epidemics they show a strong central tendency.

The simplest hypothesis not contradicted by this evidence is that in the devastating outbreaks of the plague, age made no difference to this particular risk of death. This is consistent with the general picture of a disease so devastating that, once contracted, it was almost always fatal. The risk of contagion would then be the only significant variable, and there is no reason to expect that to have been a function of age. Considering how ill understood was the nature of the disease, there is not much more reason to think that it was a function of social status, at least until it became a custom for the rich to flee to the country, as Creighton claims to have been the case after 1465.[15]

On this hypothesis, the best estimate of overall plague mortality in the various epidemics would be the averages of the last columns in Table 5. If younger age groups, including infants, were cut down at the same rate, the population declined by some 22 per cent in the first epidemic, 18 per cent in the second, 10 in the third, and 12 in the fourth.

Decimation on such a scale must have given rise to some recuperative response. The vacancies of society must have stimulated early marriages; on the other hand, the mood of the times may have discouraged fertility. One advice, at least, was that in times of pestilence 'every fleshly lust with women is to be eschewed'.[16] In the end, we can only guess at the course of fertility. If we assume that in the long run it remained at the pre-plague level, the combined impact of the first four epidemics of the plague would have been to reduce the population in 1377 to roughly 51 per cent of its level in 1347 ($0.78 \times 0.82 \times 0.90 \times 0.88 = 0.51$). This is lower than Russell's 60 per cent, but in view of his extraordinary method, it is surprising that the figures are as similar as they are. The margins of uncertainty are large enough to envelop both estimates charitably, and if we assume some positive fertility response between the epidemics it may even be reasonable to think that the drop between 1347 and 1377 was 40 per cent rather than 50.

Russell also cites evidence relating to the declining number of landholders in various villages, but there is no particular reason to expect the number of homesteads or landholders to follow total population very closely. Then there is the matter of the high mortality recorded in ecclesiastical establishments during the Black Death. In the first onslaught, between 35 and 50 per cent of the clerics perished in most dioceses, and in monasteries too this seems to have been an average level, although some were virtually extinguished. If such rates were indicative of general fatality in the first epidemic alone, the total loss between 1348 and 1377 would necessarily have been even greater than just concluded.

Although institutional mortality would be expected to be particularly severe in any plague epidemic, the Black Plague rates reported from the dioceses are surprisingly high, especially since their mortality in the following outbreaks seems to have been commensurate with that of Russell's heirs. Only if the age of clergymen in 1348 was very high or if they were especially exposed to contagion are those figures compatible with our earlier inference. They are, moreover, based on larger samples although their age distribution is unknown.

With this and other caveats in mind, we might tentatively conclude that the Black Death and the succeeding three outbreaks of the plague reduced English population by 40 and perhaps even 50 per cent in the span of little more than a quarter of a century. What happened later—whether the population continued to decline and if so for how long—Russell's data cannot possibly be made to reveal.

LAMPRECHT AND THE MOSEL VALLEY

The thesis that European population expanded spectacularly in the three centuries before 1300 is widely respected and lends colour to most accounts of the vitality of the High Middle Ages. It is actually only in Western Europe and Italy that there is evidence of such growth, and even there the indications are not compellingly clear except in the case of Britain. For France, Russell resorts to the device of premising that the rate of growth was the same as in England, and he is then able to extend a series back from Lot's estimate for 1328.[17] In Italy, city walls were expanded in the period 1100–1250, and there is a sprinkling of evidence about urban population at various times, but estimates of overall population are breathtakingly conjectural. German urbanization presents similar evidence. The medieval population of the Mosel Valley, however, was studied in detail by Lamprecht, some 80 years ago.[18]

'This meticulous study', as Russell calls it, is probably the only source of actual growth rates for a Continental population in the High Middle Ages, and in consequence it is frequently cited. The idea that Europe's population trebled in these 300 years seems to have its origin here. However, Russell has also given currency to a complete misinterpretation of it in his *Late Ancient and Medieval Population* and Lamprecht's procedure does not seem to be widely understood.

Lamprecht's idea was to rely on toponymical research and convert the documented emergence of new place-names into a picture of population growth. Although the difficulties of toponymical research are forbidding, the qualitative impression of rapid growth in the Middle Ages is based in no small measure on the profusion of new names. An attempt to lend precision to that impression is of obvious interest.

Lamprecht started from the population figures for the area in 1821 and 1828, which were 640,000 and 720,000 respectively. The rate of growth in this seven-year period was thus, he said, 1·4 per cent per annum (actually it was 1·6), and he extrapolated back to 1800 on the assumption that it had remained constant. The population at the end of the eighteenth century would thus have been about 450,000.[19]

He then introduced the place-name counts, and in a crucial but obscure passage he presented his results as follows:

Die zwischen dem 13. und 18. bis 19. Jh. liegende Periode einer im ganzen weitgehenden Ruhe im Ausbau gestattet also sehr wohl, die Zustände am Anfange und am Schluss der Periode

selbst zum Vergleich zu bringen. Betritt man nun diesen Weg unter Vermittlung der Ortsstatistik
... so würde:

Im Jahre	800	900	1000	1050	1100	1150	1200	1237	1800	
einer Anzahl von ca	100	250	350	470	590	810	990	1180	2000	Orten seine
Bevölkerungsziffer von ca	20	60	80	100	140	180	220	250	450	Tausend Seelen

entsprochen haben.[20]

From these figures he derived the rates of growth for the population:

800– 900	1·1 per cent
900–1000	0·3
1000–1050	0·45
1050–1100	0·7
1100–1150	0·5
1150–1200	0·4
1200–1237	0·35

I have retained the awkward form of Lamprecht's table in the above quotation in order to clarify Russell's misreading of it. According to him, 'Lamprecht assumed that the average size of the villages increased greatly in the period A.D. 800–1300', and Russell presents the bottom line as estimates of the average village population: 20, 60, 80, etc.[21] He then proceeds to dispute these estimates by computing his own series for the number of villages and comparing its rate of growth with that of English population. (It is not clear why he does not use Lamprecht's middle line.) Because the rates of growth for the number of Mosel villages and the number of Englishmen were comparable, he infers that village size did not change.

But Lamprecht says nothing about village size, and the series that Russell quotes is the estimate of *total* population (in thousands). If he had meant what Russell thought he meant, he would have believed that the population of the Mosel valley in 1237 was 150 times as large as in 800, about 10 times as large as in 1000, and that the annual growth rate was over 1 per cent per annum. Actually, he thought it was one-half of 1 per cent which, sustained over such a long period, was high enough to be remarkable.

And what did Lamprecht assume about village size? In listing the place-names he included for each one its population in 1825–8, a procedure suggesting that to Lamprecht each village had sprung up fully equipped with its nineteenth-century complement of inhabitants.[22] Actually, his procedure was even simpler. From the estimated population in 1800 he derived an average village size of 225, which he applied to the numbers of villages existing between A.D. 800 and 1237. That the ratios between his population figures and village figures are not constant but swing between 200 and 240 is all explained by the word 'about' in his table. He rounded off his figures to the nearest ten and computed his growth rates on the basis of the rounded population figures. Because he rounded them to one or two digits, the growth rates for the population differ slightly from those of the number of villages, which creates the tantalizing suspicion that some inscrutably sophisticated technique was being used. In actual fact, however, nothing whatever besides the number of place-names was drawn upon.

What is one to make of this procedure? Two *a priori* considerations push in opposite directions. There can hardly be any doubt of the direction of the bias of toponymical statistics. We cannot from historical documents know of a village before it is founded, but we are quite likely to ignore it for a considerable period of time. Increasing literacy, pacification, and the consolidation of law and litigation all contributed to the likelihood that a village should come to our attention only in the course of the High Middle Ages although it might then have existed for some considerable time. The distinction between Roman, Celtic, and German names in the Mosel Valley makes it possible to avoid flagrant error, but the late appearance of certain of the older forms also points up the danger of the procedure. There can be no doubt that Lamprecht's figures overstate the rate of growth of village communities.

But how valid is the assumption of proportionality between villages and population? This question arises not only in the expanding phase of medieval history to which Lamprecht turned his attention, but also in the controversial fourteenth century where the continued abandonment of homesteads and villages has been interpreted as a sign of sustained decline in population. Serious doubts arise in both cases. Even in an orderly but imaginary process of settlement, in which every new village ceases to grow when it reaches a certain limit, there will be an approximate correspondence between the growth of villages and that of the population only if villages reach their limiting size very rapidly. Otherwise, the growth in size of the villages must obviously be added to that of their numbers. It seems unlikely that the new villages of medieval Europe immediately filled to the brim, although there are fair grounds to suspect that the oldest ones had filled up at the end of the period. Hallam's Lincolnshire censuses, to mention only one example, show spectacular growth in numbers of households between Domesday and 1287:[23]

	1086	1287
Spalding	91	587
Pinchback	57	646

If the toponymical basis of Lamprecht's estimates is sound, his figures would represent a lower limit, and the actual rates of growth of population should have been a good deal higher. They would thus be higher than those estimated for England before the Black Death on the basis of entirely different, and on the whole probably more reliable sources.

This would not be outrageously implausible, but when the two sources of error—the inevitable toponymical oversights of villages, and the neglect of village growth—are simultaneously considered, one must conclude that Lamprecht's figures are fairly worthless. Those who use Lamprecht's work to illustrate the rate of medieval expansion should at least be aware that what he offers is the rate of growth of place-names, not of population.

THE HERIOTS ON THE WINCHESTER MANORS

Professor Postan and J. Titow have made ingenious use of records of certain medieval death duties to trace the course of mortality during the century before the Black Death.[24] The heriots were duties levied on holdings of customary tenants at the death of the tenant and were paid in animals or money. If the number of tenancies remained approximately constant, the number of heriots should reflect the course of the crude death rate among tenants.

The series of heriots that Postan and Titow extracted from the accounts of five of the manors of the Bishop of Winchester is of special interest when it is compared with the movements of grain prices. Deaths and prices were for the most part fairly well synchronized, though a few peaks of mortality in years of low prices suggest epidemics unaccompanied by poor harvests; after 1325 the correlation is much less impressive than at earlier times.

No doubt the contours of mortality are reflected in those figures. To derive a meaningful measure of it is none the less difficult. Postan affirms that the number of customary tenants must have been approximately constant at 1,725, the number of tenants liable to heriot in 1321. The annual number of heriots paid was high, particularly in the first half of the fourteenth century, for which the figures seem most accurate, and the crude death rate among tenants in that period approached 50 per thousand.

Customary tenants were, in general, male adults, and Postan therefore treats this figure as an estimate of the death rate of the population over 20. By comparison with other societies, particularly Russia around the turn of the century where death rates were considerably higher for the population under 20 than over 20, Postan–Titow arrive at the conclusion that overall death rates at Winchester must have been spectacular:

If these differential death rates of the Russian adult population were used to convert the Winchester death rate of adults into those of the population as a whole, a crude rate as high as 70–75 per thousand would result. Somewhat similar results would emerge from the comparison of Winchester rates with the adult death rates of Indian population between 1890 and 1920. There is thus very little doubt that the mortality on the Winchester manors in the second half of the thirteenth and the first half of the fourteenth centuries was at least as high, and probably much higher, than the mortality in any other preindustrial society whose evidence is available to us.[25]

Indeed, death rates of this magnitude in an almost stationary population would be extraordinary. They would correspond to a life expectancy at birth of about 14 years, which is less than that of the unhealthiest metropolitan centres of the eighteenth century, and considerably less than that of primitive societies.

Temporarily, mortality rates may attain any level including total extinction, but an approximately stationary population must match mortality and fertility. No estimates of fecundity in the Western world in recent centuries would suffice to maintain a population at birth and death rates around 70 per thousand.[26] This estimate of medieval mortality is therefore suspect from the outset. Actually, the Winchester heriots do not constitute evidence of such sensational rates of mortality.

The records may of course be less than perfect. The recorded number of heriots paid in money is assumed to have been seriously deficient in the thirteenth century, before it jumped to rough parity with those paid in animals. (Table 6) Money heriots were levied on holdings too small to pay in animals, and the collection or recording of such heriots apparently left out of account

TABLE 6. *Heriots and Mortality Rates of Customary Tenants on Five Winchester Manors, 1245–1348*

Years	Animal	Money	Total	Death rate (per thousand)	'Life expectancy' of tenants (years)
1245–9	38	9	47	27	37
1250–9	38	10	48	28	36
1260–9	30	2	32	19	54
1270–9	32	14	46	27	38
1280–9	37	12	49	28	35
1290–9	33	28	61	35	28
1300–9	44	30	74	43	23
1310–9	49	57	105	61	16
1320–9	44	41	84	49	21
1330–9	38	47	85	50	20
1340–9	39	56	95	55	19

Source: Prepared from figures in Longden, 'Statistical Notes on Winchester Heriots', *Econ. Hist. Rev.*, 11 (1958–9), 412–417.

many of the poorer tenants in the first half of the thirteenth century. After 1270, we are told that the records appear complete, in spite of the continued rapid increase in money heriots. The annual death rates before 1300 were considerably below those of the fourteenth century, and it is tempting to conclude that mortality was rising around 1300. The authors, however, refrained from stressing this trend, but there is no particular reason for such reticence—one thing their material suggests very forcefully is an increase in secular morality.

But the crucial question is what the age distribution of the tenant population was like. It cannot have been that of an ordinary population as the authors imply. The Winchester customs for accession to property were undoubtedly complex, but we may be certain that the entry into tenancy occurred at an average age higher than 20. It is in error that the authors say: 'the death rates on the five manors, as measured by heriots, suggest that the expectations of life of the substantial tenants, i.e., the intervals between their accession at 20 and their death, should have varied from about 24 at the beginning of our period to just under 20 in the period following 1292.'[27]

Tenants did not acquire their holdings at 20—indeed, the very next sentence mentions 'uncertain guesses as to the average age of accession to property'.

The death rate (or its inverse, the 'expectation of life') of these customary tenants can therefore not be compared with that of the age group over 20 in a regular population. A group of this kind, consisting of heads of households, may however be compared with other groups of similar nature. Death rates for such groups are usually not conceded any statistical significance and are therefore rarely published, but two cases will show that the death rate in such a group is not necessarily lower than that of the population as a whole.

In 1851, Farr investigated mortality in different occupations. He found the crude mortality rate of farmers over 20 to be 28 per thousand. This was a high rate—that of tailors was 20 per thousand. Yet his analysis showed that the age-specific mortalities of farmers were the lowest of any occupational group: they were 'the oldest and the longest livers'.[28] Farr suspected that the number of farms had been stationary for some years, and as the age group of 45–55 was greater than any other, it was clear that more men entered than left the group up to that age. Now, 28 per thousand was a high rate for Victorian England, and if we assumed that infant and child mortality, still extremely high at the time, should raise our estimate of overall mortality, we would be led in the wrong direction, for the overall death rate in England at the time was about 22·5 per thousand.

It would thus be quite possible that the Winchester population was not regularly subjected to the conflagration inferred by Postan and Titow. The overall death rate may have been lower or of the same magnitude as among customary tenants.

Between 1674 and 1742 in the parish of Crulai, in Normandy, which Gautier and Henry have subjected to intensive analysis, the average age of death of married men was between 50 and 55 (depending on the attribution of borderline cases). The average age at marriage for men was about 27 years, and the life expectancy at marriage would therefore have been about 25 years, which in a stationary population corresponds to a death rate of 40 per thousand for married men. For the population as a whole, the death rate is estimated at 31 per thousand, and the life expectancy at something close to 30 years.[29] In this case, then, the mortality of the population as a whole was lower than that of heads of households.

The customary tenants at the five Winchester manors were not identical with the population of married men; we are told there may even have been a few teenage girls among them. But there can be no doubt that their age distribution must have been more like that of married men than like that of the population over 20. The manorial custom for accession to property did not lay down hard and fast rules; minors of both sexes sometimes succeeded to holdings, and 'a surprisingly large number of successors were men who married the dead men's widows'. Succession by a grown-up son (or son-in-law) will not always occur even where it is favoured by law and custom. All possible permutations of family survivorship may occur at the death of a husband originally counted as the head of household; in slightly more than half the cases he will leave a widow who may be childless or not, whose children may be minors or not, and so forth. However, it is not unreasonable to assume that in many cases the accession to a tenancy was connected with marriage, which would make the tenants of the Winchester manors roughly comparable with the married men at Crulai. In that case, their rate of mortality was not startlingly high.

Over the whole century between 1245 and the Black Death, the heriot rate at Winchester was actually almost identical with the Crulai death rate of 40 per thousand. The heriots were fewer in the first half of that century—the rate was only about 27 per thousand for 1245–99— and it was only in the second half that deaths of tenants were numerous enough to raise the death rate to about 50. Postan and Titow suspect that the records of money heriots are incomplete before 1270, but in the 1280s and 1290s the rates were still only 28 and 35 respectively. It is true that the proportion of money heriots was still curiously low, and Longden, who assisted them in the statistical analysis of the heriots, was apparently suspicious enough of that portion of the material to disregard the tenancies liable to money heriots before 1300. Instead, he assumed that the tenancies that paid their heriots in animals formed a constant share of the total number; he was thus able to extend the series of high death rates back into the thirteenth century (since the number of animal-paying heriots was roughly constant all the time).

This is questionable procedure. We are told that the records appear complete and 'bear no trace of a change in the administration of the heriots', and the rise in money heriots would seem rather to call for an explanation than for the scrapping of the lower figures. Money heriots were paid by the tenancies that were too small to pay in animals, and subdivisions would appear to be a possible explanation. We are told that they were few, and that the total number of tenancies was more likely to decline than to increase.[30] It is worth considering, however, that an increase in the number of small tenancies would not only explain the anomalies of the money-heriot series but would also temper the exceedingly sharp rise in the turnover rate (i.e., the death rate) as calculated on the assumption of a constant number of tenancies. Subdivision would be an exceedingly probable phenomenon in the circumstances. For that matter, one can imagine an increasing tendency to pay heriots in money even on marginal tenancies. Money heriots, as Postan and Titow stress, in a number of cases also represented 'anticipated death duties' levied on sales of land *inter vivos* sometimes paid by substantial tenants selling parts of their holdings, and in all such cases tending to understate the actual life of the tenant. Finally, one might consider the possibility that there was a rise in the death rate, as the authors very reasonably hold, and that it tended to hit poorer tenants much harder than substantial ones. This may go some way towards explaining why the annual rate of money heriots should have doubled or tripled around the turn of the century, but this part of the data remains troubling.

The rates from the fourteenth century are on firmer ground. They are perfectly compatible with a level of mortality for medieval society indicated by the discussion of Russell's material in the previous pages. There is no reason to believe that the overall death rate around Winchester was higher than that of the customary tenants. If it were roughly the same or slightly lower it was of the order of 40–50 per thousand, which corresponds to a life expectation at birth of 20–25 years. For a period that included one of the most devastating famines in European history, that of 1315, this is about what we should have expected. The Postan–Titow evidence also, interestingly enough, seems to point to a deterioration between the thirteenth and the fourteenth centuries. Such a deterioration has a place in the interpretation of the turn of events in the early fourteenth century, but actual statistical evidence of it is sparse.

EPILOGUE

It is possible to argue that to the progress of historical inquiry the most important thing is not the historian's answer to some specific question but his unearthing of the sources, their processing, and presentation. As G. N. Clark once remarked, 'even in the few instances where the answer is in such a form as "Yes" or "No" or "$5\frac{1}{2}$ million souls" or "£1,753,000," the most valuable part of the investigation will be not that conclusion but what has been ascertained on the way to it'.[31] The reasonable part of this proposition is clear enough. Yet there is something not wholly satisfactory about the view that the conclusion of an investigation is less valuable than the investigation itself, as if the principal purpose were not to arrive at that conclusion. When the purpose is that of ascertaining some isolated historical statistic, such a view may be acceptable. What, indeed, does it matter whether the population of England and Wales at the beginning of the eighteenth century was 5 million, 6 or 5·5?

The answer is that it acquires considerable significance when historical statistics are combined into a greater perspective of historical change. The three problems of statistical interpretation that have been briefly considered here may in themselves seem trifling, but when the estimates of mortality in medieval Europe are to be fitted into the picture of the evolution of Western mortality and when rates of demographic expansion become cornerstones in interpretations of the economic dynamics of pre-industrial growth, it is more important to know the range of confidence of such estimates and the reasons for that confidence. Statistical estimates are not 'facts' of history, first to be ascertained and then to be interpreted; the estimation of historical statistics is merely an aspect of historical interpretation.

NOTES

[1] Joseph Lottin, *Quetelet, Statisticien et Sociologue* (Louvain and Paris, 1912), p. 176.

[2] Lance Davis *et al.*, 'Aspects of Quantitative Research in Economic History', *Jour. Econ. Hist.*, 20 (1960), 542.

[3] John Durand, 'Mortality Estimates from Roman Tombstone Inscriptions', *Amer. Jour. Sociol.*, 65 (1959–60), 365–73.

[4] To take only one example, Arthur E. R. Boak in *Manpower Shortage and the Fall of the Roman Empire in the West* (Ann Arbor, 1955), assumes that Russell managed to calculate medieval life expectancy at birth 'with reasonable certainty' and cites his figures to the second decimal (p. 11).

[5] For the method of computing standard deviations for estimates of life expectancy, see Edwin B. Wilson, 'The Standard Deviation of Sampling for Life Expectancy', *Jour. Amer. Stat. Assoc.*, 33 (1938), 705–8.

[6] Chi-square for the first four groups is 9·8, which with four degrees of freedom suggests that the difference is significant on the 2 per cent level. Above the age of 50, chi-square for eight age groups is 18·1 and the difference is significant on the same level. For the six age groups in between, chi-square is 5·2, and P over 50 per cent.

[7] To illustrate, the average birth date for the generation of 1301–25 is assumed to have been mid-1312; more than half the deaths that occurred between 30 and 35 would therefore have occurred before 1348. This method, to be sure, takes no account of the fact that the plague did not leave deaths evenly spaced, but systematic differences in mortality should nevertheless appear.

[8] Almost all his tables suffer from mistakes in the calculation of the number of years lived in these intervals. The formula he used between one and four should be

$$1^L4 = 0\cdot034\ 1_0 - 1\cdot184\ 1_1 - 2\cdot782\ 1_5$$

and was used in that form in his Table 8·2. But the formula was misquoted with the first coefficient as 0·34 (p. 178) and this is the form in which it was used in the other tables. Similarly the separation factors used to estimate $_n{}^L{}_1$ are actually not what they are claimed to be (0·8 and 0·2), but 0·812 and 0·208 which does not add up to unity. The resulting error is trifling but not confidence-inspiring.

[9] *British Medieval Population*, pp. 262–3.

[10] T. H. Hollingsworth, 'A Demographic Study of the British Ducal Families', *Population Studies*, 11 (1957), 8–9. Life expectations at 15 are given only for the generation of 1480–1679, but at age 20, the expectations for males born in 1330–1479 were 21·7 years; excluding violent deaths, they were 31·5 years.

[11] Charles F. Mullett, *The Bubonic Plague and England* (Lexington, Ky., 1956), p. 18.

[12] pp. 216, 262–3.

[13] To make things worse, he grouped his plague cases in age groups 1–5, 6–10, etc., whereas his life tables were conventionally arranged in terms of 0–4, 5–9, etc. He thought 'the results would probably not be sufficiently different to justify the effort of revising the data'. Although this may be true for most other age groups, it cannot hold for the youngest where the absence of infants robs it of all significance.

[14] He did not state this explicitly, but he deducted twice the 'normal annual mortality' from his death rates for the plague of 1360–1 and slightly more from that of 1348–50 which indicates that he included all deaths from the plague-ridden periods, and it is hard to see what else he could have done in the absence of reliable indications of the cause of death.

[15] Charles Creighton, *A History of Epidemics in Britain* (Cambridge, 1894), i. 226.

[16] Ibid., i. p. 213.

[17] Josiah Cox Russell, 'Late Ancient and Medieval Population', *Trans. Amer. Philos. Soc., n.s.*, 48, Part 3 (Philadelphia, 1958), 105.

[18] Karl Lamprecht, *Deutsches Wirtschaftsleben im Mittelalter, 1886*. See particularly i. 161–4 and ii. 20.

[19] Ibid. i. 161.

[20] Ibid. i. 163.

[21] Russell, 'Late Ancient and Medieval Population', p. 95.

[22] Lamprecht, op. cit. ii. 20.

[23] H. E. Hallam, 'Some Thirteenth-Century Censuses', *Econ. Hist. Rev.* 10 (1957–8), 340.

[24] M. M. Postan and J. Titow, 'Heriots and Prices on Winchester Manors', ibid. 11 (1958–9), 392–417.

[25] Ibid., p. 400.

[26] It is true that in recent years demographers have discovered African populations with birth rates far above the level around 50, which was long regarded as a maximum. Rates above 60 or even 70 have now been claimed. See Blanc and Théodore, 'Les populations d'Afrique noire et de Madagascar', *Population*, 15 (1960), 407–432.

[27] Postan and Titow, op. cit., p. 395.

[28] William Farr, *Vital Statistics* (London, 1885) p. 395.

[29] E. Gautier and Louis Henry, *La population de Crulai, paroisse normande*, I.N.E.D., Travaux et documents, Cahier no. 33 (Paris, 1958), pp. 181, 191, 232.

[30] Postan and Titow, op. cit., p. 399.

[31] G. N. Clark, 'History and the Social Sciences', in *The Social Sciences: Their Relations in Theory and Teaching* (London, 1936), p. 89.

3

The Geographical Distribution of
Wealth in England, 1334–1649

R. S. SCHOFIELD

Editor's note. This article was first published in *Econ. Hist. Rev.* 18 (1965), 483–510.

The two statistical methods used in the article, Spearman's rank-order correlation coefficient and Pearson's product moment correlation coefficient, are discussed above, pp. 15–16 and pp. 16–17. For further reading see footnotes to those pages.

I

THIS article seeks to discover whether a critical examination of taxation data can be made to yield any conclusions as to broad changes in the geographical distribution of wealth between the fourteenth and seventeenth centuries. It takes as its starting-point an earlier article, published by E. J. Buckatzsch in 1950, which attempted to measure statistically changes in the distribution of wealth between the counties over an extended period of eight centuries.[1] By employing two statistical measures,[2] Buckatzsch was able to show that statistically significant redistribution of wealth occurred only in the periods 1086–1150, 1150–1283, 1503–1641, and 1693–1803; while at all other times between 1086 and 1843 the distribution of wealth between the counties remained relatively stable.[3]

For the period now under review Buckatzsch summarized his arguments as follows: 'The geographical distribution of wealth appears to have remained remarkably stable from the Middle Ages to the end of the seventeenth century, and to have changed very greatly during the eighteenth century.'[4] More precisely, he argued that the tax assessments of 1453 and 1504 showed that practically no redistribution of wealth had taken place between the counties since 1334, while the tax assessment of 1641 showed that a marked, and statistically significant, redistribution of wealth had occurred after 1504.[5] In contrast, I shall argue in this article that Buckatzsch's picture of a stable geographical distribution of wealth during the later Middle Ages, followed by a significant redistribution of wealth during the sixteenth and early seventeenth centuries, is false; and that while little can be inferred from the tax assessments about the distribution of wealth in the later sixteenth and early seventeenth centuries, the best evidence available points to a very considerable redistribution of wealth during the later Middle Ages, very nearly equal to that ascribed by Buckatzsch to the eighteenth century.

I should perhaps make it clear at once that I do not consider that the falseness of Buckatzsch's conclusions stems either from the theoretical difficulties involved in the use of taxation data for measuring economic change, or from the nature of the statistical procedures which he used. Buckatzsch, indeed, carefully argued a convincing theoretical case for the validity of taxation data as evidence of economic change, providing that the data met certain basic conditions.[6] Accepting his theoretical arguments, I shall show rather that the tax assessments which he used to establish the stability of the geographical distribution of wealth in the later Middle Ages do not in practice fulfil the theoretical conditions which he formulated. Next I shall consider whether any other tax assessments can be found for the period from the mid-fourteenth to the mid-seventeenth century which do satisfy these theoretical conditions, and which can provide us with a measure of the geographical distribution of wealth at certain dates. Such assessments should enable us first to recalculate the extent of geographical redistribution of wealth within this period, and then to compare this with the extent of redistribution of wealth which Buckatzsch calculated for other periods. Finally I shall describe the geographical distribution of wealth as measured by tax assessments in the mid-fourteenth century, and again in the early sixteenth century, in greater detail, in the belief that the pattern of these distributions and the nature of the redistribution that occurred between them will be of interest to economic historians.

II

First of all, however, something should be said about Buckatzsch's arguments concerning the general limitations of tax assessments as measures of the geographical distribution of wealth. Buckatzsch began by making a 'major assumption', namely that tax assessments not only accurately reflected the geographical distribution of the items of wealth being assessed, but also the distribution of over-all wealth, that is of all 'important income-generating resources'.[7] But the practical implications of this assumption were considerably reduced by the fact that, for the purposes of a statistical comparison of wealth of the counties, no more accuracy was required of the tax assessments than that they should be able to rank the counties in the same order of wealth, and, for one of the statistical tests, in the same sort of proportions, as would have resulted from a complete and accurate survey of all forms of wealth.[8] The statistical tests which Buckatzsch used therefore made relatively light demands on the accuracy of the tax assessments; but they did impose one basic requirement, namely that at each date the conditions of assessment had to be the same for each county: each county, that is, had to have an equal chance of appearing wealthy. This fundamental rule has two main corollaries. First of all, if Buckatzsch's assumption that tax assessments can be taken to reflect the distribution of over-all wealth is to be sustained, then in each county the wealth actually assessed for taxation must always stand in the same proportion to the whole of that county's wealth. Tax assessments, for example, which only take notice of metalliferous mines, would give a markedly distorted picture of the geographical distribution of over-all wealth. In practice Buckatzsch used a combination of tax assessments on movable property, and tax assessments on annual incomes derived mainly from real property; but he considered that, although these two forms of taxation measured the distribution of different types of wealth, provided both types of assessment gave all counties an equal chance to appear wealthy, it was quite legitimate to compare the two as reasonable measures of the distribution of over-all wealth.[9] Whether the capital value of movable property and the value of annual incomes derived mainly from real property do in fact comprise more or less constant proportions of over-all wealth in all sorts of economic situations is probably somewhat of an open question. Clearly, however, since the possibility of a divergence between the level of these two sorts of wealth, either as between different regions or over a period of time, cannot be safely disregarded, it would be preferable for comparisons to be restricted as far as possible to assessments on one type of wealth alone. Of the two, tax assessments on the capital value of movable property in practice reached a much wider cross-section of the population in a variety of economic circumstances than did taxes on rents and other annual incomes, and for this reason movable property taxes are probably the better guide to the geographical distribution of over-all wealth.[10]

The second corollary of the basic requirement of comparability in the conditions of assessment as between the counties is that flaws in the process of assessment and other deficiencies in the compilation of the tax data are not prejudicial to the use of the data as measures of the geographical distribution of wealth, provided that the occurrence of these flaws and deficiencies is not itself regionally patterned, and that the wealth of each county is misrepresented to more or less the same extent. Buckatzsch distinguished three main possible sources of regionally patterned distortion in the compilation of the tax data: undervaluation, the exclusion of wealth in the hands of the clergy, and the assessment of wealth according to the location of the ownership of wealth rather than according to the location of the wealth itself. This last possibility he dismissed as unimportant before the mid-nineteenth century because of the relatively small number of geographically extensive enterprises then in existence. The problem of the exclusion of wealth in the hands of the clergy from the tax assessments he admitted that he had not been able to overcome, but suggested that variations in the assessments of the wealth of the counties attributable to this cause 'might turn out to be a second-order effect'. The possibility of regional patterns in the efficiency of assessment he did not really face, except to point out that the broadness of the statistical tests which he used made them insensitive to quite large variations in the accuracy of the assessments. This indeed was the main burden of his argument, for while admitting that his assumption of favourable answers to all the questions he raised concerning the accuracy of the tax data severely limited the validity of his conclusions, he emphasized that the general outline of his conclusions was so bold that it was beyond the reach of 'minute criticism'.[11] The three possible sources of distortion, undervaluation, the exclusion of wealth in the hands of the clergy, and a divergence between the location of wealth and the location of the ownership of wealth, are discussed in some detail below; but here it might be said that very much the same sort of conclusion is reached, namely that the degree of distortion which might be expected from these sources is insufficient to account for the magnitude of the variations in the geographical distribution of wealth suggested by the tax assessments.

But Buckatzsch also pointed out that there was another essential condition which the tax data had to meet, and this was that the assessments had to be genuine assessments, made in the year to which they purported to refer, and should not merely be repetitions of assessments made at an earlier date. He believed that the fact that the assessments which he used always differed, however slightly, in the wealth which they ascribed to the counties meant that they were genuine assessments, and that he had avoided using spurious data.[12] Unfortunately this was not so; and it is on this relatively simple question of the true nature of the tax assessments which he used, rather than on the more complex question of the limitations of the validity of his techniques, that his conclusions as to the geographical redistribution of wealth between the mid-fourteenth and mid-seventeenth centuries can be challenged and overthrown.

III

Buckatzsch's picture of a stable geographical distribution of wealth during the century and three-quarters between 1334 and 1504, followed by a statistically significant redistribution of wealth during the next century and a half between 1504 and 1641, is particularly vulnerable, because he relied for his basic data entirely on tax assessments available in print, and this restricted his choice to only four assessments: for the fifteenth and tenth in 1334, for the support of 13,000 archers in 1453, for the subsidy in lieu of two feudal aids in 1504, and for the subsidy of £400,000 in 1641.[13]

The first of these assessments, for the fifteenth and tenth in 1334, is satisfactory in every respect. The 1334 assessment was a revision of an assessment made in 1332, undertaken by two special commissioners, appointed by the Crown for each shire, in consultation with the inhabitants of each vill within the shire. The 1332 assessment had been a local assessment of all movable property, though with certain exceptions, at current values. Although undervaluation is known to have occurred in connection with this earlier assessment, there is no evidence that it was regionally patterned, and it was in some measure retrieved by the revision of 1334. The revised assessment of 1334 therefore relates with reasonable accuracy to the year 1334, and it is based on a genuine local assessment of movable wealth, without any discernible regional bias.[14]

The other three assessments, made in 1453, 1504, and 1641, are not so satisfactory. First of all they are not genuine assessments, that is the county totals are not the aggregate sums of the assessments of the wealth of the inhabitants of each county assessed locally at current values. Rather they were arrived at by the division among the counties of a certain total sum to be levied on the whole country. The county totals for these taxes are therefore allocations rather than assessments.[15] This means that the validity of data derived from these taxes as measures of the geographical distribution of wealth depends entirely on the validity of the criteria governing the allocation of the total tax due among the counties. And since it is difficult to conceive of any criteria available to those responsible for these allocations more accurate than a local assessment of wealth, it follows that county allocations of this nature are likely to be inferior to locally assessed taxes as measures of the geographical distribution of wealth. Indeed, the divergence between the patterns of distribution of wealth exhibited by four mid-seventeenth-century allocation taxes, levied over a period of only thirteen years, is so startling as to cast serious doubts on the reliability of any one of these taxes as a reasonable guide to the actual geographical distribution of wealth at the date.[16] These doubts are increased by the lack of any local assessment in which confidence can be placed after the beginning of Elizabeth's reign.[17] The 1641 assessment, which Buckatzsch used, was one of these mid-seventeenth-century allocation taxes, and therefore shares with them the dubious character of a rough estimate based on stereotyped local assessments, probably more indicative of the distribution of wealth at the beginning of Elizabeth's reign than in the mid-seventeenth century.[18]

But even more serious objections can be brought against Buckatzsch's two remaining assessments, those of 1453 and 1504. Thorold Rogers described the 1504 assessment as 'the most unsuspicious estimate of the comparative wealth of England, town and country alike'.[19] In fact even on the most superficial inspection, this assessment is one of the most suspicious. Suspicion is first aroused by the fact that Henry VII reduced the sum first granted by the Commons in lieu of two feudal aids from £40,000 to £30,000, which was almost exactly the net yield of the fifteenth and tenth at the beginning of the sixteenth century.[20] And suspicion is immediately confirmed by the patent fact that the allocations of most of the counties were exactly the same sums which these counties traditionally paid to the fifteenth and tenth.[21] Now, although these sums were not the same as those assessed on the counties when the fifteenth and tenth was revised and standardized in 1334, they stood in a simple proportional relationship to them, because the difference between the two sets of figures was brought about by the deduction of £6,000, which was allowed from 1446 for decayed areas, and which was divided amongst the counties, not according to current needs, but proportionally to their share of the total assessment of 1334.[22] The county allocations of 1504 were therefore nothing more than a re-issue of the fifteenth and tenth assessments of 1334 in the form that these had become standardized during the fifteenth century. Consequently the 1504 allocations show a geographical distribution of wealth precisely the same as that shown by the 1334 assessments, and have no connection whatsoever with the actual geographical distribution of wealth at the beginning of the sixteenth century. Nor do the sums allocated to the counties in 1453 bear any relationship to the actual geographical distribution of wealth in the mid-fifteenth century. Although the connection is not immediately apparent, the 1453 allocations can also be shown to have been based on the by then traditional fifteenth and tenth assessments of 1334. The object of the 1453 allocations was to apportion between the counties the costs of supporting an army of 13,000 archers for one year. The way in which this was done was to allocate the cost of the upkeep of a certain number of archers to each county and to a few towns, so that the counties provided for about 10,900 archers, and the towns for the remaining 2,100.[23] The significant point is that it can be shown that the archers were allocated to the counties in the ratio of one archer for every 50 marks assessed on the counties in 1334, net of the sums currently allowed for expenses of collection. The remaining 2,100 archers were allocated to ten towns; but the ratio of archers to the 1334 assessments of these towns was much higher than it was for the counties, ranging from one archer for every £2. 10s. 0d. for Newcastle-upon-Tyne to one archer for every 13s. 10d. for London.[24] When they are included in their respective counties, the allocations of these ten towns modify the strictly proportional relationship of the county allocations to the 1334 assessments, and produce the appearance of a very slight redistribution of wealth which Buckatzsch observed. But the 1453 allocations are again basically a reissue of the 1334 assessments, only very marginally altered; they bear no relationship whatsoever to the distribution of wealth in the mid-fifteenth century. The assessments of 1453 and 1504 are therefore spurious in that they have nothing to do with the actual geographical distribution of wealth in the years to which they purport to refer. Equally spurious therefore are both the 'remarkable' stability of the distribution of wealth which Buckatzsch inferred from these assessments for the period between 1334 and 1504, and the significant redistribution of wealth which he discerned between 1504 and 1641.

IV

Having discredited the allocations of 1453, 1504, and 1641, we are left without any assessments after 1334 acceptable as measures of the geographical distribution of wealth for the period from the mid-fourteenth to the mid-seventeenth century. But are there any other assessments which might be used in their place? Unfortunately for our purposes the standardized fifteenth and tenth assessments of 1334 remained for a long time the normal form of taxation, and during the rest of the fourteenth and during the fifteenth century fresh assessments were rare.[25] Those that there were comprise three rather different types, none of which is really suitable as a measure of the geographical distribution of wealth.

First of all there were the poll taxes of 1377, 1379, and 1380.[26] The difficulty of comparing any one of these taxes with the 1334 assessments is that this would involve the assumption that at both dates there was a perfect correlation between the wealth of a county and the number of its inhabitants; and such an assumption would be difficult to sustain, especially in a period of plague.[27] In addition the interval between 1334 and the levy of these taxes is rather short for much redistribution of wealth to have taken place. Secondly there were two taxes on parishes. The first of these was levied in 1371 at the flat rate of 22s. 3d. (later increased to 116s.) on each parish; while the second, levied in 1428, involved the imposition of a rate calculated according to the extented value of the parish church.[28] Neither of these taxes therefore provides any information as to the geographical distribution of wealth at the dates at which they were levied. The third group, however, looks more promising. This comprises a series of income taxes levied in the fifteenth century, in 1404, 1411, 1431, 1435, 1450, 1472, and 1489.[29] The last two of these taxes can be disregarded because no reliable figures for the county assessments have survived.[30] But the five remaining taxes are not really suitable for our purposes. In the first place they were all taxes on annual incomes, usually derived from lands, but sometimes also including other sources such as fees, annuities and corrodies; while the tax of 1334 was assessed on the capital value of movable possessions. This difference in the form of wealth on which the two types of tax were assessed may well mean that the pictures which they provide of the geographical distribution of wealth are not strictly comparable. This is made all the more likely by the relatively restricted nature of these fifteenth-century income taxes, which were levied only on those with incomes above a certain level. In 1404 the exemption limit was 500 marks; in 1411 this was reduced to £20; in 1431 and 1435 it was brought down to £5; and in 1450 it was reduced still further to £2.[31] Now taxes with high exemption limits, certainly those at £20 or above, are unsuitable as measures of the geographical distribution of wealth because they give those counties in which wealth is concentrated in relatively few hands a greater opportunity to appear richer than counties where the wealth is spread more evenly.[32] On these grounds, therefore, we must reject the assessment of 1404 and 1441. The relatively low exemption limits specified by the taxes of 1431, 1435, and 1450 would probably not unduly distort the true distribution of wealth; but other objections can be brought against these taxes. The tax of 1431 was very restricted in that it was levied only on incomes from demense lands. In addition, by equating the value of a knight's fee with socage land worth £20 a year, it introduced a further possible element of distortion. The taxes of 1435 and 1450 were much wider in their incidence in that they were levied on all annual incomes; but unfortunately they were levied at progressive rates so that the highest incomes were charged at four times the rate of the lowest. As with high exemption limits, the effect of progressive rates is to distort the true geographical distribution of wealth by allowing counties in which wealth was concentrated in fewer hands than elsewhere a greater opportunity to appear richer than other counties.

None of the fifteenth-century income taxes is therefore suitable for use as a measure of the geographical distribution of wealth. Fortunately, however, at the beginning of the sixteenth century a new system of taxation was introduced which had a very wide incidence. This new system of taxation, generally known as the Tudor subsidy, was developed in a remarkable series of statutes between 1512 and 1515, and endured substantially unaltered as the main form of direct taxation until well into the seventeenth century.[33] The Tudor subsidy was, for its period, a very complex form of taxation, so much so that it would be altogether impossible to give an adequate account of the system of assessment here. Discussion will therefore have to be confined to those features which are relevant to the use of the subsidy assessments as measures of the geographical distribution of wealth.[34] Each time that a Tudor subsidy was levied, every person throughout the country was assessed at current values on two or three categories of wealth, namely:

(1) All annual incomes, net of expenses. In practice this usually meant income from lands, but included such things as annuities, corrodies, and fees.

(2) The capital value of all movable goods. From 1515 debts owing to the taxpayer were also to be assessed, while debts owed by the taxpayer were to be deducted. From 1524 personal apparel, other than jewellery, was exempt.

(3) Wages and profits for wages. These constituted a separate category only up to 1525; after this they were taxed, if so liable, as annual incomes.[35] Before 1525 wages received casually, that is on a non-annual basis, were taxed only in 1513, 1524, and 1525.

Each category was taxed at separate rates; but the taxpayer, although assessed initially for all the categories for which he was liable, only paid on the category which yielded most tax to the crown.

The Tudor subsidies were therefore a combination of the thirteenth- and fourteenth-century tax on capital values of movables with the fifteenth-century tax on annual incomes, and should thus provide a particularly good measure of the distribution of over-all wealth. But although all Tudor subsidies adhered to this basic pattern, they were levied at a great variety of rates and with a variety of exemption limits below which no tax was payable.[36] This means that some of the Tudor subsidies are very much more suitable than others as measures of the geographical distribution of wealth. In selecting subsidies for this purpose we must first of all exclude those with progressive rates and high exemption limits because of the distortions which these produce. Secondly, because the sixteenth-century assessments should be as comparable as possible with the 1334 assessments, we must prefer those subsidies in which the rates put the greatest possible emphasis on tax derived from assessment on movable goods, as against tax derived from assessments on annual incomes and wages. Briefly, progressive rates, high exemption limits, and higher rates on annual incomes than on movable goods soon became standard features of the Tudor subsidies, so that the only three subsidies which altogether avoid these drawbacks are the three first rate-per-pound subsidies, levied at identical rates in 1514, 1515, and 1516.[37] The subsidy of 1514 is less suitable than the subsidies of 1515 and 1516 for comparison with the assessments of 1334 because, unlike the other taxes mentioned, it excludes all forms of wealth in the hands of the Church.[38] On the other hand this makes it the most suitable assessment of lay wealth for use in conjunction with an independent assessment of clerical wealth. Between the subsidies of 1515 and 1516 there is a slight preference for that of 1515, because the returns are complete for this subsidy, while for the subsidy of 1516 returns for five hundreds, situated in five different counties, are missing.[39]

V

Of all the taxes levied since 1334, therefore, the subsidies of 1514 and 1515 are best fitted for comparison with the assessments of 1334; the former in conjunction with estimates of clerical wealth, and the latter in a straight comparison of the distribution of lay wealth in the early fourteenth and sixteenth centuries. Nevertheless there are certain differences in the nature of these assessments of lay wealth, which may affect their comparability as measures of the distribution of wealth, and which therefore should be made quite explicit.

First of all there is a difference in the nature of the wealth assessed, for while the 1334 assessments were on movable goods alone, those of 1514 and 1515 were on movable goods, annual incomes, and annual wages. Unfortunately details of individual assessments were not returned to the exchequer in 1514 and 1515, so we cannot discover what proportion of the total assessment is accounted for by assessments on annual incomes and wages. However, this information is available for the subsidy of 1524, when the rates in force favour a higher proportion of assessments on annual incomes, and possibly on wages too, than in 1514 and 1515.[40] A sample check of a few areas shows that in 1524 only 7 per cent of the total value of the assessments in these areas came from annual incomes, and only 6 per cent of the total value from wages.[41] Since, however, those who were assessed on annual incomes and wages would doubtless have possessed some movable goods, and since in some cases their disregarded assessment on movable goods may have been only marginally less than their recorded assessments, the interference from assessments on annual incomes and wages in the composition of wealth assessed in 1514 and 1515 will have been much less than 13 per cent. But in 1514 there was additional interference from a poll tax which was levied on everyone too poor to be otherwise liable to the subsidy.[42] Once more it is not known what proportion of the total assessment in 1514 is accounted for by these poll payments; but it is clear that in some counties in the north and west it was quite considerably higher than elsewhere, indicating the existence of a much larger proportion of very poor people in this region.[43] But these counties were in general very much poorer than the rest of the country,[44] so the effect of the intrusion of the 1514 poll payments is confined to a marginal lessening of the substantial gap in wealth between these counties and the rest of the country. Thus, although there were some differences in the nature of the wealth assessed in 1334 and in 1514 and 1515, the amount of distortion which these differences produced would seem to have been somewhat limited in its extent.

A second, and rather more hypothetical, difference between the assessments may lie in the interpretation each assessment put on the scope of the category of wealth assessed: movable goods. Strictly speaking, the 1334 assessments made no stipulations as to the scope of the category of movable goods; but, since these assessments were revisions of assessments made in 1332, they were clearly dependent in part on the scope of these earlier assessments.[45] On the other hand it is possible that the effect of the 1334 revisions was to remove some of the divergencies which we shall notice between assessment practice in 1332 and in 1514 and 1515; and it is this possibility, together with an uncertainty about the actual details of assessment practice in 1514 and 1515, which makes this comparison between the range of movable goods assessed in 1334 and in 1514 and 1515 somewhat tentative. First of all, the assessment of 1332 was wider in scope than the assessments of 1514 and 1515 in that it exempted only those with movable goods worth less than 10s. (6s. on the ancient demesne and in towns), while the assessments of 1514 and 1515 exempted everyone with goods worth less than £2.[46] On the other hand, the scope of the 1332 assessment was narrower than that of 1514 or 1515 in that it excluded certain classes of movable goods which were not excluded in 1514 and 1515. In 1332 formal exemption was granted for the armour, riding horses, jewels, clothing and vessels of gold, silver, and brass, of knights, gentlemen, and their wives; and for the basic clothing, furniture, and personal ornamentation of townsfolk.[47] But in practice exemption appears to have been extended to foodstuffs intended for personal consumption, and, in rural districts only, to household furniture and utensils, clothing, poultry, and light farm tools.[48] In 1514 and 1515, in contrast, no formal exemptions were granted under the subsidy acts, apart from the deduction of debts owed by the taxpayer which were allowed in 1515; and other items, wholly or partially exempted in 1332, such as grains, household furniture and utensils, coin, and precious metals, were specifically required to be assessed in 1514 and 1515.[49] Although we do not know whether customary unofficial exemptions, such as those for foodstuffs in 1332, were also observed in the sixteenth century, formally at least the assessments of 1514 and 1515 covered a wider range of wealth than did the assessment of 1332. But how far this was cancelled out, either by the lower exemption limit in 1332, or by the upward revision of the assessments in 1334, is impossible to estimate. In any case, any difference between the assessments on this score is unlikely to have been so patterned as to upset the balance of wealth as between the counties.

A third difference between the assessments lies in the areas or groups exempted entirely from liability to the taxes. Some of these exemptions were common to all three taxes: all three excluded Wales, Cheshire, Cumberland, Westmorland, Northumberland, the Bishopric of Durham, and the Cinque Ports.[50] These exemptions therefore merely restrict the area over which we can measure changes in the distribution of wealth; and, in the case of the Cinque Ports, unfairly depress the wealth of Kent and Sussex *vis-à-vis* the other counties. Other exemptions were peculiar to one assessment or the other.[51] In 1514 the colleges of Oxford, Cambridge, Winchester, and Eton, together with a few religious houses, were exempted, and in 1515 these were joined by three more religious houses, and Brighton.[52] Apart from the omission of the Cinque Ports, which unfortunately cannot be rectified, these exemptions involved insignificant sums, too small to upset the balance of wealth between the counties.

A fourth difference between the fourteenth- and sixteenth-century assessments is somewhat more serious, if only because it is very difficult to establish the magnitude of the distortion of the true distribution of wealth which may be involved. This is the question, raised by Buckatzsch, but dismissed by him as unimportant before the mid-nineteenth century, of a possible divergence between the actual location of wealth and the location of the ownership of wealth as shown by the tax assessments.[53] Unfortunately it is rather uncertain how far such a divergence existed in 1334. Under the assessment rules for 1332 it would appear that wealth was assessed on individuals where they were resident; but it is possible that the revision of these assessments in 1334 on an area basis may have involved an adjustment of the total assessment of each vill so as to correspond with the value of property actually situated within the vill, rather than with the property of the inhabitants of the vill wherever this property might be located.[54] But we cannot be sure that this occurred, and the question of whether the 1334 assessments refer to the location of wealth, or to the location of the ownership of wealth, must remain an open one. The assessment rule in 1514 and 1515, however, was substantially the same as the one for 1332; it differed only in being more thorough in providing machinery to cope with foreseeable complications. The Tudor subsidy acts recognized that those who were resident in more than one place might well find themselves assessed several times over, and devised a system of inhibitory certificates to overcome this problem.[55] In the absence of anything explicit in the subsidy acts, the clear implication of this system of certificates was that the taxpayer was normally assessed where he was resident for all his property, wherever this might be situated. And that this corresponds to normal early sixteenth-century practice is shown by the fact that where taxpayers were assessed by assessors in different parts of the country, in one-third of the cases the assessors produced identical assessments, a far higher proportion than can possibly be explained by chance.[56] The assessments of 1514 and 1515, therefore, measure the location of the ownership of wealth rather than the location of wealth itself, and because of this some counties may be credited with more wealth, and others with less, than is properly attributable to them. On the other hand, it may be that the pattern of cross-ownership was evenly distributed, and that errors of this kind in the county totals in practice cancel out. Unfortunately we have no means of knowing how far this was in fact the case, and in consequence the possibility of a divergence between the location of the ownership of wealth as shown by the tax assessments and the true location of wealth must remain a hazard of unknown magnitude. Equally unfortunately, this hazard is increased by the Tudor practice of assessing the royal households as separate units.[57] This means that those counties in which property belonging to members of the royal households was situated are undervalued in 1514 and 1515. Again we have no way of knowing whether this missing wealth was spread more or less evenly between the counties, or whether some counties were affected worse than others. But we do at least know that the sum excluded from the county totals in this way was only a very small percentage (0·8 per cent in 1514 and 1·4 per cent in 1515) of the total assessed wealth of the country,[58] and quite insignificant in relation to the wide differences in the relative wealth of the counties which the assessments of 1514 and 1515 imply.

A fifth difference refers to the assessments of 1334 and 1515 alone. It is that the assessment of 1515 had the opportunity of recording a higher proportion of clerical wealth than had the assessment of 1334. This is because both assessments included movable goods on lands acquired by the Church after 1291, and the passage of another 180 years clearly favoured the assessment of 1515 in this regard.[59] Once again, however, differences in the range of wealth assessed appear to be small in comparison with differences in the total value of wealth assessed at both dates, for a rough calculation shows that increases in wealth acquired by the Church between 1291 and 1535 comprised only 12 per cent of the general increase in wealth as assessed in 1334 and 1515.[60]

The differences between the fourteenth- and sixteenth-century assessments have been discussed in some detail because the comparability of the methods of assessment is crucial for the acceptability of any conclusions which we may wish to draw from these assessments about changes in the geographical distribution of wealth. Despite the differences which have just been noticed, the assessments of 1334, 1514, and 1515, are as comparable and as satisfactory measures of the distribution of wealth as can in practice be obtained. All three are local assessments of a wide, and almost identical, category of wealth; all three were levied under standard conditions over the whole country, and all three assess the wealth of the counties according to current values. So far as they can be determined, the differences between the assessments would seem to have been too small to have had more than a marginal effect on the considerable differences in the distribution of wealth by county which these three assessments imply; and there would therefore appear to be a *prima facie* case for accepting the evidence of these tax assessments as genuine, if crude, measures of regional economic differences in the distribution of wealth in the early fourteenth and sixteenth centuries.

None the less, two considerations remain, either of which might render any of the assessments invalid as measures of the distribution of wealth. The first of these is the possibility of the existence at each of the dates of regionally patterned differences in the accuracy of the assessments. Unfortunately this is a possibility which it is very difficult either to prove or to disprove. Some undervaluation has been observed both in connection with early fourteenth-century assessments and later sixteenth-century assessments; but the only pattern that has so far been discerned is social, and it is doubtful whether this would have any relevance to the question of regional bias.[61] At present the most that can be said is that, for the assessment of 1334, a recent detailed study of the village assessments over much of the country has found no reason to suspect the existence of regionally patterned undervaluation, and has concluded that these assessments appear to provide an economically plausible picture of the geographical distribution of wealth at that date.[62] The accuracy of the early Tudor subsidy assessments has suffered from uncritical generalizations based on evidence relating to the later part of Elizabeth's reign. No evidence of under-valuation has yet been found for the subsidies of 1514 and 1515; and what evidence there is for the existence of undervaluation in the first half of the sixteenth-century gives no indication of having been regionally patterned.[63] Distortion through regionally patterned undervaluation cannot therefore definitely be excluded. However, by the same token, it should not be advanced as an explanation of the results which taxation data provide until all other possible explanations have first been exhausted.

The second possibly invalidating factor is the exclusion from the tax assessments of most of the wealth in the hands of the clergy, which may well have been distributed in such a way that the apparent variations in the wealth of the counties as shown by the lay taxes merely reflects the presence or absence of large quantities of clerical wealth. Fortunately the distribution of clerical wealth in the early fourteenth and sixteenth centuries can be recovered from two reasonably comprehensive assessments, which were made not long before, and after, the two lay assessments selected, namely the Taxation of Pope Nicholas of 1291, and the *Valor Ecclesiasticus* of 1535. The assessments of clerical wealth given in these two surveys have been broken down and rearranged so as to assign clerical wealth to the counties from which this wealth was derived; a precaution which is particularly necessary in the case of sees and religious houses drawing incomes from widely scattered possessions.[64] In fact at both dates the distribution of clerical wealth amongst the counties was rather different from the pattern of distribution of lay wealth, and this difference was more marked in the early fourteenth century than in the early sixteenth century.[65] It would therefore seem to be desirable to include some assessment of clerical wealth in any general estimate of the geographical dis-tribution of wealth. Unfortunately, however, the assessments available are on two rather different forms of wealth: on movable goods in the case of the laity, and on annual incomes in the case of the clergy. Apart from the possibility of some double counting of certain items, the main problem posed by a combina-tion of these two forms of wealth lies in achieving some sort of equivalence between them. In this instance we must estimate the equivalent value of clerical incomes in terms of movable goods assessable for lay taxes. Evidence from the lay assessments suggests that although the ratio between the value of incomes and movable goods varies considerably from person to person, it also varies more generally according to wealth, so that poor people on average possess taxable movable goods worth more than their taxable annual incomes, while very rich people on average have taxable annual incomes worth more than the value of their taxable movable goods.[66] For the clergy in the early sixteenth century a sample of 34 stipendiary priests and 26 beneficed clergy in two hun-dreds in Norfolk, with average annual incomes of £4. 9s 0d. and £10. 10s. 0d. respectively, suggests that parish clergy with incomes at this level had movable goods worth approximately twice their annual incomes.[67] Further up the income scale, a sample of 20 suppressed monasteries with an average annual income of £96. 14s. 0d., shows that at this higher level the value of movable goods was worth approximately the same as the annual income.[68] Since the average clerical income was probably about £12. 10s. 0d.,[69] the value of the movable goods of the clergy as a whole was probably greater than the value of their annual incomes, but not more than twice this amount. Because it is difficult to be more precise about the probable ratio of clerical incomes to movable goods, all figures have been calculated twice, once combining clerical incomes and lay movable wealth pound for pound, and a second time with the value of clerical incomes doubled. In practice both methods were found to provide very similar results. Since, however, the average clerical income, at least for the early sixteenth century, appears to be nearer the range of incomes where movable goods are worth twice the value of annual incomes, detailed figures are given here only for the combination of lay movable wealth with twice the value of clerical annual incomes.[70] In this combination clerical wealth is probably slightly over-represented.

There are two further reservations which should be made about this combination of clerical and lay wealth. First, the estimates of clerical wealth refer to different years from the estimates of lay wealth; but this is perhaps not so serious in the context of the very long interval between the two lay assessments being compared. Secondly, there seems to be considerable doubt as to the accuracy of some of the assessments in the two surveys of clerical wealth, and especially serious in this respect is the fact that undervaluation in 1535 appears to have been regionally patterned in that it was worse in the north than elsewhere.[71] Thus although a combination of clerical and lay wealth at least removes the possibility of distortion through the omission of an unevenly distributed clerical wealth, it also provides some additional disadvantages and inaccuracies of its own. For this reason some may prefer to disregard clerical wealth altogether and to compare the distributions of lay wealth alone as assessed in 1334 and 1515. Accordingly two sets of figures have been prepared, one referring to lay wealth alone, and the other to a combination of lay and clerical wealth. That these two sets of figures produce almost identical results underlines once again the relative immunity of bold comparisons such as are undertaken here to all kinds of flaws in the compilation of the basic data.

VI

Subject, none the less, to all the reservations outlined above, how far do the clerical and lay assessments show the existence of any geographical redistribution of wealth between the early fourteenth and the early sixteenth centuries? In answering this question the same two statistical tests which Buckatzsch used have been applied; that is Spearman's rank correlation coefficient, which measures the similarity in the order of wealth of the counties at the two dates, and which makes little demand on the accuracy of the data, and Pearson's product moment correlation coefficient, which takes into account changes in the actual value of the wealth of the counties, and which therefore makes considerably greater demands on the accuracy of the data.[72] This will provide us with two numerical measures of the amount of geographical redistribution of wealth that occurred, and these can then be compared with similar measures which Buckatzsch calculated for the redistribution of wealth in other periods.

For 1334 I have followed Buckatzsch in using the county assessments given by Willard; and for 1514 and 1515 I have calculated the county totals from the exchequer enrolled accounts.[73] I have also accepted Buckatzsch's practice of including the assessments of cities and towns in the county assessments, although this masks important differences in the rates of growth of town and countryside.[74] In the case of Bristol and York, which straddle administrative boundaries, the assessments have been divided arbitrarily between the areas concerned.[75] Ideally, for statistical reasons, London on account of its great wealth should be separated from Middlesex and excluded from the calculations.[76] Buckatzsch, however, includes London in Middlesex, so accordingly I have calculated the correlation coefficients both with London included in Middlesex and with London excluded from the county order. Similarly, although there are differences in wealth between the three traditional divisions of Yorkshire and Lincolnshire, Buckatzsch treats them as single counties, and accordingly I have calculated the correlation coefficients with Yorkshire and Lincolnshire both divided and undivided.[77] Thirdly, because the 1334 tax was levied at a double rate, and the 1514 and 1515 subsidies at other rates, to make the county assessments comparable at all dates, the yields of the taxes from each county have to be multiplied by the rate, or rates, in force so as to arrive at the assessed wealth of each county.[78] Finally the figures for the assessed wealth of each county have to be adjusted to allow for the very different sizes of the counties. I have reduced the county assessments to the ratio of £s per 1,000 acres, because this gave the most convenient range of units. There is, however, an element of uncertainty in this because we cannot be sure of the exact areas of the counties in the fourteenth and sixteenth centuries; amongst other things, land reclamation and coastal erosion would be difficult to estimate with any degree of accuracy. But this is no excuse for not doing the best we can. Buckatzsch used some early nineteenth-century estimates of county areas, which are very inaccurate, and which led him into misplacing several counties in the order of wealth for 1334.[70] As surveying techniques improved during the nineteenth century, the areas of the counties expanded and contracted at widely differing rates.[80] Clearly, therefore, the latest available figures for the historical counties must be taken, corrected to take into account the boundary changes of 1844 and 1536.[81] Having thus standardized the county assessments, we are in a position to compare the relative wealth of different counties in 1334 and in 1514 and 1515, both with and without clerical wealth. For interest I have also calculated the correlation coefficients between the 1515 lay assessments and those provided by an average of five mid-seventeenth-century estimated assessments of doubtful accuracy.[82]

Buckatzsch calculated four statistics for each comparison, but only two will be employed here.[83] The first of these, ρ, Spearman's rank correlation coefficient, measures how far two assessments agree in the order in which they rank the counties according to wealth. This coefficient is so designed that when the two assessments produce identical rankings of the counties, ρ has the value $+ 1$; and when the two rankings are as greatly in disagreement as possible, that is when one ranking is exactly the reverse of the other, ρ has the value $- 1$. The second statistic, r, Pearson's product moment correlation coefficient, also takes into account the actual values of the county assessments at both dates; but it is also designed to give the same range of values as ρ. Thus when the assessments provide not only identical rankings of the counties, but also the same proportional relationships between the assessed values of the counties at both dates, r attains the value $+ 1$; while when the two assessments provide rankings which are not only exactly the reverse of each other, but which also retain the same proportional relationships between the assessed values of the counties, r has the value $- 1$. When there is no correlation whatsoever between the county assessments at the two dates, r has the value 0. In practice, as might be expected, there was always some positive resemblance between the geographical distribution of wealth at all dates, and accordingly the values of ρ and r fall between 0 and $+ 1$, indicating between these limits a greater or lesser

TABLE 1. *Correlation Coefficients of County Assessments of Wealth*[1]

(all values positive)

Years	A		B		C	
	Lay wealth only London in Middx. Yorks. and Lincs. undivided		*Lay wealth only London excluded, Yorks. and Lincs. divided*		*Lay + 2 × clerical wealth*[3] *London excluded, Yorks. and Lincs. divided*	
	ρ	r	ρ	r	ρ	r
1086–1150	*0·690*	*0·427*				
1150–1283	*0·231*	*0·267*				
1283–1334	*0·825*	*0·895*				
1334–1515	*0·643*	*0·806*	0·547	0·487	0·526	0·531
1515–1636/49	0·892	*0·948*	0·875[2]	0·922[2]		
1641–1693	*0·797*	*0·940*				
1693–1803	*0·794*	*0·751*				
1803–1843	*0·865*	*0·947*				

[1] Figures in italic type from Buckatzsch, Table 3, p. 193.
[2] Yorks. and Lincs. undivided.
[3] $1334 + 2 × 1291 - 1514 + 2 × 1535$. When clerical and lay wealth are combined £ for £, $\rho = 0·547$ and $r = 0·513$.
Sources for new figures: 1636/49, J. E. T. Rogers, *History of Agriculture and Prices in England*, v, Tables I–IV, pp. 104–11. Other dates, see Table 2 below.

degree of similarity in the geographical distribution of wealth at the two dates being compared.[84]

The accompanying table gives these two coefficients calculated in three ways. In section A lay wealth alone is considered. Buckatzsch's procedures, namely the inclusion of London in Middlesex, the treatment of Yorkshire and Lincolnshire as undivided shires, and the use of the logarithms of the values, are followed, and Buckatzsch's figures for other periods are given in italic type. In section B lay wealth is again considered alone, but London is excluded, and Yorkshire and Lincolnshire are divided into their three traditional divisions. In section C lay and clerical wealth are combined, in the ratio 1 : 2, while London remains excluded and Yorkshire and Lincolnshire divided. If we take the cruder measure, ρ, first, this shows that there was more change in the ranking of the counties in order of wealth in the period 1334–1515, however calculated, than in any other period except 1150–1283. On the other hand, during the period 1515–1636/49 there was less change in the order of wealth of the counties than during any other period covered by Buckatzsch's figures. On the simplest test, therefore, Buckatzsch's picture of a stable distribution of wealth during the later Middle Ages, followed by an extensive redistribution of wealth during the sixteenth and early seventeenth centuries, is precisely reversed. This reversal is confirmed by the values of the more sensitive statistic r for the two periods, which in section A of the Table show a relatively low correlation between the wealth of the counties in 1334 and 1515, and the highest correlation of all between the wealth of the counties in 1515 and 1636/49. It is interesting that although the statistics ρ and r both have the same range of -1 to $+1$, the value of ρ is rather less than the value of r for the period from 1334 to 1515. This suggests that the steps taken by Buckatzsch, and repeated here for section A of the Table, to avoid the theoretical objections to the inclusion of London in the figures have not been altogether effective, and that the very great wealth of London at both dates has had an undue effect on the value of r. This is confirmed by section B of the table in which the exclusion of London and the division of Yorkshire and Lincolnshire into their three traditional divisions reduces the value of r very much more than it does the value of ρ, so that the two coefficients are much more in agreement as to the extent of the redistribution of wealth during this period. The figures in section B are therefore probably superior to those in section A as measures of changes in the distribution of wealth at different dates, and the low values of ρ and r in section B suggest that quite considerable changes in the distribution of wealth had occurred between 1334 and 1515.

If we now also take clerical wealth into account, as in section C of the table, we find values of ρ and r very similar to those in section B of the table, which referred to lay wealth alone. The inclusion or omission of clerical wealth would therefore seem to have little effect on the calculation of a general statistical measure of changes in the distribution of wealth during the later Middle Ages. No figures have been calculated in section C of the table for the subsequent period, 1515–1636/49, because the figures for lay wealth, in sections A and B of the table, appear to be suspect. The values of p and r for this period in fact remain almost exactly the same both when London is included in the calculations and when it is omitted, in marked contrast to the fall in values noticed in similar circumstances for the period 1334–1515. This suggests that the very high correlation of the distribution of wealth at the two dates shown by these figures in fact extends right through the counties, and the implausibility of such a degree of similarity in the distribution of wealth over a period of one hundred and twenty-five years in turn suggests that the mid-seventeenth century assessments were quite conventional in character, being based, as has already been suggested, more on the mid-sixteenth-century distribution of wealth than on the actual distribution of wealth of the day. Nothing, therefore, can safely be inferred from the taxation material considered here as to any changes in the geographical distribution of wealth between the early sixteenth and mid-seventeenth centuries.

VII

It now only remains to describe the pattern of the geographical distribution of wealth which the tax assessments show for the early fourteenth and the early sixteenth centuries, together with the pattern of the redistribution of wealth that occurred between these dates. The assessed wealth of each county, expressed in £s per 1,000 acres, is shown for each date in Table 2. The table also shows the increase in the wealth of each county between the two dates, expressed as the ratio of the assessed wealth in the early sixteenth century to the assessed wealth of the county in the early fourteenth century. The table is divided so that the first six columns refer to lay wealth alone, and the second six columns to lay and clerical wealth combined. To bring out the regional patterns in the distribution of wealth more clearly, much of the information in the table has been transferred to six maps, showing the distribution of wealth in 1334, the distribution of wealth in 1515, and the distribution of the rates of increase between 1334 and 1515, both for lay wealth alone and for lay and clerical wealth combined.[85] First of all, however, it should be said that the county unit is, of course, a very rough way of measuring the geographical distribution of wealth, and, indeed, local variations within a county, such as those between rural and urban areas, may be of considerably greater economic significance than the

---

Notes for Table 2

[1] For the possible exemption of the Stannary men, see below, n. 51.

[2] Bristol divided 77 per cent to Glos., 23 per cent to Somerset, see below, n. 75.

[3] Omitting the Cinque Ports.

[4] Omitting London, see foot of table.

[5] York divided equally among the Ridings, see below, n. 75.

[6] Returns missing for Trigg Hundred in 1514; these have been interpolated proportionally from the 1515 returns.

Sources: Col. (1) Willard, *Eng. Hist. Rev.* 30 (1915), 73.

Col. (3) PRO, E. 359/38, 6 Henry VIII, *passim.*

Col. (7) Col. (1) and *Taxatio Ecclesiastica, passim.*

Col. (9) PRO, E. 359/38, 5 Henry VIII, *passim,* and *Valor Ecclesiasticus, passim.*

Acreages: see above, p. 93.

TABLE 2. Comparative Wealth of Thirty-eight Counties

County	Lay wealth only						Lay and clerical wealth combined					
	1334 £/'000 acres (± £0·05)	Rank	1515 £/'000 acres (± £0·05)	Rank	Growth Ratio col. (3) col. (1) (± £0·005)	Rank	1334 + 2 × 1291 £/'000 acres (± £0·05)	Rank	1514 + 2 × 1535 £/'000 acres (± £0·05)	Rank	Growth Ratio col. (9) col. (7) (± £0·005)	Rank
	(1)	(2)	(3)	(4)	(5)	(6)	(7)	(8)	(9)	(10)	(11)	(12)
Beds.	33·6	4	80·4	13	2·39	24	47·3	8	128·2	8	2·71	20
Berks.	31·4	5	88·0	10	2·80	21	47·2	9	130·8	6	2·77	18
Bucks.	21·3	19	70·8	17	3·32	14	34·1	22	96·0	21	2·81	16
Cambs.	26·9	11	65·7	21	2·44	23	48·8	5	104·0	19	2·13	27
Cornwall[1]	7·7	35	50·8	27	6·60	3	11·1	38	61·9[6]	31	5·58	3
Derby	10·2	33	18·7	34	1·83	29	17·2	31	35·6	35	2·07	28
Devon[1]	7·9	34	67·4	18	8·53	1	12·5	37	108·6	15	8·69	1
Dorset	19·4	22	72·0	16	3·71	10	31·2	25	103·0	20	3·30	9
Essex	18·5	25	102·0	3	5·51	4	30·7	26	120·4	11	3·92	7
Glos.[2]	28·0	8	93·3	6	3·33	13	39·5	16	137·8	3	3·49	8
Hants.	18·2	26	67·1	20	3·69	11	35·0	21	94·9	23	2·71	19
Herefs.	14·4	30	38·4	30	2·67	32	30·2	27	66·6	28	2·20	26
Herts.	22·2	17	90·0	8	4·05	9	36·7	18	118·5	12	3·23	10
Hunts.	27·6	10	89·8	9	3·25	16	48·6	6	135·1	4	2·78	17
Kent[3]	24·5	14	100·5	4	4·10	8	44·2	11	129·5	7	2·93	13
Lancs.	4·6	38	3·8	38	0·83	38	16·6	33	16·4	38	0·99	38
Leics.	20·8	21	61·2	23	2·94	18	38·0	17	95·1	22	2·50	22
Lincs.												
(Holland)	46·4	1	67·3	19	1·45	34	68·0	1	106·4	18	1·56	33
(Kesteven)	27·8	9	42·5	29	1·53	36	42·4	13	62·4	30	1·47	37
(Lindsey)	22·6	15	45·6	28	2·02	33	45·1	10	68·9	27	1·53	34
Middlesex[4]	29·0	7	238·1	1	8·21	2	47·4	7	304·1	1	6·42	2
Norfolk	38·9	3	86·0	12	2·21	25	54·3	3	108·4	16	2·00	29
Northants.	26·3	12	73·8	15	2·81	20	40·5	15	116·2	14	2·87	15
Notts.	18·7	24	32·2	31	1·72	32	36·5	19	65·5	29	1·79	32
Oxon.	42·2	2	73·8	14	1·75	30	59·2	2	117·2	13	1·98	30
Rutland	31·4	6	61·7	22	1·96	28	48·8	4	91·5	25	1·87	31
Salop	11·9	31	15·5	35	1·30	35	15·2	34	36·8	34	2·42	23
Somerset[2]	19·3	23	104·5	2	5·41	6	33·9	23	145·1	2	4·28	4
Staffs.	10·9	32	21·7	33	1·99	27	16·8	32	42·4	33	2·52	21
Suffolk	22·0	18	90·4	7	4·11	7	43·2	12	125·6	9	2·91	14
Surrey	17·3	28	94·1	5	5·44	5	28·9	29	123·5	10	4·27	5
Sussex[3]	17·4	27	55·9	25	3·21	17	32·4	24	72·5	26	2·24	25
Warwicks.	21·2	20	59·8	24	2·82	19	30·0	28	92·2	24	3·07	12
Wilts.	26·2	13	86·4	11	3·30	15	42·4	14	131·7	5	3·11	11
Worcs.	15·5	29	54·1	26	3·49	12	27·4	30	107·5	17	3·92	6
Yorks.[5]												
(East Rdg.)	22·2	16	25·0	32	1·13	37	36·1	20	53·2	32	1·47	36
(North Rdg.)	7·0	36	8·1	37	1·16	36	15·2	35	22·5	37	1·48	35
(West Rdg.)	6·5	37	11·3	36	1·74	31	13·7	36	31·6	36	2·31	24
Average	21·5		66·0		3·14		35·4		97·6		2·90	
City of London	16,290·0		239,200·0		14·68		19,070·0		284,000·0		14·90	
Middx. with London	89·3	(1)	1,123·0	(1)	12·57	(1)	118·0	(1)	1,355·0	(1)	11·48	(1)

differences between the aggregate wealth of the counties.[86] Nevertheless for two reasons the county would seem to provide a useful and valid first unit of measurement. First, as is clear from the maps, counties of similar wealth are to be found adjacent to each other, which suggests that despite local variations within the counties there are broad regional patterns in the distribution of wealth which the county unit conveniently locates and measures. Secondly, at least for 1334, the county totals produce in a cruder way results which are similar to those obtained by an examination of very much smaller areas.[87]

If we take first the distribution of lay wealth in 1334, it is clear from column 1 of Table 2 that the range of wealth (London excepted) was quite wide, ranging from £4·6 per 1,000 acres in Lancashire to £46·4 per thousand acres in Holland. But Holland, together with Oxfordshire (£42·2) and Norfolk (£38·9) were some way ahead of the rest of the counties, most of which fell fairly evenly over the more restricted range of £10–30 per thousand acres. The average assessment was £21·5 per 1,000 acres. If we consider those counties which were wealthier than average (roughly those ranked 1–19), it is plain from Map 2 that, with the exception of Kent, they lie grouped along a fairly narrow band, starting in Gloucestershire and Wiltshire in the south-west and moving north-east across the south Midlands to northern East Anglia, and then extending along the east coast to the East Riding. The twelve wealthiest counties, those shaded darkest on the map together with those numbered 10–12, almost exactly comprise the midland belt, bounded on the north-west by a line from Gloucester to Lincoln and on the south-east by a line from Reading to Yarmouth, which was distinguished as the area of greatest wealth by a detailed study of the 1334 assessments.[88] Counties to the north-west and to the south and west of this band become progressively poorer. Particularly striking is the line from Flamborough Head to the Severn estuary which marks off a northwestern region which contains all but two of the nine poorest counties.

If we now consider the distribution of lay wealth in 1515, the first point that becomes clear from column 3 of Table 2 is that the range of wealth, again with London excepted, is very much wider than it was in 1334. Lancashire was again the poorest county, this time at £3·8 per 1,000 acres, while Middlesex was by far the richest at £238·1 per 1,000 acres. Most counties, however, were spread fairly evenly over the range £10–100, and the average county assessment had risen from £21·5 to £66 per 1,000 acres. Secondly, Map 4 shows that the geographical distribution of wealth was rather different in 1515 to what it had been in 1334. Those counties which were wealthier than average (again roughly those ranked 1–19), instead of falling along a band from Gloucestershire through the south Midlands to, and then up, the east coast, in fact comprised all England south of a line from the Wash to the Severn estuary, with the exception of only four counties. On the other hand the distribution of lay wealth in 1515 resembled that of 1334 in that the region north-west of a line between the Humber and the Severn estuary was by far the poorest. But the difference between the distribution of lay wealth at the two dates is best shown up by a comparison of the location of the twelve richest counties. While in 1334

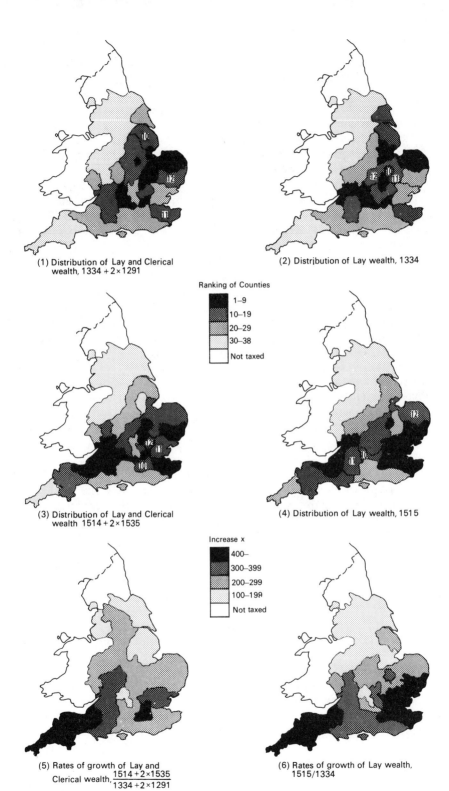

(1) Distribution of Lay and Clerical wealth, 1334 + 2×1291

(2) Distribution of Lay wealth, 1334

Ranking of Counties

- 1–9
- 10–19
- 20–29
- 30–38
- Not taxed

(3) Distribution of Lay and Clerical wealth 1514 + 2×1535

(4) Distribution of Lay wealth, 1515

Increase x

- 400–
- 300–399
- 200–299
- 100–199
- Not taxed

(5) Rates of growth of Lay and Clerical wealth, $\dfrac{1514 + 2\times1535}{1334 + 2\times1291}$

(6) Rates of growth of Lay wealth, 1515/1334

these lay in a belt from Gloucestershire and Berkshire in the south-west to Holland and Norfolk in the north-east, in 1515 they formed two well-defined areas, joined together by Berkshire. In the west there was a group comprising Gloucestershire, Somerset, and Wiltshire, and in the east a block of counties grouped around London, comprising Kent, Surrey, Middlesex, Hertfordshire, Essex, and Suffolk. A detailed study of the 1334 assessments has shown a close correlation between high lay assessments and the production of wheat.[89] The configuration of the richest counties in 1515 would seem to suggest that by the sixteenth century the greatest lay wealth may have been associated with other commodities, such as wool and cloth. But clearly a comparison of the wealth of the counties cannot take us very far in determining the main source of wealth; this can only be discovered by the comparison of the wealth of very much smaller areas.

If we now also take clerical wealth into account as it was estimated in 1291 and 1535, the first point of note, as is clear from a comparison of columns 8 and 10 with columns 2 and 4 of Table 2, is that the inclusion of clerical wealth had relatively little effect on the order of wealth of the counties at either date. Although many of the counties gained or lost between one and four places in the county order, the over-all ranking of the counties remained much the same at both dates as that for lay wealth alone. So too did the regional pattern of the distribution of wealth. A comparison of Maps 1 and 2 shows that for the early fourteenth century, with a few exceptions, the twelve richest counties remained located in a belt from the Cotswolds to the Wash, while other counties became progressively poorer the further north-west and south and west of this belt they were situated. Again, a comparison of Maps 3 and 4 shows that for the early sixteenth century, with a few exceptions, the twelve richest counties remained located in a concave southern belt stretching from Somerset and Gloucestershire to Suffolk and Kent, while the wealthier than average counties still comprised almost all of England south of a line from the Wash to the Severn estuary, and the nine poorest counties still comprised the extreme north-west. The inclusion of clerical wealth therefore more reinforces than modifies the over-all pattern of the distribution of wealth in the early fourteenth and early sixteenth centuries based on lay wealth alone.[90]

So far we have been concerned only with the pattern of the distribution of wealth in the early fourteenth and sixteenth centuries; we have yet to consider the question of which counties or areas increased most in wealth between these two dates. The first point which perhaps should be made is that the average increase in wealth (London excluded) between the early fourteenth and early sixteenth centuries, whether calculated on lay wealth alone or on lay and clerical wealth combined, was almost exactly threefold. There are, however, certain considerations which prevent us from taking this as a general measure of the increase in wealth during the later Middle Ages. First of all it is possible, though neither demonstrable nor inherently probable, that assessments in the early sixteenth century were very much more accurate than they were in the early fourteenth century. Secondly, it is not altogether certain that the prices of the items of wealth assessed were at the same level in the material years, 1332–4 and 1514–15. The best available price index refers mainly to foodstuffs, and so is not perfectly fitted to our purpose, unless it happened that other prices behaved similarly to the prices of these commodities. Nevertheless the prices of these selected consumables were at almost exactly the same level in 1332–4 and in 1514–15, at index numbers of 117 and 113 respectively.[91] Thirdly, and most important of all, marginal differences in the nature of the movable wealth actually assessed at the two dates, as discussed above, may mean that a slightly broader spectrum of wealth was included in 1515, and that the total assessed values of the two dates are therefore not strictly comparable as general measures of the absolute increase in over-all wealth. However, our concern here is rather with the relative rates of increase in wealth as between different counties and regions, so that, providing that there were no significant regional variations, uncertainty as to differences in these three aspects of assessment between the two dates is irrelevant.

If we take first the increase in lay wealth alone, the first point to be made is that London, although very much more wealthy than the rest of the country in 1334, like most other towns increased in wealth much faster than the rest of the country, so that by 1515 it was almost 15 times more wealthy than it had been in 1334, accounting for 8·9 per cent of the total assessed lay wealth of the county as opposed to 2·0 per cent in 1334.[92] Among the counties two were oustandingly more wealthy in 1515 than they had been in 1334: Devon, which was rated 8·53 times more wealthy, and Middlesex, which was rated 8·21 times more wealthy. These were followed by Cornwall at 6·60 times, Surrey, Essex, and Somerset, all more than five times more wealthy, and then Suffolk, Hertfordshire, and Kent, all between four and five times more wealthy in 1515 than they were in 1334. As is clear from Map 6, these nine counties which increased more than four-fold in lay wealth between 1334 and 1515 comprise two well-defined areas: the south-west peninsula, and a block of counties grouped around London. The counties which increased between three and four times in lay wealth, still above the average, with two exceptions form an equally well-defined area in the shape of an 'L', with its base along the middle three south-coast counties and its stem stretching upwards from Dorset to Worcestershire. The counties which increased between two and three times in lay wealth, again with a few exceptions, are grouped so as to cover all the Midlands south of the Wash together with northern East Anglia. In general all counties north of the Wash failed even to double their lay wealth between 1334 and 1515. There were therefore marked differences in the rate of increase of lay wealth between different counties over the period 1334 to 1515, and equally marked differences between the rate of increase of wealth between different regions. In general the south was pulling further ahead of the north, while of the southern counties those in the south-west and the south-east were increasing much more rapidly in wealth than the Midland and the more northerly East Anglian counties.

If, however, we include clerical wealth in calculating the different rates of increase in wealth between the counties, the picture is in some respects a little different. First, as is clear from a comparison of columns 5 and 11 of Table 2, a much greater proportion of the counties increased in wealth at nearer the average rate. Most of the counties which showed a high rate of growth in lay wealth show a reduced rate of growth when clerical wealth is also taken into account; and several of the counties which experienced little growth in lay wealth show a much greater rate of growth of lay and clerical wealth combined. The counties which appear to gain most from the inclusion of clerical wealth comprise a north-western belt from Yorkshire, through Derbyshire, Staffordshire, and Salop to Worcestershire, together with Bedfordshire. But as a comparison of Maps 5 and 6 shows, despite some differences, the general pattern of the different rates of growth of different regions remains substantially the same. The south is still, though to a lesser degree, pulling further ahead of the north, for the rates of growth are now quite similar in several of the northern, midland, and southern counties. But it is still in the south-western counties and in a few counties grouped around London that the highest rates of growth are to be found. And although some northern counties show improved rates of growth when clerical wealth is taken into account, the east-coast counties north of the Wash, and Lancashire, continue to be areas of relatively little growth.

VIII

It is believed that, despite the admitted imperfections of the basic tax data, the changing patterns of the distribution of wealth described here are sufficiently bold and coherent in outline to make it more likely that they represent genuine differences between counties and regions in the level of wealth assessed, than that they merely reflect deficiencies in the techniques of assessment.[93] The economic reasons behind both the differences in the geographical distribution of wealth in the early fourteenth and early sixteenth centuries, and the differences in the rates of increase in wealth both as between regions and individual counties between these two dates, can only be explained adequately by a more detailed examination of very much smaller areas, especially urban areas where the increase in wealth appears to have been greatest. An examination on this scale would have been impossible within the scope of this article. Its purpose has been rather to establish, against previous opinion, that a considerable geographical redistribution of wealth took place during the later Middle Ages, and to draw attention to the magnitude and general direction of this redistribution.

NOTES

[1] E. J. Buckatzsch, 'The Geographical Distribution of Wealth in England, 1086–1843', *Econ. Hist. Rev.*, 2nd series, 3 (1950), 180–202 (subsequently referred to as Buckatzsch).

[2] Spearman's rank correlation coefficient and Pearson's product moment correlation coefficient.

[3] Buckatzsch, p. 192.

[4] Buckatzsch, p. 200.

[5] Buckatzsch, p. 192. The apparent inconsistency between these two statements would seem to be explained by the fact that the latter is based on a period by period analysis (Table 3*a*, p. 193), and the former on an analysis of cumulative change measured from the base year 1283 (Table 4*b*, p. 194).

[6] Buckatzsch, pp. 180–4.

[7] Buckatzsch, p. 180.

[8] Buckatzsch used Spearman's rank correlation coefficient which simply measures the degree to which two assessments agree in the order in which they rank the counties according to wealth, and Pearson's product moment correlation coefficient which also measures how far the tax assessments agree in the proportional relationships which they indicate between the wealth of the counties (pp. 181–2, 184–90).

[9] Buckatzsch, pp. 181–3; the assessments he used are listed on p. 201.

[10] In the West Riding of Yorkshire in 1545, for example, when the exemption limit for both annual incomes and movable goods was £1, about two-thirds of all taxpayers were taxed on movable goods and had no taxable annual incomes. R. B. Smith, 'A Study in Landed Income and Social Structure in the West Riding, 1535–46' (Ph. D. thesis, Leeds, 1962), chap. 4, s. 3.

[11] Buckatzsch, pp. 182–4.

[12] Buckatzsch, pp. 183–4. He rejected possible comparisons between 1319 and 1327, and between 1636 and 1641, because they showed suspiciously large differences for such short periods (p. 191).

[13] Buckatzsch, p. 201. The ship-money assessments of 1636 were also available; it is not clear why the 1641 assessments were preferred.

[14] J. F. Willard, *Parliamentary Taxes on Personal Property, 1290–1334* (Cambridge, Mass., 1934), pp. 5, 11–12, 57 (for 1334); chaps. 3–7 (for 1332). These assessments are discussed in greater detail below.

[15] (1453) *Rot. Parl.* v, 232; (1504) 19 Henry VII, c. 32, schedule; (1641) 16 Charles I, c. 32, s. 2. All reprinted in J. E. T. Rogers, *A History of Agriculture and Prices in England* (Oxford, 1866–1902), iv. 86–8; v. 105–7.

[16] Rogers, op. cit. v. 104–11, 118. The taxes are 1636 (ship money), 1641 (£400,000 for Ireland), 25 Mar. 1649 (£90,000 per month for six months), and 25 Dec. 1649 (£90,000 per month for three months and £60,000 per month for three months).

[17] Complaints of undervaluation in Elizabeth's reign are numerous. See, for example, D'Ewes, *Journals* (1708), pp. 151–2; PRO, S.P. 12/116, no. 115; also H. Miller 'Subsidy Assessments of the Peerage in the Sixteenth Century.' *Bull. Inst. Hist. Res.*, 28 (1955), 15–34; and S. A. Peyton, 'The Village Population in the Tudor Lay Subsidy Rolls', *Eng. Hist. Rev.* 30 (1915), 234–50.

[18] No evidence has yet been forthcoming on the criteria by which these allocations were made. The bodies responsible for the allocations were: (1636) probably the council, PRO, P.C. 2/45, pp. 71–80; (1641) a committee of the House of Commons, *H. of C. Journals*, iii. 63, 69; (25 Mar. and 25 Dec. 1649) the committee of the army, ibid. vi. 172, 324, 327–8. For the resemblance of the pattern of distribution of wealth suggested by these assessments to that suggested by an early sixteenth-century assessment, see pp. 96–7.

[19] Rogers, op. cit. iv. 82–3.

[20] 19 Henry VII, c. 32, preamble. For the net yield of the fifteenth and tenth after 1485, see R. S. Schofield, 'Parliamentary Lay Taxation, 1485–1547' (Ph.D. thesis, Cambridge, 1963), Table 40, facing p. 416.

[21] 19 Henry VII, c. 32, schedule; PRO, E. 359/39, *passim*. In some counties the sums usually payable to the fifteenth and tenth were reduced slightly because of the exemption granted to the colleges of Oxford, Cambridge, Eton, Winchester, and the Charterhouses (19 Henry VII, c. 32, s. 13).

[22] *Rot. Parl.* v. 69. A similar deduction of £4,000 had been effective since 1433, ibid. iv. 425.

[23] *Rot. Parl.* v. 230–3.

[24] The ten towns were: London, Bristol, Coventry, Hull, Lincoln, Newcastle-upon-Tyne, Norwich, Nottingham, Southampton, and York. Figures for the 1334 assessments from J. F. Willard, 'The taxes upon movables of the reign of Edward III', *Eng. Hist. Rev.* 30 (1915), 73, supplemented for the towns by PRO, E. 164/7. Costs of collection from PRO, E. 164/7 and E. 359/39, *passim*.

[25] The fifteenth and tenth continued to be levied frequently until 1623 (21 James I, c. 33).

[26] *Rot. Parl.* ii, 364; iii, 57–8, 90.

[27] In fact there is a high correlation between the distribution of wealth in 1334 and the distribution of the population in 1377 ($\rho = +0.847$); but this could be produced by regional differences in the incidence of the plague and does not necessarily imply a stable distribution of wealth. Willard, *Eng. Hist. Rev.* 30 (1915), 73; E. Powell, *The Rising in East Anglia in 1381* (Cambridge, 1896), pp. 121–3.

[28] *Rot. Parl.* ii. 303–4; iv. 318.

[29] *Rot. Parl.* (1404) iii. 546–7; (1411) iii. 648–9; (1431) iv. 369–70; (1435) iv. 486–7; (1450) v, 172–4; (1472) vi. 4–6; (1489) vi. 420–4.

[30] Ibid. (1472) vi, 111–9, 149–53; (1489) Schofield, op. cit., pp. 175–9.

[31] £1 on incomes derived from freehold property, *Rot. Parl.* v. 172.

[32] The subsidies of 1535 (exemption limit £20) and 1525 (exemption limit £1–2) imply very different geographical distributions of wealth. PRO, E. 359/44, 26 Henry VIII, 1st payment; E. 359/41, 14 & 15 Henry VIII, 2nd payment.

[33] For the evolution of the Tudor subsidy, see Schofield, op. cit. pp. 198–218.

[34] For the details of each subsidy see the subsidy acts, printed in *Statutes of the Realm*. The structure and implementation of the early Tudor acts are discussed in Schofield, op. cit. pp. 219–342.

[35] From 1553 all wages, other than those of royal servants receiving more than £5 a year, were exempted from assessment (7 Edward VI, c. 12, s. 5).

[36] Subsidy acts in *Statutes of the Realm*. Rates and exemption limits of subsidies before 1547 are tabulated in Schofield, op. cit. pp. 248–9.

[37] 5 Henry VIII, c. 17; 6 Henry VIII, c. 26; 7 Henry VIII, c. 9. In 1514 a poll tax was also levied on those not otherwise taxed. The better-known subsidies of 1524 and 1525 (14 & 15 Henry VIII, c. 16) are less suitable because movables under £20 are taxed at half the rate of annual incomes. Nevertheless the 1524 subsidy ranks the counties in much the same order as the subsidy of 1515 ($\rho = + 0.952$). The subsidies of the later sixteenth century also suffer from serious undervaluation, see above, n. 17 and below n. 61.

[38] 5 Henry VIII, c. 17, s. 9 exempted those liable to the clerical subsidy of 1512. For the unusually wide incidence of this subsidy, see M. J. Kelly, 'Canterbury Jurisdiction and Influence during the Episcopate of William Warham, 1503–32' (Ph. D. thesis, Cambridge, 1963), pp. 298–300.

[39] PRO, E. 359/38, 6 Henry VIII, 7 Henry VIII.

[40] Certification to the exchequer of individual assessments was first required by 14 & 15 Henry VIII, c. 16, s. 14. In 1514 and 1515 movable goods and annual incomes were both taxed at 6d./£; while in 1524 and 1525 only goods up to £20 were taxed at 6d./£, goods above £20 and all annual incomes being taxed at 1s./£. In 1514 and 1515 only annual wages were taxed at 6d./£; in 1524 and 1525 the tax was a 'poll' payment of 4d., but all wages, including casual wages, aggregating £1 a year, counted towards this. In 1514 those not otherwise taxed paid 4d. 5 Henry VIII, c. 17, s. 1; 6 Henry VIII, c. 26, s. 2; 14 & 15 Henry VIII, c. 16, s. 2.

[41] Sample of c. 6,200 individual assessments, of which c. 3,200 from Bucks. (Buckingham, Cotteslow, and Newport hundreds), c. 2,300 from Sussex (Chichester Rape, excluding Chichester and Midhurst boroughs), and c. 700 from Suffolk (Loes hundred). The *number* of persons assessed on annual incomes was fairly constant at c. 2 per cent; the number assessed on wages ranged from 7 to 33 per cent. A. C. Chibnall and A. V. Woodman, 'Subsidy Roll for the County of Buckingham, Anno 1524', *Bucks. Record Society*, 8 (1950), 47–89; J. Cornwall, 'Lay Subsidy Rolls for the County of Sussex, 1524–5', *Sussex Record Society Publications*, 56 (1956), 8–34; S. H. A. Hervey, 'Suffolk in 1524'. *Suffolk Green Books*, 10 (1910), 231–42.

[42] That is those with movable goods worth less than £2, or in receipt of annual incomes or annual wages worth less than £1 per annum (5 Henry VIII c. 17, s. 1).

[43] The ratio of the wealth of poor people paying the poll to that of other taxpayers can be calculated roughly by comparing county assessments in 1514 with similar assessments in 1515 when the poll was not levied. Apart from economic change during the 12 months interval, the only difference between these assessments was the inclusion in 1515 of clerical wealth on lands acquired since 1291. This can be crudely estimated by subtracting the 1291 Taxatio from the 1535 Valor for each county, and can then be subtracted from the 1515 assessments. The average ratio 1514/1515 was 1·21. The highest ratios were Lancs. 4·39, Yorks. W. R. 2·17, Salop 2·03, Yorks. N. R. 1·74, Worcs. 1·72, Staffs. 1·63, Yorks. E. R. 1·51. PRO E. 359/38, 6 Henry VIII, 7 Henry VIII; *Taxatio Ecclesiastica* (1802); *Valor Ecclesiasticus* (1810–34).

[44] See Maps 1–4, above.

[45] *Rot. Parl.* ii, 447–8.

[46] Except that in 1514 those not otherwise taxed paid a poll of 4d. *Rot. Parl.* ii, 447; 5 Henry VIII, c. 17, s. 1; 6 Henry VIII, c. 26, s. 2.

[47] *Rot. Parl.* ii. 447.

[48] Willard, op cit. pp. 79–86.

[49] 5 Henry VIII, c. 17, s. 1 (grain not specified); 6 Henry VIII, c. 26, s. 2.

[50] Willard, op. cit. pp. 26, 29, 115–16, 124; 5 Henry VIII, c. 17, s. 11, schedule; 6 Henry VIII, c. 26, ss. 17–18, schedule. In 1334 some (?) outlying members of the Cinque Ports were assessed in Kent; but to maintain comparability between the assessments, these have been disregarded. PRO, E. 179/123/12. m. 26d; Press List 6/22B, p. 72, s. 4.

[51] Willard, op. cit., p. 119, does not say whether the stannary men were omitted from the 1334 assessments, or whether they were assessed and sued their charter of exemption later. The evidence points towards the latter, but is not conclusive. Stannary men in Devon were assessed in 1332 and claimed exemption later. For Cornwall there may be an exemption claim after 1334; for Devon there was no such claim, but numerous claims were made for subsequent assessments. PRO, E. 359/14, mm. 19, 19d, 21, 21d; E. 368/108 Stat. et vis. comp. Trin. r. 2; E. 363/4, mm. 24d, 25, 25d. Correction for possible omission, taking previous stannary claims, would not affect the figure calculated for Devon in column 1 of Table 2, while that for Cornwall would be slightly increased from 7·7 to 9·1. Willard, op. cit. pp. 118–19.

[52] Charterhouses, Syon, and Dertford, in 1514; with Denny, Minories, and Bruisyard, in 1515. 5 Henry VIII, c. 17, s. 10; 6 Henry VIII, c. 26, ss. 16, 18. Much of the wealth of the colleges and religious houses was exempt in any case, because it was taxed by convocation. See above, n. 39, and below, n. 59.

[53] Buckatzsch, p. 184.

[54] *Rot. Parl.* ii. 447–8.

[55] 5 Henry VIII, c. 17, s. 3; 6 Henry VIII, c. 26, s. 8.

[56] PRO, E. 359/38, 41, 42, 44, *passim*, discussed in Schofield, op. cit., pp. 258–69, and tabulated ibid. p. 265.

[57] The king's household and the queen's household. 5 Henry VIII, c. 17, schedule; 6 Henry VIII, c. 26, s. 4. In 1515 Wolsey's household was also assessed separately. PRO, E. 359/38, 6 Henry VIII, r. 5*d*.

[58] PRO, E. 359/38, 5 Henry VIII, 6 Henry VIII.

[59] Willard, op cit., pp. 93–109. 6 Henry VIII, c. 26, s. 21. The virtually total exemption of clerical wealth in 1514 has already been explained.

[60] Figures for clerical wealth are necessarily those of annual incomes, and the value of movables on these new possessions may have been higher than this (see, pp. 91–2). On the other hand the values of incomes in the 1535 survey may be higher than the actual values in 1515. *Taxatio Ecclesiastica; Valor Ecclesiasticus*; Table 2, below.

[61] Willard, op. cit., pp. 79–86, 138–41, 207–19; *Calendar Fine Rolls*, iv. 480; *Acts Privy Council*, xvii. 413–15; xxviii. 625–7; PRO, S.P. 12/107 ff. 97–8*b*. See also n. 17 above.

[62] R. E. Glasscock, 'The distribution of Lay Wealth in South-East England in the Early Fourteenth Century' (Ph.D. thesis, London, 1962), i. 67–74.

[63] Interim discussion in Schofield, op. cit., pp. 326–42. I have assembled fresh evidence which I hope to discuss in a future publication.

[64] *Taxatio Ecclesiastica; Valor Ecclesiasticus*. In almost every case where these surveys omitted the location of items of wealth, this has been recovered from ministers' accounts and other surveys. PRO, S.C. 6 and E. 315, *passim*; St George's Chapel Windsor MSS., IV B 5. Cambridge colleges from a 1545 survey proportionally reduced to 1535 totals. *Documents Relating to the University and Colleges of Cambridge*, published by direction of the Royal Commission on Cambridge (1852), i. 107–294.

[65] Rank correlation coefficient ρ is $+ 0.658$ for 1291/1334, and $+ 0.814$ for 1514/1535. The significance of this coefficient is explained on p. 94.

[66] See, for example, *Norfolk Record Society*, 1 (1931), 48–68; and, for the rich, PRO, Wards 9/ 129 ff. 48*b*, 49*b*, 55–5*b*, 56*b*, 57*b*, 80, 254–4*b*, comparing these with PRO, E. 179/203/183, m. 9*d*, /133/117, m. 9, /78/99, m. 8, /113/215B, fo. 3, /159/122, m. 11, /136/320, m. 4, /87/144, m. 4. A recent study of the wealth of the early Tudor gentry suggests that in the early sixteenth century the values of movable goods and annual incomes achieve parity at the level of approximately £100. J. Cornwall, 'The Early Tudor Gentry', *Econ. Hist. Rev.* 2nd ser. 17 (1965), 462, 467–9. This figure is very close to that calculated below for clerical wealth at the same date.

[67] The ratios were 1·94 for stipendiaries and 1·82 for the beneficed clergy. Figures from the 1522 loan/muster valuation, one extraordinary case omitted. *Norf. Rec. Soc.* 1 (1931), 47–8; *Norfolk Archaeology*, 22 (1926), 49–52.

[68] Incomes from A. Savine, 'English Monasteries on the Eve of the Dissolution', *Oxford Studies in Social and Legal History*, I (Oxford, 1909), 274–5, 281, 283–4. Movables and debts from *Letters and Papers, Henry VIII*, x, no. 1191; xi, App. no. 2. Houses where debts are greater than value of movables have been disregarded. Possible swollen debts and possible concealment of movables may make these figures untypical, see Savine, pp. 188–93, 210–17. Disregarding debts, average value of movables was £129. 18*s*. 0*d*., net of debts it was £87.

[69] Assuming that the number of clergy was about the same as it was in 1381. If the same assumption is made for 1291, the average clerical income comes out at about £7. Since the number of clergy at both dates was probably greater than it was in 1381, these figures for average clerical incomes are probably too high. If, however, the religious house is taken as the taxable unit, rather than the individual religious, in 1535 the average clerical income is slightly higher at about £18. *Taxatio Ecclesiastica; Valor Ecclesiasticus*; E. Powell, op. cit. pp. 123–4; M. D. Knowles, *The Religious Houses of Medieval England* (1940), p. 147; F. A. Gasquet, *Henry VIII and the Monasteries* (1906), pp. 359–60.

[70] Where figures obtained by a pound for pound combination of clerical and lay wealth differ from these, they have been noted.

[71] R. Graham, *English Ecclesiastical Studies* (1929), pp. 271–301; A. Savine, op cit., pp. 31–5; M. D. Knowles, *The Religious Orders in England*, iii. (1959), 244–7.

[72] For the nature of these tests, see Buckatzsch, pp. 184–90, and further references cited there.

[73] Willard, *Eng. Hist. Rev.* 30 (1915), 73; PRO, E. 359/38, 5 Henry VIII, 6 Henry VIII. The improvements in the accuracy of the 1334 assessments made by Glasscock, *op. cit., passim* are too small to affect the figures calculated here. 1334 Kent Cinque Ports assessments excluded, see above, n. 50.

[74] A. R. Bridbury, *Economic Growth: England in the Later Middle Ages* (1962), pp. 77–82, 111.

[75] Bristol according to area in each county: Glos. 77 per cent, Somerset 23 per cent. E. Boswell, *The Ecclesiastical Division of the Diocese of Bristol* (Sherborne, s.a.), p. 1, no. 3; *1891 Census*, II, Parl. Papers, 1893–4, cv, 525. York has been divided between the three Ridings in equal parts.

[76] Pearson's product moment correlation coefficient is dominated by abnormally high values; but Spearman's rank correlation coefficient is not affected in this way. F. C. Mills, *Statistical Methods* (1938), pp. 370–8. Buckatzsch tried to minimize this effect by using the logs of the values, Buckatzsch, p. 188, n. 1, p. 199, n. 1.

[77] For calculations with London included and Yorks. and Lincs. undivided I have followed Buckatzsch and used the logs of the values, otherwise not.

[78] An elementary precaution; by omitting to take it Hoskins produces a false ranking of the counties for 1334. W. G. Hoskins and H. P. R. Finberg, *Devonshire Studies* (1952), pp. 215–17. The clerical surveys usually give the assessed value of the wealth.

[79] Buckatzsch, pp. 184, 186–7, taken from G. R. Porter, *Progress of the Nation* (1847), p. 156. There are also one or two other errors in Buckatzsch's rank list of the counties.

[80] *Census of England and Wales*, Parl. Papers, 1831 *et seq.*

[81] *1901 Census*, preliminary report, Parl. Papers, 1910, xc, 3. Changes consequent upon the Divided Parishes Acts of 1876 and 1882 were 'inconsiderable in extent', and may be disregarded, *1891 Census*, iv, P.P. 1893–4, cvi, App. A, Table 6, p. 97. Acreages involved in the elimination of detached parts of counties by 7 & 8 Victoria, c. 61, s. 1 are given in *1851 Census*, I, P.P. 1852–3, lxxxv, p. lxxv. Changes on the Welsh border consequent upon 27 Henry VIII, c. 26, ss. 9–11, where whole hundreds have been taken from *1871 Census*, I, P.P. 1872, lxvi, pt. I, pp. 137, 308 and where parishes, from *1901 Census*, P.P. 1902, cxx, Monmouth, p. 15. The area of the lordship of Ellesmere (Salop) has been estimated from *Transactions of the Shropshire Archaeological and Natural History Society*, 5 (1905), 55–80, and *Ordnance Survey*, 1 inch to a mile, 7th ser. no. 118. Clun hundred (Salop) was not taxed. Glasscock, op. cit., ii, 239; PRO, E. 359/38, 5 Henry VIII, 6 Henry VIII.

[82] For these assessments see above, pp. 82–4.

[83] One of these, p', is complementary to p. The second, z, is a transformation of r which enables the statistical significance of changes in the amount of redistribution of wealth as between different periods to be established. It has been omitted here because statistical significance appears to be dependent on the (arbitrary) length of the periods chosen.

[84] For a fuller explanation of these coefficients, see Buckatzsch, pp. 184–90, and the references cited there.

[85] I am grateful to Dr. E. M. Rawstron and the Department of Geography of Queen Mary College, London, for assistance in the preparation of the maps.

[86] For local differences in 1334, see Glasscock, op. cit., *passim*; for urban areas, see Bridbury, op. cit., pp. 77–82, 111.

[87] See further, p. 102.

[88] Glasscock, op. cit., i. 70. Other less extensive areas of great wealth were situated in east Kent; on the Sussex and Hampshire coast, and in the Thames valley.

[89] Ibid., pp. 71–4.

[90] If clerical wealth is combined with lay wealth pound for pound, instead of being doubled in value, the county orders are again very slightly different as far as individual placings are concerned; but substantially the same in over-all ranking. The grouping of the counties as shown on the maps remains substantially the same; only two counties exchange groups at each date.

[91] Average figures; 1451–75 = 100. E. H. Phelps-Brown and S. V. Hopkins, 'Seven Centuries of the Prices of Consumables', *Economica*, new series 23 (1956), 311–12.

[92] This greatly under-estimates the expansion of London, much of which was into the suburbs, and which is reflected in the great increase in wealth of Middlesex and Surrey. For urban rates of expansion, including Westminster and Southwark, see Bridbury, op. cit., p. 112–13.

[93] Except always that the wealth of Kent and Sussex is irremediably under-estimated because of the exemption of the Cinque Ports from taxation.

4

The Social Distribution of Land and Men in England, 1436–1700

J. P. COOPER

Editor's note. This article was first published in *Econ. Hist. Rev.* 20 (1967) 419–40. Mr. Cooper has provided a note, printed at the end of the article, for which the Editor is grateful.

A short discussion of one aspect of this article, the use of estimates based on means, can be found above, pp. 8–11.

DR. THOMPSON has provided a fruitful and fascinating conspectus of the distribution of landed property.[1] His main purpose was to consider how and why England became 'overwhelmingly a land of tenant farmers by the end of the eighteenth century' and the consequences of this for the subsequent development of the economy. Nevertheless it may be worth seeing whether there is more material available about the situation at the beginning of his inquiry which may at least provide a basis for slightly better-informed guessing. It may also be possible to provide more information about the numbers in the various categories of landowners, or at least show why more accurate information about this would be desirable. Likewise both Thomas Wilson's and Gregory King's findings can be considered in more detail and compared with other contemporary estimates and evidence. The only general criticism of Dr. Thompson which I would venture to make is that it is not always clear what data are being used in his calculations (e.g. the size of the cultivated area at various dates seems elusive). In dealing with approximations and guesses of this order, such minor variations cannot seriously affect the general argument, yet it may be instructive to have the guesses identified and more fully expounded, even at the cost of sacrificing some clarity of exposition.

I

Dr. Thompson does not profess to offer any signposts or resting places between Domesday Book and that of Professor Stone. However an attempt to set up another basis for comparison can be made for the fifteenth and early sixteenth centuries. The returns for the income tax of 1436 analysed by Professor H. L. Gray make a convenient starting-point.[2] They probably underestimate total wealth, they certainly underestimate that of the peerage and perhaps that of the greater landowners,[3] but they do give a minimum figure for income from land of those laymen with £5 a year and above, while conveniently distinguishing between greater landowners and lesser ones. Professor Gray estimated that 51 barons had a landed income of £40,000 (average £768) and that 183 'greater knights' with incomes over £100[4] had a total of £38,000 (average £208). Some 6,950 others had incomes of £5–£100 amounting to £113,000.[5] Thus 234 greater landowners had almost 40 per cent of the income from land of £5 a year and above.

Very tentatively, these can be translated into acreages. Thorold Rogers considered that rent of arable land in the first half of the fifteenth century seldom exceeded sixpence an acre and was often below it.[6] More recent evidence would seem to confirm this.[7] As the tax is likely to understate the area of their estates at just over 3 million acres, at fivepence an acre this would be nearer 4 million acres.[8] The average income of the 'greater knights' would give an acreage of 8,000–9,000 acres. This is well above the minimum of 5,000 acres for great landlords in 1790 proposed by Dr. Mingay.[9] The tax of 1436 should have included all lay estates over 200 acres whose total acreage would be 8 or 9 million acres.

We are now left with the problems of deciding plausible figures for the total cultivated area and the proportions held by Crown, Church, and smaller lay owners. Dr. Thompson appears to favour estimates of from 20 to 30 million acres for the cultivated area around 1600.[10] If we believe only a fraction of Professor Postan's assertions,[11] we must suppose that it was smaller in 1436, so that 20 million may be taken as a maximum. For crown lands a minimum value of £13,333 can be arrived at by taking the estates of the two queens dowager alive in 1436.[12] Lord Cromwell's statement of 1433, excluding Wales and wards' lands, but including fee farms and farms, gives a total of some £13,300 gross receipts.[13] In the case of the Duchy of Lancaster the total is clearly too low and a grand total of £20,000 is conceivable.[14] This would give a total of 800,000 to 1,000,000 acres. Any estimate of the Church's lands involves even more speculation. Inferences from the clerical tenth would give the Church an income of £150,000 or more,[15] a considerable proportion of which must have consisted of tithe. A better approach may be provided by the *Valor Ecclesiasticus*. Savine judiciously decided against any attempt to estimate the area of monastic lands,[16] but we must be rasher, while acknowledging the difficulties which he described.

Savine found that the monasteries had total rural landed revenues of £100,000, £10,000 from demesnes and the rest from tenurial payments.[17] The demesnes' arable averaged sixpence an acre in the *Valor* and sevenpence in the 'Paper Surveys', with pasture roughly twice as valuable.[18] If we value all the (tenurial) income at eightpence or ninepence an acre we shall arrive at a fictional acreage, representing what the monasteries would have owned if all their land had been let as demesne. This comes to 3 million acres at eightpence, 2·7 million at ninepence. To guess the land owned by the rest of the Church is even more difficult. But if we take the clerical tenth of 1535[19] and assume that half the income did not come from ownership of land, we get a total of 4 million acres at eightpence an acre. Similar assumptions applied to the clerical tenth of Henry V give 3·6 million acres at fivepence an acre. However, it might be argued that this is an underestimate, as tithe and spiritual income were only a quarter of the monasteries' gross income.[20] Thus 4,000,000 notional acres may be a minimum for the Church.[21]

Thus we may draw together our shaky and inconsistent approximations for 1436 into the following table, bearing in mind that the 1436 tax did not cover Wales and the Marches:

TABLE 1.

	Landed income £	Millions of acres	Percentage acres
Great landowners	78,000	3–4	20
Landowners £5–100	113,000	4·5–5·5	25
Landowners under £5	100,000	3–4	20
Church	75–100,000	4–5	20–25
Crown	20,000	1–1·5	5

The most plausible of these estimates may be that a minimum of about 20 per cent of the land was owned by great landowners. This is very similar to Dr. Thompson's estimates for the seventeenth century and naturally raises the question as to whether it is possible to provide any further estimate for the sixteenth century. Here an attempt to estimate the numbers of great landowners may be of use.

II

Dr. Cornwall has shown that some 30 knights of Suffolk, Sussex, Buckinghamshire, and Norfolk were assessed to the subsidy of 1524 with average incomes from land of £180. He found the median of 26 knights at court £225 and of 18 in feodary surveys £206.[22] He and Professor Hoskins found that the annual value of land in the subsidy for Surrey and parts of Suffolk and Rutland was £32 for 1,000 acres.[23] This gives an average value per acre of 7·7 d. Presumably the average value for the whole country would be less than this, so we may take sevenpence an acre. This would give the average knight an estate of 6,200 acres, if his income was £180, or 6,900 acres, if £200, still well above Dr. Mingay's minimum figure.[24]

We must now try to estimate the number of knights around 1524. Thomas Wilson at the end of the century considered that all knights would be members of the commissions of the peace 'unless they be putt by for religion or some particular disfavor'.[25] The first of these could scarcely apply before the Reformation and there is no reason to suppose that the commissions of the peace will provide a reliable minimum for the number of knights. However, it must be admitted that Professors Thrupp and Stone have given their blessing to an estimate by Colonel Wedgwood which is very much higher.[26] This puts the number at 375 in 1491 on the assumption, for which no evidence is offered, that there were 'half as many again' as in 1434 when there were 250, according to returns in the patent rolls.[27] Table 2 shows that the highest estimate that can be derived from the commissions would be 250 for 1509–14 without making any allowance for deaths during the period. For the early 1520s 200 would seem a likely total and might include all the wealthy ones.

If we assume 200 knights with an average income of £200 and 50 peers with an average income of £800, this gives a total of £80,000,[28] which at sevenpence an acre would amount to 2·7 million acres, about 14 per cent of a total cultivated area of 20 million. As the 1436 estimate was arrived at by estimating incomes all of which were over £100 for the greater landowners who were not peers, while the 1524 one is an average of incomes of knights some of which were under £100, it would be likely to produce a smaller figure. Nevertheless the two results are of roughly the same order of magnitude and thus perhaps lend some support to each other. Dr. Cornwall's findings show that for the knights landed wealth and social status went together in the 1520s as Thomas Wilson believed they still did in 1601. It may be permissible to think that they did in the mid-sixteenth century.

One difficulty about this assumption is Professor Stone's belief that there were 600 knights by the accession of Elizabeth. If these 600 knights still had estates of the same average size as in the 1520s, then the proportion of land owned by knights would have increased by an amount roughly equal to the whole of the monastic lands. This would certainly have been the most dramatic change in favour of greater landowners ever to happen; even on Professor Stone's assumption of an increase in number of only 225, the increase would still be formidable. Now the only justification for the figure of 600 is that 'there were 374 creations from 1537–58'.[29] Even after allowing for the fact that there may have been a misprint, since by my count there were 472 creations down to November 1558, excluding Irishmen and peers, this scarcely supports an estimate of 600 for 1559. As those knighted were usually adults, some unknown, but appreciable, proportion of those knighted in the 1540s must have died by 1559, some of them as a result of war.[30] Lacking information about the ages at which they were knighted, we can only guess at the numbers surviving and suggest 300–50 as a possible maximum.

Clearly the numbers of knights in the commissions of the peace in 1564 in Table 2 are too low. Dr. Hassall Smith has shown that the commissions of the peace were purged in the early years of Elizabeth and many recusants were excluded, so that for this reason alone the 1564 figure must be too low.[31] The 1554 figure is the better one, though this may be too low, for religious reasons and because the commissions do not cover all counties. The *Libri Pacis* for 1559 and 1561 taken together overcome most of these deficiencies and provide the names of some 268 individual knights. The number of peers in 1559 was 63, so that, if we accept the view that the commissions of the peace normally included all knights, especially those of substance, the number of greater landowners would have been about 400, or at least 350.

TABLE 2. *Numbers of Knights on the Commissions of the Peace*

Date	Number of English counties	Number of knights*	Others, excluding[1] peers, clergy, law officers
1429–36[2]	36[3]	129 } c. 180[16]	—
[1434[4]	29[5]	163]	
1477–84[6]	36[3]	185	
1485–94[7]	36[3]	195	
1509–14[9]	35[8]	218	580
1519–26[10]	35[8]	170	—
1554[11]	36[3]	216	630
1559[12]	39[14]†	*195* } 268[16]	—
1561[13]	40[15]†	*203* }	670
1564[17]	39[14]†	(180)[21] *188*	(600)[21] 720
1595[18]	37[19]	214 } 237[16]	—
1596[20]	39[14]†	*184* }	1100

[1] These figures are only rough approximations.

[2] *Cal. Patent Rolls 1429–36*, pp. 613 ff.

[3] Excluding Cheshire, Durham, Lancashire.

[4] *Cal. Patent Rolls 1429–36*, pp. 370–413, persons certified by knights of shire to take an oath not to maintain peace-breakers and commissions to take these oaths.

[5] Excluding, in addition to those in n. 3, Cornwall, Hertfordshire, Leicestershire, Northampton, Somerset, Suffolk, Worcester.

[6] *Cal. Patent Rolls 1476–85*, pp. 553 ff.

[7] *Cal. Patent Rolls 1485–94*, pp. 481 ff.

[8] Excluding Rutland, Cheshire, Durham, Lancashire.

[9] *Letters and Papers . . . Henry VIII*, 2nd ed. (1920), i, pt 2, 1533–47.

[10] *Letters and Papers . . . Henry VIII*, iii, pt. 2, nos. 1451 (1), (9); 2074 (14); 2214 (24); 2415 (6), (20), (26); 2587 (22); 2694 (30); 2862 (14), (15); 2993, 3586 (28); 3677 (12); iv, pt 1, nos. 137 (4), (10), (12), (14), (23); 297 (18); 390 (2), (6), (12); 464 (2); 961 (12); 1610 (11).

[11] *Cal. Patent Rolls 1553–4*, pp. 16 ff.

[12] B.M., Lansdowne MS. 1218, fos. 4–43.

[13] Ibid., fos. 57–92.

[14] Excluding Lancashire, including Monmouth.

[15] Including Lancashire.

[16] This is the total of different individuals in both books.

[17] *Cal. Patent Rolls 1563–6*, nos. 108–63.

[18] Northants. Record Office, Wingfield (Tickencote), Box x.511, Bdle. 'Other counties and Miscellaneous'.

[19] Excluding Durham, Lancashire, Monmouth.

[20] PRO, S.P.13/Case F, no. 11.

[21] Excluding Wales.

* While an effort was made to avoid double counting, some may have occurred, so that the totals may be too high.

† The totals in the last two columns include the commissions for Wales.

This in turn raises another important problem, since Dr. Thompson[32] accepts Professor Stone's view that the peerage in 1641 formed 'about two-thirds' of the greater landowners, or in Professor Stone's own words 'the titular peerage . . . together with a further thirty or forty families . . . formed a single economic class . . .'[33] This would give a total of 150–60 families, though Dr. Thompson suggests a round number of 200. Thus between 1559 and 1641 the number of great landowners fell by a half, more or less; more surprising still, the number in 1641 had fallen by about a third compared with 1523 or 1436.[34]

Now it would certainly not be beyond the resources of our latter-day model-builders to fill this gap with an explanation. Indeed there is a vintage model to hand already, the rise of the gentry; but before driving off in this, we may still wonder whether the figures for 1641 are plausible, especially if they imply a fall in the number of great landowners in a period of substantial increase of population.

In fairness to Professor Stone, it may be argued that he was thinking of a much higher figure for a great estate than the 5,000 or 6,000 acres minimum proposed by Dr. Mingay for 1790, or that of 10,000 acres used by Dr. Thompson for 1873. He speaks of '30 or 40 upper gentry families who were as rich as the middling barons and richer than the poor ones'. If the term barons is meant to exclude those of higher rank, his statistics do not permit the reader to discover their landed income, but £3,000 seems a plausible guess, which gives 14,300 acres. The average landed income of all peers in 1641 was nearly £5,000 including casualties.[35] However, given the high proportion of the total owned by the ten richest peers, the median would be appreciably lower. Even at £4,000 a year this supposes an estate of nearly 20,000 acres, using Dr. Thompson's assumption about average rents. Thus it is possible that different criteria of size are being applied at different dates in Dr. Thompson's estimates, which may raise the question of how far they do allow even rough comparisons of the growth of great estates to be made.[36] It is worth noting that there were only 127 owners of 20,000 acres and more in England and Wales in 1873.[37]

III

None of this necessarily affects Dr. Thompson's main thesis, but it is still worth looking more closely at his use of Thomas Wilson's estimates. He believes they 'must be taken seriously in view of the substantial support they receive from Stone's calculations of peerage incomes . . .'[38] Professor Stone also considers that Wilson's estimate of 500 knights, excluding those made by Essex, tends to be supported by the figures of new creations over the previous forty years, though he himself puts the number at about 420 (550 including Essex's knights).[39] Certainly one would expect Wilson's estimate of the number of knights to be more reliable than his estimate of their income, which Dr. Thompson rejects. Nevertheless it is open to question.

Wilson reckoned his 500 knights to be landowners in England,[40] but the creations included an appreciable number of Irish and a few Scots. Between 1580 and 1600 some 556 knights were created, of these 77 were peers, Irishmen, or foreigners and 166 were knighted by Essex, leaving 313.[41] After making some allowance for deaths and survivals from before 1580, Wilson's figure for 1601 seems impossibly high and one of 350 might seem more likely. It might be argued that Shaw's figures are incomplete, but Professor Stone apparently accepts them. It is worth noticing that Sir Henry Spelman considered there were only 300 knights at the end of Elizabeth's reign, though he did not explicitly exclude Essex's knights,[42] and although Professor Stone declares he 'undoubtedly underestimated'.[43] The last known surviving *Libri Pacis* of Elizabeth's reign are for 1595 and 1596 and suggest a total of well under 300 knights on the commissions of the peace for England and Wales;[44] some 250 would be a maximum, after allowing for the omission of Lancashire from the total shown in Table 2. If Wilson made his count from the commissions in 1600 and excluded Essex's knights, the total could not have been very much higher. One explanation might be that he failed to allow for the considerable reduplication of names among commissions for different counties. His figure of 1,400 for the number of gentry in the commissions of the peace is almost certainly too high for the same reason.[45]

If Wilson who claimed to have made his reckoning from the commissions of the peace could be so mistaken, how reliable are his other statements?

We could wish that at least one of them was more reliable, when he puts the numbers of freeholders in England and Wales at 'about the number of 80,000, as I have seen in sheriffs' books'.[46] First we may wonder whether Wilson had eliminated all the gentry from the freeholders' books. In some counties these were a considerable proportion of the total, the extreme example is Lancashire in 1600 where out of 770 freeholders only seven were not styled gentleman or higher.[47] The freeholders' lists of eight counties for the early Elizabethan period give an average of some 400 non-gentry freeholders.[48] A more doubtful calculation for five more counties would give a general average of about 540.[49] This would leave 24 English counties and Wales to share the remaining 73,000 freeholders proposed by Wilson; allocating a generous 10,000 to Wales would still leave the English counties with the very high average of 2,600 each.[50] Even after allowing for an increase of freeholders between 1562 and 1601, Wilson's figure would seem to be too high. If we reduce them by a quarter, this will still leave some margin for substantial copyholders.

Wilson clearly envisaged his freeholders as substantial yeomen with five or six horses and stocks of £300–£500.[51] Professor Hoskins considers that the typical Leicestershire farm of the sixteenth century was about 50 acres.[52] Dr. Thirsk suggests that the wealthier husbandmen's and yeomen's farms on the Lincolnshire claylands and marshlands were 30–80 acres, while on the wolds the normal farm was 80–100 acres.[53] In the fens, farms were much smaller. Mr. Kenyon considers that in the Wealden clay region the typical farm was about 120 acres.[54] The mid-Essex yeoman's farm 1639–1700 was about 50–60 acres.[55] The Oxfordshire inventories from the Thames valley suggest an average holding of over 60 acres in the second half of the sixteenth century.[56] A similar number from the Trent valley in mid-sixteenth century Nottinghamshire suggest the same.[57] On this totally inadequate basis we may perhaps guess at holdings averaging at least 70–80 acres for Wilson's substantial yeomen. If there were 60,000 of them, this would give 4·2 to 4·6 million acres; if there were 80,000, 5·6 to 6·4 million. This last figure might be thought of as including the secure copyholders and would be about 20–25 per cent of Dr. Thompson's suggestion for the cultivated area in the early seventeenth century.

We must now confront Wilson's estimates with those of Gregory King. King apparently gives two different totals for the freeholders in 1688—160,000 and 180,000.[58] The lower figure would fit more comfortably with recent estimates of the electorate.[59] For the better sort of freeholders the estimates remained the same at 40,000. The question arises as to how much land this represents. King valued arable at 5s. 10d. an acre, pasture and meadow at 9s. and commons at 3s. 6d.[60] Thus the rent of a notionally typical holding might be put at 6s. 6d. or 7s. an acre. King put the better sort of freeholders' average income at £84. He reckoned that the produce of arable land was about three times its rental and that of pasture and common about twice. Thus the income of the freeholders was presumably the value of the produce, less the cost of wage labour, and other lesser costs. This might suggest that the income could represent twice to two and a half times the rental value of the land. On this assumption, the better sort of freeholders' holding was 100–30 acres.[61] An unpublished estimate in which King attempted to estimate acreages and rent valued the 40,000 freeholders' lands at 6s. an acre and put their average holding at 166 acres.[62] This would seem to suggest that King did intend to attribute holdings of well over 100 acres to this group. This again suggests that Wilson's figure for substantial freeholders was too high; while small freeholders might have declined in numbers 1601–88, it is difficult to believe that the numbers of substantial ones declined so drastically.

Similar assumptions about 140,000 lesser freeholders whose income averaged £50 would give an average holding of 60 acres or more.[63] Thus the freeholders together could hold 12·5 million acres, 32 per cent of the cultivated area, according to King.[64] Professor Habakkuk considers that King included the copyholders among his freeholders and certainly this seems the most likely category for them.[65] However if the copyholders were more than 60,000 or 70,000 strong this would leave too few freeholders to make up the parliamentary electorate, even after allowing that some copyholders were also freeholders. The demand for parliamentary votes may have inflated the number of 40-shilling freeholders in a misleading way. For example there were only 179 freeholders in the book for Nottinghamshire about 1561 which may be incomplete, there were over 1,000 in 1612, while 1,778 voted in 1698 and 2,100 in 1710.[66] In some counties it is even clearer that the number of freeholders had grown long before there was a demand for votes; for example in Essex the numbers recorded doubled between 1561 and about 1634.[67] Given a substantial increase in population and an active market in land between the mid-sixteenth and the mid-seventeenth century, such an increase in the number of freeholders does not seem surprising. The present view is that from the Restoration stagnation in agricultural prices and in the trend of population led to increasing difficulties for smaller landowners in general. These difficulties grew worse after 1688 partly as a result of taxation, and ultimately led to an increase of substantial tenant farmers at the expense of both small tenants and freeholders.[68] But it has been argued that in some areas down to 1700 at least the substantial yeoman prospered.[69] The long-term trend was towards large tenant farms based on mixed farming on the lighter soils, while family farms and owner-occupiers survived or even increased in pastoral areas, though the first phase of converting mixed arable farms on the heavy clay lands to predominantly pastoral farms may have eliminated many small family holdings and owner-occupiers.[70] This recent work partly supports A. H. Johnson's view that 'the really critical period was somewhere after 1688'.[71]

The estimates of Wilson and King can be compared in another way. If we assume that King's greater freeholders' average holding was 115 acres and that the lesser ones' was 60 acres, this would give a general average for all the 180,000 freeholders of 80 acres. This suggests that the acreages are too high, especially perhaps for the lesser freeholders. But if we accept them and Wilson's figure of 80,000 freeholders, this would give an increase in the number of freeholders of nearly 40 per cent between 1601 and 1688, even after removing 70,000 supposed copyholders from King's total. If we accept both Wilson's and King's estimates, they are difficult to reconcile with what little we know about the trend of landownership by small men in the seventeenth century. There are some more data which ought to be considered in relation to both estimates.

IV

These are the knighthood fines raised by Charles I in 1631–2. In theory these should have been paid by all those who had not been knighted at or before the coronation of the king and who had freeholds for life only or 'lands or rents to fortie pounds yearely valewe although held in Soccage, or though held of Common persons or of us by a meane tenure'. The commissioners were also instructed to assess wealth from the freeholders' books, subsidy and muster rolls, and the poor-rates. The minimum composition was to be £10, but higher rates were to be paid in accordance with wealth; J.P.s were to pay at least £25.[72] In fact, this last instruction was largely ineffective in producing compositions realistically graduated according to wealth. The great majority compounded at £10. But for our purposes what matters most is whether the names of compounders, recorded by the Auditors of the Receipt of the Exchequer, can be used for an estimate of the numbers of those below the rank of knight with lands over £40 a year. For some counties, such as Hertfordshire, Essex, Norfolk, and Cambridge, the numbers compounding look impossibly low and it is not even clear that all those who compounded have been recorded. However, for many counties the record of compounders is reasonably complete. This is true of Cheshire, Lancashire, Yorkshire, Staffordshire, Leicestershire, and Somerset, when comparisons are made with the commissioners' returns.[73] The book contains some 7,350 names, which can be classified according to styles given, but unfortunately the clerks compiling the book did not always copy the styles given in the returns of the commissioners.[74] For what little it is worth, there were in round numbers 900 esquires, 2,200 gentlemen, 300 yeomen, 50 knights and baronets, 4,000 unstyled.

As the total number of names is too small (apart from incomplete entries for counties, there are none for London), some attempt must be made to estimate the true total. In all £173,537 9s. 6d. was received from fines.[75] The average composition in the book was £13·1,[76] so that the number compounding should have been 13,250. Of course, if those omitted paid larger than average sums the number would be lower.[77] On the other hand, if it is thought that many more with lands worth £40 or more escaped, then the figure we are seeking should be higher. The first and perhaps the only thing which is clearly shown by these figures is that the number of lesser freeholders was much greater than those with £40 or over in counties where comparison can be made with seventeenth-century freeholders' books (Lancashire, Staffordshire, Leicestershire, Somerset, and Nottinghamshire).[78] It is perhaps of some interest to note that £40 should have indicated an average holding of about 200 acres, the same as the lower limit of the 1436 income tax. Professor Gray reckoned there were 7,133 lay landowners, excluding peers. If we assume there were 1,500 baronets and knights in 1631, this would give a total of at least 14,750. After allowing that both figures may be too low, they still suggest that the number of lay owners of over 200 acres doubled between 1436 and 1631. Given the increase of population, this seems plausible, but of course it unfortunately tells us little about the distribution of landownership.

Nevertheless the inferences from the knighthood fines have some negative use. The most important is that they are almost impossible to reconcile with Wilson's statements about landownership. These suppose there were 16,500 knights and esquires who with perhaps at least half the 80,000 yeomen had £40 or more in land; this gives a total of 56,000. Even if we double the estimate derived from the compositions, we still only reach a total of 28,000. The same objection would apply to King's 56,000 landowners who were greater freeholders or above, but it is more conceivable that the number of greater freeholders had increased in the two generations after 1631 than that they had been decimated in the one generation after 1600.

V

However it is worth comparing King's estimates with other estimates by his contemporary Edward Chamberlayne. This has already been done in a general way and for a different purpose by Professor Aylmer.[79] But Chamberlayne's figures can be considered in more detail and from a somewhat different aspect. First, although Chamberlayne in 1669 put the average income of the peers absurdly high at £10,000 a year, Professor Aylmer did not remark that in 1670 he reduced this to £8,000 and continued to use this figure in the editions published in his lifetime.[80] The last edition of 1702 shows that he was aware of King's estimates as published by Davenant and that he accepted these for the value of land and houses in place of his own earlier ones.[81] Not unreasonably Chamberlayne did not accept King's estimate of the average income of the peerage which both Dr. Mingay and Dr. Thompson consider to be too low. Chamberlayne's figure is nearer the average gross income in 1641, proposed by Professor Stone, than King's, though not the figure for gross landed income.[82]

In all the editions the total income of the peerage is given as a varying proportion of 'the yearly Revenue of all England' which was between £13 and £14 million. Professor Aylmer rightly pointed out that it is not clear what 'the yearly Revenue' was meant to represent and that if it was national income it was absurdly low. However the 1702 edition makes it reasonably clear that it was not national income, but is basically a fiscal valuation of real property.[83] It is tempting to believe that Chamberlayne based his first estimates upon those current in official circles and debated in the commons in 1671. These put the yearly value of the land of England and Wales at £12 million and money at interest and net stock of trade at £24 to £35 million on which interest at 6 per cent would produce somewhere around £2 million of income.[84] However this may be, it is possible to lay out Chamberlayne's estimates for the reign of William III in Table 3. An obvious difficulty is that it is not clear whether the figures for income consist solely of income from land, but given the composition of national 'revenue' of which the incomes are fractions, they must be predominantly from real property. If we take the peers and baronets as greater landowners their incomes are around the 20 per cent of landed income postulated by Dr. Thompson,[85] after revising Gregory King. But the numbers involved are too large for his assumptions and the average estate of the baronets would be too small. Even if we accept the view that Dr. Thompson's number of 200 greater landowners is too small, in the light of probabilities in the sixteenth century, Chamberlayne's 900 seems far too large.[86] Similarly

TABLE 3. *Chamberlayne's Estimates c. 1692*

	No.	Average income £	Total income £	Total income as % of 'revenue'	Same as % of rent of land	Same as % of last + rent of houses
Peers	159	8.000	1.272.000	9[1] }15	13 }22	11 }18
Baronets	749[2]	1.200	898.000	6	9	7
Knights	1.400	800	1.120.000	8 }31[3]	11	9
Esquires and gentlemen	6.000	400	2.400.000	17	24	20
			5.690.800	40	57	47
Remaining landowners	—	—	?4.300.000[4]	60	43	53
Total in millions £			10	14	10[5]	12[5]

Unless otherwise stated the information comes from the 1692 edition.
[1] p. 236, 'about the eleventh part of the yearly Revenue of England'.
[2] Before 1692 and after 1694 'above 700'.
[3] In 1694 and subsequent editions 'about a third part of the yearly Revenue . . .'. p. 442.
[4] This must include lands belonging to 16.000 younger brothers; the figure is arrived at by subtracting the totals specified above from £10 million.
[5] 1702, p. 36.

Chamberlayne's figure for knights is clearly too large, only about 1,000 were dubbed between the Restoration and 1689.[87] King's figure of 600 might be too low, but it must be nearer the truth. Chamberlayne's figures imply that between 40 and 50 per cent of the income from land belonged to landowners not in his main categories, presumably the Church, Crown, the lesser gentry, and freeholders. His account suggests a society in which the only gentry who did not have substantial estates were 16,000 younger brothers 'who have small Estates in lands, but are commonly bred up to Divinity, Law, Physick, to Court and Military Emploiements, *but of late too many of them to Shopkeeping*'.[88] If 25–30 per cent were allocated to the freeholders, this would leave 10 per cent for the gentry and 5–10 per cent for Church and Crown. Thus Chamberlayne's estimates still imply a society in which a substantial amount of land was held by freeholders and would be compatible with the estimate derived from King of about 30 per cent.[89] An unpublished estimate by King had attributed 43 per cent of the acreage and half the rental value of England to them, rather more in acres and considerably more in value than all the baronets, knights, and gentry.

VI

Whatever Chamberlayne's defects as a political arithmetician in demographic matters,[90] his guesses are not necessarily worse than King's in matter of land-ownership. King's explicit statement about the social distribution of land-ownership as against his well-known statements about the distribution of incomes has never been published. It was written down in 1695,[91] not long before the *Observations*, which seems to have been prepared before the recoinage of 1696.[92] The notebook in which it was written contains drafts and calculations which are the basis of many statements in the finished tract. More finished versions of many of these were entered in the 'Burns journal' which seems to belong to early 1696, as far as its non-demographic entries are concerned.[93] Both the journal and the notebook contain details and estimates which are not in the tract. Most of the detailed evidence and calculations are demographic, but there are a variety of estimates of the numbers in various social groups and of the country's wealth in both the notebook and the journal.[94] The journal consistently uses much the same estimate of total population and the same estimate of total acreage as the tract, whereas the model presented in the notebook underestimates the acreage, but overestimates the population by half a million or more, and the average rent of land by a sixth, compared with the *Observations*.[95] It also includes some highly implausible estimates, notably that the landed income of the Crown was as great as that of the peerage and the acreage it possessed somewhat greater; or that twice as much rye as wheat was produced (though this may have been a slip of the pen). King's evident uncertainty about the numbers of paupers, farmers, and freeholders is perhaps a reminder that his final choice for the *Observations*, however familiar it has become by subsequent repetition, was subject to a very wide margin of error.

King himself revised the estimates of the acreage of arable, average rents, and yields of corn given in the *Observations*.[96] The vindication of his demographic work by Professor Glass[97] has perhaps obscured the need for careful study of his other estimates and their sources. The estimates for foreign trade seem to have been surprisingly bad, in the view of Professor Davis.[98] It seems very desirable that as many estimates as possible should be published and studied. Therefore the estimates about landownership and related matters seemed worth including as appendixes.

If the 180,000 freeholders of the tract seem numerous, the notebook offers estimates of 440,000 and 280,000 and the journal 240,000 and 174,000.[99] There is an equal variety in the estimates of paupers, though the differences are smaller in those of the esquires and gentlemen. The figures for the freeholders bear out the general point that most people at the time believed that the freeholders were very numerous and important. It had long been an article of patriotic faith that they were more numerous and prosperous than in any continental country. If we could believe any of the figures produced in the course of this discussion, it could be that their numbers and possessions had increased appreciably since the first half of the fifteenth century. If a serious political arithmetician like King could even momentarily entertain such exaggerated notions of the numbers and acres of the freeholders, this may help to explain the anxiety often expressed in the first half of the eighteenth century at the great decline in their numbers. Doubtless these did decline, but the decline would have seemed greater if generally inflated estimates of their wealth and numbers before 1700 prevailed. Of course it can also be argued that any apparent increase in the share of land held by small landowners since 1436 may be due only to the very defective nature of the evidence. Nevertheless the evidence of the knighthood fines does lend some support to the view that the numbers of small landowners with less than 150 to 200 acres must have been considerable. The evidence of Professor Hoskins's 'great re-building' points to their prosperity and perhaps the likelihood that their numbers were increasing down to at least 1640.

VII

Little but uncertainty emerges from these desultory investigations; nothing to disturb the general proportions of Dr. Thompson's picture, though perhaps the perspective has been lengthened so that it is conceivable that 15–20 per cent of the land was held by greater lay landowners before the Reformation. Admittedly this does conflict with Dr. Thompson's assumption that in the mid-sixteenth century great estates were 'of the order of 10 per cent',[100] since it is difficult to believe that the generation after 1524 saw a marked decline in the proportion of land in great lay estates. However, Dr. Thompson's conclusion seems to arise from his other assumption that the peers 'remained a substantial majority of the great landowners as a whole', and we have seen that there is considerable reason to doubt this, especially for the first half of the sixteenth century. There is some reason to think that the peerage was not 'a majority of great landowners' in 1436, probably not in 1523 and 1559, unless the definition of a great landowner is put so high as to exclude a majority of the peers themselves. By 1641 the peers may have been nearer to forming such a majority, but they may still not have formed an actual majority of greater landowners. If these suggestions are true, they seriously weaken the significance which Professor Stone wishes to attach to his view that the peerage did not constitute a majority of the greater landowners in 1601. For his claim that this was a unique state of affairs, is one of his general arguments in support of his thesis that there was an acute structural crisis afflicting the peerage at the end of the sixteenth century.

If we accept the hypothesis that the share of greater landowners was very roughly constant from the later Middle Ages to 1700, this does not necessarily mean that the composition of this élite remained the same. For example, the share held by great magnates may have been greater in 1436 than around 1600. Our guesses, in so far as they highlight our areas of greatest ignorance, may help to define problems and priorities for investigation. If the greatest and most significant amount of social and economic change was among the smallest landowners, their numbers rising with the inflation of agricultural prices and falling when these prices stagnated, the ultimate result, as Dr. Thompson remarks, was the emergence of large tenant farmers with appreciable amounts of working capital. The early history of this process remains obscure. In the seventeenth century it may have been mainly at the expense of more or less customary tenures, while there may also have been a growth in the number of substantial freeholders and a decline in the number of lesser ones. The most extreme example of the opposite evolution is the development of *mezzadria* in central Italy where the tenant came to own less and less stock, while an increasing share of the working capital was provided by the landlord; yet in England in the fifteenth century stock and land leases had been common on great ecclesiastical estates. An important question is how far the leasing of demesne in the later Middle Ages led to parcellation and the lasting creation of smallholdings. On many ecclesiastical estates large leasehold farms certainly existed in the early sixteenth century, quite apart from those created more recently in some areas for large-scale pastoral farming. It is possible, though disputable, to claim that in some general sense in France 'les structures rurales n'ont guère subi de transformations' between the late thirteenth and the eighteenth century. There was some basic continuity which produced broadly similar responses to alternating periods of prosperity and depression.[101] If such a conception does apply to any area of France, it certainly does not apply to England. New structures emerged in English villages in the fourteenth and fifteenth centuries and probably in the seventeenth century, when in the second half of that century substantial changes in the use and cropping of land, in marketing, and in production were continuing.

The fact that there were massive transfers of land from the Church and the Crown perhaps provides the temptation to think in crude Harringtonian terms. These imply a picture of long-term changes in which some small homogeneous group was replaced as owners of the major part of the land by some other group with different social or economic characteristics. But if no distinctive social or economic group in either contemporary or later terminology owned a predominant share of the land, or even as much as half of it, such a picture becomes a mirage. England was not Bohemia, where, after and possibly even before the White Mountain, a comparatively tiny nobility did own a high proportion of the land. Some more complex process of change within and between groups must be envisaged.

However this may be, it is surely clear that we urgently need more reliable estimates of the numbers in social groups in the sixteenth and seventeenth centuries.[102] Even if we had these, reliable estimates of the social distribution of wealth might still elude us, but without the first, effective economic, social, and political analysis will be frustrated. The studies of Professor Hoskins and Dr. Cornwall in the lay subsidies hold out hope that substantial advances in our knowledge will soon be achieved for the early sixteenth century. While for the later seventeenth century, if we had more studies of the excellence and thoroughness of those by Mr. Styles,[103] we should be able to discriminate more effectively between the bewildering variety of alternatives offered by Gregory King.

APPENDIX I

Extracts from Gregory King's Notebook

Suppose England to contain 30,000,000 of Acres[1] [*39 million*][2] And the Rents thereof 8,000,000 of Pounds [*10 million*] Then one acre with another is worth about 5s per acre. [*6s. 2d.*]

The 30 Millions of Acres may be thus apportioned

	acres		
Arable[2]	9,000,000	at 3s. 4d. *p*[3] acre	1,500,000[li]
	[*11*]	[*5s. 10d.*]	
Pasture[4]	13,000,000	at 6s. *p* acre[5]	3,900,000
Meadow for Hay	4,000,000	at 10s. *p* acre	2,000,000
Heaths and Barren	3,000,000	at 2s. *p* acre	300,000
grounds	[*10*]	[*1s.*]	
Roads Rivers	1,000,000[6]	at 6d. *p* acre	25,000
and Lakes	30,000,000[7]		7,725,000

		acres		
at 3s. 4d. *p* acre	The Crown Lands	3,000,000[8]	[?]	300,000[li]
at [?] 4s. *p*[9] acre	150 [*160*] Temporal Lords at			
	2000[l] *p* ann each [*2800*]	1,500,000		300,000
5s. *p* acre	26 Spiritual Lords at 1200[L]	124,800		31,200
	[*£1300*] *p* ann			
	4000 Dean and Chapters Lands			
	Colleges and Corporations	400,000		100,000
5s. *p* acre	10,000[10] Gleab Lands of the Clergy	80,000		20,000
5s. *p* acre	1,400 [*800*] Baronets and [*600*]			
	Knights at 600[l] *p* ann[11]	3,360,000		840,000

5s. p acre	4,000 [*3,000*] Esquires at 300[L]		
	[*£450*] *p* ann	4,800,000	1,200,000
5s. 6d. per acre	12,000 [*12,000*] Gentlemen		
	at 100[l] per ann [*280*]	4,363,636	1,200,000
6s.[12] per acre	40,000 [*40,000*] Freeholders at		
	50[l] per ann or upwards [84]	6,666,666	2,000,000
6s. per acre	400,000 [*140,000*] at 5[l] per ann		
	or under 50[l] per ann [50][13]	6,666,666	2,000,000
		30,561,768 [sic]	7,991,200

Acres	of the Arable land
1,000,000	Wheat at 20 bushels per acre . . .[14]
2,500,000[15]	Rye at 20 bushels per acre . . .
1,500,000	Oats at 15 bushels per acre . . .
2,000,000	Barley at 16 bushels per acre . . .[16]
1,000,000	Peas and Beans at 10 bushels per acre . . .
2,000,000	Fallow
9,000,000[17][sic]	

Pasture land may winter Summer each acre 1[18] Beeve besides Calves and 5 sheep besides lambs to another acre Which would make the Stock of Cattle to be 6,000,000 of Beeves, Whereof 3 millions consumed annually and 30,000,000 of muttons whereof 15 million consumed. . . . This quality will answer to 7 oz and $\frac{1}{2}$ of Mutton and Beef together including swines flesh and Goats flesh for each Head per diem for 2 millions of People[19] which is not much above what may reasonably be allowed. So the Pasture ground at 13,000,000 of Acres seems a good Computation or at least not much over.

Hay ground

Pasture 3,000,000 of acres at 1 Load per acre—	3,000,000
Loads at 20 C per load 60,000,000 C worth	1,000,000[l][20]
Meadow 4,000,000 of acres at 2 Load per acre—	8,000,000
—at 20[C] per Load 160,000,000[cwt]—	3,000,000[l]

Which for near 4 millions of Cattle is 3 Load per Head per ann. or 55 or 60[C].

And allowing 2[C] per week for each Head, in a maintenance for 30 weeks and the other 22 weeks to be allowed for grazing.

[Estimates of the total consumption of food-stuffs which follow are very much higher than those in *Two Tracts* pp. 37–40.[21]]

Which for 6 millions of People is 4[l] per head per ann.

Whereof the Dyet for 1,000,000 of Infants or children at 20[s]	1,000,000
3 Of 2 millions of Paupers and Day Labourers at 40[s] per ann.[22]	4,000,000
1 Of 2 millions of Farmers and Freeholders at 5[l]	10,000,000[20]
Of $\frac{1}{2}$ million of Tradesmen at 6[l] per ann	3,000,000
Of 400,000 Freeholders of 50[l] per ann or upwards at 6[l]	2,400,000
Of 150,000 or 250,000 Retainers to Noblemen and Gentlemen at 8[l]	1,400,000
[or]	1,600,000
Of 100,000 Noblemen and Gentlemen and their Children at 20[l][23]	2,800,000
	22,600,000 [sic]
wch wants 2 or 3 million[24]	24,000,000

So the Expenses of the Nation are

Dyet	24,000,000
Cloaths	24,000,000
Incident Charges and Expenses.	12,000,000
	60,000,000

So that if the Rents are 12 millions The Product of the Land is five times as much. So the greatest Taxes are to be raised upon the Product of the Land and of Trades Employments and Offices and not upon the Rents.

Families			
	200	Lords Spiritual and Temporal	at 40 per Family
	1,500	Knights and Baronets	at 24 per Family
	3,000	[or] 3,800 Esquires	at 16 per Family [*10*]
	15,000	Gentlemen	at 10 per Family [*8*]
	80,000	Freeholders at 50[1] per ann	at 8 per Family [*7*]
	200,000[25]	Freeholders at 10[1] per ann	at 6 per Family [*5*]
	400,000[26]	Farmers	at 5 per Family [*5*]
	100,000	Cotagers and day labourers and paupers	at 4 per Family[27]
	300,000	Tradesmen and professions	at 5 per Family[28]
	1,100,000	[sic] [*1,360,586*]	

NOTES

[1] Acreage is just under 32·5 million.

[2] Figures in square brackets and italics are from *Naturall and Political Observations . . .*; unless otherwise stated they refer to England and Wales.

[2A] The 'Kashnor' MS. of the *Observations* in the National Library of Australia, Canberra, shows that in 1697 in reply to criticisms by Robert Harley, King reduced his estimate of the arable to 9 million acres and the rent per acre to 5s. 6d. He also reduced the rent of meadow and pasture to 8s. 6d. and increased his estimate of the yield of grain 'I agree the seed corn in general to be about one seventh of the Produce.' I am indebted to the Librarian of the National Library for kindly providing a microfilm of this document.

[3] 4s struck out.

[4] '10,000,000 acres Grazing 3,000,000 acres Hay.'

[5] [*Pasture and Meadow 10 million at 9s an acre.*]

[6] [*Rivers, Lakes 500,000 acres at 2s.; Roads and Waste Land 500,000 acres.*]

[7] The journal (p. 169) gives the following acreages for 1695: Arable 9 million, 'Pasture and Profitable Land' 19 million, 'Woods and Waste' 11 million.

[8] If the number of acres is correct, the rent should be £500,000. It is difficult to believe that King could have meant this, so perhaps the number of acres should be 1,800,000.

[9] This is probably a slip for 5s. in view of the figure for the clergy.

[10] [*8000 clergymen.*]

[11] [*Baronets' income £880, knights' £600.*]

[12] Possibly originally 6s. 8d.

[13] The original total reading 32,864,800 has been struck out. The acreages for the baronets, esquires, gentlemen, and both sorts of freeholders were all apparently altered to achieve the new total.

[14] [*12 million bushels, exclusive of seed corn, and quarter or a fifth of the produce.*]

[15] The first figure seems to have been altered, perhaps in error for the one above.

[16] [*25 million net.*] This is the only instance where both estimates agree.

[17] P.R.O. T64/302, fo. 14, Crown Copyright.

[18] Originally 2.

[19] [*2·7 million eat flesh constantly average 6⅔ oz. per head per day, p. 38.*]

[20] The first figure is not clearly legible.

[21] e.g. 3 million beeves and calves against 800,000; sheep and lambs 11 million and 3·2 million; swine 6 million and 3·2 million; only the 24 millions of bushels of malt are the same.

[22] The figures in the margin are interesting examples of King's uncertainty about the number of paupers.

[23] 50,000 has been crossed out.

[24] The last two figures were increased in order to reach the required total of £24 million. The adjustments have not been completed successfully in the estimate of retainers. The expense of Noblemen and gentlemen was originally a figure less than £20, probably £16.

[25] The first figure was altered to what looks like 2.

[26] The first figure is not clearly legible, it could be a 5.

[27] [*Labouring People and outservants 3¼; paupers and cottagers 3¼.*]

[28] P.R.O. T64/302, fos. 18, 18v, Crown Copyright.

APPENDIX II

Journal pp. 280–1, figures in [] from p. 74

That the Lords Spiritual and Temporal and Peers of Scotland
and Ireland commonly residing in England are about 200
their eldest and younger Sons of all ages „ „ 160
Baronets of this Kingdom „ „ 780
Knights of this Kingdom „ „ 620
Sargeants at Law and Deans of Cathedral and Collegiate „ „
Churches „ „ 70
Esquires and reputed Esquires including such as are or have been
Parliament men, Sheriffs of counties, Justices of Peace, Deputy
Lieutenants, Mayors and Sheriffs of London and some of the
principal Cities, Commission Officers, Barristers at Law etc. „ „ 3,500
or 3,000
Gentlemen or reputed Gentlemen paying as such[1] „ „ 20,000
[12,000] or 13,000
Cannons and Prebendaries are about 400
the Clergy of England charged as Gentlemen or having a living
of 50[1] or 60[1] p.a. „ „ 2,000
the Dissenting Ministers and Teachers „ „ 500
the Widows of all Degrees and qualities and the Widows of
100[1] p.a. or 1000[1] personal estate [1200] „ „ 3,000
the Drs of Divinity Law and Physick „ „ 400
the Double Beneficed clergymen of 120[1] p.a. „ „ 200
merchants of London living in or within 10 miles of London
and not free of London „ „ 60
Tradesmen Shopkeepers and Vintners worth 300[1] „ „ 10,000
Merchants, Tradesmen or Artificers living in a house of 30[1] p.a.
in London or within 20 miles of London „ „ 10,000
whereof the merchants and brokers to merchants are about
500 [400]
. . . [2]the Merchants Strangers 60
Merchants Jews 30
Jews Brokers 8
Jews of 16 years old 250
rather
. . . [3]the Servants having about 3[1] p.a. or upwards 150,000 200,000
the Servants having under 3[1] p.a. 350,000 400,000
[4]the Cursiters, Philazers, Attorneys, Solicitors, Clerks in
Chancery, or Exchequer, or other Courts in Law or Equity,
Scriveners, Chancellors, Commissaries, Advocates, Proctors,
publick notaries and other officers are about 2,000
unmarried women worth 1000[1]   are about [500] 1,000
the persons finding a horse to the Militia   are about 4,000
the persons keeping a Coach, Chariot or Calash not finding
a Horse are about 2000 or one moiety of the Coaches
the persons keeping Hackney and Stage Coaches are about 1,500
the Gentlemen of 300[1] and 16 years of age and not taking the
Oaths are about 300

the Men and Women in the Kingdom who receive Alms [700,000]	800,	750,	700,000
their children under 16 are [300,000]	500, 540,	440,	300,000
poor Housekeeping Men and Women not paying to Church and Poor [740,000]		700, 650,	700,000
their children under 16 [460,000]		500	450,000
the Day Labourers and their Wives are about 400,000 and their children under 16 [250,000 + 150,000 Servants in Husbandry]		300	250,000
Servants in Husbandry and their wives are about 300,000 and their children under 16		160,	150,000
the Parents who have 4 Children or more and are not worth 50[1] are about 150,000 [200,000] and their children under 16			150,000

3,900,000 2,850,000
3,060,000 2,700,000
[sic]

That those 3,060,000 Poor People usually exempt from Taxes in all Polls are equal to the Inhabitants of 860,000 houses at above 3½ to a House.

and that the remaining 2,400,000, 2,340,000 upon whom the Poll Tax is raised are equal to the Inhabitants of 540,000 450,000 Houses at 5½ to a House[5]

So that in Round Numbers the Insolvent Persons in a Poll Tax where the non-Contributors to Church and Poor are Exempted as well as their Children under 16 are 3 millions or 2,850,000 and the Solvent are 2,400,000 or 2,550,000

NOTES

[1] In the margin 'That the Gentlemen and those who are above Gentlemen and under a peer having 300[1] p.a. or upwards are about 6000 [3500].'

[2] 'Stock of East India, Guinea, and Hudson Bay is now but £600,000; Shares in the New River, Thames, Hide Park and Marybone Waters and King's Printing House about 10,000.'

[3] Persons taxed for personal estate not taxed for above £2 million; profits of offices, places, and public employments taxed for about £80,000; pensions and annuities out the king's revenue for £30,000; the article judges and judicial officers in 1 Wm. and Mary for £30,000.

[4] In the margin.

[5] Margin '2,850,000 Insolvent, 805,000 houses at 3½ per House; 2,550,000 Solvent, 485,000 houses at 5¼ per House; Houses insolvent 800,000, solvent 500,000.'

These estimates are related to those on pp. 74–5 of the Journal and all give higher figures for those receiving alms and not paying rates than in *Two Tracts*, p. 42. They show that these are attempts to relate the estimates of population and social groups to the quarterly poll tax of 1691, knowing only its total yield and assuming (p. 74) that 150,000 were omitted by neglect and that the yield of the special rates on various groups was £122,700, which was too high for the estimates of those excused or paying at ordinary rates.

POSTSCRIPT

Table 1 was presented as 'shaky and inconsistent approximations' and Mr. R. B. Pugh has recently shown[104] that the 1436 tax returns, besides seriously underestimating the landed income of the peerage, overestimated that of some commoners, because they taxed fees and annuities granted for life. The income of the 183 'greater knights' came partly from such annuities which were mainly[105] transfers of landed income from other greater landowners (mostly peers) which were deductable from their taxable incomes.[106] The figure for the greater landowners retains its validity as a minimum estimate; though the proportions held by those with under £100 per annum might be affected, the indicated margins of error were already wide enough.

For the sixteenth century Dr. Leonard has produced estimates of the numbers of knights which completely supersede mine. His totals are 1500, 225–300; 1523, 336; 1550, 539; 1577, 247; 1600, 330 (including Essex's knights).[107] The estimate of knights in 1523 on p. 110 is clearly too small, though 200 for those who were greater landowners may not be. Henry VIII had dubbed many knights for his wars, many of whom might well have been less wealthy.[108] Nevertheless the estimate of landed wealth may not be too low.[109] There was another increase in military knights in the 1540s[110] and the total around 1560 would have been smaller than that in 1550. The higher figure on p. 110 of 350 knights as greater landowners now seems the more likely. Dr. Leonard's researches confirm Spelman's estimate for 1601 and demolish Wilson's (pp. 112–13).

What may be King's last notes on the distribution of land should have been considered.[111] In 1697 he reduced the freeholders to 140,000 each averaging 50 acres of arable (5/9 of the total);[112] '100,000 freeholders and farmers using their own teams' averaged 75 acres, while '60,000 freeholders and farmers hiring their teams' averaged 25 acres each. Taking his original estimate of 150,000 farmers, this would leave 130,000 freeholders and farmers and 10 million acres of meadow and pasture. If we give the 160,000 arable farmers 3 million acres of pasture, this leaves the 130,000 with an average of 54 acres. Returning to the 140,000 freeholders, if they had 2 million acres of pasture, this would give them a quarter of 28 million productive acres. The estimate on p. 114 that 180,000 freeholders had 12.5 million acres is too high;[113] while, if there were only 140,000, the revised valuations would give them 30 per cent of the productive acres.[114] Thus the estimate of 25–30 per cent on p. 118 is compatible with King's last thoughts.

So far as more general interpretations are concerned, the most stimulating one has again come from Professor Thompson. He read the article as implying 'a conjuring trick on the monastic and crown lands which seem to have disappeared without leaving a trace' and a lack of 'any pronounced shifts in the overall structure in the seventeenth century which could then be construed as imparting momentum to the economy.[115] My silence about the former was not meant to deny them any significance. For what little it is worth my guess is that the peerage owned less land in 1523 than in 1436, while by 1560 they had more than in 1523, partly as a result of dispersal by the Crown. This also encouraged much smaller landowners to round off holdings and stimulated the land market without completely dominating it in the only county so far studied fully.[116]

As for the seventeenth century there are changes which would have affected the economic functioning of landownership. Apart from stagnating prices interacting with agrarian improvements after 1650 to encourage more market conscious farming, Mr. Habakkuk has argued that a true market for land and mortgages, as against one ruled by conventional rates, was emerging from about 1620 and was established by the 1660s.[117] It has also been argued that demographic and other factors favoured the growth of large estates and decline of small ones from about 1670.[118] King's last notes seem to suggest fewer lesser freeholders with smaller holdings than his *Political Observations*, but they do reaffirm his belief in the existence of large numbers of freeholders with around 100 acres each. These latter may already have existed in 1601, as Wilson implies, but I suspect their numbers increased in the seventeenth century.

What is distinctive about England is not the existence of large farms, or their increase in the seventeenth century; both phenomena can be found in France.[119] Small landowners may well have *owned* as high a proportion of the land as in many parts of France, but the rural structures were different.[120] In terms of farming and ownership Bavarian agriculture was much more completely dominated by peasants than France.[121] A crucial difference between England and both countries was the relative unimportance of income from seigneurial rights. Faced with difficult times from the mid-seventeenth century or earlier, some French landowners, from both old and new families, could maintain or even increase seigneurial incomes.[122] They could and often did reduce peasant property rights, while preserving peasant social and agrarian structures and to some extent protecting them from the full impact of market forces.

NOTES

[1] F. M. L. Thompson, 'The Social Distribution of Landed Property in England since the Sixteenth Century', *Econ. Hist. Rev.*, 2nd series, 19 (1966), 505–17.

[2] H. L. Gray, 'Incomes from Land in England in 1436', *Eng. Hist. Rev.* 49 (1934), 609–39.

[3] Pugh and Ross in 'The English Baronage and the Income Tax of 1436', *Bull. Inst. Hist. Res.* 26 (1953), 1–28, have shown that Prof. Gray left out some peers altogether, as well as a considerable number of dowagers, while some of the incomes assessed are demonstrably too small. The tax did not include income from Wales and the Marches which provided a larger part of the income of some peers.

[4] Ten of these were estimated to be over £400 (average £557), the remainder under £400, ibid., pp. 620–1.

[5] Ibid., p. 630.

[6] *A History of Agriculture and Prices in England* (Oxford, 1866–1902), iv. 128.

[7] R. H. Hilton in *V.C.H. Leics.* ii. 183–4: *The Economic Development of some Leicestershire Estates in the Fourteenth and Fifteenth Centuries* (1947), pp. 157–8.

[8] 3,100,000 and 3,700,000 acres respectively. Allowance for the understatement of the peers' income would make even the higher figure a minimum.

[9] G. E. Mingay, *English Landed Society in the Eighteenth Century* (1963), p. 19. F. M. L. Thompson, *English Landed Society in the Nineteenth Century* (1963), pp. 28–9, puts great estates as those of 10,000 acres and over in the late nineteenth century.

[10] Thompson, 'The Social Distribution of Landed Property . . .', p. 509; 1601 'one million acres . . . can be taken as a full 5 per cent of the cultivated acreage'; 1641 'not far short of three million acres, or from 10 to 15 per cent of the cultivated area', 'four and a half million acres, or from 15 to 20 per cent' (i.e. 21, 22·5, or 30 million acres).

[11] *Cambridge Economic History of Europe* (2nd ed. 1966), i. 587–9.

[12] Each had 10,000 marks; Pugh and Ross, op. cit., p. 4 and *Rot. Parl.* iv. 186–9.

[13] J. L. Kirby, 'Lord Cromwell's Estimates of 1433', *Bull. Inst. Hist. Res.*, 24 (1951), 132.

[14] R. Somerville, *Duchy of Lancaster* (1953), pp. 188, 238, gives gross values of £13,000 for 1419 and £10,000–£12,500 around 1460.

[15] Kirby, op. cit., p. 137 n. 2, the tenth realized £15,000, 1413–16. W. E. Lunt, *Financial Relations of the Papacy with England 1327–1534* (Cambridge, Mass., 1962), pp. 82, 112, shows that the yield of a tenth in 1330–3 was £17,700 and in 1376 £18,000.

[16] A. Savine, *English Monasteries on the Eve of the Dissolution* (Oxford Studies in Social and Legal History, i, 1909), 77–86, 165.

[17] Ibid., pp. 140, 156, 165.

[18] Ibid., pp. 171, 173.

[19] Ibid., p. 77 n. 2, gives £32,000 for 1535.

[20] Ibid., p. 101, while the monasteries paid about half the tenth.

[21] Taking only one-third of the total income as spiritual would give 4·8 million acres at 8*d.* in 1535.

[22] J. Cornwall, 'The Early Tudor Gentry', *Econ. Hist. Rev.* 2nd series, 17 (1965), 462–3.

[23] J. Cornwall, 'The People of Rutland in 1522', *Trans. Leic. Arch. Soc.*, 37 (1961–2), 26 n. 9.

[24] At 7·7 pence the acreages would be 5,600 and 6,200 respectively.

[25] T. Wilson, *The State of England Anno Dom. 1600*, ed. F. J. Fisher, *Camden Miscellany*, 16 (1936), 23.

[26] S. L. Thrupp, *The Merchant Class of Medieval London* (Chicago, 1948), p. 276; L. Stone, *The Crisis of the Aristocracy 1558–1641* (Oxford, 1965), p. 71. Prof. Thrupp's acceptance of the figures is more qualified than Prof. Stone's.

[27] J. C. Wedgwood, *History of Parliament 1439–1509, Register* (1936), p. lxxxvii. The returns of 1434 are for commissions to take oaths against maintaining peace-breakers (*Cal. Patent Rolls 1429–1436*, pp. 370–413). In fact these give some 163 knights and cover 29 counties. The commissions of the peace 1429–36 (ibid., pp. 613–40) give some 130 names for 36 counties. Together, the two give about 180–90 knights. Allowing for absences in France, 250 may be a reasonable guess. No reasons or evidence are given for the estimate of 1491.

[28] Helen Miller, 'Subsidy Assessments of the Peerage in the Sixteenth Century', *Bull. Inst. Hist. Res.*, 28 (1955), 18–20, shows that the incomplete returns of the subsidy of 1523 give an average landed income of £801. This average may be too low; in 1534 it was £921, when seven were assessed on goods, so that this average may also be too low. Miss Miller considers that the numbers of the early Tudor peerage fluctuated around 50, ibid., 24 (1950), 80.

[29] Stone, op. cit., p. 71.

[30] W. A. Shaw, *The Knights of England* (1906), ii, 48–70, gives 60 creations for 1530–7 and 170 for 1538–45. T. H. Hollingsworth, *The Demography of the British Peerage* (Supplement to *Population Studies*, 18 no. 2), p. 66, Table 51, shows that in the second half of the sixteenth century half of the males alive at 15 were dead 35 years later; ibid., p. 60, Table 46, gives the mortality of the age group 25–40 as 700 per 1,000.

[31] A. Hassall Smith, 'The Personnel of the Commissions of the Peace 1554–64', *Huntington Library Quarterly*, 22 (1958–9), 301–12. This studies Norfolk, Sussex, and Northants. *A Collection of Original Letters from the Bishops to the Privy Council 1564*, ed. M. Bateson, *Camden Miscellany*, ix (1893), gives the names of some dozen knights apparently not in the commissions.

[32] *Econ. Hist. Rev.* 2nd series, 19 (1966), 509.

[33] Stone, op. cit., pp. 57, 59.

[34] It could be argued that the discrepancies are even greater, since 22 out of 121 peers in 1641 had gross rentals below £1,094, averaging £772 (Stone, p. 761); adding something for casualties, this would come to £900, which at 4*s.* 6*d.* an acre represents 4,000 acres, well below the minimum of 5,000 acres proposed by Dr. Mingay. This would reduce the number of great landowners in 1641 to about 140.

[35] Stone, op. cit., pp. 57, 761–2.

[36] In *English Landed Society in the Nineteenth Century* (1963), pp. 28–33, Dr. Thompson clearly defines great estates as those over 10,000 acres, but it is not clear whether this is the measure used in his article.

[37] This figure comes from a count of the estates listed in J. Bateman, *The Great Landowners of Great Britain* (1883); about half a dozen more had over 19,000 acres.

[38] Thompson, 'Social Distribution . . .', p. 508.

[39] Stone, op. cit., p. 74.

[40] T. Wilson, op. cit., p. 23.

[41] W. A. Shaw, op. cit., ii. 80–98; the number knighted from 1575 to 1600 was 660, the number of peers, etc. 89, leaving 405, after excluding Essex's knights. Including Essex's knights, but excluding peers, etc., the numbers knighted from 1580 to 1600 were 460, and from 1575 to 1600, 550.

[42] *The English Works of Sir Henry Spelman Kt. . . . Together with his Posthumous Works* (1723), p. 179, is comparing the creations of Elizabeth and James, so he might be thought to be excluding those of Essex. He explicitly refers to England only. From 1580 to Elizabeth's death 340 knights, excluding Essex's, peers, Irishmen, and foreigners, had been made. From 1575 the total is 430.

[43] Stone, op. cit. p. 74n. 1.

[44] See T. G. Barnes and A. Hassall-Smith, 'Justices of the Peace from 1558 to 1688—a revised list of sources', *Bull. Inst. Hist. Res.*, 32 (1959), 238.

[45] T. Wilson, op. cit., p. 23. This, with the 500 knights alleged to be on the commissions, gives 1,900. The *Libri* for 1595 and 1596 contain some 2,100 names for England and Wales, including those of peers and of perhaps 50 clergy and civilians. The 1595 book gives 1,800 to 1,900 names for England, excluding Lancashire. These totals do not allow for recurrence of names in more than one commission.

[46] T. Wilson, op. cit., p. 19.

[47] *Miscellanies, relating to Lancashire and Cheshire*, i, Lancs. and Cheshire Record Society, 12 (1885), 229–51. In 1695, out of a total of 763, 101 were yeomen or unstyled; Lancashire County Record Office, DDK/1740/2.

[48] I am indebted to Dr. R. M. Jeffs of Sheffield University for these statistics. Suffolk had the highest total

of almost 1,200, Oxford the lowest at 130; the other counties were Essex, Bedford, Berkshire, Hereford, Nottingham all for 1561–2, and Cheshire for 1580.

[49] The other counties are Yorkshire, Lincolnshire, and Northamptonshire, where the lists are incomplete and the total has been estimated. Totals for Leicestershire and Somerset for 1630 and 1647 have been used.

[50] Making the same assumptions, but taking the first eight counties, would give an average of 2,000 each to the remaining ones, which still seems too high.

[51] T. Wilson, op. cit., p. 19.

[52] *Essays in Leicestershire History* (Liverpool, 1950), p. 145. Of 161 husbandmen's and yeomen's inventories 1638–42, 11 were over £300 and 21 £200–300, Prof. Hoskins found the average yeoman had a personal estate of £176 10s 0d., *Provincial England* (1963), pp. 154–5.

[53] J. Thirsk, *English Peasant Farming* (1957), pp. 75, 84, 96, 134. The larger Laxton leasehold farms were 60–70 acres or more. C. S. Orwin, *The Open Fields* (1938), pp. 137–9, 294–5, 302.

[54] G. H. Kenyon, 'The Kirdford Inventories, 1611–1776', *Sussex Archaeological Collections*, 93 (1955), 94. This was 'about 50 acres of arable, 45 acres of meadow or pasture, and the remainder woodland and furze'. The stock included six oxen and four horses, but the average farm stock was £123, ibid., p. 102.

[55] This is based on 20 yeomen's inventories before 1700 in F. W. Steer, *Farm and Cottage Inventories of Mid-Essex 1635–1749* (Colchester, 1950). The average was 55 and the average value of the inventories £355. In Devon 21 yeomen's inventories of the seventeenth century, mostly before 1660, give an average value of £333, or £255 after deducting the value of leases, *Devonshire Inventories of the Sixteenth and Seventeenth Centuries*, ed. M. Cash (Devon and Cornwall Record Society, n.s. 11, 1966).

[56] M. A. Havinden (ed), *Household and Farm Inventories in Oxfordshire 1550–1590*, Oxfordshire Record Society 44 (1965), 37, Table 9. The largest and four smallest farms in the table were excluded, leaving ten farms with an average of 38 sown acres.

[57] P. A. Kennedy, *Nottinghamshire Household Inventories,* Thoroton Society, Record Series 22 (1963), 33, 34, 39, 44, 47, 49, 50, 98, 116. Five inventories give an average of 29 sown acres, another five average, including fallow and some meadow, 61 acres. It is perhaps worth noticing that John Smyth of Nibley considered that a yardland in the richer soils of Berkeley Hundred consisted of 40 acres and rather more in the wolds. *The Berkeley Manuscripts. A Description of the Hundred of Berkeley*, iii (Gloucester, 1885), 2.

[58] Sir George Clark, *The Wealth of England 1496–1760* (1946), p. 194, considers that they are estimates for 1688 and 1696 respectively. But the second figure appears in King's own tract, *Two Tracts*, ed. G. E. Barnett (Baltimore, 1936), p. 31, as belonging to 1688, while the first was published by Davenant in 1699 and ascribed to 1688, *Political and Commercial Works*, ed. C. Whitworth (1771), ii, 184; possibly this, like the higher income of the peerage, represents Davenant's opinion.

[59] J. H. Plumb, *The Growth of Political Stability in England 1675–1725* (1967), p. 29, puts the total electorate at 200,000 as a minimum. Sir Lewis Namier, *The Structure of Politics at the Accession of George II* (1957), p. 81, put the borough electorate at 85,000. It was presumably smaller in the 1690s.

[60] *Two Tracts*, p. 35.

[61] In the 'Kashnor' MS in the National Library of Australia, Canberra, King revised these estimates to three and three-quarters the rent for the produce of arable and two and one-fifth for pasture. This would suggest an income nearer three times the rental value and a holding of about 90 acres.

[62] PRO, T64/302, 6,666,666 acres were attributed to them. This was a calculation for England only, assuming that it had 30 million rentable acres.

[63] On the revised estimate, the holding would be nearer 50 acres.

[64] *Two Tracts*, p. 35; King overestimated the area of England and Wales, putting it at 39 million acres. On the other hand he thought there were 10 million acres of 'Heaths Moors Mountains and barren Land', though he valued them at 1s. an acre. There were also a million acres of waste, roads, rivers, and lakes, leaving 27–8 million acres of more productive land.

[65] 'La disparition du paysan anglais', *Annales*, 20e année, no. 4 (1965), 654–5.

[66] I owe the first two figures to Dr. R. M. Jeffs. The poll book of 1698 is in B. M. Harley 6846, fos. 306–40, and gives 1,778 'persons that polled'. Thoroton Society Record Series 18, *Poll Books of Nottinghamshire, 1710*, by counting voters in the county book.

[67] I am again indebted to Dr. R. M. Jeffs for this.

[68] C. Wilson, *England's Apprenticeship 1603–1763* (1965), pp. 153, 250–3.

[69] W. G. Hoskins, *Provincial England* (1963), pp. 165–9, believes that this conclusion based on study of Leicestershire 'will almost certainly be found to be true of the greater part of the clayey Midland plain . . . from the Trent down to the Chiltern hills'. His study of Wigston shows the emergence of half a dozen families of 'present gentry' in the later seventeenth century with holdings of up to 200 acres, *The Midland Peasant* (1957), pp. 198–9, 203–4, 213–14.

[70] E. L. Jones, 'Agricultural Change in England 1660–1750', *Jour. Econ. Hist.*, 25 (1965), 8–9, 14; H. J. Habakkuk, 'English Landownership 1680–1740', *Econ. Hist. Rev.* 1st series, 10 (1939–40), 15–16, gives examples of the decline of freeholders before 1720 in Northamptonshire and Bedfordshire. E. Kerridge, 'Agriculture 1500–1793', *V.C.H. Wiltshire*, iv (1959), 58–9, finds a decline in the number of family farms and owner-occupiers in the corn and sheep areas and growth in their numbers in the cheese areas, especially after about 1650. Mrs. M. Spufford, *A Cambridgeshire Community: Chippenham from Settlement to Enclosure* (Leicester, 1965), pp. 37–53, shows that the number of free and copyholders declined from 1470

to 1636 and later, while the size of farms grew. By about 1660, yeomen farmers had virtually eliminated smallholders with under 50 acres; by 1712 nearly two-thirds of the land was in three farms, all over 240 acres, and most of the rest in four farms of about 100 acres each, although the common fields were not enclosed until 1780.

[71] *The Disappearance of the Small Landowner* (1909), p. 135.

[72] Rymer, *Foedera*, xviii, 278; *Miscellanies relating to Lancashire and Cheshire*, i, Lancs. and Cheshire Record Soc., 12(1885), 200–1. Those charged with three pounds or less in the subsidies were to be at the minimum rate, those with over three pounds at three and a half times the amount charged.

[73] Lancs. and Cheshire Record Soc. *Miscellanies*, i. 203–23; Yorks. Archaeological Soc., Record Series, lxi, *Miscellanea*, i (1920), 88–107; William Salt Soc., *Historical Collections for a History of Staffordshire*, ii, pt 2 (1881), 13 ff. Bodleian, MS. Carte 78, fos. 95–6, 99; PRO. E 178/5614. The return for Suffolk E178/7356 is too damaged for comparison to be made. The rest suggest that omissions of those who refused or compounded later are under 5 per cent of the total in the auditor's book, E 407/35.

[74] This clearly took place in the Suffolk entries and to a less striking extent for Leicestershire, Yorkshire, and Somerset. Wiltshire, Lincolnshire, and Cornwall are examples of entries where the great majority of names are unstyled.

[75] B. M. Harley 3796, fo. 36; of this £49,844 8s. 4d. was from 'particular compositions', the rest from collectors, fo. 22.

[76] The total recorded in the book was about £96,000; the average omits three counties where the totals are unclear.

[77] The original intention, as the instructions show, was for the peers to compound separately. If this took place, it would mean that the composition omitted from the book were larger than average, the more so as London was omitted. The considerable amount of the particular compositions also suggests this.

[78] Freeholders' books give some 3,600 freeholders, excluding knights and above, the book of compositions some 1,050 names. If all those styled yeoman, gentleman, and esquire in the Gloucestershire musters of 1608 were freeholders, this gives 1,350; if only half the yeomen were, there would have been 890, as against 163 compounders. The most striking case is Lancashire, where there were 662 names in the 1600 freeholders' book, all except nine styled gentlemen or above; while 282 compounded. Mr. J. S. Morrill of Trinity College, Oxford, has made a careful investigation of the Cheshire gentry. He has kindly sent me his finding that most of those not in the lists of compounders were either too poor or were wards; some 14 might have been eligible, but were not included. This gives a rate of omission of under 10 per cent. Like Lancashire, Cheshire had no compounders below the rank of gentleman, apart from some aldermen of Chester.

[79] G. E. Aylmer, *The King's Servants* (1961), pp. 327–9, Tables 32 and 33.

[80] *Angliae Notitia* (1669), p. 454; ed. 1670, pp. 436–7; ed. 1692. p. 236; ed. 1700, p. 285; ed. 1702, p. 292.

[81] Ed. 1700, p. 36, put the rents of the land in England and Wales at £8 million and of houses at £4 million; in 1702, p. 36, these are changed to £10 million and £2 million, with acknowledgement to King.

[82] £6,030 and £5,200; Stone, op. cit., p. 762.

[83] p. 36 rents £10 million, 'houses (not let with lands)' £2 million, 'all other Hereditaments' £2 million. This ultimately derives from King, *Two Tracts*, p. 35, but there 'all other Hereditaments' are put at £1 million and another item 'Personal Estates etc' £1 million follows. I must confess that I am not clear what this constitutes, except that it is part of the assessment to the 4s. tax, so presumably it includes personal estates in money, debts, goods, and offices.

[84] *The Parliamentary Diary of Sir Edward Dering 1670–1733*, ed. B. D. Henning (New Haven, Conn., 1940), pp. 40, 58–9. The lower figure represents Dering's own opinion. He overestimated the total number of acres and the number of profitable acres whose average rent was 6s. 8d., hence the difference between his estimate and King's. Some attempt to estimate the income of office-holders was also made. Other values suggested were £7, £9·5, £10, and £12 million. Anchitell Grey, *Debates of the House of Commons* (1763), i. 323–4, 327.

[85] *Econ. Hist. Rev.* 2nd series, 19 (1966), 510.

[86] In fairness to Chamberlayne, it should be pointed out that in 1660 a list of 675 candidates for the proposed 'order of the Royal Oak' with an average income of £1,170, including only 85 knights and baronets, was produced (Aylmer, *The King's Servants*, pp. 329–30, Table 34).

[87] Shaw, *Knights*, ii, 225–65, plus 50 knights of the Bath at the coronation.

[88] 1669 ed., p. 487, the words in italics were omitted in 1692.

[89] See above p. 114.

[90] Like Davenant he used much too high a multiplier. In 1669 he put the total population at 5·4 million using a multiplier of seven to each head of a family. Later he applied a multiplier of six to Houghton's estimate of the number of houses to produce a total of 7 million, 1700 ed., p. 46.

[91] PRO, T64/302, notebook p. 7, calculation of number of houses in London 'now in 1695 are increased 5000 Houses more'; fo. 15 '10 June 1695 census of Sevenoaks'.

[92] *Two Tracts*, pp. 45, 47.

[93] So called by Prof. Glass; it belonged to John Burns and is now in the G.L.C. Record Office, p. 271, calculations about war taxes made in 1696.

[94] Notebook, p. 7 shows that the number of houses in London (*Two Tracts*, p. 17) was based on an estimate of c. 1680 and that King put their rents at £1,520,000.

[95] It could be argued that the acreage in the notebook is that of England only, that of the *Observations* of England and Wales, while the first relates to 1695 and the second to 1688, when rents may have been higher and population somewhat lower, though none of King's calculations assume an increase of population of the order this would suppose.

[96] See Appendix I, n. 2a below

[97] D. V. Glass, 'Two Papers on Gregory King' in *Population in History* (1965), ed. Glass and D. E. C. Eversley pp. 159–220, esp. 161–3; also his introduction to *London Inhabitants within the Walls 1695*, London Record Soc., 2 (1966). These provide an admirably thorough guide to the manuscripts of King, but naturally concentrate on his demographic work.

[98] R. Davis, 'English Foreign Trade 1660–1700', *Econ. Hist. Rev.* 2nd series, 7 (1954), 155 n. 6, says of the tract *The Naval Trade of England*, 'King's statistics are hardly credible . . .' Some calculations in the journal suggest they were based on the receipts of tunnage and poundage.

[99] Appendix I, journal pp. 65, 270; p. 246 gives 100,000 freeholders and 120,000 'lesser Freeholders and farmers'.

[100] *Econ. Hist. Rev.* 2nd series, 19 (1966), 512.

[101] Guy Fourquin, *Les Campagnes de la région parisienne à la fin du moyen age* (Paris, 1964), p. 530. This does not agree with E. Le Roy Ladurie's account of Languedoc, where changes in social and demographic structure are described for the sixteenth and seventeenth century. His study of the *compoix* shows a growth of large holdings in the fifteenth century continuing more slowly in the next two centuries, during which increasing population led to a decline in the share and number of middling peasant holdings and a great increase in tiny holdings (*Les Paysans de Languedoc* (Paris, 1966), pp. 142–4, 150–60). This type of evolution still contrasts with England, where in most areas middling and minuscule peasant holdings probably both declined in numbers in the seventeenth century.

[102] Unfortunately some recent estimates of even the higher groups are not very well founded on evidence. For example Professor W. T. Maccaffery says that Burghley 'counted no more than a hundred names among the inner core of county notables . . . in 1579', that there were 'above 800 names' listed as 'assessed at £20 a year, or more in land'. 'Place and Patronage in Elizabethan Politics', *Elizabethan Government and Society*, ed. S. T. Bindoff, J. Hurstfield, C. H. Williams (1961), pp. 98–9. The document cited for the first statement (B.M., Lansdowne MS. 683, p. 71) gives the names of 65 men below the rank of peer and covers only 34 English counties (including Rutland and Monmouth). The inference that there were only 100 peers and notables for the whole country seems unwarranted. The second statement refers to a document (B.M., Lansdowne 32, no. 27) which is headed 'Taxacio Commissionarorum assign' ad taxend' et assidend' primam solucionem subsidii A° 23 Eliz'. The list includes a considerable number of assessments under £20 (e.g. fo. 64r and v).

[103] Philip Styles, 'The Social Structure of Kineton Hundred in the Reign of Charles II'. *Essays in Honour of Philip B. Chatwin* (Oxford, 1962); 'The Heralds' Visitation of Warwickshire in 1682–3', *Trans. and Proceedings of the Birmingham Archaeological Society*, 80 (1962) and 71 (1953).

[104] 'The magnates, knights and gentry', in *Fifteenth Century England*, ed. S. B. Chrimes, C. D. Ross, R. A. Griffiths (Manchester, 1972), pp. 97–105.

[105] Some would also come from the Crown, but at most would probably have been under 7 per cent of the 'greater knights' income, ibid., pp. 98 and 122 n. 63.

[106] Remarriage of widows also produced some temporary transfers of income from peers' estates to commoners.

[107] H. H. Leonard, 'Knights and Knighthood in Tudor England' (London Ph.D. thesis, 1970), p. 102 Table 12. I am most grateful to Dr. Leonard for kindly allowing me to quote his thesis.

[108] In 1523 at least 151 are classified as military knights, ibid., p. 106.

[109] 300 knights with £150 p.a. and 50 peers with £900 p.a. would have 3·1 million acres, 15 per cent of the cultivated area; 300 knights with £200 p.a. and 50 peers with £800 p.a. would have 3·4 million acres and 17 per cent. Thus the range of estimates would be 14–17 per cent.

[110] Dr. Leonard classified 167 as military in 1550, op. cit., p. 107.

[111] Bodleian MS. Rawlinson D 924, fo. 430, printed J. Thirsk and J. P. Cooper, *Seventeenth Century Economic Documents* (Oxford, 1972), p. 811.

[112] 9 million acres was the revised total for arable, ibid. p. 797; it is worth noting that this was also the total of arable in 1939. 50 acres is a slip, the average should be 35 acres. The 140,000 may originally have been written 100,000.

[113] The revised valuations, above n. 61 and n. 63 would give 10·6 million acres.

[114] Assuming there were still 40,000 of the better sort of freeholders, the total would be 8·6 million acres which would be 43 per cent of all the arable, meadow and pasture.

[115] F. M. L. Thompson, 'Landownership and economic growth in England in the eighteenth century', *Agrarian Change and Economic Development*, ed. E. L. Jones and S. J. Woolf (London, 1969), pp. 42–3.

[116] J. Kew, 'The Disposal of Crown Lands and the Devon Land Market 1536–58', *Agric. Hist. Rev.*, 18 (1970), 94–105, shows 25–30 per cent of the county's land changed hands, less than half as a result of crown grants. There were considerable regional variations, J. Kew, 'Regional Variations in Devon Land Market', *The South West and the Land*, ed. M. A. Havinden and C. M. King (Exeter, 1969), pp. 27–41.

[117] H. J. Habakkuk, 'The price of Land in England 1500–1700', *Wirtschaft, Geschichte und Wirtschafts*

Geschichte. Festschrift fur Friedrich Lütege. ed. W. Abel (Stuttgart. 1966). pp. 119–28.

[118] C. Clay, 'Marriage, Inheritance and the rise of Large Estates in England 1660–1815', *Econ. Hist. Rev.*, 2nd series, 21 (1968), 503–18.

[119] J.-M. Constant, 'Gestion et revenus d'un grant domaine aux XVI et XVIIe siecles', *Revue D'Histoire Economique et Sociale*, 50 (1972), 165–202; L. Merle, *La Metairie et l'evolution agraire de la Gatine poitevine* (Paris, 1959).

[120] By 1780 French peasants are reckoned to have owned 40–45 per cent of the land, with regional variations of 22–98 per cent in Acquitaine and averaging a third over northern France. Most of this would have been customary tenures rather than freehold in English terminology, M. Vovelle, *La Chute de la Monarchie* (Paris, 1972) pp. 13–15. In 1808 18 per cent of the annual value of agricultural land belonged to owner-occupiers, Habakkok, *Annales*, 20 (1965), 655 n. 2, but in some counties they had 25 per cent, P. K. O'Brien, 'British Incomes and Property in the early nineteenth century, *Econ. Hist. Rev.*, 2nd series, 12 (1960), 263 n. 4.

[121] E. Weiss, 'Engebnisse eines Vergleiches der grundherrschaftlichen Strukturen Deutschlands und Frankreichs vom 13 bis zum Ausgang des 18 jahrhunderts', *Vierteljahrschrift für Sozial- und Wirtschaftegeschi cht,* 57 (1970), 1–13.

[122] J.-M. Constant, op. cit., pp. 192–9, 202; P. Leon and others, 'Regime seigneurial et regime feodale dans la France du Sud-Est (XVII–XVIIIe siecles', *L'Abolition de la Feodalitè* Centre national de la recherche scientifique (Paris, 1971), i. 152–68, ii. 613–15; P. de Saint Jacob, *Les Paysans du Bourgogne du Nord* (Paris, 1960), pp. 169–70.

5

Profit Inflation and Industrial Growth: The Historic Record and Contemporary Analogies*

D. FELIX

Editor's note. This article was first published in the *Quarterly Journal of Economics*, 70 (1956), 441–63.

Price and wage indices used in this article are discussed above, pp. 10–11. For further reading as an introduction to this very complex subject, see Allen (1966), ch. 6.

Chronic inflation in industrializing underdeveloped countries has been widely analysed in recent years, although thus far no fully authoritative judgement as to its effect on industrial growth has emerged. Instead, as they tend to do on complex social issues, economists have divided into disputant groups matching the number of logical possibilities.

Can the prolonged inflationary experience of Western Europe during much of the sixteenth to eighteenth centuries offer any insight on this issue? No economic historian has devoted more effort to answering this question than Professor Earl J. Hamilton. His view that inflation was a powerful promoter of industrial growth during the Price Revolution is well known, providing Keynes with the theme of an approving sermon in his *Treatise on Money*. His demonstration of the importance of inflation during the English Industrial Revolution has found an honoured place in a recent economic history anthology[1] and has been used by Professor W. Arthur Lewis to make a case for inflation in currently underdeveloped countries.[2] Recently, in his Presidential Address to the Economic History Association, Hamilton reviewed the evidence and broadened his claim.[3] Inflation in his view has been a powerful stimulant in a wide number of historical instances and could perform a similar function in currently underdeveloped countries.

The importance of Hamilton's views does not rest on the originality or ingenuity of the hypothesis. The theoretical core is, in fact, appealingly simple and familiar. During long periods of inflation, rising prices tend to outrun compensating wage adjustments. The result is 'profit inflation', a widened spread between labour costs and industrial receipts. This windfall to industrialists, partly ploughed back into capital formation, was, according to Hamilton, the chief boon from inflation during the Price Revolution and in many subsequent inflationary eras. Profit inflation in these periods enabled a much more rapid rate of industrial growth to occur than would have obtained under stable

* I am grateful to Professors Sanford A. Mosk of the University of California, Douglas F. Dowd of Cornell University, and I. B. Goodman of Wayne University for various suggestions on the organization of this paper.

prices. By profit inflation, it should be stressed, is meant a relationship between industrialists as a whole — broadly defined to include merchants, on the reasonable assumption that the two groups are closely intertwined in the early phases of industrialization — and labour. Windfalls gained merely at the expense of others in the mercantile–industrial class redistribute but do not add to the over-all profit gain.[4] The simplicity of the thesis does prove to be somewhat deceptive; as will be shown later, Hamilton beclouds its austere lines with a number of *ad hoc* qualifications. The chief strength of the thesis, however, lies in the large array of empirical proof Hamilton presents in its support. His is, therefore, more than a mere speculative generalization. If the proofs are adequate, not only is a major insight into the cause of European industrial growth prior to the nineteenth century established, but also the analogy which Hamilton draws concerning the efficacy of secular inflation in today's underdeveloped countries is considerably strengthened.

The purpose of this paper is to explore the adequacy of Hamilton's proof and the relevance of his analogy between past and present inflation in newly industrializing countries. To eschew needless suspense, may it be said at the outset that I believe Hamilton has misread the evidence; industrial profit inflation is not so much in evidence in the periods to which he refers. It is even possible that it was non-existent, although this may be too bold a counterclaim in view of the gaps and obscurities in the evidence. But even if it did exist in a much reduced degree, it does not appear to have been a decisive force determining rates of industrial growth. Furthermore, the data point up similarities between the results of inflation in low-productive agricultural societies past and present during the incipient phases of industrialization, which undermine rather than support the notion that inflation is a major stimulant of industrial growth in such an institutional context. The following sections, therefore, are devoted respectively to an evaluation of Hamilton's evidence on profit inflation during the Price Revolution, the era of the Industrial Revolution, to his more general survey of the evidence in his Presidential Address, and finally to suggesting some leading analogues between earlier and contemporary inflation to which the data point. The concern, it should be noted, is primarily with profit inflation, as defined above, and not with other arguments for inflation, e.g. the psychic stimulus to economic activity which some writers associate with secularly rising prices.[5]

I. PROFIT INFLATION DURING THE PRICE REVOLUTION

Hamilton's original article on the Price Revolution[6] was eclectic and rather tentative in its conclusions, suggesting a number of relations other than profit inflation: the inflow of American treasure enlarged overseas trading opportunities, drawing in capital and merchant enterprise and stimulating ship-building and more advanced forms of business organization; in particular, it enabled Europe to support an import surplus with the Far East on which Eastern trade depended; the discoveries and the quest for treasure had a leavening effect on European thought and imagination; rents, in addition to wages, lagged behind rising prices, creating windfalls for merchants and entrepreneurs. But subsequently, perhaps influenced by the authoritative benediction of Keynes, who, peeling away Hamilton's compound layers of effects, isolated 'profit inflation' as the quintessential contribution of the Price Revolution to capitalist development,[7] Hamilton has increasingly emphasized lagging wages and rising prices as the chief gain from the Price Revolution.

Thus in a later article, dealing with Spain's economic decay in the midst of a prolonged inflation, he wrote, 'inasmuch as the lag of wages behind prices, the chief cause of industrial progress in all countries during the Price Revolution ... was considerably less than in England and France, Spanish manufacturers advanced less rapidly than the English and the French in the sixteenth century.'[8] And more recently he stated,

'It is difficult, however, to see how anything else could have been more important than the great lag of wages behind prices in economically advanced countries during the Price Revolution. Capitalism requires capital, and it would not be easy to imagine a more powerful instrument for providing it than forced savings through a highly favourable price-wage ratio. The high rate of profit when prices were rising and wages, the chief cost, were lagging gave a strong inducement to savings in productive enterprise.... Other things anywhere near equal, capitalism could hardly have failed to flourish.'[9]

A. Variations in Wage Lags Among European Countries

The most obvious criticism of the profit inflation thesis is that there is no correlation either between the degree of price inflation and the degree of profit inflation, or between the rates of profit inflation and the apparent rates of industrial growth. Spain, undergoing the greatest price inflation during the 150 to 200 years of the Price Revolution, had the least profit inflation — limited to a few decades in the sixteenth century. France, with the least price inflation, had the greatest profit inflation. England with less profit inflation than France had a greater rate of industrial growth.[10] Moreover, during the seventeeth century English wages rose more rapidly than prices with no apparent retarding effect on the rate of industrial growth.[11] Clearly, price inflation was not synonymous with profit inflation, and a widening spread between wage and price indices did not necessarily mean a more rapid rate of growth.

Demographic and institutional influences on the supply curve of wage labour — largely independent of inflation — seem to underly much of the wide discrepancies between price and profit inflation. For as Weber points out, with some oversimplification, '. . . it depends entirely on the nature of the wage system what tendency will result from an inflow of precious metals'.[12] Thus, while England's expanding population during the sixteenth and much of the seventeenth century enlarged its labour supply, Spanish population began a substantial decline by the end of the sixteenth century, after a period of earlier growth. English enclosures, particularly in the sixteenth century, forced dispossessed peasants into the labour market at a time when an extension of mortmain and latifundism was reinforcing feudal agriculture in Spain.[13] In both

England and France, legal wage fixing, growing guild exclusiveness, and harsh treatment of vagabondage helped hold down wage rates.[14] In Spain, on the other hand, a more charitable handling of the poor, the swelling of clerical ranks with lower-class recruits, the quixotic pretensions of the 'Spanish Temper', military and colonial service, and the expulsion of the Moriscos all helped maintain a tight labour supply.[15] It is not difficult to see a rough correspondence between the timing of these demographic and institutional factors and the variations in profit inflation.[16] Rising prices may, therefore, have been no more than a marginal influence on real wages.

B. *The Deflation of Industrial Profit Inflation*

We may next ask whether English and French industry benefited from the spread between wages and prices. Hamilton's view is that 'for a period of almost 200 years, English and French capitalists . . . must have enjoyed incomes analogous to those of American profiteers reaped from a similar divergence between prices and wages from 1916 to 1919.'[17] That this is probably a gross overestimate is indicated by Tables 1–3, which break down Wiebe's price indices, the source of Hamilton's profit inflation estimates.

In the first place, it is apparent from Table 1 that sharply rising agricultural and wood product prices are responsible for much of the steep rise in Wiebe's

TABLE 1. *Price and Wage Trends in England, 1500–1702*

(1451–1500 = 100)

	1521– 1530	1551– 1560	1583– 1592	1613– 1622	1643– 1652	1673– 1682	1693– 1702
Wiebe's price index	113	132	198	257	331	348	339
Unprocessed agricultural products[1]	132	179	262	402	478	466	518
Assorted industrial products[2]	110	116	150	176	217	200	239
textile products[3]	93	121	118	130	143	153	143
Wood and wood products[4]	87	119	185	259	300	420	395
Imported food products,[5] largely tropical	151	119	146	124	151	—	163
Wiebe's wage index	93	88	125	134	175	205	233

[1] Average of price relatives of the following commodities: wheat, barley, oats, peas, beans, malt, oxen, pigs, lambs, hens, geese. These are the raw food products for which price relatives are given for all or most of the 200-year period.

[2] The components are listed in Table 2. These are manufactured items for which price relatives are given for all or most of the 200-year period.

[3] Canvas, cloth, shirting.

[4] Firewood, laths, charcoal.

[5] Sugar, cinnamon, raisins, peppers, nutmeg, cloves.

Source: Georg Wiebe, *Zur Geschichte der Preisrevolution des XVI und XVII Jahrhunderts* (Leipzig, 1895), pp. 374–77. Wiebe's price and wage series, compiled from price and wage data in J. E. T. Rogers, *A History of Agriculture and Prices in England* (Oxford, 1866–1902), iv and v, consist of a simple arithmetic average of 79 price relatives computed decennially, and a similarly computed average of 8 wage relatives.

TABLE 2. *Selected English Industrial Prices, 1500–1702*

(1451–1500 = 100)

	1521–1530	1551–1560	1583–1592	1613–1622	1643–1652	1673–1682	1693–1702
Lime	91	102	198	267	287	215	282
Salt	162	137	233	267	438	287	577
Wrought iron	93	138	100	123	171	137	149
Pewter	128	138	128	213	265	205	185
Slate	159	125	260	260	295	335	375
Gutter tiles	98	96	137	152	162	219	221
Paper	88	70	87	187	119	97	173
Shirting	101	138	140	155	172	159	170
Canvas	92	104	135	129	158	—	170
Cloth	85	—	80	106	99	146	91
Average[1]	110	116	150	176	217	200	239
Wage Index	93	88	125	134	175	205	233

[1] Same as index of assorted manufactures in Table 1.
Source: Wiebe, op. cit., pp. 374–7.

TABLE 3. *Price and Wage Trends in France, 1500–1700*

(1451–1500 = 100)

	1501–1525	1526–1550	1551–1575	1576–1600	1601–1625	1626–1650	1651–1675	1676–1700
Wiebe's price index	113	136	174	248	189	243	227	229
Selected agricultural index[1]	136	163	250	429	259	402	345	315
Index of assorted manufactures[2]	96	130	122	144	129	143	133	161
Wiebe's wage index	92	104	103	113	113	127	127	125

[1] Rye, wheat, vegetables, meat, eggs, milk.
[2] Iron, lead, copper, footwear, linen, clothing, cloth (2 grades).
Source: Wiebe, op. cit., pp. 378–9. Wiebe's price index is a simple 25-year average of 39 price relatives, based on the compilations of Comte d'Avenal.

index of English prices. When industrial products alone — see Tables 1 and 2 — are compared with Wiebe's wage index, industrial profit inflation shrinks to quite modest proportions, and disappears in such expanding industries as iron, textiles, and paper.

Secondly, it is apparent that finished good prices on the average lagged well behind the prices of their raw material components. In some cases the lag seems to have been formidable, as for example between iron and pewter and the prices of wood fuels. Partial evidence suggests the same for some other commodities. Thus, from 1501–10 to 1571–82 wool prices rose 114 per cent, while those of cloth rose 61 per cent. Butter rose 296 per cent over the 200-year period, while hay rose 350 per cent.[18] Nef also infers that bread and beer prices rose much less than did those of wheat, malt, hops, fuel, and other components.[19] We cannot know, lacking more detailed cost and wage breakdowns, the extent to which material cost pressures offset the gain from lagging industrial wages. The indices permit the impression that the offset was substantial and perhaps more than complete in many cases, particularly if Hamilton's conjecture that raw materials made up 40 per cent of produce costs is not wide of the mark.[20] This impression is further strengthened if Nef's elevation of Wiebe's wage index by 20 per cent is accepted.[21]

A similar price breakdown in Table 3 also reduces, and perhaps eliminates, industrial profit inflation for France. Moreover, while the wage lag may have lasted longer than in England, the rate of industrial growth in France was less.[22]

Finally, the evidence buttresses the contrary view, advanced by Weber and Nef, that the technological advances sparking the growth of a number of English industries in this period were called forth to overcome cost pressures from rising raw material prices.[23] Hamilton has rejected this view, as it applies to timber and fuel prices, with the assertion that the data are too contradictory to allow a firm judgement about price trends in this area.[24] Such purism, though permissible, is rather inconsistent; wood and wood fuel prices seem no more murky than other price–wage data of the period upon which Hamilton bases his profit inflation thesis. In Wiebe's collection, only laths rise less than the general price index between 1500 and 1700. Moreover, all the wood items — three covering the entire 200-year period and six covering the period from 1583–92 to 1700 — arrange themselves in rough conformity to Nef's thesis that, as English forests receded, the high-value items, less affected by rising transport costs, rose least.[25] The same is broadly true of the Beveridge price collection, covering the period after 1550; bavins (a type of brushwood faggot) in the Eton College accounts, which rose only 18 per cent between 1631–4 and 1694–8, is the only wood item rising less than Wiebe's general price index.[26] And all in all, the growing timber and wood shortage in the seventeeth century has been so widely noted as to make it hard to see why its existence should be denied.[27]

C. Agricultural windfalls

Was there a substantial net flow of windfall capital from agriculture to industry? Apparently not. True, the rigidities of Tudor and Stuart society were not ineluctable, and some capital moved between the various economic sectors. Landed wealth was invested in joint-stock trading companies and played an important role in the iron industry and to some extent in coal and copper.[28] But commercial and industrial wealth also went into the purchase of estates, as much for seignorial display as for income.[29] In sum, Lipson suggests, the capital flow from agriculture was not important. 'Speaking generally, the capital which found its way into manufactures was drawn . . . not from rents but from trade. . . . Commerce and industry reacted on each other; and capital began to play an increasingly important part in the development of both.'[30] This is also Hamilton's view, for writing of the much more economically fluid Industrial Revolution, he approvingly quotes Postan:

In the last quarter of the eighteenth and the first quarter of the nineteenth century, the country banks and the city merchants succeeded, much to the surprise of foreigners, in employing the free resources of the rural classes for financing the sale of the new industrial products. But they never attempted, and would never have succeeded if they had attempted to finance the new production, and to divert the wealth of landlords and farmers into industrial investment. In spite of the fact that rural England had long been familiar with the new financial methods, surprisingly little of her wealth found its way into the new industrial enterprises, where the shortage of capital must have been acute, and the risks, even as they might appear to the investor, not immoderate.[31]

The profit inflation thesis cannot, evidently, be rejuvenated by grafting an agricultural artery on to it.[32]

D. Other Effects of the Inflow of Specie

Derogation of profit inflation is not meant to imply that the inflow of American treasure or even the rise in prices may not have stimulated capitalist development along some of the other lines suggested in the original Hamilton article. While the notion that rents generally lagged behind rising prices during the Price Revolution has been seriously weakened,[33] fixed rents and poor estate management in a period of rising prices evidently did add to the financial agonies of the old aristocracy and facilitated the transfer of land to a more commercial-minded gentry and yeomanry.[34] Nor is there much doubt that American specie covered in the seventeenth century a chronically adverse trade balance with the East — and probably for England, an adverse balance also with Northern Europe[35] — and so facilitated the expansion of overseas trade. And certainly foreign trade was a major growing point around which mercantile capital accumulated, and various domestic industries, particularly in England and Holland, were nurtured.

The effect on trade of the treasure inflow needs clarification on one point, however. If the inflow of treasure stimulated overseas trade,[36] there is little evidence that its favourable effects operated through price inflation. In Tables 1 and 2 tropical products and cloth, respectively the chief English imports and export during the Price Revolution, both rise much less in price than Wiebe's general price index.[37] The inflow of internationally vendible specie was a 'real' asset gain. It is scarcely arguable that a mere inflation through coinage debasement would have been equally stimulating.

II. PROFIT INFLATION IN THE ERA OF THE INDUSTRIAL REVOLUTION, 1750–1800

A new surge of prices in the second half of the eighteenth century gave another powerful push to industrial growth, according to Hamilton. For the period

Quantitative Economic History

1750–1790 the rise is attributed chiefly to revived silver output in Mexico and the Brazilian gold discoveries. After 1790 war expenditure is acknowledged as the prime cause of the inflation.[38] Price inflation and lagging wages allegedly played a major role in the quickening of industrial growth in France, Spain, and England during this half-century. That the Netherlands went into a pronounced economic decline during this same inflationary period is silently passed over.[39]

A. Profit Inflation in France

For French evidence, Hamilton relies on the elaborate studies of Labrousse.[40] Between 1726–41 and 1771–89 prices rose 54 per cent and wages only 16–17 per cent. With 1785–9 as the terminal period, the increases are 64 per cent and 22 per cent respectively.[41] For part of this era, according to Labrousse (for all of it, according to Hamilton), rising prices and lagging wages coincided with a degree of prosperity and economic growth.[42]

Labrousse's sectoral statistics, however, do not indicate industrial profit inflation. Grains rose 60 per cent; all food products, 56 per cent; raw wool 41 per cent; and firewood, 63 per cent, between 1726–41 and 1771–89. But wool cloth rose only 22 per cent, linen cloth 36 per cent, and iron prices — Labrousse ventures no firm numerical guess here — rose little. In general, Labrousse believes the increase in industrial prices did not exceed the rise in wages, with industrial wages rising more than agricultural wages.[43]

How does Labrousse interpret his data? Essentially, that income and price fluctuations in eighteenth-century France, predominantly agricultural and with relatively stagnant productive techniques, were dominated by harvest fluctuations. The generally favourable harvests which marked the period 1733–1770 raised national income and stimulated industrial expansion. Poor harvests and high food prices after 1770 plunged France into a prolonged depression. In both prosperous and depressed years, however, agricultural rents reaped the major gains. Before 1770 the gains were shared in part with commercial farmers, merchants, and manufacturers; after 1770 rental gains continued to pile up despite declining incomes for almost all other economic classes.[44]

Moreover, the evanescent eighteenth-century prosperity has, according to Labrousse, been considerably overrated by some observers, misled by the expansion of foreign trade under the *ancien régime*. International trade expansion largely ceased in the late 1760s, while the composition of French exports shifted increasingly toward re-exports of colonial products at the expense of domestically produced goods.[45] Although some of the gains of the landlords were invested in mining and manufactures, far more of them sweetened the demand for luxuries, colonial imports, and urban building, and little was invested in agricultural improvements.[46] But even prior to 1770, the gains were too narrowly concentrated greatly to stimulate industrial markets. Wage workers, métayers, small peasants, comprising the bulk of the population, provided a thin market for manufactures, and during the poor harvest years were forced to divert almost all of their purchasing power to food. Large-scale unemployment, chronic throughout the prosperous years, increased in severity after 1770. A one-fourth rise in population during the century, land enclosures, and a shift to pasturage swelled the labour force and depressed real wages. All in all, improvements in industrial and agricultural techniques were limited. 'A rapid increase in population, a relatively mediocre increase in production' is Labrousse's judgement on the last six decades of the *ancien régime*.[47]

Finally, threading through Labrousse's studies is the theme that rental engrossment, rising unemployment, and a succession of poor harvests increased social tensions during Louis XVI's reign, setting the stage for the Revolution. With much of the rental gains accruing to the clergy and nobility, who were exempt from most taxes, the crown was trapped between its increased fiscal needs and a shrunken and discontented tax base. A fiscal crisis set off the Revolution, but the seeds of revolt are to be found in the profound economic crisis which racked the country.[48] There is thus little doubt as to how Labrousse would answer Hamilton's rhetorical question: 'It is interesting to speculate how far the industrial progress of France would have gone if she had been spared the violence and unbridled inflation of the French Revolution. . . .'[49]

B. *Profit Inflation in Spain*

Spanish prosperity and industrial growth is dated by Hamilton from around the fourth decade of the eighteenth century until the 1790s, beginning in a period of secularly stable prices and extensive mercantilist reforms under Philip V (1701–46), and carrying through an era of rising prices, lagging wages, and vigorous economic reforms by succeeding regimes. It terminates, despite an upward sweep of prices, in war and corrupt and inept administration under Charles IV (1788–1808).[50]

Why rising prices and profit inflation should be held chiefly responsible for the economic gains, is, however, not made clear in Hamilton's account. For example, public works and institutional reforms are acknowledged as important factors in the economic growth of the period.[51] Did the public works and industrial subsidies depend chiefly on rising prices or on fiscal improvements and increases in state revenues from colonial mines? Would the economic gains have been substantial if currency debasement alone had swelled the money supply? Moreover, in his admirable compilation of Spanish monetary, wage, and price trends, one finds that prices in the textile industry, an area of 'revolutionary advances', rose far less than the price of grains or animal products.[52] And we are also told that 'the lag of wages behind commodity prices . . . apparently resulted from the increase in the Spanish population by almost 100 per cent in 1701–1800, the mass migration into urban districts of rural workers displaced by agricultural reforms, and the undermining of craft guilds by liberalizing legislation. . . .'[53] Did the industrial growth, after all, depend on profit inflation from rising prices or on independent institutional factors and the increased inflow of specie?

C. Profit Inflation in England

Price and profit inflation is also alleged to have played a major role in England's far more spectacular and lasting industrial growth in this period.[54] Although Hamilton now believes that his original presentation overestimated the fall in real wages,[55] nevertheless, 'that forced savings through the lag of wages behind rising prices played a vital role in the eighteenth century, its [English Industrial Revolution] critical incipient stage, can hardly be questioned.'[56]

Yet both this conclusion and a peripheral point can be roundly questioned. On the peripheral issue — the source of the increased money supply in England — Hamilton is apparently incorrect in attributing most of the increase to specie inflow. On balance, England gained little additional specie during the five or six decades preceding the suspension of specie payments in 1797, such inflows as occurred in peace being sharply reversed during the numerous war years.[57] The increased money supply is largely accounted for by country bank note expansion and the Bank of England's monetization of the public debt, swollen by sizeable government deficits during the two major mid-century wars and the French Wars in the 1790s;[58] nor were transfusions of gold and silver as important to English overseas trade as they may have been a century earlier.

The more basic criticism is that Hamilton's price index, when decomposed, shows little or no profit inflation in industry. The index, apparently unweighted, is constructed from sixteen series taken from the accounts of two London hospitals as compiled by Sir William Beveridge and associates.[59] Table 4 lists nine of the agricultural items and four of the industrial series as well as a few other indicative products not included in Hamilton's index.[60] Price movements between 1750–90 and 1790–1800 are given separately, since most of the price increase in the half-century occurred in the latter decade.[61] The following conclusions are evident from Table 4.

1. Prices of unprocessed agricultural items rose far more than the general average. They also rose markedly more than the price of processed agricultural products such as beer, bread, candles, and flour, suggesting something of a cost squeeze on the producers of the latter which must have at least partly counterbalanced any putative gains from lagging wages.[62]

2. Prices of industrial products rose much less than the over-all index; in the case of felt and woven textiles there was virtually no rise. The profit inflation assumption fares poorly for industrial products; with the exception of coal there is no evidence of any such inflation.

A number of other industrial products, not areas of 'revolutionary advances', rose more. Wood and wood products, for example, rose substantially according to the Beveridge data.[63] However, Hamilton's thesis is that profit inflation, by greatly swelling industrial capital accumulation, was a major cause

TABLE 4. *Hamilton's Price and Wage Indices and*
Price Trends in Individual Commodity Series for England, 1750–1800

(1750 = 100)

			1790	1800
Hamilton's indices[1]		Prices	132	255
		Wages	115	117
Prices of agricultural products and of commodities produced from domestic agricultural materials	Items included in the Hamilton price index[2]	Peas	214	366
		Hops	129	435
		Bread	114	269
		Meat	149	256
		Cheese	149	233
		Oatmeal	131	434
		Malt	161	363
		Candles	145	189
		Beer	149	189
		Unweighted average	149	304
	Other agricultural products[2]	Wheat[3]	190	538
		Flour[2]	106	300
Industrial and mineral products[2]	Items included in the Hamilton price index	Coal	142	163
		Hats	104	104
		Stockings	100	100
		Shoes	99	133
		Unweighted average	111	125
	Other industrial prices	Gowns and coats	102	108
		Blue cloth	100	95
		Nails	113	121

Sources: [1] Earl J. Hamilton, 'Profit Inflation and the Industrial Revolution, 1750–1800', Chart
I, p. 258.
[2] Beveridge and others, *Prices and Wages in England from the Twelfth to the Nineteenth Century*, i.
291–300. Greenwich and Chelsea Hospital accounts.
[3] Ibid., pp. 81–84. Winchester College accounts.

of the rapidity of industrial advances. 'If prices and wages had not behaved as
they did, or in similar fashion, it is doubtful that industrial progress would have
been rapid, pervasive, or persistent enough to appear revolutionary to
succeeding generations.'[64] This his data fail to show for most of the dynamic
industrial growth sectors listed above. If, as appears to be the case, capital in
the technically advancing industries came predominately from reinvested
profits, it was more likely the great increases in productivity rather than rising
prices which accounted for the expanded profits. If real wages fell during the
Industrial Revolution, it was because of rising agricultural prices, conjoined
with a major increase in wage labour supply from population growth and
enclosures. Hamilton's price index, heavily loaded with agricultural items, has
misled him as to the chief beneficiaries of the rising prices. The classical

economists who made favourable agricultural terms of trade the focus of their concern were not wrong in their assessment of the facts.

III. HAMILTON'S *TOUR D'HORIZON*

By pointing to an alleged concurrence of inflation and quickened economic growth in a wide variety of instances, Hamilton, in his recent Presidential Address, has attempted to elevate the profit inflation thesis more nearly to the level of a universal generalization. And as a corollary, he concludes that today's underdeveloped countries would be well advised, since more drastic recourses are probably politically unfeasible, not to disregard the contribution which chronic inflation could make to industrial growth.

The quasi-universal generalization is, however, modified by numerous *ad hoc* qualifications which seriously weaken its claims to universality. Hyperinflation is excluded; no good can come of it. The most favourable results, he states at one point, came from a secular inflation of perhaps 1 to 2 per cent per annum.[65] Yet, although this would be virtually price stability for a majority of underdeveloped countries today, where annual price rises of 10 per cent and more have been more common, these higher rates are also beneficial, if one may judge from his qualified benediction on current inflation in underdeveloped countries.

The inflation should, however, be gentle; severe price fluctuations create an uncertain and therefore unfavourable climate for industrial enterprise.[66] Yet to speak of gentle secular inflation comes rather close at times to dangling a statistical illusion before the reader. In the price computations cited by Hamilton, the 'gentleness' often represents an averaging of much sharper short-run peaks and valleys and abrupt individual and sectoral price shifts. This is even more often the case in contemporary 'shortage economies', pressing for scarce industrial resources and pressed by expanding population. The frequent and wide variation in monthly and annual price data in, for example, the United Nations' *Monthly Bulletin of Statistics* is impressive. Price and wage adjustments, exchange rate devaluations, variations in export prices, fluctuating harvests, and other factors affecting the price level work their impact usually in discrete, and often sizeable jolts. Periodic fiscal and monetary checks to keep price increases in bounds tend similarly to operate in jolting fashion. Few underdeveloped countries seem to have been able to avoid this jolting price pattern under inflation.

Furthermore, it is by no means as evident as Hamilton implies that accelerated economic growth and secularly rising prices went hand-in-hand in the nineteenth century. For Britain the issue is notably unsettled.[67] For example, Rostow finds that in nineteenth-century Britain, 'periods of falling or stagnant prices were, normally, the intervals when the largest increases in production occurred and the greatest decline in unemployment',[68] Unfortunately, Hamilton explains away 1815–50, the period in which Rostow, incidentally, thinks the British rate of economic growth reached its zenith, only by falling into the fallacy of extrapolation,[69] remarking, 'No one will deny that economic progress was great in England and in the United States in 1815–1850; but would it not have been greater if the low level of output of precious metals had not depressed the price level?'[70]

In short, far from clinching the case for inflation, the *tour d'horizon* merely emphasizes the difficulty of generalizing about the relationship between prices and economic growth.

IV. PROFIT INFLATION IN UNDERDEVELOPED COUNTRIES

Historical comparisons are fraught with pitfalls. With this incense on the altar of scholarly caution, the following analogies are suggested between the incipient industrialization of the seventeenth and eighteenth centuries and the similar process in underdeveloped countries today. First, in today's underdeveloped countries, as in the past, inflation as far as industry is concerned has been more cost inflation and less profit inflation than Hamilton would have us believe. Secondly, one of the persistent sources of cost pressures in both periods has been rising agricultural prices. Thirdly, for both periods care must be taken not to attribute gains from an inflow of specie (or foreign exchange, its modern equivalent) to the inflation sometimes accompanying the inflow.[71]

A. Inflationary Pressures from Agriculture

Lagging agricultural output and rapidly growing demand brought on by population growth and expanding urbanization account for the strong upward trend in agricultural prices.[72] This has, in turn, periodically forced compensating wage adjustments; for despite similarly ample labour reserves, a somewhat lower degree of labour docility seems to distinguish contemporary from past industrializing societies. These wage increases, in conjunction with higher costs of agricultural inputs for industry, periodically depress industrial profits. To an important degree inflationary credit expansion — Latin America is replete with examples — is induced by efforts to offset the profit squeeze by easing credit, or to restrain wage pressures through governmentally subsidized distribution of food.

Inflating industrial prices have, however, typically failed to prevent a favourable trend in agricultural terms of trade;[73] agricultural incomes continue to corner a large part of the windfall gains from inflation.[74] And as in the past, little of the agrarian windfalls seems to flow into industrial investment.[75] Indeed, because of institutional rigidities in the agricultural sector, not very much of the gain tends to be invested productively in agriculture without considerable government development efforts and institutional reforms to prepare the way.[76]

B. Foreign Exchange Earnings and Inflation

Mere historical analogy would grossly understate the significance of the 'real' gain provided by an increased inflow of specie, or foreign exchange. It may have been no more than a marginal factor during the Price Revolution, but given the technological imperatives of modern industry, ample foreign exchange to finance capital goods imports is vital for countries lacking a well-developed structure of producer goods industries.[77] And over and above this, ample foreign exchange enables critically deficient supplies of fuels, food, and raw materials to be supplemented.[78]

There is thus a direct and well-recognized correlation in Latin America between export receipts and domestic investment rates. With the added margin of resources provided by rapidly expanding foreign exchange proceeds, not only may inflation generate some profit inflation but the profit inflation may also translate into an increase in productive investment. Doubtless, this is a grossly inefficient means of channelling resources into economic development, tending to favour 'consumption by the classes benefiting thereby, and speculative investment, to a greater degree than basic economic activity',[79] and to 'broaden very considerably the scope of profitable investment where the use benefits are low and the ownership benefits high'.[80] Hamilton's point, however, is merely that more rational methods of allocating resources for development are precluded in most underdeveloped countries by institutional resistances and government ineptitude and weakness[81] — a quite plausible observation.

Internal cost pressures, however, tend to create a momentum which propels inflation to a pace insupportable by foreign exchange earnings, unless these are also expanding rapidly. At this point import controls and deteriorating exchange rates create external pressures on costs and prices to supplement the already potent internal pressures. Inflation now shifts almost completely from profit to cost inflation and economic growth slows down, despite the accelerating inflationary momentum. It is significant that among the industrializing Latin American countries in the postwar period, Venezuela and Colombia, with considerably higher rates of export expansion, have also had higher rates of domestic investment and much less inflation than have Brazil and Chile, where exports have expanded less rapidly.[82] Hamilton can thus be criticized for attributing productive powers to inflation in contemporary underdeveloped countries, which rightfully belong to expanding foreign exchange earnings.

To some extent, of course, shortages of capital goods imports can be circumvented by substituting underemployed labour and other domestic resources. However, the countries most successfully industrializing today despite severely restricted access to import capital goods are the Soviet countries, who are circumventing these limits by Spartan efforts to build up a producer goods base at a pace hardly likely to be duplicated, under the demand conditions prevailing in underdeveloped countries, by market inducements and private incentives. In capitalistically oriented underdeveloped countries, the pronounced tendency for domestic investment to decline when exports slacken, inflation or no, suggests that inflation has not been for them an effective means of exploiting under-utilized domestic resources without the aid and stimulus of rising exports. In the Soviet countries, on the other hand, profit inflation is a superfluous addition to the State's potent arsenal of economic techniques. The inflation which has paralleled their efforts from time to time has been cost inflation, the result of planning miscalculations, bad harvests, and war destruction, according to most experts on Soviet economics.[83]

V. CONCLUSION

Profit inflation does not appear to have been a major industrial stimulus either in the salad days of European industrialization or in newly industrializing countries today. In the prolonged inflationary periods at times paralleling these industrial transformations, wages have often lagged behind rising prices. However, the extent of the wage lag — or its absence — relates much less to the intensity of the price rise than to the relative buoyancy of the labour market. The chief gain, moreover, has not been industry's; rather agricultural and raw material prices have tended in virtually all cases to rise more rapidly than industrial prices. For industry, inflation has appeared more as cost than as profit inflation. Population growth, institutional rigidities, and resource limitations account for the upward press of agricultural prices in the early phases of industrialization. That these factors in conjunction with the related institutional forces affecting the labour supply explain so much of the price and wage trends under inflation, suggests that inflation per se is not nearly the dynamic reallocator of resources that Hamilton implies.

The inflow of specie during the Price Revolution did stimulate Western Europe's foreign trade; and today an expanded inflow of foreign exchange is undoubtedly far more important to newly industrializing countries. The stimulus derives, however, not from inflation, but from the added margin of resources purchasable with specie or foreign exchange. It is questionable, moreover, whether, as Hamilton implies, such expanded inflows adequately account for the prolonged periods of inflation. This point scarcely needs argument for underdeveloped countries today, where for the most part the rhythm of monetary expansion is set by internal cost pressures. But similar pressures seem to have functioned during England's Industrial Revolution, and may also help explain the divergences in national price levels during the Price Revolution. For we must not overlook that precursor of central bank credit — royal currency debasement.

Nef concluded his assessment of profit inflation during the Price Revolution with the comment, 'Industry was responding in different ways in the various European countries to the strains and stimuli provided by the inflow of American treasure and the debasement of the coinage. Whether or not the response took the form of greatly increased activity in sinking mine shafts and setting up new manufacturing enterprises, depended mainly on conditions independent of the price revolution.'[84] This judgement seems equally appropriate for eighteenth-century inflation and for inflation in currently underdeveloped countries. Despite his forceful efforts, Hamilton has not succeeded in forging the historical material into a keen blade cutting through the knotted controversies over the inflation issue. What the historical material does cut down in size is perhaps the scope of issue at stake. By indicating no clear correlation between inflation, or its absence, and variations in the rate of economic growth, the data suggest that the long-run inclination of the price level may have only a relatively minor influence on growth rates.

NOTES

[1] Frederic C. Lane and Jelle C. Riemersma, *Enterprise and Secular Change* (Homewood, Ill., 1953).

[2] *Aspects of Industrialization,* National Bank of Egypt, Fiftieth Commemoration Lectures (Cairo, 1953), pp. 15–19.

[3] Earl J. Hamilton, 'Prices and Progress', *Jour. Econ. Hist.* 12 (1952), 325–49.

[4] Ibid., p. 327. In an earlier article, however, this distinction was not made; all windfalls were cited as part of the putative gain without regard for offsetting windfall losses. See 'American Treasure and the Rise of Capitalism', *Economica,* 9 (1929), 355.

[5] Cf. n. 49 below.

[6] 'American Treasure and the Rise of Capitalism', pp. 338–57.

[7] Keynes, *Treatise on Money,* ii. 152–63.

[8] Hamilton, 'The Decline of Spain', *Econ. Hist. Rev.* 8 (1937–8), 168.

[9] 'Prices and Progress', pp. 338–9.

[10] Cf. John U. Nef, 'Prices and Industrial Capitalism in France and England, 1540–1640', *Econ. Hist. Rev.,* 7 (1936–7), 155–85. Nef also shows by a comparison of 'profit inflation' and industrial trends during subintervals of the Price Revolution the low correlation between the two in both France and England.

[11] According to Wiebe, between the decades 1593–1602 and 1643–52, English prices rose 36 per cent and wages 40 per cent. For the period 1593–1602 to 1693–1702 prices rose 40 per cent and wages 84 per cent. See Georg Wiebe, *Zur Geschichte der Preisrevolution des XVI and XVII Jahrhunderts* (Leipzig, 1895), pp. 374–9.

[12] Max Weber, *General Economic History,* trans. F. H. Knight (London, 1929), p. 363.

[13] Rafael Altamira y Crevea, *Historia de España y de la Civilización Española* (3d ed.; Barcelona, 1913), iii. 447–54; Earl J. Hamilton, *American Treasure and the Price Revolution in Spain* (Cambridge, Mass., 1934) p. 296.

[14] Maurice Dobb, *Studies in the Development of Capitalism* (London, 1946) pp. 224–38.

[15] Altamira, op. cit., pp. 487–508; Hamilton, 'Decline of Spain', *passim.* Hamilton convincingly argues that the Morisco expulsion has been overplayed by many historians as a major cause of Spanish demographic and economic decline.

[16] Just as there is a correlation between declining population, a labour shortage, and rising real wages in England during the fourteenth and fifteenth centuries.

[17] 'American Treasure and the Rise of Capitalism', p. 355.

[18] Wiebe, op. cit., pp. 375–6. The cloth figure is the average of two grades. Wiebe's wool series unfortunately ends in 1571–82.

[19] Nef, op. cit., pp. 166–9.

[20] Hamilton, 'Prices and Progress', p. 335. Keynes's assumption that wages were 50 per cent of costs and that material costs rose uniformly with the price level is also evidently conjectural, and on the second point, largely incorrect. See Keynes, op. cit., ii. 159–61.

[21] Nef, op. cit., pp. 163–5.

[22] Nef, 'A Comparison of Industrial Growth in France and England from 1540 to 1640', *Jour. Pol. Econ.* 44 (1936), 289–317, 505–33, 643–66.

[23] Weber, op. cit., p. 311; Nef, 'Prices and Industrial Capitalism', *passim.*

There seems less basis for Nef's contention that there was little decline in English real wages during the Price Revolution. He accepts, for example, Knoop and Jones's conjecture—advanced in order to extricate the English worker from the horrible predicament of having his real wages apparently halved by rising food prices—that there must have been an increase in truck payments relative to money wages. As Hamilton points out, such an increase in payments in kind would seem unlikely in an era of increasing commercialization. See D. Knoop and G. P. Jones, 'Masons' Wages in Medieval England', *Econ. Hist.,* 2 (1933), 473–99. Hamilton, 'Prices and Progress', pp. 333–4. Cf. also, Sir John Clapham, *A Concise Economic History of Britain from Earliest Times to A.D. 1750* (Cambridge, 1949) p. 212.

Nef may have also overemphasized the extent to which industrial workers doubled as farmers. In Lipson's judgement such dual activity was not important in many branches of industry, notably textiles, and declined generally with industrial growth. E. Lipson, *The Economic History of England* (London, 1956) ii. 65—6, 79–81, 123–6.

[24] 'Prices and Progress', pp. 336–7.

[25] Nef, 'Prices and Industrial Capitalism', pp. 180–1.

[26] Sir William Beveridge and others, *Prices and Wages in England From the Twelfth to the Ninteenth Century* (London, 1939) vol. i. In this compilation, the accounts of various schools, hospitals, and government bureaus are sterilized separately; no general price index is constructed. The small rise in Eton's bevins may perhaps be explained by the fact that the prices are derived from *sales* by the college from its own forests to dealers. In the accounts of the Westminster School and Abbey, located in treeless London, bavins rose by 209 per cent between 1574–9 and 1639–43, and faggots by 56 per cent between 1664–8 and 1699–1704. Eton's charcoal prices (*purchases*, not sales) rose 151 per cent between 1550–4 and 1665–9, levelling off at the latter date, at which time coal purchases were now being made on a steady basis. Wooden tilepins and laths in the Office of Works accounts also show larger price increases than the Wiebe general index, although less than the increases in charcoal prices. However, lath prices in the above accounts, though covering only the period 1558–64 to 1635–9, show a substantially greater increase than does Wiebe's lath series. Ibid, pp. 116–27, 493, 707–9, 712–13, 726–7.

[27] Cf. Rogers, op. cit., v. 529–30. On the effect of high timber prices on English shipbuilding costs, see Violet Barbour, 'Dutch and English Merchant Shipping in the Seventeenth Century', *Econ. Hist. Rev.,* 2 (1929–30), 267–70, 275. On state efforts during Elizabeth's reign and in the seventeenth century to restrict iron production in order to conserve the dwindling forests, see Lipson, op. cit., ii. 156–9.

[28] Lipson, op. cit., ii. 118–23, 162–8, 178; iii. 208. M. B. Donald, *Elizabethan Copper* (Oxford, 1955). Davis states, however, that the bulk of shares in joint-stock companies of the Restoration period were held by wholesaling and overseas merchants and bankers. K. G. Davis, 'Joint Stock Investment in the Later Seventeenth Century', *Econ. Hist. Rev.,* 2nd series 4 (1952), 293–301.

[29] R.H. Tawney, 'The Rise of the Gentry, 1558–1640', *Econ. Hist. Rev.,* 12 (1941), 187–8.

[30] Lipson, op. cit., iii. 208.

[31] Hamilton, 'Profit Inflation in the Industrial Revolution', *Quarterly Jour. Econ.* 56 (1942), 265–6; M. Postan, 'Recent Trends in the Accumulation of Capital', *Econ. Hist. Rev.,* 6 (1935–6), 2.

[32] Needless to say, the stimulus to consumer demand from inflated agricultural incomes is irrelevant, unless a net gain can be shown after deducting the effect of depressing wage income. It is unlikely that this can be shown; workers' tastes were probably more conducive to standardizing production than the more luxurious tastes of the wealthier landed classes.

[33] See Eric Kerridge, 'The Movement of Rent, 1540–1640', *Econ. Hist. Rev.,* 2nd series, 6 (1953), 16–34. Kerridge presents data suggesting that, with the exception of royal lands and noble estates where patronage and 'social power' motivated the owners, rents rose as much if not more than did agricultural prices.

[34] Tawney, 'Rise of the Gentry', *passim.* Lawrence Stone, 'The Anatomy of the Elizabethan Aristocracy', *Econ. Hist. Rev.,* 18 (1948), 1–53; idem, 'Elizabethan Aristocracy—A Restatement', *Econ. Hist. Rev.,* 2nd series, 4 (1952), 302–21.

[35] Cf. C. H. Wilson, 'Treasure and Trade Balances; the Mercantilist Problem', *Econ. Hist. Rev.,* 2nd series, 2 (1949), 152–61; idem, 'Treasure and Trade Balances: Further Evidence', *Econ. Hist. Rev.* 2nd series, 4 (1951–2), 231–42.

[36] Weber points out that the flow of specie from Europe to the East had no markedly inflationary effects on the Eastern Economies, nor did it unleash any great and lasting economic transformation. Evidently the major gains from specie inflow go to the economies already institutionally adapted to exploit the opportunities which the inflow presents. Op. cit., p. 353.

Schumpeter makes the same point, concluding, however, that the net effect of the Price Revolution was retrogressive. It cannot be said, however, that the argument is adequately buttressed by his analogy with World War I inflation. See *Business Cycles* (New York, 1939), i. 231–32.

[37] The meagre rise in cloth, linen, and canvas prices throughout the seventeenth century is also borne out by all the Beveridge price series. See op. cit. i. 702–33. See also F. J. Fisher, 'London's Export Trade in the Early Seventeenth Century', *Econ. Hist. Rev.,* 2nd series, 3 (1950), 151–61.

[38] 'Prices and Progress', p. 339. 80 per cent of the rise in English prices during the period 1750–1800 occurred in the last decade.

[39] C. H. Wilson, 'The Economic Decline of the Netherlands', *Econ. Hist. Rev.,* 9 (1939), 111–27.

[40] C. E. Labrousse, *Esquisse du mouvement des prix et des revenus en France au XVIIIᶜ siècle* (Paris 1933), 2 vols.

[41] Ibid., ii. 361–2, 492. The price index, it should be noted, does not include manufactures (*produits ouvres*).

[42] Ibid., ii. 509–12. Labrousse, *La Crise de l'économie française à la fin de l'Ancien Règime et au début de la Révolution* (Paris 1944), pp. xxiv–xxxi. Hamilton, 'Prices and Progress', p. 341.

[43] *Esquisse*, i. 240; ii. 315–17, 329–30, 346, 349–53, 362, 491.

[44] *Esquisse*, ii. 379–425, 514–67; *La Crise*, pp. xv, xxxiii–iv.

[45] *La Crise*, pp. xxxvi–xxxvii.

[46] *Esquisse*, ii. 509–11; *La Crise*, pp. xxvi–xxvii.

[47] *Esquisse*, ii. 512. Cf. 501–67.

[48] *Esquisse*, ii. 617–42; *La Crise*, pp. xlii–xlv.

[49] Hamilton, 'Prices and Progress', p. 341. Labrousse does take the position that secularly rising prices and wages along a broad front stimulate economic growth. The stimulus derives, however, from a euphoria

allegedly associated with rising prices and wages broadly shared, not from profit inflation at the expense of falling or stagnant real wages. See his remarks on the Napoleonic and 1851–73 periods. *La Crise,* pp. xvi–xx.

[50] 'Prices and Progress', pp. 341–2; Hamilton, *War and Prices in Spain, 1651–1800* (Cambridge, Mass., 1947) p. 151. The period was marred, to be sure, by frequent food riots, increased hordes of vagrants, and other less attractive manifestations of prosperity. See ibid., pp. 93, 158–9, 163–4.

[51] Ibid., pp. 100, 219–22. Hamilton, 'Money and Economic Recovery in Spain under the First Bourbon', *Jour. Mod. Hist.,* 15 (1943), 306.

[52] *War and Prices in Spain, 1651–1800,* pp. 178–9, 185–6, 266–7. Hamilton's Chart V (p. 173), shows agricultural prices rather consistently leading nonagricultural prices both in the up- and down-swings.

[53] Ibid., p. 216.

[54] 'Profit inflation and the Industrial Revolution, 1750–1800', *passim.*

[55] 'Prices and Progress', pp. 342–3.

[56] Ibid., p. 340–1.

[57] Elizabeth Boody Schumpeter, 'English Prices and Public Finance, 1660–1822', *Rev. Econ. Stat.,* 20 (1938), 30; Sir John Clapham, *The Bank of England: A History* (Cambridge, 1944), i. 217–21, 231–66, 295–8.

[58] Schumpeter, op. cit., pp. 27–31. Government expenditures during the Seven Years War and the American Revolution tripled over peacetime levels, with over 40 per cent of the expenditures financed by short-term borrowing, chiefly from the Bank of England. Cf. Clapham, *The Bank of England: A History,* i. chap. 4, pp. 210–13, 241–8, 251–4, 293–9.

[59] Beveridge and others, op. cit. i. 291–300, 313.

[60] The excluded items are milk, butter, and salt. Only monthly milk prices, averaged for a period of years rather than annually, are given in the Beveridge volume; the increase between 1749–58 and 1796–1802 was 77 per cent. Butter prices are given only until 1795; the over-all rise was 8 per cent. Salt prices rose 17 per cent between 1750–90, and 250 per cent in the entire period, 1750–1800. This rise in the last decade, however, was heavily influenced by increasingly heavy salt taxes. See ibid., pp. 262, 264.

[61] 1800 is actually a poor terminal date. Preceding harvests had been particularly bad and there was an unusually sharp rise in grain prices in that year.

[62] 'On a number of occasions the brewer [supplying Chelsea Hospital] complained that, through the exceptional cost of malt or hops, the prices allowed him for beer involved him in loss. . . .' Beveridge and others, op. cit., i. 309.

[63] In the 1790s there were frequent petitions from carpenters, joiners, and other contractors for increased contract prices because of 'the great rise in prices of labour and materials.' Ibid., i. 253.

[64] 'Prices and Progress', p. 341. Cf. Lewis, op. cit., pp. 16–17. for a similar deduction.

[65] 'Prices and Progress', pp. 346–7.

[66] Loc. cit.

[67] E. H. Phelps-Brown and S. A. Ozga, 'Economic Growth and the Price Level', *Econ. Jour.,* 65 (Mar. 1955), 1–18, contend that secularly rising prices and slower economic growth went together, both the result of adverse terms of trade with raw materials.

[68] W. W. Rostow, *British Economy in the 19th Century* (Oxford, 1948), chap. 1. Phyllis Deane even suggests that English national output grew less rapidly in the last third than in the first two-thirds of the eighteenth century. 'The Implications of Early National Income Estimates for the Measurement of Long-term Economic Growth in the United Kingdom', *Economic Development and Cultural Change,* 4 (Nov. 1955), 20–38.

[69] That is, attempting to verify a hypothesis empirically, while explaining away negative evidence by drawing corollaries from the hypothesis being tested.

[70] 'Prices and Progress', p. 344.

[71] The following brief comments are based on material contained in my Ph.D. dissertation, 'Industrialization and Secular Inflation in Underdeveloped Countries' (Department of Economics, University of California, 1955).

[72] Engel's law evidently does little to dampen food demand while per capita calorie consumption remains within daily rates of 1800–2500 and daily protein intake between 40 and 60 grams, as is the case in underdeveloped countries.

[73] See U.N.F.A.O., *Monthly Bulletin of Agricultural Economics and Statistics* (May 1955). Table 24; (Sept. 1955), Table 20; U.N. Economic Commission for Latin America, *Economic Survey of Latin America, 1951–1952,* Tables 43, 54, 62.

[74] The importance in the early stages of the Japanese and Soviet patterns of industrialization, respectively, of the Meiji land taxes, siphoning off agricultural incomes for use in government industrial subsidies, and the Soviet method of compulsory agricultural deliveries at low prices, can thus be appreciated.

[75] Cf. U. N. Economic Commission for Latin America, *Economic Survey of Latin America, 1950: Recent Developments and Trends in the Economy of Latin America,* pp. 146–7 (mimeo.).

[76] U.N.F.A.O., *Propects for Agricultural Development in Latin America* (Rome, 1953); Charles E. Rollins, 'Economic Development in Venezuela', *Economic Development and Cultural Change,* 4 (Nov. 1955), 86–9.

[77] For industrializing Brazil, Chile, and Mexico the ratio between capital goods imports and gross domestic investment has averaged, respectively, 36, 55·4, and 54·7 per cent during 1945–52. *Economic Survey of Latin America, 1951–1952,* Tables 42, 52, 63.

[78] Brazil's fuel imports alone now average over 13 per cent of total imports. Venezuela in some recent years has imported half her marketed food supply. Peruvian imports of food, beverages, and tobacco averaged 24 per cent of total imports during 1948–52. U. N. Economic Commission for Latin America, *Economic Survey of Latin America, 1953,* pp. 175, 238; *Prospects for Agricultural Development,* p. 33.

[79] *Economic Survey of Latin America, 1953,* p. 72.

[80] E. M. Bernstein, 'Financing Economic Growth in Underdeveloped Economies', *Savings in the Modern Economy,* ed. Walter W. Heller (Minneapolis, 1953), p. 290.

[81] 'Prices and Progress', pp. 347–8.

[82] This observation, which obviously needs further amplification, is the subject of another paper in preparation. Suffice it to say at this point that cost pressures on the export industries from inflation seem to have been a minor factor (because exchange rate concessions are used as offsets) in accounting for these variations in export expansion. More important by far have been the relative buoyancy of foreign markets for the respective products of these countries and the varying natural resource and institutional limits to the expansion of these products.

[83] Cf. Franklyn D. Holzman, 'Financing Soviet Economic Development', Universities-National Bureau Committee for Economic Research, *Capital Formation and Economic Growth* (Princeton, 1955). Raymond P. Powell, 'Soviet Monetary Policy' (Ph.D. dissertation, University of California, 1952). Gregory Grossman, 'National Income', and Alexander Gerschenkron's comments in *Soviet Economic Growth,* ed. Abram Bergson (Evanston, Ill., 1953).

As for Soviet economic doctrine, it unqualifiedly rejects inflation, and like Von Mises, Hayek, and Schumpeter—though for different reasons—favours a secularly falling price level.

[84] 'Prices and Industrial Capitalism', p. 185.

6

Long-Run Changes in British Income Inequality

L. SOLTOW

Editor's note. This article was first published in *Econ. Hist. Rev.* 21 (1968), 17–29.

Lorenz curves and the Gini coefficient are discussed above, pp. 17, 19. For further reading see footnotes to those pages. Methods for fitting curves, in particular Pareto distributions, to data are mentioned on pp. 29–30, and notes on further reading are given in footnotes.

It is difficult to measure the extent of improvement of various social and economic groups during the Industrial Revolution. There seems to be a growing body of evidence showing that lower-income segments shared in economic growth.[1] However, the idea still prevails that a dynamic industrial group developed in the eighteenth and nineteenth centuries which made the rich richer even if the poor did not become poorer. The consequence of such a movement would mean that relative inequality among all income groups would increase. This belief is often accepted in the United States because of the large body of literature dealing with the era of the robber baron. It is accepted by economists as being true for Germany mainly because of the study of annual income distributions available for the years from 1873 to 1913 and the one year 1854.[2]

There is a degree of silence about the British experience, even though income tax distributions exist for various income years[3] since 1801. This stems from the fact that from 1803 to 1910 there were no comprehensive definitions of income. Distributions were available only for Schedule D income, that is, income from trade or business, the professions, and some miscellaneous items including small interest payments. The large amounts of property income, including interest and rents, were subject to separate flat rates so that any exact statements about income were difficult to make. It is the purpose of this paper to bring together available distributions before and after the Industrial Revolution in an attempt to make those data that are available more meaningful within the context of a long period of economic growth. This will involve the use of distributions for 1962–3, 1801, 1688, and, brazenly, for 1436.

I. DISTRIBUTIONS FOR THE TOTAL LABOUR FORCE

For 1688 there are Gregory King's well-known estimates. He gives the number and average incomes of 26 classes of persons in England and Wales as follows:

Number of families in class	Class	Yearly income per family £
160	Temporal lords	3,200
26	Spiritual lords	1,300
800	Baronets	880
600	Knights	650
3,000	Esquires	450
12,000	Gentlemen	280
5,000	Persons in greater offices and places	240
5,000	Persons in lesser offices and places	120
2,000	Eminent merchants and traders by sea	400
8,000	Lesser merchants an l traders by sea	198
10,000	Persons in the law	154
2,000	Eminent clergymen	72
8,000	Lesser clergymen	50
40,000	Freeholders of the better sort	91
120,000	Freeholders of the lesser sort	55
150,000	Farmers	$42\frac{1}{2}$
15,000	Persons in liberal arts and sciences	60
50,000	Shopkeepers and tradesmen	45
60,000	Artisans and handicrafts	38
5,000	Naval officers	80
4,000	Military officers	60
35,000	Common soldiers	14
50,000	Common seamen	20
364,000	Labouring people and out-servants	15
400,000	Cottagers and paupers	$6\frac{1}{2}$
30,000 (persons)	Vagrants, beggars, gipsies, thieves, and prostitutes	2 (per head)

Phyllis Deane, who has used King's data as the basis of an estimate of national income for 1688, states that King had access in some main respects to better data than we do.[4]

By ordering King's 26 average incomes from lowest to highest, and weighting each by the number of families involved, data may be obtained for the Lorenz curve given in Chart 1. A measure of relative inequality, Gini's coefficient of concentration or R, is calculated by determining the area between the actual Lorenz curve and the straight-line curve of perfect equality. This area as a ratio of the triangular area under the line of perfect equality was 0·551 in 1688. This procedure neglects dispersion within each economic class which, if accounted for, might increase R by 5 or 10 per cent.

Patrick Colquhoun was the next person to make a serious estimate of annual income distribution in England and Wales, considering data from 1801 to 1803. Superficially at least, he used King's framework.

Number of families in class	Class	Yearly income per family £
287	Peers	8,000
26	Spiritual lords	4,000
540	Baronets	3,000
350	Knights	1,500
6,000	Esquires	1,500
20,000	Gentlemen	700
2,000	In high civil offices	800
11,000	Persons of the law	350
1,000	Eminent clergymen	500
10,000	Lesser clergymen	120
120,000	Better freeholders	200
120,000	Lesser freeholders	90
160,000	Farmers	120
16,300	Liberal arts and sciences	260
74,500	Shopkeepers	150
445,726	Artisans, mechanics, labourers	55
3,000	Naval officers	347
5,000	Military officers	363
50,000	Common soldiers	110
38,175	Marines	129
67,099	Seamen	107
340,000	Labourers	31
40,000	Labourers in mines	40
260,179	Paupers	26
222,000	Vagrants	10

Colquhoun significantly added 20 more classes to his list.[5] Some of these were classes emerging as a result of industrialization so that, with a few exceptions, these additions could perhaps be thought of as a partial accounting for the effects of eighteenth-century economic growth:

1	The Sovereign and Queen	200,000
5,000	Ship-owners letting ships	500
25,000	Manufacturers	800
500	Wholesalers	800
300	Employing capital in shipbuilding	700
25,000	Employing capital in textiles	150
5,000	Engineers	200
30,000	Clerks and shopmen	75
2,500	Dissenting clergymen	120
500	Educators in universities	600
20,000	In education	150
500	Families in theatrical pursuits	800
800	Hawkers and pedlars	125
2,000	Debtors in prisons	43
40	Lunatic keepers	500

Number of families in class	Class	Yearly income per family £
2,500	Lunatics	30
50,000	Innkeepers	100
2,000	Part military	45
30,500	Pensioners	20
50,000	Having trusts	100

The Lorenz curve for these 45 classes is given in Chart 1. There is some little tendency to show betterment among lower-income classes, but vagaries associated with subsistence non-cash income perhaps make it advisable to conclude that there is no evidence of change in the eighteenth century. The concentration coefficient, R, for the 1801–3 data is 0·555. A further elaboration of the above lists obtained by weighting families by size does not materially alter the calculations.

CHART 1. *Lorenz Curves of Frequency Distributions of Income of Persons in Great Britain in Selected Years from 1688 to 1963*

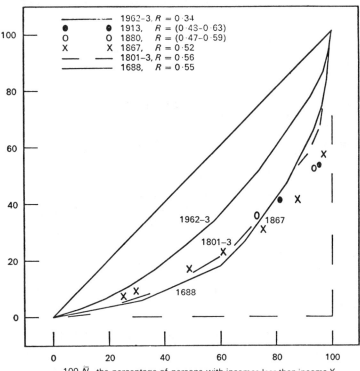

100 $\bar{A}_x$, the percentage of total income of persons with income less than X

```
——— · ——   1962–3, R = 0·34
●      ●    1913,    R = (0·43–0·63)
O      O    1880,    R = (0·47–0·59)
X      X    1867,    R = 0·52
——   ——   1801–3, R = 0·56
————————   1688,    R = 0·55
```

100 $\bar{N}_x$, the percentage of persons with incomes less than income X

Source: See Table 1.

Colquhoun's total for annual national income in 1801–3 of £222 million for England and Wales is almost the same as might be expected on the basis of later research. Phyllis Deane and W. A. Cole estimated total gross national income for Great Britain to be £232 million in 1801. Colquhoun again made estimates of income for social and economic classes for 1812. This time his total of £430 million was for Great Britain and Ireland. This can be compared to a Deane–Cole estimate for Great Britain[6] of £301 million for 1811. It thus seems that Colquhoun's data are not unreasonable. One may construct the Lorenz curve for the 1812 data of Colquhoun in the manner already described. It is not surprising that it is similar to that for 1801 and has a concentration coefficient of 0·536. A list of findings to this point is given in Table 1.

One now turns to distributions based on income-tax data for at least the upper-income classes. The first of these is by R. Dudley Baxter, who presented 1867 estimates to the Statistical Society of London. The frequency table for England and Wales based on family income unweighted by family size is

TABLE 1. *Summary Information Concerning Complete Distributions of Income of Persons in Great Britain for Eight Selected Years*

Year	Name of investigator	Region	Use of income-tax data	Number of persons in data	Arithmetic mean, $\overline{X}$ (£)	Concentration coefficient R
1688	Gregory King	England and Wales	No	1,350,000 families and single individuals	32·2	0·551
1801–3	Patrick Colquhoun	England and Wales	No	2,210,000 families and single individuals	99·8	0·555
1812	Patrick Colquhoun	G.B. and Ireland	No	4,379,000 families and single individuals	98·0	0·536
1867	R. Dudley Baxter	England and Wales	Yes	5,229,000 men	112·0	0·500
1867	R. Dudley Baxter	G.B. and Ireland	Yes	13,720,000 men, women, and children with income	59·3	0·521
1880	Arthur Bowley	United Kingdom	Yes	14,770,000 with occupations and assessments	76·2	0·474–0·6
1913	Arthur Bowley	United Kingdom	Yes	20,700,000 with occupations and assessments	105·0	0·467–0·5
1962–3	Inland Revenue	United Kingdom	Yes	22,242,000 married couples[1] and single	853·0	0·338

[1] A married couple (whether separately assessed for tax or not) is counted as one person.

Sources: Charles Davenant, *The Political and Commercial Works*, ed. Sir Charles Whitworth (1771), ii. 184. Slight variants of these figures will be found in Gregory King, *Two Tracts*, ed. George Barnett (Baltimore, 1936), and in George Chalmers, *An Estimate of the Comparative Strength of Great Britain* (1804); Patrick Colquhoun, *A Treatise on Indigence* (1806), p. 23; Colquhoun, *A Treatise on the Wealth, Power and Resources of the British Empire* (1815), pp. 124, 125; R. Dudley Baxter, *National Income, The United Kingdom* (1868), frontispiece, p. 60, appendix 1; Arthur Bowley, *The Change in the Distribution of the National Income, 1880–1913* (Oxford, 1920), pp. 13, 16; *Report of the Commissioners of Her Majesty's Inland Revenue, Report 107* (1965), p. 83; B. R. Mitchell, *Abstract of British Historical Statistics* (Cambridge, 1962), pp. 8, 11.

Lower limit of income class £	Number in class[7]	Lower limit of income class £	Number in class[7]
5,000	4,609	52	582,000
1,000	25,812	46	1,028,000
300	92,188	$36\frac{1}{2}$	260,360
100	522,401	33	1,148,500
73	616,433	30	73,400
60	42,200	20	34,500
60	798,600		

The Lorenz curve for this case, as presented in Chart 1 and stated in Table 1, yields a concentration coefficient of 0·500. A similar calculation considering the number of income earners per family gives an R of 0·521. Examination of Chart 1 shows greater equality in the lower portion of the curve in 1867 than in 1801–3. The upper portion of the 1867 distribution has greater inequality than in 1801–3. At least part of this is due to the fact that Schedule D income-tax data were used in the latter but not in the former year. Information for the upper tail based on income-tax data will be presented shortly. It is best to hold in abeyance any conclusion that the rich got richer from 1801 to 1867.

Professor Bowley made estimates[8] for three income classes in 1880 and 1913, using income-tax data for the highest class with incomes over £160.

| | 1880 | | 1913 | |
Income class	Number of persons (millions)	Income (£ millions)	Number of persons (millions)	Income (£ millions)
Wages	12·30	465	15·20	770
Income under £160	1·85	130	4·31	365
Income over £160	0·62	530	1·19	2,165

It is difficult to compute R measures with only three classes. If one assumes perfect equality in the modal class, R is 0·48 in 1880 and 0·47 in 1913. If one assumes a Pareto distribution within each based on the relationship between the three points, R is 0·63 in 1880 and 0·59 in 1913. The main point to note is that there is no indication of increased inequality in the third of a century before the First World War.

One completes the final half-century by comparing the 1962–3 distribution for families and single individuals, as compiled by the Inland Revenue, with the earlier distributions of 1913 and 1867. The concentration coefficient of 0·34 is at most two-thirds of that in 1867 and probably two-thirds of that in 1913. The tentative hypothesis is that long-run inequality did not change in the eighteenth and nineteenth centuries. Only since the First World War has there been a decrease, and this decrease has been substantial.

II. DISTRIBUTIONS LIMITED TO HIGH-INCOME GROUPS

It is possible to add three more important distributions which have a bearing on inequality changes. These distributions, based on income-tax data, are for upper-income groups in 1436, 1801, and 1911–12. These data are summarized in Table 2 and presented graphically in Chart 2 in conjunction with the eight distributions previously described.

Unfortunately, one cannot use a Lorenz curve approach as such when dealing with incomplete distributions, since the total income and perhaps even the total labour force are not known. The alternative approach, using Pareto curves, will be employed because certain estimates from these curves have attractive ramifications. Although Pareto curves may be considered inappropriate by some for distributions today, they can be used to make effective generalizations if handled with care. It must continually be borne in mind that these curves put an emphasis upon the incomes of high-income and upper-income groups and neglect the poor.

One might begin by examining the 1962–3 cumulative curve in Chart 2, where X is defined as the income variate, and L_X is the number of persons having an income greater than X. It may be seen that a straight line unfolds for incomes above £400 or £500 which encompasses 75–80 per cent of the cases. One may fit a straight line of the form $X = aL_X^{-b}$ to the data by the method of least squares with the following results:

> 1962–3, £500 $\leqslant X \leqslant$ £20,000, $N = 11$ points or classes,
> $\log X = 5 \cdot 0226 - 0 \cdot 435 \log L_X$, $b = 0 \cdot 435$, implied lower
> (0·009)
> limit = £499, implied arithmetic mean = £883, implied
> concentration coefficient = 0·278.

It is of interest to know some of the properties of this distribution were it to continue to be distributed below £500 in logarithmic fashion to an L_X equivalent to the total number of cases. The implied lower limit may be obtained by substituting the total number of cases ($L_X = 22,242,000$ in 1962–3) in the formula. It can be demonstrated by using a continuous distribution that the implied arithmetic mean for this inverse Pareto curve[9] is $\bar{X} =$ (implied lower limit)/$(1 - b)$ and its concentration coefficient is $R = b/(2 - b)$. This procedure thus yields an $\bar{X} = $ £883 and an R of 0·278 which differ from the actual $\bar{X} = $ £853 and $R = 0 \cdot 338$. The theoretical R is less than the actual R because lower-tail incomes have been raised with an implicit lower limit of £499 instead of the actual lower limit of £180.

If the inverse Pareto line had been fitted to all points, one would have obtained:

> 1962–3, £180 $\leqslant X \leqslant$ £20,000, $N 3_4$ 16 points or classes,
> $\log X = 5 \cdot 2265 - 0 \cdot 503 \log L_X$, $b = 0 \cdot 503$, implied lower
> (0·032)
> limit £345, implied arithmetic mean = £694, implied
> concentration coefficient = 0·336.

The point to be emphasized is that when the procedure is applied only to upper-tail income for a distribution like that in 1962–3, $\bar{X}$ has an upward bias. The estimate for R has a downward bias but the slope of the line, b, is a measure of inequality with a larger value associated with a larger R.

We are now in a position to examine the ramifications of the various slopes which are presented in Chart 2 and Table 2. H. L. Gray has made estimates for six income classes in the year 1436, obtaining:

Class	Number of families in class	Yearly income per family £
Barons	51	865
Knights	183	208
Lesser knights and other men of government	750	60
Esquires (who were beneath the squirearchy,	1,200	24
including gentlemen, merchants, artisans,	1,600	12
but largely artisans)	3,400	5–9

CHART 2. *Cumulative Frequency Distributions of Income of Persons in Great Britain for Selected Years from 1436 to 1963.*

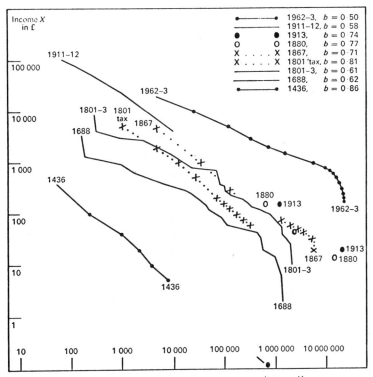

L_x cumulative number of persons with incomes above income X

TABLE 2. *British Income Data Featuring Upper-Income Groups*

Year	Name of investigator	Region	Number of persons in data	Lower limit of smallest class (£)	Per cent of total persons covered by data	Number of classes used	Inverse Pareto curve Slope b	Implied R for all persons	Implied mean X̄ of all persons (£)	Implied income of top person when $L_x = 1$ (£)	Standard error of b	Correlation coefficient squared and adjusted, R^2
1436	H. L. Gray	England and Wales	7,184 men	5	1	6	0.856	0.748	0.78	12,000	0.042	0.99
1688	Gregory King	England and Wales	1,350,000 families and single persons	2	100	26	0.616	0.446	33.8	77,000	0.040	0.94
1801-3	Patrick Colquhoun	England and Wales	2,210,000 families and single persons	10	100	45	0.610	0.438	105	320,000	0.023	0.94
1812	Patrick Colquhoun	G.B. and Ireland	4,379,000 families and single persons	25	100	12	0.520	0.351	109	150,000	0.028	0.96
1801	Parliamentary returns	Great Britain	320,759 persons	65	15	33	0.807	0.677	64.2	1,600,000	0.008	0.99
1867	R. Dudley Baxter	England and Wales	5,229,000 men	20	100	13	0.705	0.544	94.2	1,500,000	0.027	0.98
1867	R. Dudley Baxter	G.B. and Ireland	13,720,000 men, women, and children with income	15	100	8	0.726	0.570	27.6	570,000	0.036	0.98
1880	Arthur Bowley	United Kingdom	14,770,000 with occupations and assessments	below 160	100	3	0.772	0.629	76.2	4,600,000	0.033	0.99
1913	Arthur Bowley	United Kingdom	20,700,000 with occupations and assessments	below 160	100	3	0.740	0.588	105	4,900,000	0.038	0.99
1911-12	Josiah Stamp	United Kingdom	12,399 assessed persons	5,000	0.1	11	0.575	0.403	—	1,200,000	0.009	0.99
1913-14	Josiah Stamp	United Kingdom	13,231 assessed persons	5,000	0.1	11	0.575	0.403	—	1,300,000	0.013	0.99
1962-3	Inland Revenue	United Kingdom	22,242,000 married couples[1] and single	180	100	16	0.503	0.336	694	170,000	0.032	0.95
			15,981,000 married couples[1] and single	500	72	11	0.435	0.278	883	110,000	0.009	0.99

[1] A married couple (whether separately assessed for tax or not) is counted as one person.

Sources: H. L. Gray, 'Incomes from Land in England in 1436'. *Eng. Hist. Rev.*, 49 (1934), 607–39; Charles Davenant, *The Political and Commercial Works*, ed. Sir Charles Whitworth, (1771), ii. 184; Patrick Colquhoun, *A Treatise on Indigence* (1806), p. 23; Colquhoun, *A Treatise on the Wealth, Power, and Resources of the British Empire* (1815), pp. 124, 125; R. Dudley

Kingdom (1868), frontispiece, p. 60, appendix 1; Arthur Bowley, *The Change in the Distribution of the National Income, 1880–1913* (Oxford, 1920), p. 16; Josiah Stamp, *British Incomes and Property* (1916), p. 338; *Report of the Commissioners of Her Majesty's Inland Revenue, Report 107* (1965), p. 83; B. R. Mitchell, *Abstract of British Historical Statistics* (Cambridge, 1962), pp. 8

When the inverse Pareto curve is fitted to these six classes the slope, b, is 0·86.
(0·042)
One might consider the extension of the curve to an L_X of 750,000 persons,[10] shown as a dot at the bottom of Chart 2. Such a distribution has an implicit R of 0·75, which is larger than any other implied or actual income R computed in this study. It will be remembered that the implied R is more likely to be a minimum than a maximum R. The author has never found a complete distribution with an R less than the implied R of the upper tail having a substantial number of classes.

The next upper-tail distribution is that stemming from the income tax in 1801. This included:

Lower limit of income class £	Number in class	Lower limit of income class £	Number in class
5,000	1,020	200	42,694
2,000	3,657	150	33,554
1,000	6,927	100	70,381
500	14,762	60	147,764

The slope, b, of 0·81 is substantially greater than the $b = 0.61$ from
(0·008)   (0·023)
Colquhoun's data, and one should try to resolve the discrepancy if one is to link 1436 to 1801, and 1801 to 1867 [$t(0·81, 0·61) = 3·67$; $t_{05} = 1·67$].[11] At least part of the difference can be explained by statistical calculations. Let us reshuffle the Colquhoun data by granting a modest dispersion within each socio-economic class by assuming within each class a Pareto distribution with an R of 0·25. When this is done, some persons in each class spill over into higher- or lower-income classes, yielding an overall cumulative curve with a slope, b, of 0·68, based on a laborious calculation involving 14 points. The value 0·68 is substantially higher than that value without internal class dispersion, 0·61. One might argue, then, that at least one-third of the inequality discrepancy between Colquhoun's 1801–3 data and the 1801 income-tax data can be explained by the statistical formulation.

The 1801 tax data are criticized because they are considered to account for only a small part of national income. High evasion is suspected. If one uses the concepts of implied lower limit and implied $\bar{X}$, however, average income from the income-tax data is calculated to be £64·2. This was 64 per cent of Colquhoun's annual average income in the 1801–3 period.

One is left to make judgements about inequality. These might be:

1. No change occurred from 1688 to 1801–3. This is based on the King–Colquhoun data with $b_{1688} = 0.62$, and $b_{1801-3} = 0·61$.
[$t(0·62, 0·61) = 0·10$; $t_{05} = 1·67$]

2. Income inequality in 1436 was perhaps a little greater than in 1801 (and, thus, than in 1688). This is based on the income-tax data of Gray and the

parliamentary returns with $b_{1436} = 0.86$, and $b_{1801} = 0.81$.

$$[t(0.86, 0.81) = 1.83; \; t_{05} = 1.68]$$

3. Inequality in 1867 and 1880 was similar to that in 1801. This stems from the parliamentary returns of 1801, the Baxter estimates for 1867, and the Bowley estimates of 1880. All are based on income-tax returns with $b_{1801} = 0.81$, $b_{1867} = 0.71$, and $b_{1880} = 0.77$. One might conclude that there is evidence that inequality was less in 1867 and in 1880 than in 1801. However, Colquhoun's estimates might dampen one's ardour.

$$[t(0.81, 0.71) = 4.46; \; t_{05} = 1.68]$$
$$[t(0.81, 0.77) = 1.36; \; t_{05} = 1.69]$$

4. Inequality was not greater in 1911 and 1913 that it was in 1867 and 1880. It might even have been 10 per cent less. These results are based on $b_{1867} = 0.71$, $b_{1880} = 0.77$, and $b_{1913} = 0.74$, coupled with additional data yielding $b_{1911-12} = 0.58$ and $b_{1913-14} = 0.58$. These latter two coefficients, coming from data of Sir Josiah Stamp, are rather startling. The Stamp 1911–12 cumulative curve is given in Chart 2. Particular details are listed in Table 2.

$$[t(0.71, 0.74) \text{ has wrong sign}]$$
$$[t(0.71, 0.58) = 3.56; \; t_{05} = 1.73]$$
$$[t(0.71, 0.58) = 3.47; \; t_{05} = 1.73]$$
$$[t(0.77, 0.74) = 0.63; \; t_{05} = 2.92]$$
$$[t(0.77, 0.58) = 2.69; \; t_{05} = 1.81]$$
$$[t(0.77, 0.58) = 6.12; \; t_{05} = 1.81]$$

5. Inequality decreased substantially from 1911–13 to 1962–3, with $b_{(1962-3 \text{ above } £500)} = 0.44$.

$$[t(0.74, 0.44) = 7.56; \; t_{05} = 1.80]$$
$$[t(0.58, 0.44) = 9.44; \; t_{05} = 1.73]$$
$$[t(0.58, 0.44) = 8.40; \; t_{05} = 1.73]$$

6. Upper-tail income-tax data show evidence of continuous decline in inequality based on the 1436, 1801, 1911–12, and 1962–3 data, where $b_{1436} = 0.86$, $b_{1801} = 0.81$, $b_{1911-12} = 0.58$, and $b_{1962-3 \text{ above } £500} = 0.44$.

III. ECONOMIC GROWTH AND INEQUALITY

Emphasis in this paper is placed on upper-income groups and their relative income shares. In traditional society, property income was the more substantial portion of total income. If the Industrial Revolution had not taken place, incomes in 1873 might have been distributed in the fashion shown in Table 3. The concentration coefficients for gross rentals are not quite as high as they would have been had sorting been by rentals rather than by acres. With this allowance, one can say that the concentration coefficients are substantially greater than those of Chart 1 and Table 1. The inverse Pareto slopes are close to unity. A continuous geometric distribution of this shape would lead to perfect inequality. The 1,688 peers and great landowners owned almost 50 per cent of the land. The 10,207 persons having landholdings of 500 acres or more had two-thirds of private landholdings and 40 per cent of gross estate rentals.

TABLE 3. *British Landownership, 1873–5*

(a) *In England, 1873*

Class	Number of owners	Acres (thousands)
Peers and peeresses	400	5,728
Great landowners	1,288	8,497
Squires	2,529	4,319
Great yeomen	9,585	4,782
Lesser yeomen	24,412	4,144
Small proprietors	217,049	3,931
Cottagers	703,289	151
Public bodies	14,459	1,443
Waste		1,524
Total	973,011	34,519

Concentration coefficient, R, of private holders is $0 \cdot 817$ excluding cottagers and $0 \cdot 944$ including cottagers.

(b) *In England and Ireland, 1874–5*

Lower class limit (in acres)	Number of persons	Acreage (thousands)	Gross revenue estimates (£ thousands)
100,000+	1	181	161
50,000+	3	194	188
20,000+	66	1,917	2,331
10,000+	223	3,098	4,337
5,000+	581	3,974	5,522
2,000+	1,815	5,529	9,579
1,000+	2,719	3,799	7,914
500+	4,799	3,317	6,427
100+	32,317	6,827	13,680
50+	25,839	1,791	4,302
10+	72,640	1,750	6,509
1+	121,983	478	6,438
0+	703,289	151	29,127
Total	966,275	33,006	96,515

The concentration coefficient for acreage was $0 \cdot 858$ for those holding 1 acre or more, and $0 \cdot 774$ for those holding 10 acres or more. The concentration coefficients of gross revenues based on these same classifications were $0 \cdot 697$ and $0 \cdot 678$.

Sources: Table 3 (a): John Bateman, *The Great Land Owners of Great Britain and Ireland* (1883), p. 515; this table is culled from *The Modern Domesday Book* and correspondence to correct for variation in spelling of landowners holding land in several counties. Table 3 (b): Charles B. Spahr, *The Present Distribution of Wealth in the United States* (1893), Library of Economics and Politics, ed. Richard T. Ely, p. 162, as taken from the Domesday Book for 1874–5. Bateman suggests several changes above 2,000 acres showing greater concentration (lower class limit in acres–frequency): 100,000–44; 50,000–71; 20,000–299; 10,000–487; 6,000–617; 3,000–982; 2,000–1,320. There is some question of Irish holdings.

This is probably the element determining the configuration of the 1436 data and the element dominating that of the 1801 tax data. It was noted that there could have been a slight lessening of inequality from 1436 to 1688. One might engage in somewhat questionable calculations to demonstrate that economic growth took place during this period and, thus, that property income might not have been as dominant in the latter year. The implicit arithmetic mean for 1436 was given earlier as £0·78. The King average for 1688 was £32·2. If prices doubled in this 253-year period, the average annual rate of growth was 1·2 per cent. If prices quadrupled, it was 0·9 per cent.[12] It will be recalled that the implicit arithmetic mean projected internally from the 1436 figures is more a maximum than a minimum estimate. One may still question the absolute level of the 1436 figures.

It would seem that the onslaught of the Industrial Revolution, with growth in profits from trade and professional income, could not have introduced an element of greater inequality than that existing with property income. Two pieces of evidence which have some bearing on this point can now be introduced.

First, as mentioned earlier, Patrick Colquhoun's estimates for 1801 had 20 socio-economic classes listed which were not stated in King's 1688 data. These 20 classes, given earlier, included shopowners, manufacturers, merchants, etc., which in general might be considered as the emerging groups. The analysis from Lorenz curves for the 1801–3 data yields:

	Number of families and single individuals	$\overline{X}$	R
25 classes similar to those of King	1,958,000	£87·9	0·545
20 classes including those emerging with economic growth	252,000	£198·1	0·501
45 classes	2,210,000	£99·8	0·555

The new element at this stage has not increased total inequality, even though its income average is higher. Its internal relative dispersion is less than that for more traditional classes.

Secondly, the introduction of evidence from British 1812 and 1849 income-tax data, using Schedule D income from trade and the professions, shows the following results:

$$1812, X \geqslant £150, \text{ 13 income classes, } b = 0·85$$
$$1849, X \geqslant £150, \text{ 13 income classes, } b = 0·74$$
$$[t(0·85, 0·74) = 7·31; \ t_{05} = 1·72]$$

Inequality in the developing trade and professional sector in 1812, as measured by $b = 0·85$, was at least as large as that of the total taxable income inequality in 1801, with $b = 0·82$. By 1849, Schedule D income had a slope b of 0·74. This was sufficient to elicit the conclusion[13] in the Parliamentary Papers, 'this remarkable fact that the incomes have increased more under the smaller classes of income than the larger ones'. It will be recalled that R. Dudley Baxter's data for 1867 employ Schedule D income, yielding a *b* of 0·72. One has access again to a concept of total income in 1911 where the slope is 0·58. From 1811 to 1911 the number of males employed in the agricultural sector with its great inequality remained relatively unchanged while the male labour force expanded more than five times in other endeavours with less inequality.[14]

The argument is thus one that there was a continued widening of opportunity for non-propertied income groups. Statistical evidence indicates that income inequality, particularly in upper-income groups, has decreased for several centuries. This trend has been accelerated in the twentieth century.

NOTES

[1] A. J. Taylor in 'Progress and Poverty in Britain in 1780–1850; A Reappraisal', *History*, 45 (Feb. 1960), lists four major works supporting this thesis. The list is headed by the remarkable work of Dorothy George, *London Life in the Eighteenth century* (1925).

[2] S. N. Procopovitch, 'The Distribution of National Income', *Econ. Jour.* 36 (Mar. 1926); Simon Kuznets, 'Quantitative Aspects of the Economic Growth of Nations', *Economic Development and Cultural Change*, 11 no. 2, pt. ii (Jan. 1963).

[3] *Parl. Papers*, 1801–2, iv. 152–5, also 1852 (in 510), ix. 463; Josiah Stamp, *British Incomes and Property* (1916), *Wealth and Taxable Capacity* (1922); Inland Revenue Reports beginning in 1857.

[4] Phyllis Deane, 'The Implications of Early National Income Estimates for the Measurement of Long-Term Economic Growth in the United Kingdom', *Econ. Dev. and Cult. Change*, 4 (1955–6), 3–38.

[5] Patrick Colquhoun, *Treatise on Indigence*, p. 23.

[6] B. R. Mitchell, *Abstract of British Historical Statistics*, pp. 8, 11, 366.

[7] R. Dudley Baxter, *National Income, the United Kingdom*, frontispiece, p. 60, appendix 1. Use has been made of the fact that 62 per cent of men, women, and children in the upper- and middle-income classes were males twenty years old and over.

[8] Arthur Bowley, *The Change in the Distribution of the National Income, 1880–1913*, p. 16.

[9] Lee Soltow, 'The Share of Lower Income Groups in Income', *Rev. Econ. and Stat.* (Nov. 1965).

[10] Gregory King used approximately 1,350,000 as the number of adult families and single adult individuals in 1688. He further estimated the total population in the year 1400 as 60 per cent of the total population in the year 1700.

[11] The *t*-statistics stem from the standard error of the difference between two sample slopes. In this and subsequent comparisons of two slopes, it is assumed that the standard errors of estimate for the two universes are the same. One-tail tests are employed, using the 5 per cent level.

[12] Wheat prices at Exeter in 1688 as a ratio of those in 1436 were 3·84.—Mitchell, op. cit. p. 484.

[13] *Parl. Papers*, 1852, ix. 593.

[14] Labour force data from Mitchell, op. cit., p. 60.

7

English Bank Deposits before 1844*

D. K. ADIE

Editor's note. This article was first published in *Econ. Hist. Rev.* 23 (1970), 285–97.

The methods of time series analysis are discussed above, pp. 25–30 and those of correlation analysis are considered on pp. 15–19. Numerous references to further reading on these subjects are given in the footnotes to those pages.

Peel's Act of 1844 has been a controversial piece of legislation because the Bank of England's authority for discretionary control of the money supply through changes in deposits was based on its provisions for over a century. The features of the Act are as follows: the prohibition of new banks of issue, the limitation of existing country note-issues, the separation of the note-issuing from the banking functions of the Bank of England, the limitation of the Bank of England's fiduciary note-issues, and the 100 per cent reserve requirement for Bank notes issued in excess of this limit. The Act also gave the Bank of England freedom in its management of deposits, since it made no mention of the control of deposits.

Basing discretionary monetary policy on the authority of the Bank Charter Act is ironical, since the Currency School which drafted the Act denied the need for central banking. The Currency School vigorously opposed discretionary control of the money supply, and in their view the 1844 Act replaced discretion with rules. The Banking School, which opposed the Currency School in theory and policy, supported discretion in the control of the money supply.

In espousing the real bills doctrine, the Banking School advocated discretionary control of bank liabilities by the banks themselves. John Fullarton of the Banking School said that money should be provided at all times in proportion to the demands of the community. 'So long as a bank issues its notes only in the discount of good bills, at not more than sixty days date, it cannot go wrong in issuing as many as the public will receive from it.'[1] The Banking School argued that economic fluctuations would be minimized if the banks regulated the size of their own liabilities by responding to the 'needs of trade'.[2]

* The author is indebted to his teachers and colleagues at the University of Chicago and in particular to Milton Friedman, Robert Mundell, and George Stigler for their direction. The author takes blame for errors. Financial assistance from the following is gratefully acknowledged: the William Lyon MacKenzie King Foundation, the Richard M. Weaver Foundation, the Workshop on Money and Banking at the University of Chicago, the Earhart Foundation, and the Ford Foundation. Secretarial assistance was provided by the College of Business Administration, Ohio University. Computer facilities were provided by the University of Chicago and Ohio University.

James Wilson of the Banking School said that 'Banking, above all other professions, is that which under entire freedom and non-interference would soonest be placed in the most perfect position.'[3]

For the Currency School, Samson Ricardo said that deviations from fixed rules tended to derange the supply of money (defined by the Currency School as all notes plus gold held for monetary purposes);[4] Peel and Robert Torrens argued that discretionary control of the money supply endangered convertibility of notes into gold.[5] The public, according to Overstone, blamed the Bank of England for failing to protect sufficiently well the convertibility of notes into gold in 1825, 1837, and 1839.[6] Overstone blamed the Bank's discretionary changes in the money supply for the unstable business climate. He said that the Bank's discretionary decisions caused widespread suffering throughout the entire country;[7] and, later, that the Act of 1844 was the public's attempt to substitute rules for discretion because of the financial crises they had suffered.[8]

Robert Torrens and Samson Ricardo maintained that control of the money supply was too important to be conducted by the Bank of England's managers, since their discretionary decisions affected all Englishmen.[9] George Norman of the Currency School added that the discretionary control of the money supply by the joint-stock and private banks also increased instability and harmed the economy.[10] To eliminate instability in the economy, Overstone advocated the control of the money supply by a fixed rule known to everyone rather than 'the private judgement and prudence' of the monetary authority.[11] Peel argued that fixed rules were needed because discretion was not sufficiently safe for regulating the amount of money.[12]

After Peel's Act was passed, Overstone triumphantly claimed, 'Never again will one great public body be entrusted with the dangerous power of creating money at its own discretion and extending or contracting the amount of the circulation uncontrolled by any fixed rule.'[13] Peel said that the essential feature of the Act of 1844 was the removal of convertible notes entirely from the discretion of any man, body of men, bank, or government.[14]

After 1844, the Bank became conscious of its power to control the activity of other banks, credit conditions, and the money supply through its deposit management, rather than through changes in its notes and deposits. The failure to regulate deposits in Peel's Act permitted this discretionary control of the money supply when automatic control was intended. Professor R. S. Sayers, who supports the present discretionary monetary policy, has said that Peel's Act

... was clutching at a slippery eel when it sought to apply a rule of thumb to the monetary situation by regulating the issue of bank notes alone. This was the design of the famous Bank Charter Act of 1844; men soon found how to escape its intentions, though the empty shell long remained, a memorial to those who believed that either nature or the law had drawn a sharp line of distinction between what was money and what was not money and that an automatic machine could sufficiently govern the monetary situation.[15]

The legal framework of the Act remained intact while its underlying principle—the control of money supply by rules instead of authority—was denied in practice because the Act left the Bank free to conduct its banking business as a central bank. Professor Hayek, who advocates rules rather than authority in monetary policy, has suggested that the intentions of the Currency School would have been implemented by applying the fixed fiduciary issue principle to deposits as well as to notes. This would have brought deposits under regulation by a fixed rule and diminished discretion in monetary management.[16]

Against the background of the 'rules versus discretion' controversy, the problem of the source of discretionary control of the money supply might be rephrased as follows: why did the Currency School omit deposits from regulation in Peel's Act, 1844?

Several reasons have been suggested why deposits were not controlled by the Bank Charter Act. First, the Currency School desired the control of notes alone because earlier financial crises had involved the convertibility of notes but not deposits.[17] Secondly, the Currency and Banking Schools believed that the limitation on note issues was an ultimate constraint on the creation of deposits. The Currency School believed further that rigid control of deposits was implicit in the control of notes. If notes were controlled, there would then be no need to control deposits explicitly.[18] Thirdly, the Currency School viewed deposit banking as a commercial enterprise, subject to the minimum regulation consistent with the shareholder's and creditor's security. No direct interference with deposit banking appeared justified since the general public could choose whether or not to hold bank deposits, whereas it had no choice in the matter of notes. Note-issues then fell within the state's responsibility for the currency while deposits did not.[19] Although the Currency and Banking Schools were generally aware of the importance of deposits in 1844, apart from a few references there was no discussion of their quantitative importance. Finally, then, deposits were not controlled by the Bank Charter Act because they were quantitatively insignificant compared to notes.[20]

This article examines the last reason suggested above. A little consideration is given to the second reason, but much more work needs to be done. In determining the quantitative importance of English bank deposits, the levels and fluctuations of deposits are considered and compared with notes.[21] Four main questions are posed, two concerning the levels of deposits and two concerning their fluctuations: (1) What were the levels of deposits relative to notes, as measured by their respective means? (2) What were the trends in deposits relative to notes, as measured by their respective percentage rates of increase? (3) Were fluctuations in deposits large relative to the fluctuations in notes, as measured where possible by their respective standard errors of estimate of logs about time trends? (4) Were fluctuations in deposits in the same direction as the fluctuations in notes, as measured where possible by the correlation coefficients between the logs of notes and deposits? The time trend is included for the long-run comparison; excluded for short-run comparisons. The deposits of each of three types of English banks are examined separately: the Bank of England which issued notes and created deposits; London banks which created deposits; and country banks which issued notes.

I

Gold payments for notes were restricted at the Bank of England in 1797 and resumed in 1821. Peel's Act in 1844 tied Bank note issues to gold reserves and took steps to eliminate country issues. These dates divide the data into useful periods which will be used throughout this article, except where the availability of data determines otherwise.

TABLE 1. *Levels of Bank of England Notes and Deposits*

	Means (£ million)		Notes/	Annual percentage rates of increase[1]	
Period	Notes	Deposits	Deposits	Notes	Deposits
1815–56	20·90	5·40	3·87	—0·42	4·69
1815–21	25·82	1·63	15·84	—3·59	—1·01
1822–44	19·38	4·80	4·03	—0·46	3·96
1845–56	20·94	8·74	2·39	0·49	0·14

[1] The annual percentage rates of increase are the coefficients β and b expressed as percentages taken from regression equations $\log N = \gamma + \beta T$ and $\log D = a + bT$ where T is the year and N and D are Bank of England notes and deposits respectively. The same kind of calculations are made throughout this article unless otherwise specified.

Source: Figures for Bank notes are averages of 28 February and 31 August taken from *Report from the Select Committee on Bank Acts*, P.P. (1857), 2nd Sess. x, pts i and ii, app. eleven. Figures for Bank deposits are taken from the same source with government deposits and banker's balances at head office subtracted.

TABLE 2. *Fluctuations of Bank of England Notes and Deposits*

	Standard deviations of logs about trend		Correlation coefficients between logs of notes and deposits[1]			
Period	Notes	Deposits	$r^2 \cdot T$	$r \cdot T$	r^2	r
1815–56	12	33	4	—0·19	19	—0·43
1815–21	5	45	36	0·60	11	0·33
1822–44	8	30	4	0·19	2	—0·12
1845–56	7	18	24	0·49	23	0·48

[1] $r^2 \cdot T$ is the square of the correlation coefficient between the logs of Bank notes and deposits excluding the trend and expressed as a percentage. r is the correlation coefficient including the trend. The same terminology is used throughout the article.

Source: Same as source to Table 1.

The means of bank deposits in Table 1 are less than the corresponding means of Bank notes for all periods. With respect to relative levels during the Restriction (1797–1821) when the Bank was released from its obligation to buy its notes with gold, the ratio of notes to deposits rose to its highest level. After the resumption of gold payments in 1821, this ratio fell from 15·84 to 4·03. After Peel's Act, when Bank notes were tied to gold reserves, the ratio fell to 2·39. Except perhaps during the Restriction, the levels of deposits were at no time low enough to be regarded as economically insignificant.

The annual percentage rates of increase in Table 1 indicate that the level of deposits increased after 1821. During 1822–44 deposits increased at 3·9 per cent per annum, while notes decreased. This was the period during which the Currency and Banking Schools tried to influence policy.

The standard deviations of logs about trend in Table 2, expressed in percentage terms, indicate that deposits fluctuated more widely than notes throughout the whole period and in each sub-period from 1815 to 1856. The correlation coefficients indicate that during the Restriction and after Peel's Act deposits fluctuated in the same direction as notes. The highest proportion of the variance in deposits 'explained' by the contemporaneous variation in notes is only 36 per cent and occurs during the Restriction period. Hence for Bank of England notes and deposits, there is little support for the proposition that fluctuations in notes closely controlled fluctuations in deposits.

II

No private London banks published balance sheets before the 1890s. Consequently, it is difficult to obtain data on London bank deposits. I have been able to get estimates for only nine dates between 1796 and 1857. The periods in Table 3 differ from those in Table 1 in order to make better use of these sparse estimates.

TABLE 3. *Levels of Bank of England Notes and London Bank Deposits*

Period	Means (£ million)		Notes/Deposits	Annual percentage rates of increase	
	Notes	Deposits		Notes	Deposits
1796–1857	19·93	38·25	0·52	0·4	1·1
1796–1824	19·85	13·00	1·53	2·6	1·3
1824–44	19·48	22·25	0·88	−0·8	2·4
1844–57	20·97	48·00	0·44	0·3	3·3

Sources: Calculations involving Bank of England notes are based on figures described in source to Table 1. Annual percentage rates of increase for deposits were calculated directly from estimates in Feaveryear, op. cit., p. 304, and my estimates based on Elmer Wood, *English Theories of Central Banking Control, 1819–1858* (Cambridge, Mass., 1939), p. 21n., and figures for London joint-stock bank deposits in *Report from the Select Committee on Bank Acts*, P.P. 1857–8, v, Q. 1134.

The means and the annual percentage rates of increase for London bank deposits in Table 3 were greater than those for Bank notes over the whole period and in each sub-period, except during the Restriction. The level of London bank deposits surpassed the level of Bank notes and increased at a greater annual rate than Bank notes between 1824 and 1844. This evidence indicates that London bank deposits were a quantitatively significant item in the inventory of financial assets.

Sufficient data are not available to make direct calculations of fluctuations of

London bank deposits. In attempting to measure fluctuations indirectly, I have considered the London joint-stock banks for which information is available. The London and Westminster Bank which began operations in 1834 was the first joint-stock bank in London, apart from the Bank of England. By 1857 there were eight such banks in London with 28 offices. The correlation coefficient between the logs of the number of London joint-stock bank offices and London joint-stock deposits, excluding the time trend for the period 1834–57, is 0·78. This provides some support for using the number of offices as a proxy for deposits.[22]

An indirect comparison of the fluctuation of London bank deposits and country bank deposits is made in Table 4. The availability of data accounts for the periods.

If the number of bank offices is taken as a proxy for deposits, the standard deviations of logs about trends in Table 4 indicate that the fluctuations in London bank deposits were less than those of country banks. This result is supported by the testimony of Overstone who said that 'you will not find the fluctuations in the amount of deposits with London bankers as nearly so great as the fluctuations in the amount of deposits with country banks.'[23]

TABLE 4. *Fluctuations in the Number of London Bank Offices and Issuing Country Bank Offices*

Period	Standard deviation of logs about trends		Correlation coefficients between logs of the number of London bank offices and issuing country bank offices			
	London bank offices	Country bank offices	$r^2 \cdot T$	$r \cdot T$	r^2	r
1809–32	2	8	4	0·21	46	0·68
1809–21	2	9	45	0·67	4	0·22
1822–32	5	5	29	0·54	40	0·63

Sources: The numbers of country bank offices are taken from the licences to issue notes. See Wood, op. cit., p. 14. A licence was required for each office up to a total of four offices. Before 1819, there were few non-issuing banks except in Lancashire. After 1819 these figures understate the number of offices. The number of London bank offices is taken from F. G. H. Price (comp.), *A Handbook of London Bankers* (1890–1). L. S. Pressnell has brought to my attention the fact that these yearly lists inflate the true statistics of bank offices by including merchant bankers and others who were not strictly 'bankers' for the public. Probably this does not affect broad trends.

TABLE 5. *Correlation Coefficients between Logs of Joint-stock Deposits and Bank Notes or Deposits*

Period	Bank notes				Bank deposits			
	$r^2 \cdot T$	$r \cdot T$	r^2	r	$r^2 \cdot T$	$r \cdot T$	r^2	r
1834–56	1	−0·08	38	0·62	11	−0·34	0	−0·04
1834–44	15	−0·39	13	0·36	16	−0·42	24	−0·46
1845–56	17	0·41	14	0·37	2	0·15	2	0·15

Sources: Same as sources to Tables 1 and 3.

In Table 5, the negative correlation coefficients between the joint-stock deposits and Bank notes or deposits, excluding the time trend, suggest that the short-run fluctuations in London deposits were in the opposite direction from Bank notes or deposits before 1845. The long-run fluctuations in London deposits tended to be in the same direction as Bank notes but the tendency was not strong as measured by the percentage of variation in joint-stock deposits 'explained' by the fluctuations of Bank notes.

J. H. Palmer, Director of the Bank of England from 1811 to 1857 and Governor in 1830–3, said in 1840 that fluctuations in Bank of England deposits were greater than those of private banks, since as much as one-third of the Bank's deposits might be withdrawn during an unfavourable exchange.[24] Palmer also said that the deposits of London bankers varied, at most, only £3 million to £4 million.[25] I conclude that Bank of England deposits (relative to their size) fluctuated more than London deposits or country deposits.

III

In Table 6 country notes and deposits are compared. The periods differ from those of Table 1 in order to make better use of the sparse estimates.

The levels of the notes–deposits ratio indicate that the level of country deposits exceeded country notes between 1821 and 1844. As early as 1828, Thomas Attwood estimated the total liabilities of all bankers in England and Wales to be £200 million which, while an inflated figure, suggests that country deposits were 'important' by this date.[26]

The annual percentage rates of increase for country deposits in Table 6 exceeded those of notes in all periods. In the period 1821–44, a very large

TABLE 6. *Levels of Country Notes and Deposits*

Period	Means (£ million)			Annual percentage rates of increase	
	Notes	*Deposits*	*Notes/Deposits*	*Notes*	*Deposits*
1808–50	15·3	45·9	0·33	−4·0	2·3
1808–21	26·8	20·5	1·31	−3·7	2·2
1821–44	10·7	34·1	0·31	−1·9	4·3
1844–50	7·0	59·6	0·12	−5·2	4·9

Sources: Country notes for 1807–32 are crude estimates derived from stamp duties. The reader is warned that these figures should be used only to indicate broad movements. Country notes for 1807–25 are calculated from L. S. Pressnell, *Country Banking in the Industrial Revolution* (Oxford, 1956), p. 188, by taking notes stamped in each year and adding notes stamped in the previous two years. For procedure see Viner, op. cit., pp. 163–5. For 1826–32, the annual figures for country notes are calculated in the same way from *Report from the Committee of Secrecy on the Bank of England Charter*, P.P. 1831–2, vi, app. 99. For 1833–56 the annual figures for country notes are the averages of 28 Feb. and 31 Aug. in *Committee* (1857), app. 15. My estimates for country deposits are based on Pressnell, op. cit., pp. 512–13, 526–31; Wood, op. cit., pp. 21–2; Feavearyear, op. cit., p. 289; *Committee* (1857), apps. 15 and 21.

growth took place in country deposits. William Rodwell said that all banks had shared in the joint-stock bank expansion in 1836 which extended the deposit system throughout the country. The large increase in country deposits, he said, accounted for the decrease in country notes from £11·7 million in 1839 to £7·7 million in 1843.[27] William Newmarch, a Wakefield banker and supporter of the Banking School, stated that the aggregate quantity of notes in the United Kingdom increased only £1·5 million from 1834 to 1855, while trade transactions increased five or six times and population increased 30 or 35 per cent.[28] Although Newmarch's estimate of the increase in trade transactions seems to be exaggerated, his argument that deposit banking must have expanded considerably to support the increased trade was not opposed by any contemporary authors known to me.

The distribution of joint-stock banks established in the country between 1837 and 1844 between issuing and non-issuing banks also supports an early development of deposit banking. In 1837–44 only seven issuing banks as against 30 nonissuing banks were established. This indicates that deposits grew substantially compared with notes before 1844. [29]

Since country deposits exceeded country notes in levels and annual percentage rates of increase, and the Currency School regarded country notes as important enough to be eliminated, country deposits were also important enough on quantitative grounds to have deserved consideration in policy-making.

Figures of savings banks deposits, and from Barnard, Leyland, and Gillett, who were country bankers, may be taken to stand for country deposits. The standard deviations of logs about trend in Table 7 indicate that, except for savings bank deposits in the period 1845–56, all series of country deposits fluctuated at least as much (relative to their size) as Bank notes. This means that

T A B L E 7. *Fluctuations in Bank of England Notes and Country Deposits Series*

(Standard deviations of logs about trend)

Period	Bank notes	Savings bank deposits	Barnard's deposits	Leyland's deposits	Gillett's deposits
1800–45	16		24		
1812–45	10			26	
1817–56	12	61[1]			
1800–21	10		25		
1812–21	9			9	
1822–45	8		18		
1826–45	9				21
1822–44	8	12			
1845–56	7	6			

[1] This figure is high because savings bank deposits increased at a much higher rate in the first five years than in subsequent years.

Sources: Barnard's, Leyland's, and Gillett's deposits all taken from Pressnell, op. cit., pp. 512–13, 516–17, 518–19. Savings bank deposits are taken from B. R. Mitchell and Phyllis Deane, *Abstract of British Historical Statistics* (Cambridge, 1962), p. 453. Also see source to Table 1.

the degree of fluctuations of country deposits was quantitatively significant.

Table 8 indicates that except for Barnard's deposits in the period 1807–21 and Leyland's deposits in the period 1822–45, country notes fluctuated more (relative to their size) than the country deposit series. Newmarch said that although country notes and deposits were stable in 'quiet times', in periods of unrest country deposits fluctuated more than country notes.[30] This statement is confirmed by the evidence if interpreted in absolute terms, but denied if fluctuations are expressed in percentage terms. Tentatively, it seems that country deposits fluctuated more than Bank of England notes but slightly less than country notes, relative to their respective sizes. Fluctuations in country deposits were greater than those of London deposits, but not greater than Bank deposits. This indicates that fluctuations in country bank deposits were quantitatively significant.

Thomas Tooke's statement that country bank notes fluctuated more, relative

TABLE 8. *Fluctuations in the Country Bank Notes and Country Deposit Series*

(Standard deviations of logs about trend)

Period	Country notes	Savings bank deposits	Barnard's deposits	Leyland's deposits	Gillett's deposits
1807–45	27		23		
1812–45	29			26	
1817–56	26	61[1]			
1807–21	18		25		
1812–21	17			9	
1822–45	26		18	26	
1826–45	24				21
1822–44	27	12			
1845–56	8	6			

[1] This figure is high because savings bank deposits increased at a much higher rate in the first five years than in subsequent years.

Sources: Same as sources to Tables 1, 6, and 7.

TABLE 9. *Fluctuations in Bank of England and Country Bank Notes*

Period[1]	Standard deviations of logs about trend		Correlation coefficients between logs of Bank of England and country bank notes							
	Bank notes	Country notes	$r^2 \cdot T$	Simultaneous				Country notes lagged one year		
				$r \cdot T$	r^2	r	$r^2 \cdot T$	$r \cdot T$	r^2	r
1807–56	13	26	14	0·37	20	45	6	0·24	14	0·37
1807–21	12	18	53	0·73	0	0·01	36	0·59	6	−0·25
1822–44	8	27	3	−0·18	0	0·01	21	−0·46	1	−0·10
1845–56	7	8	9	0·30	3	0·17	55	0·74	31	0·56

[1] Periods refer to country notes even when lagged one year.

Sources: Same as sources to Tables 1 and 6.

185 of 264

TABLE 10. *Fluctuations in Bank of England Notes and Country Deposit Series*

Correlation coefficients between logs of Bank of England notes and logs of

Period	Savings bank deposits				Barnard's deposits				Leyland's deposits				Gillett's deposits			
	$r^2 \cdot T$	$r \cdot T$	r^2	r	$r^2 \cdot T$	$r \cdot T$	r^2	r	$r^2 \cdot T$	$r \cdot T$	r^2	r	$r^2 \cdot T$	$r \cdot T$	r^2	r
1808–45					0	0.05	0	0.02								
1812–45									21	−0.41	55	−0.74				
1817–56	39	−0.63	35	−0.59												
1800–21					0	−0.01	61	0.78								
1812–21									67	0.82	38	0.62				
1822–45					50	−0.71	30	−0.55	13	−0.36	15	−0.39				
1826–45													1	0.12	10	−0.31
1822–44	38	0.62	3	−0.16												
1845–56	28	0.53	30	0.55												

Sources: Same as sources to Tables 1 and 7.

TABLE 11. *Correlation Coefficients between Logs (1834–45)*

	Savings bank deposits				Barnard's deposits				Leyland's deposits				Gillett's deposits			
	$r^2 \cdot T$	$r \cdot T$	r^2	r	$r^2 \cdot T$	$r \cdot T$	r^2	r	$r^2 \cdot T$	$r \cdot T$	r^2	r	$r^2 \cdot T$	$r \cdot T$	r^2	r
Bank notes	1	0.10	25	0.50	38	−0.62	10	−0.33	64	−0.80	49	−0.70	14	−0.37	53	0.23
Bank deposits	2	−0.13	1	−0.11	62	−0.79	59	−0.77	30	−0.55	1	−0.09	31	−0.56	15	−0.39
Country notes	50	0.71	59	−0.77	49	0.70	1	0.10	52	0.23	66	0.81	69	0.83	17	−0.41
Joint-stock deposits	29	0.54	92	0.96	86	0.93	36	0.60	1	0.09	79	−0.89	85	0.92	90	0.95

Sources: Same as sources to Tables 1, 3 and 7.

TABLE 12. *Fluctuations in Country Notes and Country Deposit Series*

Correlation coefficients between logs of country notes and logs of

Period	Savings bank deposits				Barnard's deposits				Leyland's deposits				Gillett's deposits			
	$r^2 \cdot T$	$r \cdot T$	r^2	r	$r^2 \cdot T$	$r \cdot T$	r^2	r	$r^2 \cdot T$	$r \cdot T$	r^2	r	$r^2 \cdot T$	$r \cdot T$	r^2	r
1807–45					0	−0·04	69	−0·93								
1812–45									16	−0·40	55	−0·74				
1817–56	17	−0·41	62	−0·79												
1807–21					1	−0·11	32	−0·57								
1812–21									4	0·16	8	−0·28				
1822–45					14	0·37	6	−0·24	3	−0·17	6	−0·25				
1826–45													17	0·41	0	0·05
1822–44	0	0·81	15	−0·39												
1845–56	83	0·91	12	0·35												

Sources: Same as sources to Table 11.

to their size, than Bank notes[31] is supported by the standard deviations of logs about trend in Table 9. Tooke also said that if deposits were added to notes, the fluctuations in country bank liabilities would be still greater (relative to their size) than fluctuations in Bank liabilities, but only if the effects of the East and West India deposits at the Bank were excluded.[32] This suggests that the fluctuations in country deposits were not greater than those of Bank deposits, if the East and West India deposits at the Bank are included. This conclusion is supported by a comparison of the standard deviations of logs about trend for Bank deposits in Table 2 with those of the country deposits series in Table 8.

Table 10 indicates that 38 per cent of the variation in savings bank deposits can be 'explained' by the variation in Bank notes in period 1822–44; 28 per cent in period 1845–56. Also 67 per cent of the variation in Leyland's deposits can be 'exglained' by the variation in Bank notes in period 1800–21. Except for these cases, there is no evidence that country deposit series fluctuated consistently in the same direction as Bank notes. In many cases country deposits fluctuated in the opposite direction from Bank notes. Table 10 offers no evidence that fluctuations in country deposits were closely controlled by fluctuations in Bank notes; so there is no justification on this account, from the Currency School's point of view, for failing to regulate country deposits.

The correlation coefficients between joint-stock deposits and Barnard's, Leyland's, and Gillett's deposits in Table 11 are all positive, suggesting that country deposits fluctuated in the same direction as London deposits. The positive coefficients in Table 5 reinforce this opinion. The negative correlation coefficients between country deposits and Bank notes suggest that country deposits fluctuated in the opposite direction from Bank notes, discrediting the Currency School theory. The percentage of short-run fluctuations in Bernard's and Gillett's deposits 'explained' by the fluctuations in joint-stock deposits are 86 and 85 respectively. This suggests that country deposits might have been controlled quite closely by changes in London bank deposits.

Table 12, which compares the direction of fluctuations in country notes with those of some country deposit series, indicates that 83 per cent of the variation in savings bank deposits can be 'explained' by the variation in country notes in the period 1845–56; 14 per cent of the variation in Barnard's deposits can be 'explained' by the variation in country notes in the period 1822–45 and 17 per cent of the variation of Gillett's deposits can be 'explained' by the variation in country notes in the period 1826–45. Only 4 per cent of the variation in Leyland's deposits can be 'explained' by the variation in country notes. In all other cases country deposit series tended to fluctuate in the opposite direction from country notes. There is no justification here for failing to regulate country deposits in 1844.

The correlation coefficients between the log values of country notes and Bank notes in Table 9 are not great enough to support the proposition that fluctuations in Bank notes controlled country notes. Lagging country notes one year does not alter this conclusion before 1844. Country notes tended to fluctuate in the opposite direction from Bank notes between 1822 and 1844.

IV

A summary of the quantitative conclusions concerning deposits is contained in Table 13 from which a judgement can be made about their importance.

From Table 13, it is clear that deposits were at least as quantitatively important as notes in the period 1822–44 before Peel's Act. If deposits were negligible in amount, decreased, or fluctuated only slightly compared with notes, the

TABLE 13. *Summary of Quantitative Conclusions Concerning Deposits*

	Bank of England	London banks	Country banks
1. Level	Bank deposits were lower than Bank notes in all periods, but nevertheless were significant before 1844.	London deposits surpassed Bank notes between 1824 and 1844.	Country deposits exceeded country notes and Bank notes between 1821 and 1844.
2. Trend	Bank deposits increased at a greater rate than Bank notes between 1822 and 1856.	London deposits increased at a greater rate than Bank notes between 1824 and 1844.	From 1808 country deposits increased at a greater rate than Bank notes and country notes.
3. Degree of fluctuation	Bank deposits fluctuated more than Bank notes in all periods.	London deposits fluctuated less than Bank notes.	Country deposits fluctuated more than Bank notes and slightly less than country notes.
4. Direction of fluctuation	Bank deposits fluctuated only slightly in the same direction as Bank notes.	Short-run fluctuations in London deposits were not in the same direction as Bank notes or deposits.	Country deposits fluctuated in the same direction as country notes.

suggestion that the Currency School neglected deposits in Peel's Act on quantitative grounds would have been supported by evidence. However, the evidence does not show this and the few casual empirical statements made by members of the Currency and Banking Schools seem to indicate that they were aware of the true magnitudes involved.

The suggestion that the Currency School omitted deposits from regulation because they believed fluctuations in Bank notes caused fluctuations in deposits depends on an examination of the literature. Simple empirical tests suggest that a strong positive relationship did not exist between the fluctuations in Bank notes and deposits. Not finding a positive relationship does not discount this suggestion. Further research comparing the views of the Currency and Banking Schools concerning sources of change in the supply of notes and deposits, and comparing these with the actual sources of change, would clarify some important details surrounding the origin of discretionary monetary policy.

NOTES

[1] John Fullarton, *On the Regulation of Currencies* (2nd edn., 1845), pp. 206–7.

[2] Ibid., pp. 152, 226; *First and Second Reports from the Select Committee on Banks of Issue*, Parl. Papers, 1841, v, Q. 957 (J. W. Gilbart) Thomas Tooke, *A History of Prices, and the State of the Circulation, in 1838 and 1839* (6 vols., 1840), iii. 185; *Report from the Select Committee on Banks of Issue*, P.P. 1840 iv, Q. 3851 (T. Tooke); *Report from the Select Committee on Bank Acts*, P.P. 1857, 2nd Sess. x, pts i and ii, Q. 2057 (J. S. Mill). Government reports of committees are subsequently called *Committee* and distinguished by dates.

[3] James Wilson, *Capital, Currency and Banking*; being a collection of a series of articles published in *The Economist* in 1845, on the principle of the Bank Act of 1844: and in 1847, on the recent monetarial and commercial crisis; concluding with a plan for a secure and economical currency (1847), p. 29.

[4] Samson Ricardo, *A National Bank. The remedy for the evils attendant upon our present system of paper currency* (1838). Appendix. 'Plan for a national bank by (the late) David Ricardo' p. 32.

[5] *Debates in the House of Commons on Sir Robert Peel's Bank Bills of 1844 and 1845*. Reprinted verbatim from Hansard, *Parliamentary Debates* (1875), pp. 233–4 (Robert Peel); (Robert Torrens, *The Principles and Practical Operation of Sir Robert Peel's Act of 1844, Explained and Defended* (3rd edn., 1858), pp. 146, 150, 154.

[6] *First and Second Reports from the Secret Committee on Commercial Distress*, P.P. 1847–8, viii, pt i; Appendix, ibid. pt ii, QQ. 1406, 1551, 1514 (Samuel Jones Loyd (Lord Overstone)).

[7] Overstone, *Thoughts on the Separation of the Departments of the Bank of England* (1844). Reprinted in *Tracts and Other Publications on Metallic and Paper Currency*, ed. John R. McCulloch (1857), p. 254; *Committee* (1840), QQ. 2764, 2805 (Overstone).

[8] *Committee* (1848). Q. 5207 (Overstone).

[9] Torrens, op. cit., p. 53; S. Ricardo, *Observations on the Recent Pamphlet of J. Horsley Palmer, Esq. on the Causes and Consequences of the Money Market, etc.* (1837), p. 37.

[10] George Norman, *Remarks upon Some Prevalent Errors with Respect to Currency and Banking, and Suggestions to the Legislature and the Public as to the Improvement of the Monetary System* (1838), pp. 87–8.

[11] Overstone, *Thoughts on the Separation* in *Tracts*, ed. McCulloch, p. 254; *Committee* (1840), QQ. 2764, 2805. (Overstone).

[12] Peel, in Overstone, 'Letter to the Editor of *The Times* on the Bank Charter Act of 1844, and on the State of the Currency in 1855–1856', in *Tracts*, ed. McCulloch, p. 349.

[13] Overstone, *Letters of Mercator on the Bank Charter Act of 1844, and the State of the Currency, 1855–1857* (1857), p. 49.

[14] Peel, Hansard, *Parl. Debates*, p. 250.

[15] R. S. Sayers, *Central Banking After Bagehot* (Oxford, 1957), reprinted in Lawrence S. Ritter (ed.), *Money and Economic Activity* (3rd edn., Boston, 1967), p. 366.

[16] P. Barrett Whale, 'A Retrospective View of the Bank Charter Act', in T. S. Ashton (ed.), *Papers in English Monetary History* (Oxford, 1953), p. 131.

[17] Lionel (Lord) Robbins, *Robert Torrens and the Evolution of Classical Economics* (1958), p. 117.

[18] Ibid., p. 111; Henry Simons, 'Rules versus Authorities in Monetary Policy', reprinted in *Economic Policy for a Free Society* (Chicago, 1948), p. 162.

[19] Jacob Viner, *Studies in the Theory of International Trade* (1953), p. 250.

[20] Ludwig von Mises and A. E. Feavearyear regarded deposits as quantitatively unimportant before Peel's Act, 1844. Von Mises argued that the development of deposit banking did not reach significant proportions until Peel's Act itself encouraged it. Feavearyear argued that deposits were a negligible factor in the economic system before the Act because their use in transactions was hindered by the lack of a national cheque-clearing system. See Ludwig von Mises, *The Theory of Money and Credit*, trans. H. E. Batson (New York, 1936), p. 369. See also Albert E. Feavearyear, *The Pound Sterling: A History of English Money* (1931), pp. 289–90.

[21] Notes are used as a criterion for assessing the economic importance of deposits because they were regulated by the Currency School and therefore were considered important. Gold also was regarded as important, but only a few estimates of the gold held by the public are available.

[22] The source of the numbers of London joint-stock bank offices and their deposits is given in the sources to Table 3.

[23] Overstone, 'Extracts from the Evidence of Samuel Jones Loyd Esq. before the Select Committee of the House of Commons on Commercial Distress in 1848', reprinted in *Tracts*, ed. McCulloch, p. 629.

[24] Palmer attributed this difference in the degree of fluctuations between the Bank and other banks to customer relations. Customers of private bankers felt more obliged to maintain a steady level of deposits because their relationship with bankers was personal. Customers of the Bank felt no such obligation.—*Report from the Select Committee on Bank Issue*, PP. 1840, iv., QQ. 1566–1996.

[25] J. H. Palmer in Tooke, *A History of Prices*, iii. 124n.

[26] See Wood, op. cit., p. 21. Robinson said that a large part of the 'capital' of every banker in 1825 was deposits—ibid., pp. 22–3. Feavearyear supported his low deposit estimates by saying that the development of deposit banking in the country did not begin until after Peel's Act because of the absence of a national cheque-clearing system—Feavearyear, op. cit., pp. 247–89. This assertion is not consistent with J. W. Gilbart's remark that each country banker was connected with a London bank and so virtually connected with all the country

banks for purposes of transmitting money. J. W. Gilbart, *The History and Principles of Banking* (3rd edn., 1837), p. 151.

[27] J. W. Gilbart, *The Logic of Banking* (*Works,* 1856), pp. 541–2.

[28] *Committee* (1857), Q. 174 (W. Newmarch). This evidence does not support Ludwig von Mises's assertion that the country deposit system was in a backward state before 1844.—von Mises, op. cit., p. 369 Deposits increased considerably after the Act of 1844 but this does not imply that deposits were economically insignificant before the Act.

[29] See *Committee* (1857), app. 21.

[30] Ibid., QQ. 1647–9 (Newmarch).

[31] Tooke, *A History of Prices,* iii. 128.

[32] Ibid.

8

American Rings and English Mules: The Role of Economic Rationality*

L. G. SANDBERG

Editor's note. This article was first published in the *Quarterly Journal of Economics*, 83 (1969), 25–43.

The article has been included as a good example of the role of theory in economic history, discussed above, pp. 3–4.

The single most important technological improvement in the cotton spinning industry during the last hundred years has been the replacement of mule by ring spinning. Most of the technical development of this process took place in the United States, and it was in the United States that it first rose to economic prominence.

As early as 1870 ring spinning had become the dominant form of spinning in the United States. In that year there were a total of 3·7 million ring spindles and 3·4 million mule spindles installed in the United States.[1] Since, for a given fineness (count)[2] of yarn, output per ring spindle exceeds output per mule spindle, a comparison of the numbers of the two types of spindles installed tends to understate the importance of ring spinning. By 1905, 17·9 million of the 23·1 million installed spindles in the United States were rings.[3] This trend, of course, continued and by the outbreak of the Second World War mule spinning was virtually extinct in the United States.

Ring spinning was also introduced into other parts of the world, but at a slower pace than in the United States. If modern cotton industries outside the United States are divided into three general groups, non-European (principally those in Japan, China, and India), Continental European, and British, then the percentage of ring spindles installed at any given point in time decreased in the order listed above. That is, Great Britain, with the largest cotton industry in the world, was last among all important cotton industries in the introduction of ring spindles.[4] As late as 1913 there were 45·2 million mule spindles but only 10·4 million ring spindles in Great Britain.[5]

Although some contemporary observers noted that Great Britain had certain special advantages in mule as opposed to ring spinning,[6] the British lag in ring spinning has usually been taken as a sign of technological conservatism, not to say backwardness.[7] This view has been reinforced by subsequent developments. Ring spinning has indeed proved to be the wave of the future

* I am indebted to Alexander Gerschenkron and the members of the Economic History Seminar at Harvard for suggestions and encouragement. A somewhat longer and more detailed version of this paper is available from the author on request.

and the British cotton textile industry has experienced a sharp decline ever since the end of the First World War. Neither of these later trends, however, in any way proves that the British made a mistake, or were irrational, in not introducing more ring spindles before the First World War. Under the conditions then prevailing with regard to factor costs, as well as the technical capabilities of the ring spindles then being built, the British may well have been acting rationally.

The question whether the difference in the ratio of rings to mules in Great Britain and the United States in some given year was justified by differing factor costs and market conditions is, however, extremely difficult to answer. Phrased in this form, the question presents several formidable obstacles to quantitative analysis. First of all, as will be discussed below, the relative efficiency of ring and mule spindles varied for different counts of yarn. Thus, a detailed knowledge of the counts of yarn spun in the United States and in Great Britain would be needed. Although it is generally presumed that Great Britain devoted a larger percentage of her spindles to high-quality yarn than did the United States,[8] no sufficiently detailed information is available for the pre-First World War period. Furthermore, installing rings when a new plant was built or when old mules were physically worn out, was quite a different thing from throwing out technically well-functioning mules and replacing them with rings. Thus, the optimal mix of rings and mules depended not only on the distribution of counts spun, but also on the past rate of expansion of the industry.

The situation is further complicated by differences in factor costs in the two countries. These differences mean that the profitability of replacing mules by rings on a given count differed in the two countries. Not only does this mean that the same count might sometimes rationally have been spun by different methods in the two countries, but also that mules would be judged ready for the scrap heap at different ages in the two countries. There is thus no doubt that in the pre-First World War period it paid to keep old mules longer in Great Britain than in the United States. Any calculation of this effect on the optimal combination of rings and mules in the two countries would require a detailed knowledge of the distribution of mule spindles by age in the two countries, as well as a huge amount of information about the effect of age and obsolescence on the costs of mule spinning. In addition, of course, the unavailable information on the distribution of counts spun would be needed. Clearly, these obstacles require that the original question be rephrased in a more convenient form.

Since it is clear that rings were considered more suitable for low- as opposed to high-count yarn, I have decided to concentrate my attention on the counts at which new investment generally shifted from mules to rings in each of the two countries. That is, the central question of this paper will be, can rational economic forces explain why American firms generally installed rings to spin all yarns up to count X while British firms continued to install mules for counts lower than X?

The date for which this question will be investigated is the period immediately preceding the First World War. This period has the advantage that a good deal of information is available for it. Unfortunately, some of the information on the technical characteristics of mules and rings needed for this study is available only for a later period. This later period is not a good one for the study as a whole, however, principally because the extremely depressed conditions that have existed since the First World War are clearly not conducive to a study of investment behaviour and technological change.

OBSERVED INVESTMENT BEHAVIOUR

The first problem of this study is to determine whether there really were fairly sharp cut-off points between rings and mules when new spindles were being installed in the United States and Great Britain, respectively, and if so, at what counts these cut-off points occurred. In his excellent study of the American cotton textile industry published in 1912, Melvin Copeland reports that 'Not much yarn finer than 40's and very little higher than 60's is produced upon the ring-frame in Europe, whereas practically all warp yarn, even up to 120's, is spun upon that machine in America.'[9]

This statement is well supported by other evidence available from the same period. The works by Uttley and Young are full of examples of high-quality yarn spun on rings in the United States.[10] Not only is this true with regard to warp, it also seems to be the case for weft,[11] although the references to high-quality weft being spun on mules are somewhat more common than those to high-quality warp yarn. On the other hand, there are no references to any yarn below 40 being spun on mules.[12]

As for new installations, the U.S. Department of Commerce reports that between 1900 and 1914, only 981,023 new mule spindles were installed in the United States as opposed to 11,888,587 new ring spindles.[13] Further confirmation of the low number of new mule spindles being installed can be obtained from the U.S. Census of Manufactures for 1914 where it is stated that 'the installation of these [mule] spindles has practically ceased'.[14] It is clear that the small number of mules still being put in were intended to make very high-quality yarns. In fact, the *Census of Manufactures, 1905*, concluded that the only reason any mules at all were being installed was that 'there are some [high] qualities of yarn which cannot be made successfully by ring spinning'.[15]

The most important evidence that rings were being installed in Great Britain for yarns up to the lower 40's but very seldom above that range comes from the Universal Wage List for Ring Spinning which was adopted in 1912 and which covered virtually all British ring spinning.[16] Because the number of spindles tended by a spinner increased as the count of the yarn being spun increased, the list was designed to give a lower piece rate per spindle as the count spun increased. This accommodation is made for counts up to and including 43, but then stops abruptly. This is true despite the fact that the tendency towards more and more spindles per spinner continued on past the 40's and that the adjustment would have created no great computational problems.[17]

The only reasonable conclusion is that the list ends because there were virtually no spinners working on higher counts.

The evidence thus makes it clear that at least some rings were being installed for counts up to the lower 40's, but virtually none for counts above that. This is of little value, however, unless it can at least be shown that installations below 40 were not unusual occurrences. Fortunately such evidence is available.

Between 1907 and 1913, the number of installed mule spindles in Great Britain increased from 43·7 million to 45·2 million, and the number of ring spindles increased from approximately 8·3 million to 10·4 million.[18] On the basis of several reasonable assumptions, it can be shown that these new rings were enough to account for all the increase in sub 40 capacity and to replace about 15 per cent of all the mules used for sub 40 yarn in 1907.[19] At the very least, it is clear that a very large percentage of the spindles installed for counts up to 40 were rings.

THE RELATIVE ADVANTAGES OF RINGS OR MULES
IN THE UNITED STATES AND GREAT BRITAIN

The purpose of this section is to examine the differences that existed in the benefits to be derived from replacing mules with rings in the United States and the benefits to be derived from doing so in Great Britain. The discussion will be divided into two parts, the first dealing with factor costs and the second with such problems as the role of labour unions and the technological interrelationships between ring spinning and automatic weaving.

A. Factor Costs

(1) *Labour Costs.* The principal advantage of ring as opposed to mule spinning was that the former used unskilled or semi-skilled female labour while the latter used highly skilled males. Good estimates of the spinning labour costs of the two methods of producing yarn in this period are available for both the United States and Great Britain in Copeland's book which presents a range of spindles per operator and a range of wages per operator.[20] I have focused attention on the high estimates for both the number of spindles tended and the weekly wage. In fact, it would not matter very much if I had used the lower estimates for both, or if I had chosen a middle position. I use the upper limits for both number of spindles and wages because these figures are most likely to apply to the new equipment in which I am principally interested.

Taking account of the difference in ring spindle speed in the United States and Great Britain and allowing for the difference in productivity between ring and mule spindles at a count around 40, the spinning labour cost for ring spinning turns out to have been about 50 cents per week, per hundred 'mule equivalent' spindles[21] in both countries. For mule spinning the cost was around $1·65 per 100 actual mule spindles per week in Great Britain and $2·15 in the United States. This, in turn, implies that at a count of 40, ring spinning labour per pound of yarn was about 1·6 cents lower in Great Britain and about 2·4 cents lower in the United States than the cost of mule spinning labour.

(2) *Capital.* Mule and ring spinning appear to have been of almost exactly the same capital intensity per unit of output in the production of yarns of a count around 40.[22] Below this count, mules tended to be more capital-intensive and above it rings were more capital-intensive. This rough equality around 40 was the result of higher machinery costs for ring spinning, including some extra roving equipment, offset by the space saving achieved in ring spinning. In view of this fact, it is difficult to believe that any difference in interest rates could have had much to do with America's greater propensity to install rings. Certainly, if rings stopped being profitable in Great Britain at a count of 40, no reasonable change in the interest rate could have made them profitable.

It does seem apparent, however, that mule spinning machinery was more expensive relative to ring spinning machinery in the United States than in Great Britain. Evidence for this comes primarily from the fact that between 1900 and 1914, 77·6 per cent of all new mule spindles installed in the United States were imported from Great Britain, while only small quantities of other types of cotton textile machinery were imported.[23] This, of course, was not due to any inherent inefficiency in mule making in the United States, but rather to the fact that so few mules were being installed that it was not profitable for American producers to make mule spinning frames.[24] While it is difficult to tell how much difference there was in the relative prices of the two types of machinery, this effect must have given some further impetus to ring spinning in the United States. On the other hand, it should be remembered that ring spinning tended to save capital in the form of buildings and required extra capital for machinery. In view of the fact that construction was relatively cheaper as compared with machinery in the United States than in Great Britain,[25] this would tend to favour the use of the 'construction-intensive' mule process in the United States.

(3) *Fuel and Lubricants.* Here, again, the costs appear to be virtually the same for the two methods. Sources can be found that disagree about which method saved fuel.[26] In any case the difference was very small when expressed in terms of cents per pound of yarn. This means, of course, that any effect of different fuel prices in the two countries on the choice of spinning technique must have been infinitesimal.

(4) *Transportation.* Transportation is treated as an input because the yarn had to be moved before it could be woven into cloth. The difference in transportation costs between rings and mules arises because mule yarn was spun either on a bare spindle or on a paper tube, while ring yarn had to be wound on a heavy wooden bobbin. Fortunately, the warp yarn could be rewound. The weft, however, had to be shipped on the bobbin.[27] Copeland quotes with approval an estimate that the paper tubes added only 10 per cent to the freight costs, while the wooden bobbins added 200 per cent. Furthermore, the bobbin had to be returned.[28]

The reason this difference in transportation costs affected Great Britain and the United States differently is that the American industry was vertically integrated while the British industry was not. Thus, much more yarn transportation was required in Great Britain than in the United States. In addition, Britain had a large export trade in yarn.

Fortunately, a good estimate can be made of the level of these extra transportation costs. Reliable information is available on the cost of shipping yarn in Lancashire in 1907 over the average distance yarn was in fact shipped.[29] If the 200 per cent cost increase figure is used together with an allowance for the extra cost of returning the wooden bobbins, it appears that shipping ring weft within Lancashire cost about three mills more per pound of yarn than shipping mule weft. The cost differential, of course, did not apply to yarn produced in integrated plants.

It is impossible to give a single cost estimate for exports, since it depended on the destination of the yarn. This extra cost of exporting ring rather than mule weft, however, could clearly be very high or even prohibitive. Nevertheless, the effect of this cost differential is severely limited by the fact that in this production period only 10 to 15 per cent of total British yarn production was being exported.[30] This means that no more than 5 to 8 per cent of all the yarn produced was weft for export. Since there were many more mules working at all counts than were needed to produce this percentage, there was probably little effect on investment behaviour. Presumably, the export transportation disadvantage of ring weft resulted mainly in the concentration of the production of sub 40 weft for export on mules installed in the pre-ring period.

B. Other Factors Affecting the Choice of Spinning Method

(1) *Labour Unions.* The literature on the history of the American cotton textile industry is full of references to the effect that the disruptive and belligerent attitude of the American mule spinners' unions was a major factor in encouraging the shift to ring spinning. Thus, it is reported that it was after the strike of January 1898 (led by the mule spinners) that the treasurer of the highly efficient and well-managed Pepperell Manufacturing Company, of Biddeford, Maine, 'made plans to get rid of all the mule frames eventually and to put in ring frames.'[31] Earlier, the cotton manufacturers of Fall River, Massachusetts, had been 'particularly anxious to introduce ring spindles' as a result of the strikes of 1870 and 1875.[32] A more general comment to the same effect appears in the *Census of Manufactures*, 1905: 'But there are reasons, not unconnected with the labor problem, which render manufacturers desirous of using frames (i.e., rings) rather than mules whenever it is (technically) practical to do so.'[33]

These observations must, however, be viewed with at least some reservations. In all cases there were other good reasons for introducing rings. Furthermore, the manufacturers had every interest in making the workers fear that aggressive union action would result in technological unemployment. Nevertheless, there can be no doubt that American manufacturers had a strong aversion to unions and that the mule spinners were probably the most efficient and powerful cotton textile union, at least until the absolute number of installed mule spindles started to decline around 1900. It is also clear that the mule spinners' union tended to encourage at least temporary organization among the other workers and that it was largely responsible for many strikes.[34] Thus, the desire to break the power of the union by replacing the obstreperous mule spinners with docile girl spinners probably did have at least some effect in encouraging the adoption of ring spinning in the United States.

In the case of Great Britain, there was also a sharp contrast between the powerful and well-organized mule spinners and the weakly organized ring spinners. The British employers, however, appeared to have been better adjusted to the fact of having to face unions than were American employers. The British mule spinners' union was far from the only strong British cotton union. Even more important, the British mule spinners were mainly dedicated simply to raising their own wages. To the extent they succeeded in this endeavour, they may, of course, have helped the cause of ring spinning, but any such effect has already been considered in the section on relative wages.

(2) *Relation of Ring Yarn to Automatic Looms.* The period under discussion in this paper was also a period during which large numbers of automatic looms were installed in the United States. Automatic looms, however, or at least these automatic looms, required the greater strength of ring as opposed to mule yarn.[35] This complementarity between ring spinning and automatic weaving meant that the existence of ring spinning made the introduction of automatic looms more appealing and, similarly, plans to install automatic looms depended on the availability of ring spinning.[36] There may, therefore, have been some American manufacturers for whom a desire to introduce automatic looms made ring spinning relatively more advantageous as compared with mule spinning than would otherwise have been the case. For the most part, however, ring spinning clearly preceded automatic weaving.[37] With regard to Great Britain, this interdependence between ring spinning and automatic looms can be ignored for purposes of this paper since automatic looms did not begin to appear there in significant numbers until the 1930s.[38]

THE ROLE OF COTTON PRICES

This discussion of factor costs and other considerations has shown that in virtually every category the advantage of replacing mules by rings was greater in the United States than in Great Britain. This fact, combined with the generally accepted fact, to be discussed in greater detail below, that the relative advantage of ring as opposed to mule spinning declined as the count spun increased, generally accords well with the observed fact that Great Britain stopped installing rings at a count of about 40, while the United States continued installing rings at much higher counts. It says very little, however, about whether the British cut-off line logically should have been drawn exactly where it was drawn. Some information on this problem can be obtained from the structure of cotton prices.

Cotton prices played an important role in the choice of spinning technique because of the technological fact that, for a given count of yarn, ring spinning required a longer cotton-staple than did mule spinning. Figure 1 is designed to show which lengths of fibre were 'suitable' for different counts.[39]

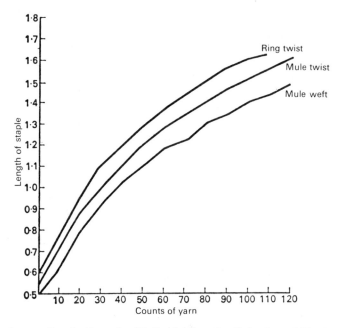

FIG. 1. *Cotton Staple Lengths 'Suitable' for the Spinning of Various Yarns*

Note: Figure 1 is based on the following equations:
  Length of staple in inches, for ring twist $= 0.35$ $(\sqrt[3]{\text{count}})$
  Length of staple in inches, for mule twist $= 0.325$ $(\sqrt[3]{\text{count}})$
  Length of staple in inches, for mule weft $= 0.30$ $(\sqrt[3]{\text{count}})$
Source: Winterbottom, p. 235.

Unfortunately, the compiler of the information used to produce Figure 1 considered only ring twist, mule twist, and mule weft. He neglected to include ring weft. This could be interpreted to mean that ring weft required the same staple length as ring twist. This was almost certainly not true, however. Most observers were of the opinion that, for a given count, a shorter staple could be used to produce weft than was needed for twist, both on mules and rings.[40] Indeed, the evidence seems to indicate that the difference in length was pretty much the same regardless of the spinning method used.[41] If this is correct, it means that the mule twist requirements would be the same as the ring weft requirements. I will, therefore, treat the difference between the staple length needed for mule twist and mule weft as representing the difference between ring weft and mule weft.

This difference in the required staple length enters as a factor in the choice of spinning technique; the price of cotton generally increased as its staple length did. This is shown in Figure 2 which contains cotton prices in New Orleans on 1 April 1913. This year and date were deliberately chosen as representing a season and period when the market was 'normal'.[42] In particular, the compiler of these data reports that the big jump in price occurring between staple lengths of $1\frac{1}{16}$ in and $1\frac{1}{8}$ in was 'common at all times.'[43] The exact size of the price jumps between different staple lengths must have varied somewhat depending on harvest conditions as well as peculiarities of final demand for cotton products, but Figure 2 can certainly be taken as representative of the period just preceding the First World War.[44]

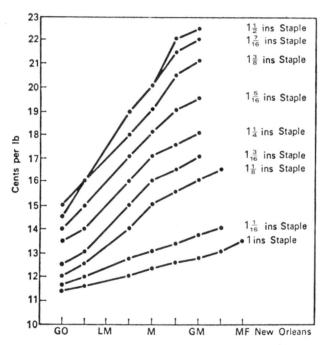

FIG. 2. *Prices of Various Cottons by Quality and Staple Lengths, New Orleans, 1 April 1913*

Combining Figures 1 and 2, it is possible to compute the differential cotton cost in spinning with rings as opposed to mules. A literal application of the technical information in Figure 1 results in Figure 3 for ring twist versus mule twist and Figure 4 for ring weft versus mule weft.

It is clear that Figure 1, and therefore Figures 3 and 4, are primarily based on technological rather than economic considerations. Since cotton prices were

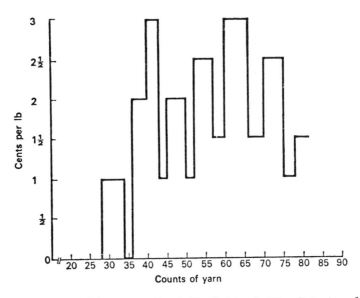

FIG. 3. *Extra Cost of the Longer Staple Needed for the Ring Spinning of Warp (Twist)*

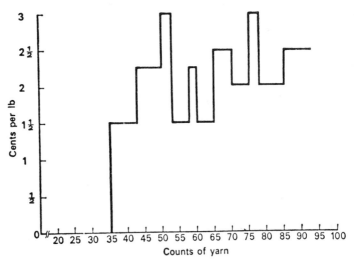

FIG. 4. *Extra Cost of the Longer Staple Needed for the Ring Spinning of Weft*

not quoted continuously by length, but by steps of $\frac{1}{16}$ in., rational producers would be prepared to accept somewhat higher costs in order to avoid the next step on the staple progression. Rather than immediately going to the longer staple when the count they were spinning required it if they were to continue with the exact production methods used at a slightly lower count, they would try to keep on using the lower staple by altering their production methods somewhat.

It follows that diagrams of the extra cost imposed on ring spinning because of the need for a longer staple would in fact differ somewhat from Figures 3 and 4.[45]

Nevertheless, some conclusions of relevance to this paper can be drawn from the information available. First, the differential in cotton costs between rings and mules for warp yarn probably starts to appear at a count around 28 and then increases to a peak somewhat below three cents per pound, probably in the vicinity of 45 or 50. In all probability, the difference reaches two cents in the low 40's. Secondly, the cost differential does not drop significantly below two cents again, at least not in the range shown in Figure 3. As for weft, the cost differential starts around a count of 35 and rises to more than two cents in the 50's. It probably reaches two cents in the upper 40's. The differential then stays at least as high as one and a half cents for higher counts.

The discussion so far has only dealt with counts below 100. This is the area relevant for Great Britain. In the United States, however, the only count range where mules appear to have been installed was above 100. The question thus arises as to whether cotton price differentials can explain at least the very partial return to mules at very high counts.

On the whole, it can be expected that price differentials of two or even three cents continued out well beyond a count of 90. This continued gap resulted from the need to resort to Egyptian and 'regular' Sea Island cotton for ring twist in the 80 to 100 range.[46] Above that range, however, it eventually became necessary to use 'Best Sea Island' cotton. In view of the very large difference in the count that could be spun by the two methods at these high counts,[47] the differential must at some point have been between using the Best Sea Island on rings or distinctly inferior types of cotton on mules. The cost differential can be estimated to be five or six cents per pound and sometimes even more. Once the count is high enough, however, even the mule would require Best Sea Island. Once this happened, the cost differential would be very much reduced, at least if the ring was physically capable of spinning such extremely fine yarn. This evidence appears to be consistent with rational manufacturers installing both mules and rings for very high counts.

RELATIVE FACTOR COSTS AS A FUNCTION OF COUNTS SPUN

I have repeatedly stated that expert opinion in the period being studied unanimously held that ring spinning was relatively less well suited to high than to low counts. It is now necessary to look at this proposition in more detail.

Changes in the relative advantage of ring and mule spinning as the count increased can be expected to result from changes in the relative cost of the raw material and other inputs, on the one hand, and the quality of the product on the other hand.

A. Input Costs

In the previous section the relative costs imposed by the cotton needed for ring and mule spinning were studied as a function of the count of the yarn spun. It appears that this cost difference did increase with the count, at least in moving from low to medium and high counts.

The other important inputs to be examined are labour and capital. It is quite clear from all contemporary evidence that labour input per pound of yarn increased faster on rings than on mules as the count increased. Even with a constant capital–labour ratio, this would also imply that the capital cost of ring spinning increased faster than that of mule spinning. In fact, however, the capital–labour ratio increased faster in ring than in mule spinning.[48] In ring, unlike mule, spinning, the number of spindles per operative increased as the count increased. The difference in capital costs thus increased even faster than implied by the changing ratio of spinning labour input.

Before jumping to the conclusion that this evidence proves that the cost of ring spinning increased faster than the cost of mule spinning, it must be remembered that mule spinners were more expensive than ring spinners. Thus, an equal percentage increase in the number of spinners' hours per pound of yarn would increase the saving per pound of yarn to be derived from using rings rather than mules.

While a good deal of vague information on the relationship between the count of yarn spun and labour input is available for the pre-First World War period, careful studies of this relationship were carried out only in a later period. Two such studies, one based on interwar conditions and one based on 1949 conditions, are available.[49] Happily, the two studies present almost identical results with regard to the relationship of output per man hour in spinning and the count of yarn spun. I therefore used the results of these studies to calculate cost differentials.[50]

In addition to an estimate of output per man, I also needed an estimate of changes in the spindles per man ratio in ring spinning. I obtained an estimate of the latter from the structure of piece rates in the British Universal Ring Spinning List 1912.[51] This structure was specifically designed to reflect the fact that spinners working on higher counts were able to tend more spindles. On the

TABLE 1. *Cost Differentials*

Difference in labour and capital costs in United States cents									
Count	40	50	60	70	80	90	100	110	120
Great Britain	1·6	1·7	1·8	1·8	1·8	1·6	1·5	1·2	0·8
United States	2·4	2·6	2·9	2·9	3·0	3·0	2·9	2·7	2·3

basis of this information, I calculated the saving per pound of yarn in spinning labour and capital charges that resulted from using rings instead of mules. Assuming a waste rate of 5 to 10 per cent, the saving per pound of cotton used would be 5 to 10 per cent less than the results shown in Table 1.[52]

B. Quality Differentials

There now remains the question of the quality of ring versus mule yarn. There is a great deal of talk, especially in British writings, concerning the superior quality of mule yarn. Clearly, however, British comments on this subject are of questionable value. After all, they can be counted on to claim superiority for the product on which they concentrated. I have also been unable to find any data that show a price differential between yarns of the same count, made of cotton of the same quality (here defined to exclude staple length), differing only in the method of production.

Nevertheless, there do seem to have been some differences between the two types of yarn. Thus, Copeland, an American, remarks that: 'Mule yarn, however, is superior . . .', and 'the harder ring-spun yarn is better adapted for warp than for weft.'[53]

My general conclusion in this matter is that mule yarn probably did have some superior qualities. It is not clear whether this advantage became greater in a technical sense as the count increased. What is clear, however, is that the *importance* of this difference increased with the count. For the low-quality cloth usually made with low-count yarns, this minor difference in the yarn probably did not matter much. As the quality of the cloth increased with the count, however, differences in the yarn undoubtedly took on added importance. Quality differences thus probably did make the ring somewhat less well adapted to high than low counts as well as more suited to warp than weft. This difference in suitability for warp and weft probably played a role in what appears to have been the greater staying power of old American mules in weft as opposed to warp spinning.

COSTS AND BENEFITS

Having estimated the various costs and benefits involved in choosing between mules and rings, it is now time to evaluate the results.[54]

Taking account of all these different costs (including labour, fuel transportation, and capital) with the single exception of cotton, it seems that in Great Britain the saving per pound of cotton spun on rings rather than mules was about 1·5 cents for warp and 1·2 cents for weft at a count of 40. This saving rose to about 1·7 and 1·4 cents, respectively, at a count around 70 and then declined slightly. On the other hand, the increase in cost due to the longer staples required by ring as opposed to mule spinning for twist (i.e. warp) rose from zero at counts below 28 to about 2 cents around 40. It then remained at that level. For weft, the differential probably reached 2 cents close to 50. It thus appears that in Great Britain rings were preferable for warp production up to a count perhaps a little below 40, while for weft they were probably to be preferred even for counts in the low 40's. In cases where the spinner contemplated using low-quality cotton, rings may have been better even at slightly higher counts. It does not appear that rings ever became profitable again at higher counts. This conclusion is reinforced by the fact that a growing effective quality differential probably worked against ring yarn at higher counts.

When these results are compared with the actual behaviour of British manufacturers, they appear to have behaved in a rational manner. At the very least, these results should throw the burden of proof onto those who maintain that the British were irrational in their choice between rings and mules.

In the case of the United States, the cost advantage per pound of yarn was over 2 cents at a count of 40 and then rose to around 3 cents. In view of these results, it is understandable that ring spinning was used for much higher counts in the United States than in Great Britain. At the same time, the price differential is down to 2·3 cents per pound at a count of 120 and heading lower. In view of this fact and the high price differentials encountered for very long staple cotton, it is also not surprising that some mules were being installed to spin very fine yarn. Indeed, my reaction is that surprisingly few new mules were installed in the United States. Although the quantitative data are not strong enough to prove the point, I suspect there may have been some substance to the many comments by contemporary observers that employer dislike of unions caused them to avoid mule spinning.

NOTES

[1] Melvin T. Copeland, *The Cotton Manufacturing Industry of the United States* (Cambridge, Mass., 1912), p. 70. For a technical description of mule and ring spinning, see John Jewkes and E. M. Gray, *Wages and Labour in the Lancashire Cotton Spinning Industry* (Manchester, 1935). chap. 1.

[2] The 'count' of a yarn is defined as the number of hanks, at 840 yards each, per pound.

[3] Copeland, op. cit., p. 70.

[4] R. Robson, *The Cotton Industry in Britain* (London, 1957), p. 355.

[5] Ibid.

[6] Copeland, op. cit., pp. 71–3.

[7] See, for example, Rockwood Chin, *Management, Industry and Trade in Cotton Textiles* (New Haven, Conn., 1965), p. 85.

[8] See, for example, Copeland, op. cit., p. 71.

[9] Copeland, op. cit., p. 301.

[10] T. W. Uttley, *Cotton Spinning and Manufacturing in the United States of America* (Manchester, 1905), pp. 9, 11, 16, 22, 23, 29, 31, 32, 34, 49, 54, 56, and 60, and T. M. Young, *The American Cotton Industry* (London, 1902), pp. 10, 16, 18, 19, 24, 35, 61, 68, 73, 86, 88, 97, and 110.

[11] Warp, also known as twist, is the yarn which is stretched in the loom. Weft, also known as filling, is the yarn inserted into the warp by means of the shuttle. Warp has to be stronger than weft.

[12] See previous references in Uttley and Young.

[13] U.S. Department of Commerce, Bureau of Foreign and Domestic Commerce, *The Cotton Spinning Machinery Industry*, Miscellaneous Series, No. 37 (Washington, 1916), Table 44, p. 77.

[14] U.S. Bureau of the Census, *Census of Manufactures, 1914*, ii. 38.

[15] Ibid., *1905*, iii. 42.

[16] Jewkes and Gray, op. cit., pp. 117 and 128.

[17] Ibid., p. 121.

[18] British Census Office, *Census of Production, 1907* (London, 1908), i. 293 and Robson, op. cit., p. 355.

[19] For a detailed discussion of this problem, see the author's longer paper which is available on request.

[20] Copeland, op. cit., pp. 298–300.

[21] I have converted ring spindles into mule equivalence so that the cost comparisons can be based on equal quantities of output.

[22] James Winterbottom, *Cotton Spinning Calculations and Yarn Costs* (2nd edn., London, 1925), pp. 213, 272, and 273. Winterbottom was lecturer in cotton spinning at the Municipal School of Technology in Manchester during the period covered in this study.

[23] *The Cotton Spinning Machinery Industry.* Table 44, p. 77.

[24] Since America was a high-cost, protected producer of textile machinery, there was no hope of capturing an export market for mule frames.

[25] Young, op. cit., p. 9.

[26] Winterbottom op. cit., pp. 272 and 273, and W. A. Graham Clark, *Cotton Textile Trade in the Turkish Empire, Greece, and Italy,* Bureau of Manufactures, Special Agents Report No. 18 (Washington, 1908), pp. 89 and 90.

[27] Copeland, op. cit., pp. 69 and 72.

[28] Ibid., p. 69.

[29] William Whittam, *Report on England's Cotton Industry,* Bureau of Manufactures, Special Agents Report No. 15 (Washington, 1907), p. 32.

[30] See Robinson, op. cit., p. 333.

[31] Evelyn H. Knowlton, *Pepperell's Progress* (Cambridge, Mass., 1948), p. 171.

[32] R. Smith, *The Cotton Textile Industry of Fall River, Massachusetts* (New York, 1944), p. 100. See also Robert K. Lamb, 'The Development of Entrepreneurship in Fall River, 1813–1859', unpublished Ph.D. thesis, Harvard University, p. xii–8.

[33] *Census of Manufactures, 1905,* iii. 42.

[34] Knowlton, op. cit., pp. 170–1, and Smith, op. cit., p. 100.

[35] Irwin Feller, 'The Draper Loom in New England Textiles, 1894–1914: A Study of Diffusion of an Innovation', *Jour. Econ. Hist.,* 26 (Sept. 1966), 331.

[36] Ibid., p. 333.

[37] See Copeland, op. cit., pp. 70 and 87, and Robson, op. cit., p. 355.

[38] In 1937, only 3 per cent of all British cotton looms were automatic. Robson, op. cit., p. 210.

[39] Winterbottom, op. cit., p. 236.

[40] Paul H. Nystrom, *Textiles* (New York. 1916). pp. 71–2.

[41] Ibid.

[42] Winterbottom, op. cit., p. 234.

[43] Ibid.

[44] Figure 2 does not include the very longest staple cottons. It should thus be added that at the very top of the scale the jump was from cotton of about $1\frac{3}{4}$ inches to about 2 inches, with virtually nothing in between, and an increase in price amounting to around 5 or 6 cents per pound at July 1914 prices. John A. Todd, *The World's Cotton Crops* (London, 1915), p. 17.

[45] A more detailed discussion of this question can be found in the author's longer paper which is available on request.

[46] Todd, op. cit., p. 17.

[47] Ibid., and Winterbottom, op. cit., p. 52.

[48] Jewkes and Gray, op. cit., p. 121.

[49] See British Ministry of Production, *Report of the Cotton Textile Mission to the United States of America* (London, 1944), and Productivity Team, *Cotton Spinning* (London, Anglo-American Council on Productivity, 1950).

[50] It is, of course, unfortunate that these studies do not refer to the exact period under study. Encouragement, however, can be taken from the fact that no noticeable change occurred between the 1930s and 1949. More important, virtually all the mules studied, and the great majority of the rings were in fact installed before the First World War. If there is any bias in using these past period studies, it is probably in underestimating the labour required on high count rings. Such a bias might be expected because technical change on the ring is generally credited with making it effective at higher and higher counts.

[51] Jewkes and Gray, op. cit., p. 121.

[52] This calculation is based on the assumption that the capital costs of mules and rings were the same at a count of 40. Account has been taken of the somewhat greater speed of rings in the United States as compared with Great Britain. The generally accepted figure of 10 per cent for loss, depreciation, and upkeep of machinery (see Winterbottom, op. cit., p. 271) is used. In addition, the interest cost of the money invested is set at 10 per cent. While the cost differential at a count of 40 is independent of these percentages, the cost differentials at higher counts would be higher if lower interest rates were used and lower if higher interest rates were used.

There is some reason to believe that the rate of growth of the capital differential is underestimated. This bias results because high-count mules have shorter 'draws' than do low-count mules and, therefore, occupy less space than do low-count mules. This is not the case with rings.

[53] Copeland, op. cit., p. 68.

[54] The longer version of this paper also contains *prima facie* evidence that French and German manufacturers were rational in choosing between rings and mules and that British and American manufacturers were rational in their replacement policies.

9

Free Trade in 'Corn':
A Statistical Study of
the Prices and Production
of Wheat in Great Britain
from 1873 to 1914

M. OLSON AND C. C. HARRIS JR.

Editor's note. This article was first published in the *Quarterly Journal of Economics*, 73 (1959), 145–68.

The methods of correlation and regression analysis, and of the treatment of time series data, are discussed above, pp. 15–30. Numerous references to further reading on these subjects are given in the footnotes to those pages. It should be noted that this article was written before the general availability of electronic computers and that such comments as that on p. 213, note 10, about the cost of regression analysis no longer apply to the use of such methods.

I. THE PROBLEM

Some economists claim that economic historians have given too much of their attention to the development of economic policy, and neglected some other aspects of economic life, especially those requiring statistical analysis. The record of historians' efforts to explain British agriculture in Victorian times shows one instance where the criticism is justified. Much has been written about the Corn Laws — they are perhaps the most celebrated statutes in all of economic history — and about the controversy culminating in their repeal. This vast literature is, of course, quite significant, for the repeal of the Corn Laws must have had *something* to do with the obviously important fact that Britain, of all major nations, is the most overwhelmingly industrialized: it has the smallest proportion of its resources in the agricultural sector.

The quantitative and economic aspects of the decline of British wheat production have been much neglected, however, and it is the purpose of this paper to examine them, rather than the political controversies. The period from 1873 to 1914 will be studied for the reason that it was only after 1873 that the price of wheat (and other kinds of 'corn') fell below the level to which British farmers had been accustomed through most of the nineteenth century. Indeed, the beginning of the drop in the production of this staple of British agriculture could hardly be set at an earlier date, for the acreage planted to wheat was at record or near record levels through the fifties, sixties, and early seventies.

This paper will attempt to show how farmers reacted to the lower prices. The elasticity of supply will be studied, along with the factors affecting farmers' price expectations. The responses of British farmers to the lower prices in this period should be of more than historical interest now, when agricultural prices are stellar subjects of political debate. The period has value as a polar case in agricultural policy, in that there has been no other period or country in which the government has stuck steadfastly to a laissez faire policy in the face of a drastic drop in wheat prices and rapidly increasing imports.

Finally, there is a demonstration of a simple method which should in many cases be helpful in getting information about the elasticities of supply or demand functions from time series data.

II. THE BACKGROUND

Almost everyone expected that the repeal of the Corn Laws in 1846 would bring lower prices immediately.[1] In fact prices stayed at about the usual level for most of the three decades following the repeal. The period from 1852 to 1862 was called a 'golden age' for British agriculture; prices averaged over 50 shillings a quarter for most of the fifties and sixties, and reached 74s. 8d., the highest since 1818, during the Crimean War. There had been a price decline beginning in 1847, during the industrial and financial panic, but this was neither deep nor long.[2]

The war with Russia, conflict on the Continent and in America during the sixties, the fact that most of the frontier lands of the new world had not yet been exploited, and rapidly increasing domestic demand helped keep the price from falling to the predicted levels. Another important fact was that transportation costs had not been reduced enough to deprive the British farmer of the 'natural protection of distance'.

The price decline began in 1873, though there was a temporary rise in 1876 and 1877 due to the Russo–Turkish War. After 1877 there was no questioning the fact that farm prices had collapsed. In 1879 the average annual price was only 43s. 10d. per quarter, well below the level common in the sixties.[3] Prices fell inexorably until 1886, reaching 31s. in that year. In 1885–6 the United Kingdom imported 147·1 million bushels of wheat; the apparent domestic utilization (production plus net imports) was 229·1 million bushels. Assuming no change in stocks, 64 per cent of the country's needs were being met by imports.[4] The price of wheat rose insignificantly for a time, but dipped below 30s. in 1889. There was a measurable strengthening of the market from 1889 to 1891.

After this respite came the final turn of the screw. Prices far cheaper than any Disraeli had contemplated confronted the British farmer. Wheat plunged first to 30s. 3d. in 1892, then set a record for cheapness the next year at 26s. 2d.; this record was broken in 1894, when wheat prices reached the nadir at 22s. 10d. This was roughly a third of the price that had ordinarily prevailed three decades earlier. By this time most British farmers were on the verge of ruin. Many indeed had been driven past that verge into bankruptcy in the two decades of price collapse before 1894. While wheat production in Britain had been cut drastically, this had no significant effect on the British price (which with free trade was the same as the world price), since British output was almost minute in relation to the world supply. Foreign competition was by now at the root of the British farmer's difficulty, for in 1895–6 the United Kingdom imported three-fourths of its grain.

The improvements in transportation and the settling of the new lands in the United States and other frontier countries were the main causes of the increase in imports and the lower prices beginning in the seventies. The steam-powered, metal ship made ocean freight less expensive at the same time that the railroads and immigration madę wheat growing important in the American Great Plains and other frontier lands. British wheat growers had many competitive disadvantages; Marshall even claimed that many farmers in the newly settled lands thought of wheat as a by-product, and the prospective increase in land values as the main source of gain.[5] The difficulties confronting the British farmer were aggravated by what was then called the 'Great Depression', which lasted from 1873 until almost the end of the century.

In 1894 prices reached bottom and a slight resurgence was soon experienced. The movement of prices was in general slowly upward at first, then the year to year fluctuations continued without any distinct, persistent tendency to move either upward or downward until World War I.

III. THE EFFECTS ON ACREAGE

Between 1873 and 1894[6] the acreage planted to wheat fell from 3·63 million acres to 1·42 million acres.[7] The fact that both price and acreage fell and the

---

Notes to Table 1

[1] The harvest year is from 1 Sept. to 31 Aug. Wheat is planted in the autumn and usually harvested in August.

[2] Wheat acreages are in millions of acres. The figures relate to the acres standing in June. (Board of Agriculture and Fisheries, *Agricultural Statistics*, tables of acreages in the Report for each year, with the exception of the years from 1897 to 1903, which were taken from p. 124 of the Report for 1903.)

[3] The rate of change in acres. The acres in year T-1 minus the acres in year T. A decrease in acres shows as a plus.

[4] Prices are the average for the previous harvest year expressed in pence per quarter. The price in T-1 is in the same row as acreage in T. (From the Board of Agriculture and Fisheries, *Agricultural Statistics*.)

[5] The rate of change in price. The price in year T-2 minus the price in time T-1. A decrease in price shows as a plus.

[6] Prices are the average for the harvest year two years previous to planting, and are expressed in pence per quarter. The price in T-2 is in the same row as acreage in T.

[7] The average price is a seven-year average, expressed in pence per quarter. It is the average of the calendar year in which the harvest year listed in the same row began, and the preceding six calendar years. The seven-year period price plotted against the 1873–4 harvest year is the average from 1 Jan. 1867 to 31 Dec. 1873. (Board of Agriculture and Fisheries, *Agricultural Statistics*.) The septennial average price was computed and recorded in the official statistics for the determination of the tithe rent charge.

[8] The barley price in time T-1 divided by the wheat price in time T-1. The ratio is in the same row as the harvest year T and the acreage in harvest year T. (Barley prices are from the Board of Agriculture and Fisheries, *Agricultural Statistics*. The harvest year price is a simple average of the monthly prices, except for the 1872 and 1873 harvest years, which were estimated by linear interpolation from the annual totals. The monthly figures were not available for those years.)

[9] Time is used as an independent variable. The origin is taken as the 1873–74 harvest year.

TABLE 1. *Table of Variables*

Harvest[1] Year	Acres[2] of Wheat	Acres[3] T-1 minus T	Price[4] T-1	Price[5] T-2 minus T-1	Price[6] T-2	Average[7] Price	Barley[8] Wheat Price Ratio	Time[9]
	Y	y	X_1	X_2	X_3	X_4	X_5	X_T
1873–4	3·63	−0·14	688	−9	679	678	0·68	0
1874–5	3·42	0·21	735	−47	688	662	0·70	1
1875–6	2·99	0·43	535	200	735	630	0·90	2
1876–7	3·17	−0·18	551	−16	535	626	0·73	3
1877–8	3·22	−0·05	655	−104	551	644	0·70	4
1878–9	2·89	0·33	610	45	655	626	0·81	5
1879–80	2·91	−0·02	499	111	610	604	0·83	6
1880–1	2·81	0·10	553	−54	499	580	0·76	7
1881–2	3·00	−0·19	527	26	553	562	0·73	8
1882–3	2·61	0·39	565	−38	527	562	0·66	9
1883–4	2·68	−0·07	504	61	565	554	0·77	10
1884–5	2·48	0·20	462	42	504	518	0·81	11
1885–6	2·29	0·19	398	64	462	494	0·92	12
1886–7	2·32	−0·03	371	27	398	472	0·89	13
1887–8	2·56	−0·24	396	−25	371	452	0·75	14
1888–9	2·45	0·11	369	27	396	428	0·91	15
1889–90	2·39	0·06	372	−3	369	402	0·83	16
1890–1	2·31	0·08	374	−2	372	386	0·94	17
1891–2	2·22	0·09	420	−46	374	388	0·80	18
1892–3	1·90	0·32	401	−19	420	384	0·82	19
1893–4	1·93	−0·03	324	77	401	376	0·92	20
1894–5	1·42	0·51	309	15	324	360	1·03	21
1895–6	1·69	−0·27	256	53	309	344	1·00	22
1896–7	1·89	−0·20	300	−44	256	338	0·90	23
1897–8	2·10	−0·21	345	−48	300	334	0·83	24
1898–9	2·00	0·10	432	−87	345	330	0·75	25
1899–1900	1·85	0·15	312	120	432	322	0·98	26
1900–1	1·70	0·15	313	−1	312	322	0·96	27
1901–2	1·73	−0·03	327	−14	313	330	0·91	28
1902–3	1·58	0·15	336	−9	327	338	0·92	29
1903–4	1·38	0·20	319	17	336	340	0·88	30
1904–5	1·80	−0·42	327	−8	319	336	0·80	31
1905–6	1·76	0·04	367	−40	327	328	0·80	32
1906–7	1·63	0·13	345	22	367	334	0·84	33
1907–8	1·63	0	336	9	345	340	0·87	34
1908–9	1·82	−0·19	393	−57	336	348	0·79	35
1909–10	1·81	0·01	437	−44	393	364	0·74	36
1910–11	1·91	−0·10	390	47	437	372	0·73	37
1911–12	1·93	−0·02	371	19	390	378	0·80	38
1912–13	1·76	0·17	419	−48	371	386	0·89	39
1913–14	1·87	−0·11	385	34	419	392	0·87	40

most venerable assumptions of economics suggest that the decisions to plant less were in response to the lower prices. This explanation can be tested by measuring the effect of the average price in the harvest year before sowing (X_1)[8] on the acreage (Y), that is by finding the correlation of prices in harvest year T-1 with acreage in year T.[9]

This correlation, r_{Y_1}, was 0·89 for the years 1873 to 1913. It is strong *prima facie* evidence that the price in the year before planting was a most important determinant of acreage. It seems that the problem under study is already largely solved. Prices fell, acreage declined: the average price in the harvest year preceding the planting apparently influenced the decisions of most wheat farmers.

The statistics have revealed a convincing correlation, but what have they concealed? Correlation *seems* to point convincingly to cause, though perhaps a third variable dictates both price and acreage, or perhaps the trend of prices *per se* is responsible for the reduction in acreage.

IV. THE TREND

Figure 1 indicates that prices fell drastically and rather persistently from 1873 through 1894, but after 1894 this trend ended and there were fairly large fluctuations from year to year around an average that was constant or perhaps

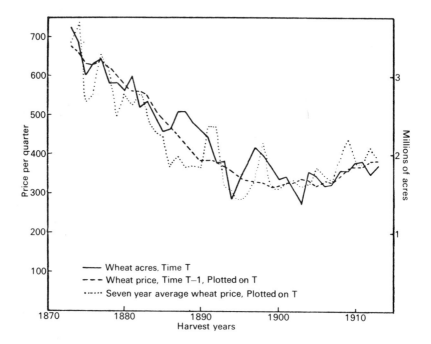

FIG. 1

rising slightly. If prices in year T-1 are intrinsically the cause of the acreage changes, and if the 0·89 correlation for r_{Y1} *really does explain most of what* happened, the correlation of the previous year's price (X_1) with acreage (Y) should be high both in the years before and after 1894, that is X_1 should explain the two distinct parts of the period. But most assuredly it does not. The correlation of X_1 and Y is only 0·37 — not enough to explain more than 14 per cent of the acreage variation — in the years from 1895 to 1913. There appears to be something misleading about the high correlation between price (X_1) and acreage for the whole period. For the years before 1895 r_{Y1} is 0·88. (The correlation for the last nineteen years is only 0·37, even though the correlations for the first twenty-two years and for the period as a whole are both about 0·9; this is due to the greater variance involved in the steep reduction of prices before 1895.)

Another method of testing the meaningfulness of the r_{Y1} correlation is to take the correlation of the first differences of the harvest year average prices and acreage. If the price in year T-1 is subtracted from the average price in year T-2, and if the difference is correlated with the change in acreage between year T-1 and year T, the result will be another measure of the influence of the price before planting on acreage. If the direction and magnitude of the price changes in the two years preceding planting help determine whether the farmer plants more or less, it should be reflected in this correlation between first differences in price (X_2) and acreage (y).

Remarkably, the r_{y2} correlation is only 0·22: while prices in year T-1 had a 0·89 correlation with acreage, first differences of price and acreage show a correlation so small as to be trivial.

The incongruity of these results is increased by the fact that when the average prices in harvest year T-2 (X) are compared with acreage, the result is a 0·86 correlation. This is further evidence that the impressive r_{Y1} result is deceptive; price two years before sowing, in isolation from prices in other years, could hardly be the basis for a farmer's decisions about acreage. Moreover, the relationship of the price difference between years T–1 and T–2 and first differences in acreage shows that both r_{Y1} and r_{Y3} do not reflect genuine causal relationships.

An additional reason for doubting the validity of the r_{Y1} correlation for the part of the period before 1895 is that both the T-1 price (X_1) and acreage (Y) are more highly correlated with time than they are with each other. Time (T) and X_1 show a −0·91 correlation, and acreage and time a −0·94 correlation. The mere passage of time is more closely correlated with acreage than is the price in the previous year, and time per se certainly could not have been a cause of the changes in wheat acreage. The partial correlations involving price in year T-1, acreage, and time are also significant. Previous to 1895 r_{Y1} is 0·88 and $r_{Y1.T}$ is only 0·21. After 1894 r_{Y1} is only 0·37, but $r_{Y1.T}$ rises to 0·51. Wheat prices in year T-1 account for less than 5 per cent of the variance in acreage in the early part of the period when the effect of time is accounted for, yet in the latter part of the period when the small correlation between X_T and Y

indicates there is no marked trend, the importance of X_1 is enhanced remarkably. All of the relevant partials tell the same tale. (See Table 2.)

The parallel movements of Y, X_1, and X_3 then are due to the time trend common to all of them. From this one might infer that some other variable was the cause of the variation in these three variables. But study of the period reveals

TABLE 2. *Correlations*

	1873–1913	1873–1894	1895–1913
Simple correlations			
r_{Y1}	0·89	0·88	0·37
r_{Y2}	0·22	0·24	0·03
r_{Y3}	0·86	0·81	0·14
r_{Y4}	0·94	0·91	0·21
r_{Y5}	−0·59	−0·70	−0·47
r_{YT}	−0·88	−0·94	−0·04
r_{14}	0·91	0·92	0·55
r_{15}	1	1	−0·69
r_{1T}	−0·72	−0·91	0·64
r_{45}	−0·53	−0·63	−0·35
Partial correlations			
$r_{Y1·T}$	0·71	0·21	0·51
$r_{Y4·1}$	0·69	0·53	0·01
$r_{Y4·5}$	0·92	0·85	0·05
$r_{Y5·1}$	1	1	−0·32
$r_{Y5·4}$	−0·30	−0·40	−0·43
Multiple correlations			
$R_{Y·45}$	0·95	0·93	1
$R_{Y·145}$	1	1	0·47

[1] Not computed.

no such variable (imports are the main cause of the lower prices and smaller acreages, of course, but imports affect acreage only through their effect on price).

The lack of some other variable which could explain the movements of acreage and price prompts consideration of the possibility that the price trend *itself* helped to determine acreage. Farmers' decisions were perhaps influenced not so much by the absolute level of price in year T-1 as by the persistent direction of the price movement.

The hypothesis that the trend of prices has intrinsic importance can be studied by correlating a moving average of the prices in some number of years before each planting with the acres planted. (See Figure 1.)[10] A fairly long series of years must be chosen or else the two- or three-year fluctuations will obscure the trend. A seven year average seems most appropriate.[11] The correlation of the seven-year average price (X_4) with acreage for the years before 1895 is 0·91. In the second part of the period the correlation is only 0·21. The seven-year average is very important when the trend is sharply downward, but accounts for less than 5 per cent of the variation in acreage when the trend is horizontal or rising slightly. This high correlation between X_4 and Y supports the thesis that the trend of prices was itself a factor affecting acreage in the years before 1895.

It would sometimes be rational for a farmer to decide what wheat acreage to plant on the basis of his knowledge of the trend of prices. It is the price at harvest time which determines the farmer's income, so he must, if rational, project *some* price ten months ahead when he decides how much to plant. What would be more natural to expect than that the farmer, in some rough and ready way, would project the trend? Or weight last year's price less heavily than the trend in his estimate of next year's price? If a farmer does in fact consider what has been happening to prices — the trend — when he decides how much to plant, it follows that he would plant less at any given T-1 price if prices had been falling for a long time, than he would have planted at the same T-1 price if prices had been at about a constant level for some time.[12]

V. BARLEY–WHEAT PRICE RATIO

The ratio of the b:rley price to the wheat price in harvest year T-1 is an important variable, as barley is the producer's closest substitute for wheat. The farmer can change from wheat to barley with little or no outlay for new equipment. Oats would also be a good substitute, except that they are used mainly as a feed, and to make the growing of oats profitable many farmers would have felt they needed to invest in livestock. Since the ratio here expresses the barley price divided by the wheat price, when the ratio gets larger there is an incentive for the farmer to change to barley.[13] The ratio varies significantly, the extremes being 0·66 and 1·03.

The correlations of the barley–wheat price ratio and wheat acreage are quite significant: −0·59 for the whole period, −0·70 in the first part, and −0·47 in the last part. These correlations are what should have been expected. When the wheat price fell relative to the barley price, the ratio became larger, and wheat acreage decreased.

Again the correlation is highest for the period before 1895. This is largely due to the fact that in the earlier part of the period wheat prices fell more precipitously than barley prices, and the ratio became greater during the years of the most striking reductions in wheat acreage. As a measure of the causal relationships the r_{Y5} correlation before 1895 is somewhat misleading. When a partial correlation is taken holding the trend factor 'constant', that is when the effect of the moving average (X_4) is taken out, the importance of X_5 is much reduced; the partial correlation $r_{Y5\cdot4}$ is −0·40 before 1895. After 1894, on the other hand, the correlation between X_5 and Y is not significantly reduced when X_4's effects are excluded; $r_{Y5\cdot4}$ is −0·43 in the later years.

These partials, in combination with other results, strengthen somewhat the argument that the trend has special importance. The best measure of factors other than trend influencing price is X_5; its correlation with acreage in the first part of the period is much reduced when trend is held 'constant', but this is not the case for the second part of the period, i.e., the roughly horizontal movement of the seven-year average price does not reduce the importance of X_5 significantly after 1894.

It will be remembered that the r_{Y5} correlation was $-0\cdot47$ after 1894. This is distinctly higher than any of the other correlations that were tried for this part of the period; X_1 is a poor second with a $0\cdot37$ correlation, and X_4, which in other years explained almost all of the variance in Y, is only $0\cdot21$. Moreover, X_5 is not reduced materially by holding other factors constant in the years after 1894, as was explained above. These facts point to the conclusion that the price ratio is an important variable. It seems that, but for the severity of the downward trend before 1895, which made farmers abandon wheat in favour of grass (or letting the land 'tumble down' to weeds) and other crops as well as barley, the price ratio would have been the most important variable for all of the years between 1873 and 1913. The importance of X_5 after 1894, and the fact that it is often easy for farmers to switch from one crop to another, suggest that it is by no means always helpful to use Marshallian analysis in its simplest, most 'partial' sense in studying supply responses and prices for particular grain crops. It is often only by using price ratios, or other methods which allow simultaneous consideration of more than two variables, that realistic analysis is possible. Yet it is often the case that the supply of wheat is considered without explicit consideration of the prices of any substitute crops.

VI. THE MODELS

The multiple regression equation that appears to be best for the period as a whole includes only the seven-year average price (X_4) and the ratio of barley and wheat prices (X_5); between these two variables almost all of the variance in acreage is explained. The collinearity between X_4 and X_5 is by no means intolerable.

Wheat prices in year T-1 will not be included in the model for the entire period because the r_{Y1} correlation is misleading, and because X_4 has a higher correlation with Y than does X_1, and the r_{14} collinearity is too great for the two to be used together. It would obviously be inappropriate to include X_3 and X_2 in the multiple regression equation.

The regression equation using X_4 and X_5 is:

$$Y = 0\cdot97 + 0\cdot0043X_4 - 0\cdot77X_5{}^{14}$$

The multiple correlation coefficient is $0\cdot95$: about 89 per cent of the variance in acreage is explained by these two variables. The simple correlation between X_4 and Y is $0\cdot94$, almost as high. The standard error of estimate is essentially the same for the simple as for the multiple correlation. This means that as a model for estimating Y the simple regression model was about as good as the model using both X_4 and X_5. The simple regression equation is:

$$Y = 0\cdot19 + 0\cdot0047X_4$$

It would have been possible to have removed the linear trend from the b coefficients in all of these regression equations by using either of the following methods: (1) $y' = a' + b'_4 x'_4 + b'_5 x'_5$ where x'_4, x'_5, and y' are deviations from the linear trend, that is $x_i' = X_i - a - b_T X_T$ and $y' = Y - a - b_T X_T$, or (2) $Y = a + b_T X_T + b_4 X_4 + b_5 X_5$. The value of the b coefficients is the same in both methods, i.e., $b_2 = b'_4$ and $b_5 = b'_5$.[15] But neither method would have been of much use here; the 'time element' should be included in the b coefficients. Any b values determined for this period after elimination of the trend will not be appropriate in other periods.

The same model which was used for the whole period seems best for the earlier part. The correlations for the earlier years of the period are usually much the same as those for the period as a whole because the largest variances are in the early years, and they are the dominant influence on the results for the whole period. The multiple regression model for the years before 1895 is:

$$Y = 1 \cdot 59 + 0 \cdot 0038 X_4 - 1 \cdot 15 X_5.$$

The multiple correlation coefficient is $0 \cdot 93$, while the correlation of X_4 alone with Y is practically the same, $0 \cdot 91$. The standard error of estimate for the multiple regression is $0 \cdot 21$, while for the simple regression equation it is $0 \cdot 22$. The model using only X_4 is:

$$Y = 0 \cdot 31 + 0 \cdot 0045 X_4.$$

For the latter part of the period it seems wise to include the variable X_1, wheat prices in year T-1. The problem of collinearity is not so great. Here X_1 can be in the equation without excluding X_4; their correlation for this part of the period is $0 \cdot 55$ — uncomfortably high, but far better than the figure of $0 \cdot 91$ for the whole period. Moreover, the partial correlations indicate that X_1 may here have some of the genuine influence that prices before planting are usually presumed to have. The correlation r_{y1} is only $0 \cdot 37$, though when time (T) is 'held constant' the correlation rises: $r_{y1 \cdot T}$ is $0 \cdot 51$. On the other hand, the correlation between first differences of (X_2 and y) was even smaller in the latter part of the period than it was when all the years studied were considered together.

The normal equations were solved by the Fisher–Doolittle method. The resulting equation is:

$$Y = 2 \cdot 35 + 0 \cdot 0028 X_1 + 0 \cdot 00017 X_4 - 0 \cdot 86 X_5.$$

This multiple correlation, $R_{y \cdot 145}$, is $0 \cdot 471$. It is no improvement over the highest simple correlation, r_{y5}, which is $-0 \cdot 465$. The simple regression equation for X_5 is:

$$Y = 2 \cdot 62 - 0 \cdot 99 X_5.$$

There is no significant difference between the standard errors of the two regressions.

It is interesting if not surprising to note that while a high proportion of the variance was explained in the first part of the period and only a small percentage was accounted for in the second part, the regression analysis in the second part gives a greater accuracy of estimate. The multiple regression equation for the years before 1895 had a standard error of estimate of 0·21, but in the latter part of the period the standard error was 0·17. Of course, different Y's are being compared; there is less variance in the later years.

VII. THE RELATIONSHIP OF REGRESSION LINES AND FUNCTION ELASTICITIES

The next problem is to determine what information the regression lines give about the economic history of the period. While the foregoing regressions relate prices and quantities (acreage is a tolerable indication of the quantity of wheat farmers intend to supply), it would be wrong to think of them as supply functions. A supply function shows the relation between price and the intentions to sell when all other things are held constant, but these regression lines, covering as many as forty-one years, reflect the effects of factors like technical change and movements in factor costs.

In a very interesting article[16] Professor W. W. Cochrane contends that the idea of the 'response relation' is often more useful than the supply function concept. The 'response relation' is the *actual* relationship between price and quantity during a particular period: unlike the supply function it does not require the heroic *ceteris paribus* assumption. It is based on the recognition that the shifts in the functions are often the largest part of the story. It does seem to be true that the response relation would generally be the most useful for historical research: it tells us (in Ranke's words about the purpose of the history) 'what really happened'.

Cochrane then offers the thesis that the response relation is more elastic in periods of rising prices than in periods of falling prices. His rationale is that during a period of rising prices farmers will have the capital and confidence to invest in new equipment, thus increasing output, but when prices are falling they will treat the expense that has been incurred on this equipment as a fixed cost, and continue to use the new production function. The data, already divided into a phase of declining prices and a series of years in which prices (though showing no distinct trend) rose slightly, can easily be used to test this contention. The regression lines of X and Y reveal that for the first part of the period the elasticity was 1·6, while for the latter part it was 1·9.[17] The thesis seems to be confirmed. In fact, the question is much more complicated. Price-quantity regression lines are derived from the points of intersection of the different supply and demand functions during a particular period. The price-quantity regression lines could not be computed but for the fact that the true demand and supply functions were shifting. Only if the true supply function were constant during the whole period, while the demand function shifted, could an ordinary regression line represent a supply function. If the demand schedule shifts farther than the supply function, the regression line is likely to have a positive slope; conversely, larger shifts in the supply function will tend to create a regression line with a negative slope.[18] It follows that generalizations about the elasticity of the regression lines (i.e., statistically derived response relations) are usually meaningless.[19]

The elasticity of a supply function can be determined if the size and direction of the shifts in the supply schedule can be specified. That this is sometimes acutely difficult is evidenced by the paucity of reliable estimates of the supply function. Statistical virtuosity can succeed in solving the 'identification problem', but only by using additional data or making further assumptions. It seems impossible to determine the elasticity of supply with precision in the case at hand, for there are not sufficiently accurate data on the factors which would cause the supply curve to shift. The shifts in the supply schedule depend on several factors, like changes in factor costs, the prices of other commodities the farmer might produce, and the extent of technical change.

The data clearly do not allow any reliable estimates of the exact size of the movements in the supply function; the most that can be done is to determine the direction of the shifts. It is, for example, impossible to say at exactly what rate technical change proceeded on British farms.

Nihilism might seem to be the only justifiable attitude about the elasticity of the supply curve. *But in fact, extremely useful conclusions can be drawn from the logic of the relationship between the supply functions and the regression line.* Examine the representation of the regression line of X and Y for the years from 1873 to 1894 (Figure 2 A). The earlier years of the period, when price and acreage were highest, are represented by the upper portion of the regression line, while the years just before 1895 take up that part of the regression line

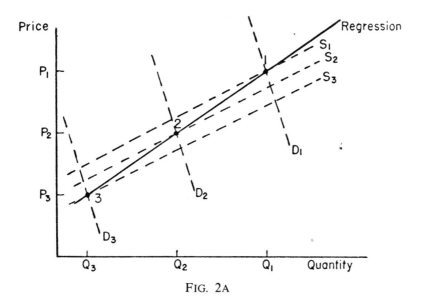

FIG. 2A

nearest the origin. Assume that the intersection of the demand and supply functions for the very earliest years of the period is represented by point 1, while points 2 and 3 are examples of the points of intersection of demand and supply functions in the eighties and early nineties respectively. It is clear (for reasons discussed below) that the supply schedule shifted to the right. *But with the supply schedule shifting to the right, it is impossible to have the supply functions cutting the regression line from the bottom. The supply functions must be more elastic than the regression line, which has an elasticity of 1·6.* This is obvious from the fact that any supply function through point 3 which has a steeper slope than the regression line must be to the left of any supply function drawn through points 1 or 2: only if all three of the supply functions have elasticities greater than the regression line could they have shifted to the right. It is obvious, too, that the demand curve shifted to the left, for prices fell.

The same logic could be used whatever the slope of the regression line. If the regression line had the negative slope of a demand curve (as in Figure 2B) and

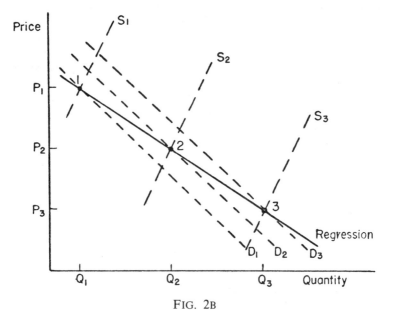

FIG. 2B

prices had been falling, it would follow that the supply function had shifted to the right. Moreover, in almost any practical case the direction of the demand shift would be evident, so it would be simple to describe the relationship between the regression lines and the demand functions: if demand had shifted to the left, it would have to be more elastic than the regression line, while the demand curve would have to be less elastic than the regression line if there had been an increase in the amount demanded at every price. If price had risen the converse would follow. The argument just developed holds whether the supply functions are curved or straight, so long as each curve does not have more than one point of intersection with the regression line.[20]

The conclusion from the logic of the function–regression relationship, then, is that it is overwhelmingly likely that the supply function had in general an elasticity greater than 1·6.

This conclusion is based on the vital, but unexceptionable, premise that the supply curve shifted to the right. One thing causing the rightward shifts was technological advance. The twenty-two years considered were roughly the ones in which the reaper and binder came into fairly general use in Great Britain. There were improvements in the methods of seeding and threshing wheat, and chemical fertilizers were beginning to be used. The old-fashioned Norfolk four-course rotation was being abandoned.[21] Several writers give evidence which implies that the rate of technological advance was, however, less than it had been in the preceding decades,[22] and this seems reasonable, for the price collapse must have reduced the marginal efficiency of investment, and left farmers without the capital or confidence necessary for rapid progress.

Colin Clark's index (in 'international units') of output per man hour in agriculture in the United Kingdom indicates that between 1870–6 and 1886–93, output increased by about 13 per cent. E. M. Ojala finds that product per worker increased by 8 per cent.[23] It seems that Ojala's index shows the smaller gain in productivity largely because his figures are net of the effects of increased purchases of non-farm inputs like fertilizer and machinery, and because he assumes no change in the number of hours worked per person. Presumably the increases in the efficiency of wheat production were not radically different from those in the rest of agriculture, and so technological improvement must have been tending to make the wheat supply function shift to the right.[24]

Moreover, factor costs decreased somewhat between 1873 and 1895, and this meant (*ceteris paribus*) that farmers would have wanted to plant more wheat at any given price. It was the time of the 'Great Depression', and the costs of the things farmers had to buy were decreasing; the Sauerbeck–Statist index of commodity prices shows that the general level of commodity prices declined from 121 in 1870–6 to 84 in 1886–93.[25] It is likely that the cost of most of the things farmers needed for their business decreased with the general price level, though probably not in the same proportion. Rents, a large item in costs, were lower in 1894 than they had been in 1873. (While rents would be considered a fixed cost to the tenant in the short run, and a change in rent would accordingly have no influence on the optimum output, a change in rents would affect a farmer's 'long-run' decisions, e.g., his decisions about whether or not to continue farming. Because most rental contracts were for periods of up to twenty-one years, land rents, in the popular sense of the word, were not determined by price in the short run.) Between 1870–6 and 1886–93, rents in England and Wales decreased by 24 per cent, according to Rhee's index of rents.[26] *The Report of the Royal Commission on Land in Wales* holds that English and Welsh rents dropped 22·6 per cent between 1878 and 1893, while

Scotch rents were said to fall 18·5 per cent.[27] Though the exact amount of the
fall in rents cannot be determined, there can be no question that they were
reduced somewhat. In that day of Henry George and Joseph Chamberlain people were sensitive to the advantages of the landlord's position, and there was
much criticism of the rent takers.

A possible exception to the generalization that factor costs fell seems to be
the case of labour, but again the data do not allow precise measurement. An index computed by Ojala shows a very slight but steady increase in farm wages
in the years before 1894.[28] Other evidence makes it seem that farm labourers'
wages sank in the late seventies and early eighties, but had risen again by
1891.[29] Though wages probably rose measurably, it is patent that this could
not have negated the several other factors pushing the supply curve in the other
direction.

The price of other commodities the farmer might have produced declined,
though not by as much as wheat prices. Agricultural prices in general fell by
about a third between 1873 and 1894.[30] As the previous discussion of the
wheat-barley price ratio indicates, the price of the closest substitute to wheat
decreased considerably. Even though the price of wheat fell more precipitously
than the prices of other products, it still paid the farmers to plant more wheat,
in response to any particular wheat price, than if the prices of other commodities had remained constant or risen slightly. So there was in the prices of
alternatives yet another influence causing the supply functions to move to the
right.

Accordingly, the conclusion that in general the supply functions between
1873 and 1894 had an elasticity greater than 1·6 seems almost as inescapable
as it is surprising. (The elasticity of supply for wheat in the United States
during recent times is widely, and probably justifiably, thought to be extremely
inelastic.)[31]

The fact that the elasticity of supply, at least before 1895, was startlingly
high, is only part of the story of the supply relationship. In conditions of uncertainty there are two elements in the farmer's reaction to a change in price: one
is the way a price change affects his estimate of the harvest price, the other is
the extent of his response to the estimated price. Since different price changes
affect estimates of the harvest price differently, the response of quantity to
prices is affected by whether, and in what way, the farmer thinks a particular
price change gives a guide to the harvest price. The conclusions in this paper
about the importance of the trend in farmers' decisions before 1895, the
relative unimportance of year to year changes in price, and the causal importance of the wheat-barley price ratio tell more about the relation of price and
quantity than the elasticity of supply does. There were conclusions about which
price changes caused most of the movement in acreage, and about when and
how British farmers responded to price changes before a supply function was
mentioned, and before any regression lines had been determined. This shows
that the correlation coefficient can often be as useful as the regression line in
the study of the supply relationship.

VIII. CONCLUSIONS

It was not until 1873 that British farmers were faced with sharply falling prices. Contrary to the expectations of 1846, the free trade policy did not bring an immediate collapse of prices. But from 1873 until 1894 prices dropped precipitously, and British wheat production fell by about 60 per cent.

The principle of the relationship between regression lines and supply functions indicates that the elasticity of the supply functions in the years from 1873 through 1894 must have been generally greater than 1·6. This surprisingly high elasticity suggests that the substitution between wheat and other products the farmer might raise was fairly rapid. That the substitution between wheat and barley was particularly important is suggested by the close correlation between the wheat-barley price ratio and the acreage of wheat. This was also the case after 1894 when the ratio of wheat to barley prices appeared to be the most important causal variable. It is probable that the substitution between wheat and other products was easier in Great Britain than it is in many other wheat-growing areas, such as the American Great Plains. With relatively ample rainfall and nearness to large markets, the British wheat grower had a larger range of alternatives than wheat farmers in most semi-arid areas. In many countries wheat is grown on land which is too dry for barley, but this is not the case in Great Britain. Another factor making for the surprisingly high elasticity of supply was the fact that in those days farmers had very little expensive, specialized equipment, and could probably switch from one product to another without great cost.

The main substantive conclusions of this paper concern the way farmers formed their estimates of the harvest price. In the first part of the period it seems clear that farmers did not expect that the price at harvest time would be the same as the price before planting. Among the evidences in support of this claim is the absence of any correlation between year to year changes in prices and year to year changes in acreage (that is, first differences in average annual prices and acreages). Farmers seemed to have thought instead that the downward trend of prices would continue. One of the arrows pointing to this conclusion (see Section IV) is the very high correlation between the average price in the seven years before planting, and acreage.[32] Farmers must have concentrated their attention on whether or not prices had on the average been falling over the last several years, and given scant attention to the smaller movements affecting the price at the time of planting. The average price in the seven years before planting was not thought of as the expected price, but when the average of past prices fell, as it almost always did from 1873 to 1895, the farmer extrapolated generally poor prospects for wheat production.

Thus price expectations, and the factors that affect them, are often vital to an understanding of a market. And sometimes expectations about prices several years hence may be important. Wheat is often planted on fallow only, and a decision about wheat acreage may require an adjustment in the rotation that must be planned two or more years in advance. Similarly when a farmer buys machinery, or decides whether or not to switch from wheat to livestock, it is the price expectations for future years that are relevant.

After 1894 the effect of price on acreage was much less distinct: the best correlation explained only one-fourth of the variation in acreage. Farmers must have felt, when prices were fluctuating considerably and there was no discernible trend, that past prices did not give a reliable basis for predicting the price that would prevail at the time of the next harvest. When the harvest price is more difficult to predict, it is natural that non-price factors, like the difficulty of changing rotations, the habits of the entrepreneur, and institutional rigidities (e.g., leases which dictated the maximum or minimum acreage that could be planted to wheat) should be more important.[33]

The contrast between the two parts of the period indicates the need for the study of an aspect of the supply relationship which is generally overlooked: the manner in which price changes affect the farmer's estimate of the price at harvest time. The elasticity of supply seems to have been greater after 1894 than it was before, yet it would not be correct to say that the effect of price on acreage was greater, or that price was causally more important, in the latter part of the period. Since farmers did not feel that past prices gave an adequate basis for predicting harvest prices in the years after 1894, they did not respond in any regular manner. It can be very misleading to think of the elasticity of supply without making a distinction between the way a particular price change affects the estimate of the harvest price and the response of quantity to price when the harvest price is known. Thus another dimension of the supply relationship comes into view. A different reaction should be expected when there is a change in the price support level than when there is a change in free market prices.

Here the analysis is directly relevant to the arguments among economists about 'forward prices' for agriculture; if prices at planting time, or in the years before, do not provide an adequate indication of the price at harvest time, presumably prices are not functioning properly as guides for resource allocation, and some system of guaranteed prices would be useful. On the other hand, when harvest prices are predicted from the trend with a fair degree of accuracy, then forward prices (that is, estimates of the equilibrium price guaranteed for a year or two in advance of the harvest) could not bring much improvement in resource allocation.[34]

The adaptation to the lower prices was fundamental and far-reaching. The reduction in the amount of wheat produced was a major factor in the decline of the whole agricultural sector. France and Germany imposed tariffs which gave their farmers some protection against the collapse in world agricultural prices. Britain is now the most urban or industrialized of all countries, partly because of her agricultural policy in the late nineteenth century. The ramifications of these *laissez-faire* policies extended even to the political and social structure. The anciently important landed gentry and the country clergy lost a measure of their power and prestige.[35]

Britain's persistence in *laissez-faire* policies at the price of a devastated agriculture is unique in the history of nations. Yet the problems discussed here have been at most cursorily treated by historians. From the attention lavished on the repeal of the Corn Laws one might assume that all that was important in British agriculture ended in 1846. But it would be more appropriate to say that the downfall of British agriculture began, not in 1846, but in 1873. The common concern of economic historians with the politics of the repeal of the Corn Laws has brought neglect of the economic developments themselves. The goal of this paper, aside from the purely statistical development, is to redress the balance and explain this most crucial part of the story of the decline of British agriculture.

NOTES

[1] 'I say, then, assuming, as I have given you reason to assume, that the price of wheat when this system is established ranges in England at 35s. per quarter, with other grains in proportion.' (The usual price before the repeal was 50 to 60 shillings per quarter. A quarter is equal to 8 bushels.) Benjamin Disraeli's speech of 15 May, 1846, on the third reading of the Corn Importation Bill, *Hansard's Debates*, quoted in the *Speeches of the Earl of Beaconsfield*, ed. T. E. Kebbel (London, 1882), i. 158.

[2] Lord Ernle, *English Farming Past and Present* (London, 1919), p. 441.

[3] It is one of the greatest ironies of British economic history that nothing significant was done about the agricultural depression in the late seventies, for Disraeli, by this time Lord Beaconsfield, was Prime Minister. Disraeli had been, of course, the most famous and eloquent opponent of the repeal of the Corn Laws. He made the following lugubrious prediction in the debate on the repeal:

'It may be vain now, in the midnight of their intoxication, to tell them that there will be an awakening of bitterness; it may be idle now, in the springtide of their economic frenzy, to warn them that there may be an ebb of trouble, but the dark and inevitable hour will arrive. Then, when their spirit is softened by misfortune, they will recur to those principles that made England great, and which in our belief, can alone keep England great.' (Disraeli, *Speeches* . . ., i. 172.)

But in 1879, when the Marquis of Huntly used quotations from Disraeli's old speeches to advocate *aid* for agriculture, Disraeli (now Beaconsfield) begrudgingly acknowledged his 'rusty words' '. . . in "another place" and another generation,' but he was not willing to act upon his erstwhile recommendations: 'I cannot for a moment doubt that the repeal of the Corn Laws has materially affected the condition of those who are interested in land. . . . But that is no reason why we should retrace our steps (*sic*) and authorize and sanction any violent changes.' (Speech in House of Lords, 28 Apr., 1879, *Speeches* . . ., i. 340.)

[4] Helen Farnsworth, *Wheat Studies*, 10, nos. 8 and 9 (1934), 348–9.

[5] Alfred Marshall, *Principles of Economics* (8th ed., London, 1949), pp. 429–30.

[6] The reference is to the harvest years beginning in calendar years 1873 and 1894. Harvest years begin 1 Sept. and end 31 Aug. All subsequent references will be to harvest years.

[7] See Table 1 for the sources of all acreage statistics.

[8] The calendar year price would be inappropriate because most of the wheat in Great Britain is planted in the autumn shortly after the end of the preceding harvest year. The harvest year average price was obtained by taking a simple, i.e., unweighted average of the monthly average prices in *Agricultural Statistics*.

[9] The wheat acreage figures give the acres standing in June of each year. For explanation of official agricultural statistics for Britain see J. A. Venn, *The Foundations of Agricultural Economics* (Cambridge, 1933), p. 432.

[10] Another way of determining trend values would involve taking the regression of price on time: $P_T = a + bX_T$. The value of P_T for each year would be correlated with acreage. But this is not ideal either, for the values of P_T depend upon which particular series of years is chosen. This means nothing more than that the linear time trend will be different for each time period selected: the trend values which are correlated with acreage will be changed whenever the researcher chooses a different year as the starting point for the trend. The seven-year average method does to some extent avoid the complications that arise from the fact that the historian using a linear trend can select a series of years to suit his argument.

Perhaps the best method of getting the trend values to correlate with acreage would entail taking a separate linear regression of price on time for the series of seven years preceding each planting. That is, the $P_T = a + bX_T$ equation that would be relevant to the year 1885 is that from 1877 to 1884, while that suitable for the farmers' 1886 planting would involve the years 1878 to 1885. Obviously this method is too costly. Though the seven-year average does not give a linear trend it does decline in all but two years between 1873 and 1895, and shows a high correlation with acreage during this time of rapidly falling prices. This is evidence for the importance of trend.

[11] The choice of seven years for the moving average is partly for convenience. The seven-year average was

computed by the government to assess tithes. The seven-year average has the further advantage that it was published and made known to many British farmers in that day.

[12] This, of course, assumes that the farmers do not expect quick and sizeable changes in costs. Since costs were very stable *by comparison* with prices, this is a reasonable assumption.

[13] The ratio of the two prices was used instead of the difference between them because at high prices a particular difference might make it profitable to plant wheat, but at low prices the same absolute difference might be consistent with barley being the better alternative: the absolute difference between the two prices has meaning only in relation to the absolute level of the two prices.

[14] This equation, involving a time series, is of course strictly correct only on the assumption that the error terms in the regression equation are uncorrelated, i.e. that the residuals in $Y^i = a + bX^i + u^i$ are not serially correlated. Several of the regressions in this paper have been tested using Von Neuman's ratio and the Durbin and Watson tables (*Biometrika*, June 1951, p. 175) at the 1 per cent significance level. It was found that the ratio was slightly below the lower limit for the simple regressions (for the whole period and the first part of the period) involving X_2, and in the range of indeterminancy using X_5. However, the highest serial correlation in any of the three equations was only 0.52. The accuracy of the test used to assess the seriousness of the serial correlation is debatable, and there is no indication of the true relationship of the residuals (e.g., no basis for assuming that $u_T = u_{T-1} + v_T$ where v_T is not correlated), so it is doubtful that there is any serious error here due to serial correlation or that there is any better method that could have been used. In any event the estimates are not biased.

[15] For proof see R. Frisch and F. V. Waugh, 'Partial Time Regressions as Compared with Individual Time Trends', *Econometrica*, 1 (1933), 387 ff.

[16] 'Conceptualizing the Supply Relation in Agriculture', *Journal of Farm Economics*, 37 (Dec. 1955), 1161.

[17] The elasticity was computed at the point of means. $E = dY/dX_1 \cdot \overline{X}_1/\overline{Y}$ where dY/dX_1 is the reciprocal of the b coefficient in the regression $X_1 = a + bY$.

[18] An example of a study which neglects to draw an adequate distinction between a price–quantity regression line and a supply function is provided by B. J. Bowlen, 'The Wheat Supply Function', *Journal of Farm Economics*, 37 (Dec. 1955), 1177.

[19] Cochrane's emphasis on the response relation is still in order. The point here concerns the pitfalls of statistical measurement of the elasticity of the response relation. It can still be most useful to study a response relation in a particular situation as a source of information about the price-quantity points themselves. The thought that in some sense the supply response will usually be more elastic in times of rising prices is still plausible, though it is best stated in terms of a tendency for the supply function to shift to the right when prices rise. Finally, Cochrane's application of his concepts to the case of aggregate food supply is not affected, for his assumption is that in the years chosen the supply function for food did not shift significantly.

[20] This is possible, but unlikely, in the present case. But even if the supply functions do intersect the regression line more than once, it still follows that the supply function is quite elastic for some distance near the regression line, for a curve obviously could not intersect the regression line twice without having a flatter slope than the regression line somewhere between the two intersections.

Another minor exception is that supply–demand intersections are not on the regression line, but clustered around it, so every supply function need not be more elastic than the regression line. Any statistical estimate of a supply function is subject to criticism on the ground that there are some observations which are a distance away from the line. Any such criticism against the results here is weakened by the high correlation. It should still be true with but infrequent exceptions that the supply functions had an elasticity greater than the regression line.

[21] Two contemporary French writers testified to a considerable technological improvement in British agriculture. See A. Dulac, *L'Agriculture et le Libre-Echange dans le Royaume Uni* (Paris, 1903); and Pierre Besse, *La Crise et L'Evolution de L'Agriculture en Angleterre de 1875 à Nos Jours* (Paris, 1910), pp. 173–91.

[22] W. B. Wall, 'The Agriculture of Pembrokeshire', *Jour. Roy. Agr. Soc.* 2nd series, 23 (1887) 83, 86; C. Whitehead, 'A Sketch of the Agriculture of Kent', ibid., 35 (1899), p. 456; A. D. Hall, *Agriculture After the War* (London, 1916); and J. H. Clapham, *An Economic History of Modern Britain* (Cambridge, 1926–38), iii. Book IV, chap. 2.

[23] Clark, *Conditions of Economic Progress* (London, 1957), p. 269. Ojala, *Agriculture and Economic Progress* (London, 1952), p. 153.

[24] The data on yields give no unambiguous information on changes in the production function for wheat. While yields increased from 24.7 bushels per acre during the harvest years 1873–79 to an average yield of 29.3 bushels from 1885–94, the inclement weather of the late seventies must have been an important factor. From 1853–73 the yield was 28.2 bushels per acre, only a little less than the figure for 1885–94. Any changes in yields must be explained partly by the tendency for the poorer land to be abandoned when acreage is reduced. From 1894 until World War I yields rose considerably. (The data for the years after 1885 are from *Agricultural Statistics*, while figures for before 1880 come from the estimates of J. B. Lawes and J. H. Gilbert, 'On the Home Produce, Imports and Consumption, and Price of Wheat', *Jour. Stat. Soc.*, 43 (June 1880) 313–40.

[25] Ojala, op. cit., p. 146.

[26] Ojala, op. cit., p. 216.

[27] King's College, Cambridge, has in its 'Mundum book' figures showing that the net receipts from the college lands in thirteen counties (with an above average proportion of land in corn) dropped by 38·9 per cent between 1878 and 1893. (J. H. Clapham, op. cit., ii. 283.) Paradoxically, the assets of King's College were later to be much augmented by the speculation of a famous Bursar noted as an advocate of 'euthanasia of the rentier'.

[28] Op. cit., p. 138. His index is constructed from data in the *Nineteenth Abstract of Labour Statistics for the United Kingdom* and J. J. Macgregor, 'Labour Costs in British Forestry since 1824', *Forestry*, 20 (1946).

[29] W. C. Little's report to the *Royal Commission on Labour* (1893–4), xxvii, Part 2, p. 44.

[30] Ojala shows three separate indices, all of which show a drop of about this amount. Op. cit., p. 146.

[31] It was probably also the case that the supply functions shifted to the right in the years after 1894. If this is true, and the elasticity of 1·9 for the X and Y regression line is correct, it would follow that the elasticity of supply is even greater, and probably above 2, in the later years of the period. But with the much less impressive correlations for the years after 1894, this conclusion seems uncautious; there is not enough correlation behind the regression line to justify confidence in the measure of its elasticity.

The elasticities of the regression lines relate the percentage change in price in the year before planting (X_1) to the percentage change in acreage. Earlier in this paper it was shown that the average annual prices were not the most important influence on acreage. This illustrates a problem in the concept of price elasticity: if the distribution of prices over time—the direction in which prices have been moving—also affects supply decisions, it is not altogether correct to speak of the elasticity of supply as a measure of the change in quantity prompted by the price before planting.

[32] Costs, in comparison with prices, were quite stable, and so prices give a good indication of the profit margin.

[33] The statistical orientation of this paper is not meant to imply that only quantitative factors were significant. The nature of the leasing arrangements, for example, was a crucial factor. When the price collapse began many tenants had contracts which bound them to pay a fixed money rent each year for the duration of the contract, which was at times as long as twenty-one years. Rents were reduced by some landlords before the expiration of the lease, but the burden of fixed charges, assumed when prices were high, bore heavily on many tenants.

The differences among regions are also concealed in a study of the statistical aggregates. On the whole the adaptation to the price collapse was faster in the West of England than in the East. In the West the land was poorer for grain, and farmers turned to livestock more quickly. The growing demand for garden products made the adaptation more rapid near larger cities. Observers in those days often suggested that the Scots moving to English farms were an important factor in the adjustment to the lower prices. The claim was that the Scots, parsimonious and accustomed to raising oats and livestock rather than wheat, were able to prosper when most of the English farmers could not.

These and other qualitative factors are discussed, albeit with some misinterpretation, by Pierre Besse, op. cit., and by Raymond Phincas Stearns, 'Agricultural Adaptation in England, 1875–1900', *Agr. Hist.*, 6, nos. 2 and 3 (1932).

[34] See D. Gale Johnson's *Forward Prices for Agriculture* (Chicago, 1947), chap. 6. Johnson lists several bases on which a farmer might predict prices: (1) he may project the current price into the future, (2) he may project the price trend, (3) he may assume that the future price will be the same as the 'normal' price, which is the long-term average price, (4) or that the future price will be somewhere between the present price and the 'normal' price, (5) he may choose some particular past price (say a war or drought year price) and use it to predict the future price, (6) he may use complex statistical techniques, or follow the advice of those who do. Model number 1 on Johnson's list—the one so often taken for granted by economists—does not fit the facts of British agricultural history in the period covered by this paper; the continuation-of-trend hypothesis appears to be best for the years before 1895, and in the later part of the period no one hypothesis describes the facts adequately. Johnson finds that in the United States between 1910 and 1943 a mechanical projection of trend (model 2) gave less reliable forecasts of prices than models, 1, 3, or 4. There is no conflict with the results in this paper, however, for Johnson's trend model was the assumption that 'the price next year will bear the same relationship to this year's price as this year's price did to last year's' (p. 81, footnote to Table 7). A trend over two years is naturally much less reliable than one which has continued over, say, seven years. Moreover, it is not the contention in this paper that farmers always project the trend of prices; it is obvious that they did not do this after 1894. The point is that when the trend is 'distinct', i.e., whenever there is an easily discernible direction to the movement of prices, farmers are apt to project the trend. Finally, Johnson compared the accuracy of the models for prediction; nothing definite can be deduced from his figures about what model(s) American farmers actually did use.

[35] Another aspect of the repeal of the Corn Laws which needs study is the hardship imposed on those who had to bear the burden of the adjustments, but this is beyond the scope of this paper. Some farmers, though lacking the facile mobility assumed in economic models, had to change occupation and domicile in the interests of the rest of the economy. The policies which were adopted to ameliorate the difficulties arising from the adjustment were only placebos.

10

British Investment in Argentina and Long Swings, 1880–1914*

Editor's note. This article was first published in *Journ. Econ. Hist.* 31 (1971) 650–63. Professor Ford has kindly provided some additional graphs, for which the Editor is grateful.

Simple and multiple regression methods, the major analytical tool used in this article, are described above, pp. 19–25, and references to further reading are given in the footnotes to those pages.

British investment in Argentina in the period 1880–1914 amounted to some 8 per cent of total British overseas investment;[1] it exhibited long swings which were roughly similar to long swings in total British overseas investment but opposite to British domestic investment, although the bursts of lending to Argentina were particularly concentrated. These swings have attracted the attention of economists and some (notably Brinley Thomas) have pointed out that emigration from Europe to North America and American investment in construction and transportation and other series in the American economy exhibited 18–20 year swings similar to those in British overseas investment, and that these were all in opposite phase to swings in British home investment and the building cycle in Britain.[2] They have then gone on to explain these inverse British patterns in terms of emigration and the growth rhythm of the Atlantic economy, with heavy stress being laid on North American effects. The analysis of movements of both labour and capital can then be conducted in terms of the varying intensities of the *pull* of opportunities at home and abroad, and the *push* of home conditions and prospects, and how these interacted with each other to produce these inverse patterns.

Some earlier studies in *The Journal of Economic History* have examined the issue of pull versus push for the migration of labour. In particular, Wilkinson has examined long swings in Swedish emigration to the United States and has concluded that, besides the major pull factor of the United States economy, the push factor, as represented by the pace of economic development of Sweden, was influential too.[3] He further suggests that the latter might have been influenced, via trade, by British economic growth, so that Sweden might be linked in various ways with the U.S./U.K. inverse patterns. Kelley has demonstrated for migration into Australia the importance of the pull factor, but has pointed out the influence of forces other than the interaction of source and

---

* I am grateful to Dr. S. K. Nath for comments on an earlier version of this paper.

receiving countries — for example, events in other British migrant-receiving areas.[4] It will emerge that these observations have their counterparts in this study, which is concerned with capital flows.

This article seeks to examine whether the pull and push factors can be applied to explain the flow of British lending to Argentina, which was closely linked to Britain through trade flows, profit and interest remittances, and capital movements, but not to any significant extent through flows of labour. First, the simple 'pull' hypothesis of Argentine opportunities on British lending to Argentina will be tested. Second, more complex hypotheses involving a push factor and a factor reflecting British attitudes to overseas investment in general will be investigated.

In discussing factors influencing the pull of Argentine prospects, attention must be paid to non-economic forces which shaped the social and political environment within which British lending took place. These were of special importance at the beginning of our period, when the military expeditions of 1878–81 had put down the Indians of the interior and had made the fertile Pampas safe for permanent cultivation. This was needed before the British investor could be tempted to lend for railways to open up these areas and the farmers to settle and expand the output of primary produce for export. Again, not without significance for the overseas investor was the assumption of power by a strong federal government which seemed capable of maintaining law and order and safety of property.

Given the environment, the pull of Argentine projects depended first on the behaviour of world demand and prices for the primary produce which Argentina was capable of producing with her endowment of resources. On account of the small size of the local market and the existing comparative cost ratios, development was seen in terms of exporting primary goods to world markets and importing manufactures. Growing population and production in Europe were raising the demand for foodstuffs and raw materials, while the growing urban population of the United States was diminishing her exportable surplus, and her growing production was increasing her raw material needs. Furthermore, in Britain free trade meant that imported foodstuffs — especially cereals — could gain at the expense of home-produced foodstuffs. Investors, therefore, realized that there was a growing world market for goods Argentina could produce and the railways could carry. With given world prices of such produce the proportion accruing to Argentina would depend on the behaviour of ocean freight rates, dramatic alterations in which would provide another pull factor. For example, the fall in freight rates in the late 1870s due to sea transport innovations enhanced the profitability of existing and contemplated Argentine ventures.

Secondly, within this background of world conditions the actual performance of individual Argentine enterprises and the behaviour of her exports became of crucial importance in pulling — or repelling — the would-be British investor. Gloomy world conditions would be outweighed by a sparkling profit record more easily than would gloomy profits by promising world conditions.

Although the latter were one important factor in determining export proceeds and profit rates of Argentine ventures, low profit rates could occur despite favourable world conditions because of adverse local conditions or because there was a time-lag following the construction of a railway, for example, before traffic and profits built up.

In order to test the hypothesis that the flow of British lending to Argentina was determined by the pull of Argentine prospects, an indicator of the 'pull' is required, or some guide to the expected profitability of new enterprises and the likelihood of Argentine governments' being able to meet foreign debt-service charges from their revenue, for the British investor was no philanthropist *ex ante*. Amongst the available information the best indicator would seem to be railway profits as a percentage of capital employed. For the railway proved the key feature in the export-biased economic development of Argentina by transforming the fertile Pampas from an unused resource into a factor of production, and was financed almost entirely from abroad, with the British share dominant. Furthermore, more than half of British new issues for Argentina were absorbed by railways.

When seeking to explain the behaviour of Argentine issues in London by reference to the railway profit percentage, it is necessary to lag the latter because information would only become available some time after the year in which profits had been earned. Furthermore some time should be allowed for investors to react to the information so that their expectations of profitability would be governed by (immediately) past behaviour. Hence the first regression equation (1a) has a lag of one year in the profit rate; it yields the following results, where the figures in brackets represent the standard errors, and the symbols are defined as follows:

A = Argentine new issues on the London Stock Exchange (in millions of pounds (£))

P = Argentine railway profits as a percentage of capital employed (in percentage figures)

$$1883–1913 \qquad A = -1 \cdot 889 + 2 \cdot 531 \, P_{t-1} \qquad R^2 = 0 \cdot 212 \qquad (1a)$$
$$(3 \cdot 750) \ (0 \cdot 906) \qquad \qquad d = 0 \cdot 705$$

Although the coefficient of the profit rate is significant, R^2 is low and autocorrelation presents a serious problem. The second regression equation has a lag of two years in the profit rate and yields somewhat improved results with a higher R^2.

$$1884–1912 \qquad A_t = -4 \cdot 516 + 3 \cdot 230 \, P_{t-2} \qquad R^2 = 0 \cdot 357 \qquad (2a)$$
$$(3 \cdot 462) \ (0 \cdot 835) \qquad \qquad d = 0 \cdot 593$$

From inspection of the data it does appear that the first three railway profit figures (for 1882–1884) are exceptionally high as a result of special circumstances, and that it may have taken a longer lapse of time before British investors were tempted to subscribe to Argentine ventures. If these are omitted, considerably improved results are obtained both for a one-year lag (1b) and for a two-year lag (2b).

1886–1913 $\quad A_t = -10 \cdot 795 + 5 \cdot 296 \, P_{t-1}$ $\qquad R^2 = 0 \cdot 607$ $\qquad$ (1b)

$\qquad\qquad\quad (3 \cdot 193) \quad (0 \cdot 836)$ $\qquad\qquad d = 1 \cdot 207$

1887–1912 $\quad A_t = -11 \cdot 511 + 5 \cdot 474 \, P_{-2}$ $\qquad R^2 = 0 \cdot 650$ $\qquad$ (2b)

$\qquad\qquad\quad (3 \cdot 116) \quad (0 \cdot 820)$ $\qquad\qquad d = 1 \cdot 190$

It will be noted that both R^2 and the Durbin–Watson statistics for each equation are more satisfactory, while the coefficient of P is also higher, both in size and significance. Undoubtedly the pull of Argentine prospects can be considered an important influence on the flow of British overseas issues to Argentina. Nevertheless, the low figures for d in the earlier regressions (1a) and (2a) do suggest that it may be fruitful to add other variables.

Among other factors influencing issues for Argentina was the receptiveness of the London capital market to overseas issues in general. The success of an issue — indeed, its placing — would depend on the climate of opinion in Britain toward overseas investment. Although Argentine ventures might seem attractive, some recent disastrous overseas investment experiences might have tarred all overseas projects with the same brush, so that the mood of the British lender was unfavourable toward all overseas ventures. Certainly it was true that Argentine issues were high when total overseas issues were high and likewise low when the latter were low (see Table 1 and Figure 1). Accordingly a second independent variable is introduced into the regression equations to represent this factor.

$F =$ New issues on the London Stock Exchange for all overseas areas except Argentina.

The regressions were calculated, as before, for one- and two-year lags in P for the whole period and for the shorter period, which omits the 1882–1884 profit observations, and the following results were obtained:

1883–1913

$\qquad A_t = -9 \cdot 304 + 1 \cdot 990 \, P_{t-1} + 0 \cdot 108 \, F_t$ $\qquad R^2 = 0 \cdot 660$ $\qquad$ (3a)

$\qquad\quad (2 \cdot 800) \quad (0 \cdot 663) \qquad (0 \cdot 020)$ $\qquad\qquad d = 1 \cdot 510$

1886–1913

$\qquad A_t = -12 \cdot 290 + 3 \cdot 616 \, P_{t-1} + 0 \cdot 080 \, F_t$ $\qquad R^2 = 0 \cdot 760$ $\qquad$ (3b)

$\qquad\quad (2 \cdot 616) \quad (0 \cdot 818) \qquad (0 \cdot 020)$ $\qquad\qquad d = 1 \cdot 624$

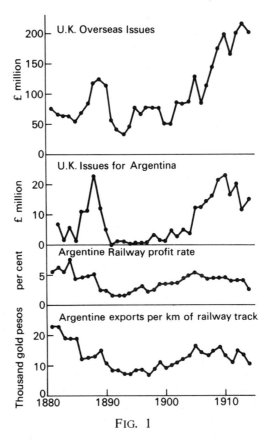

FIG. 1

1884–1912

$$A_t = -10 \cdot 890 + 1 \cdot 987 \, P_{t-2} + 0 \cdot 129 \, F_t \qquad R^2 = 0 \cdot 752 \qquad (4a)$$
$$(2 \cdot 406) \quad (0 \cdot 563) \qquad (0 \cdot 020) \qquad d = 1 \cdot 482$$

1887–1912

$$A_t = -12 \cdot 243 + 3 \cdot 223 \, P_{t-2} + 0 \cdot 098 \, F_t \qquad R^2 = 0 \cdot 788 \qquad (4b)$$
$$(2 \cdot 483) \quad (0 \cdot 873) \qquad (0 \cdot 025) \qquad d = 1 \cdot 621$$

The improvement—as compared with equations (1a) and (2a)—in explanatory power for the periods 1883—1913 and 1884–1912 in equations (3a) and (4a) is striking. All coefficients are highly significant, R^2 has risen to 0·752 in (4a) as compared with 0·357 in (2a), while the Durbin–Watson statistic has improved. There now seems much less of a case for omitting the profit rate observations of 1882–1884, as was done in regressions (1b) and (2b), as the R^2 for the longer periods has been lifted by the inclusion of the new variable, F. It is clear that the lack of influence of these 1882–4 profit rates on Argentine new issues is explicable in terms of the low level of all overseas issues in London and the general lack of interest in overseas ventures at that time.

Although F has been introduced to represent the mood of Britain with regard to overseas ventures, nevertheless implicitly it may incorporate some influence of the pull and push of British domestic prospects since, when the trend of British overseas investment was high, home investment was low and vice versa. However, it seems reasonable to introduce net home investment in Britain (at current prices) as a variable to reflect the influence of the pull of good domestic prospects or the push of bad home prospects on the assumption that investment in Britain was motivated by the prospect of profits.

In the third set of regression equations we have:

I = Net home investment in the United Kingdom.

The regressions were calculated as before for one- and two-year lags in P. The following results were obtained:

1883–1913
$$A_t = -6 \cdot 134 + 1 \cdot 590 \, P_{t-1}$$
$$(3 \cdot 537) \quad (0 \cdot 636)$$
$$+ 0 \cdot 117 \, F_t \, - 0 \cdot 0307 \, I_t, \qquad R^2 = 0 \cdot 661 \quad (5a)$$
$$(0 \cdot 020) \qquad (0 \cdot 025) \qquad d = 1 \cdot 434$$

1886–1913
$$A_t = -8 \cdot 131 + 3 \cdot 997 \, P_{-1}$$
$$(2 \cdot 670) \quad (0 \cdot 681)$$
$$+ 0 \cdot 074 \, F_t \, - 0 \cdot 056 \, I_t, \qquad R^2 = 0 \cdot 824 \quad (5b)$$
$$(0 \cdot 017) \qquad (0 \cdot 019) \qquad d = 2 \cdot 156$$

1884–1912
$$A_t = -9 \cdot 435 + 1 \cdot 890 \, P_{-2}$$
$$(3 \cdot 356) \quad (0 \cdot 590)$$
$$+ 0 \cdot 130 \, F_t \, - 0 \cdot 014 \, I_t, \qquad R^2 = 0 \cdot 756 \quad (6a)$$
$$(0 \cdot 020) \qquad (0 \cdot 022) \qquad d = 1 \cdot 501$$

1887–1912
$$A_t = -9 \cdot 685 + 3 \cdot 273 \, P_{t-2}$$
$$(3 \cdot 182) \quad (0 \cdot 863)$$
$$+ 0 \cdot 094 \, F_t \, - 0 \cdot 0271_t, \qquad R^2 = 0 \cdot 803 \quad (6b)$$
$$(0 \cdot 025) \qquad (0 \cdot 022) \qquad d = 1 \cdot 727$$

The introduction of net home investment in the United Kingdom into the regression equations for the longer period (equations (5a) and (6a)) has produced a minute improvement in R^2. The regression coefficient of I is not significantly different from zero, although it is of the right sign for the hypothesis that a rise in British opportunities, as reflected by a rise in investment, brought a fall in new issues for Argentina. Furthermore, railway profit rates lagged two years still provide a higher R^2 than if lagged one year.

However, for the shorter period the introduction of I has made a more pronounced improvement, especially in equation (5b), where R^2 has been increased from 0·760 to 0·824, and the regression coefficient of I is significantly different from zero. The improvement is less marked in equation (6b), whose explanatory power has been overtaken by (5b), with the one-year lag in profit rates.

These results do not provide much support for the hypothesis that the varying pull and push of British domestic prospects (as reflected in the behaviour of domestic investment) directly influenced Argentine new issues.[5] However it might be mistaken to dismiss it entirely since, as was pointed out earlier, British overseas new issues were implicitly linked with the state of British home prospects, as well as overseas prospects, and the variable F might pick up both influences.

In general it may be concluded that the variable flow of British funds to the Argentine which gave rise to two heavy bursts of capital formation can be explained by the pull of Argentine prospects and by the strength of the general British preference for, or aversion from, overseas ventures in any year, as measured by overseas issues to the rest of the world. Herein there would seem a distinct link with the long swings in this latter variable, whereas any direct link through British home investment claiming or releasing funds would seem weak. However there may well be features peculiar to Argentina which influenced the behaviour of the railway profit rate.

It can be suggested that Argentine prospects (as represented by the railway profit rate) might be expected to exhibit a long-run swing in the form of a development cycle, whose periodicity would certainly exceed that of a trade cycle and might well approach that of the 'long swings' previously discussed. In this development cycle, under a regime of private enterprise, I would stress as key features: (1) that there were excesses of enthusiasm and revulsion amongst leaders and (2) that overhead investment projects (for example, railways) typically take time to construct and time before they mature into their hoped-for profitability.

Such a cycle can be outlined in general terms as it may well have wider applicability than to Argentine economic development. An upsurge in overseas investment takes place in a favoured area or perhaps on an excessive scale, as enthusiasm waxes amongst promoters and lenders with consequent bunching of projects. In so far as much borrowing is in the form of fixed-interest-bearing securities, foreign debt-service charges mount while output and export proceeds are unexpanded. Speculative excesses overtake any expansion of output to bring disillusion, crisis, and cessation of lending, once it is realized that earlier judgements were excessively optimistic and short-sighted. Balance of payments strain follows the decline in the influx of funds from abroad, as service charges claim a growing portion of foreign currency receipts (which have not yet been expanded by the process of export-oriented development).

Moratoria may be sought on fixed-interest payments, while profit rates and yields on new projects may well be low or even non-existent until output and sales have built up.

In this period of revulsion among former lenders and low influx of foreign funds, the (overhead) capital projects are gradually completed and mature with growing output (and exports) of primary produce, so that with an improving balance of payments, interest and dividend payments can be resumed once again. If the projects have been bunched, considerable growth in output may be needed to absorb the large increase in capacity and bring worthwhile earnings on capital. One essential feature facilitating recovery would be the behaviour of world demand for primary produce, rapid growth and rising prices helping a recovery more than sluggish growth and sagging prices. Gradually the borrowing country comes back into favour as its economic climate continues to improve, as output now presses on existing capital stock, and the growing profits and prospects tempt lenders and induce enterprises to contemplate expansion once again. With such projects as railways to aid the expansion of exports of primary produce, the length of time between the first surge in overseas lending and its subsequent revival could easily be in the order of 15 years.[6]

Something like this was clearly at work in Argentina in our period. 1881–4 saw attractive railway profits and favourable non-economic factors, which touched off a foreign lending influx of some £140 million between 1885 and 1890, culminating in speculative mania and in disillusion amongst European investors by late 1889. The immediate result of this upsurge in foreign borrowings was to increase foreign debt-service charges to 60 per cent of export proceeds by 1890, long before productive capacity had expanded. Such a burden was not really felt as long as foreign funds flowed in, from which interest charges could be met, but was felt more keenly when foreign loans crashed in 1890 and exports (comparatively unexpanded) provided the sole source of foreign exchange. To make matters worse, export prices fell steadily from 1890 to 1896, the government repudiated its foreign debt-service payments in 1891, and the exchange rate declined precipitously between 1889 and 1891. This whole episode caused a revulsion of British interest and bitter allegations of fraud. Yet some of it was the lenders' own fault, as, greedy for gain, they were uncomprehending of the time-consuming nature of the development process. For although 1888 marked the peak of new issues for Argentina, the peak of railway length completed came in 1891 and the volume of cereal exports showed a marked rise only by 1893–4, such was the lag of the capacity effects behind the raising of funds.

In this way the size of the Argentine railway system was trebled between 1885 and 1895 and the economy was provided with the basis of her overhead capital. Perhaps, indeed, it was an overgenerous provision in the first instance, but the economy grew gradually into this railway system and railway profits steadily improved from 1895. Speedier recovery was thwarted until 1896 by falling world prices of primary products, but thereafter rising prices enhanced rising export volumes. Revival in the Argentine economy and the start of the rehabilitation of its good name among European investors seems to date from 1896, as ventures were starting to show increased profitability, the exchange-rate was appreciating, and public debt-service payments abroad were resumed in 1897. Furthermore, the problems which had been besetting the frozen meat trade from Argentina were now solved, just as the American exportable surplus was declining. Thus by the start of the twentieth century Argentina looked as if she were fulfilling her early promise. She seemed set for another bout of exter-nally financed capital formation as she was outgrowing her existing railway system, ports, and utilities. This began in 1905 after several years of rising railway profit rates and was accompanied by sustained immigration of labour.

The revived overseas investment surge reached a peak in 1910, so far as new issues for Argentina were concerned, while the railway profit rate started to sag after 1909 and new issues exhibited a downward trend thereafter. As compared with 1885–90, the expansion had been less concentrated, there had been little if any speculative mania, and far more favourable background conditions prevailed. Primary product prices were rising, the economy was broader-based and could cope more easily with the foreign debt-service problem. It was in-deed more a case of adding to a growing economy than of starting one. Nevertheless, before its effects were obscured by the economic upsets of the Great War, there were distinct signs that the upper turning point in the development cycle had been reached by 1912 for Argentina. Despite record export sales, 1913 exhibited many signs of recession as the inflow of foreign funds slackened and the gold standard mechanism brought credit contraction.

It is clear from the underlying data in Table 1 and Figure 1 that the railway profit rate exhibits a distinct long cyclical movement, much in line with the 'development' cycle sketched out above. This would suggest that as these sur-ges of foreign investment in railways took place, capital stock and capacity would be expanded relatively to existing traffic (as output in the economy was unexpanded at this stage), so that the profit rate might be expected to fall to lower levels. As primary production and exports, and hence traffic, later began to expand, so capital stock would be more fully utilized and the profit rate would rise. Eventually full capacity operation would be reached together with a high profit rate, which, other things equal, should attract fresh foreign invest-ment. (This is, of course, abstracting from other forces increasing the profit rate, such as higher rates or increased efficiency.) In the Argentine context one important determinant of the railway profit rate would clearly be the degree of capacity utilization, which might be taken to reflect the relationship between output and capital stock not only in the railway sector, but also in the economy as a whole, in just the same way as the profit rate was taken as an indicator of the 'pull' of the Argentine economy.[7]

The main task of the Argentine railway system was to convey primary products from the Pampas to the main cities and especially to the ports for export. Furthermore, Argentina was heavily dependent on export sales for her well-being, so that their performance governed the level of activity in the

TABLE 1. *Series Bearing on Economic Relations Between Argentina and the United Kingdom, 1881–1914*

	(1) U.K. issues for Argentina *(£ million)*	*(2)* Total U.K. overseas issues *(£ million)*	*(3)* Net immigration into Argentina *(thousands)*	*(4)* Argentine railway profit rate *(per cent)*	*(5)* Argentine exports per km railway length *(000 gold pesos)*
1881	n.a.	74	25	5·40	23·05
1882	7·1	68	43	6·04	22·80
1883	1·8	61	54	5·75	18·96
1884	5·9	63	63	7·34	18·70
1885	1·8	55	94	4·63	18·66
1886	11·2	70	79	4·68	11·99
1887	11·3	84	107	4·83	12·56
1888	23·4	119	139	5·05	13·21
1889	12·3	123	220	2·36	15·11
1890	4·9	117	30	2·63	10·71
1891	0·0	58	−30	1·74	8·24
1892	1·2	40	29	1·77	8·25
1893	0·6	32	36	1·90	6·79
1894	0·0	48	39	2·04	7·27
1895	0·6	78	44	2·59	8·51
1896	0·2	69	89	3·05	8·09
1897	1·0	78	48	2·31	6·77
1898	3·6	77	42	2·70	8·67
1899	1·6	78	49	3·59	11·28
1900	1·5	50	50	3·33	9·34
1901	4·9	50	46	3·67	9·94
1902	3·2	89	17	3·62	10·29
1903	5·1	83	38	4·51	12·01
1904	4·1	88	94	4·99	13·58
1905	12·1	129	139	5·14	16·31
1906	12·6	85	198	4·95	14·20
1907	14·3	116	120	4·35	13·39
1908	16·0	147	176	4·65	15·42
1909	21·7	176	141	4·71	16·02
1910	22·9	198	209	4·32	13·32
1911	16·7	169	110	3·99	10·82
1912	20·1	201	206	4·11	15·26
1913	12·0	217	145	4·17	14·89
1914	15·2	203	−61	2·77	10·41

Sources: As given in Appendix.

economy as a whole. Hence, given the availability and reliability of Argentine statistics for this period, the behaviour each year of export sales divided by the length of the railway system can reasonably be taken as a measure of capacity utilization in the whole economy.[8] When plotted, the data display the same sort of temporal pattern as the railway profit rate (see Figure 1).

This relationship can be expressed more precisely if we fit regression equation (7) for the period 1881–1914 with the railway profit rate (P) as dependent on export sales per kilometre of railway track (x—expressed in units of thousands of gold pesos per kilometre). This yields the following result (standard errors in brackets):

$$1881–1914 \qquad P_t = 0.650 + 0.257\ x_t \qquad R^2 = 0.665 \qquad (7)$$
$$\ (0.434)\ \ (0.032) \qquad d = 1.461$$

Given the nature of the information, it is pleasing to find the coefficient of x highly significant and R^2 comparatively high, with the Durbin–Watson statistic at a satisfactory level. From this we would seem justified in our approach to the factors determining the varying pull of Argentine prospects in the form of a development cycle. For the varying growth of track and its temporal pattern were influenced by the (earlier) enthusiasm—or revulsion—of the British investor, while exports depended both on world market conditions and on domestic production possibilities.

An important question now arises. To what extent do the regression results reflect short-term variations in the time series (such as the trade cycle, or even erratic fluctuations) or major movements which could be identified and called long swings?[9] Some impression of the significance of long swings can be derived from Table 1. Examination suggests that much of the observed correlations in the regressions derives from the association of the long-swing movements and can be thought of in terms of the suggested 'development cycle'. This point emerges more clearly when the data are plotted on a chart.

Circumstances specific to Argentina certainly influenced the pull of Argentine prospects on British new issues in this 'development cycle' fashion which emphasizes the type of project, the nature of finance, and the animal spirits of British investors to explain why the marginal efficiency of investment in Argentina exhibited long swings. Parts of the explanation for Argentina seem very different to that adduced for the Kuznets cycle (or long swings) in North America so that the similarity between the waves of overseas investment to North America and to Argentina may appear coincidental. Yet there are connections. The behaviour of certain primary product prices (cereals and meat especially) would affect both North American and Argentine prospects, and other common links were the state of European prospects and the receptiveness and interest of the London capital market in overseas ventures. Argentine experiences also indicate that over-precise explanations of the inverse behaviour of British home and overseas investment should be regarded with some caution and one should be prepared to allow more of a role to chance and to specific circumstances.

APPENDIX

Sources of series used:

U. K. Overseas Issues: M. Simon, 'The Pattern of New British Portfolio Foreign Investment, 1865–1914', in J. H. Adler (ed), *Capital Movements and Economic Development* (London, 1967).

U.K. Issues for Argentina: author's calculations from *The Economist* 'New Issues' sections.

Net U.K. Home Investment: C. H. Feinstein, 'Income and Investment in the United Kingdom 1856–1914', *Econ. Jour.*, 70 (June 1961), 374–84.

Net Immigration into Argentina: E. Tornquist, *The Economic Development of the Argentine Republic in the Last 50 Years* (Buenos Aires, 1919), p. 15.

Argentine Railway Length and Profit Rate: ibid., p. 117.

Argentine Exports: *Extracto Estadistico de la Republica Argentina correspondiente al año 1915*, Argentine Government Official Publication (Buenos Aires, 1916), p. 3.

NOTES

[1] Issues on the London Stock Exchange for Argentina were 8 per cent of total overseas 'calls' and it is assumed that this proportion could be applied to total overseas investment, a principal vehicle of which was overseas issues.

[2] See, for example, A. K. Cairncross, *Home and Foreign Investment 1870–1913* (Cambridge, 1953); Brinley Thomas, *Migration and Economic Growth* (Cambridge, 1954) and 'The Historical Record of International Capital Movements to 1913', in J. H. Adler (ed.), *Capital Movements and Economic Development* (London, 1967), and 'Migration and International Investment', in Brinley Thomas (ed.), *The Economics of International Migration* (London, 1958); M. Abramovitz, 'The Passing of the Kuznets' Cycle', *Economica*, 35 (1968), 349–67; J. Parry Lewis, *Building Cycles and Britain's Growth* (London, 1965).

[3] M. Wilkinson, 'Evidences of Long Swings in the Growth of Swedish Population and Related Economic Variables, 1860–1935', *Jour. Econ. Hist.*, 27 (Mar. 1967), 17–38.

[4] Allen C. Kelley, 'International Migration and Economic Growth: Australia, 1865–1935', *Jour. Econ. Hist.* 25 (Sept. 1965), 333–54.

[5] Similar conclusions follow if just P and I are used as explanatory variables:

$$1883-1913 \qquad A_t = -0.228 + 2.495P_{t-1} \qquad -0.0181_t \qquad R^2 = 0.219$$
$$ \qquad (5.075)\ (0.921) \qquad (0.036) \qquad d = 0.696$$

$$1884-1912 \qquad A_t = -4.441 + 3.226P_{t-2} \qquad -0.00069I_t \qquad R^2 = 0.357$$
$$ \qquad (5.192)\ (0.878) \qquad (0.035) \qquad d = 0.593$$

Comparison of these with (1a) and (2a) makes it clear that the introduction of I alone has virtually no explanatory power for the longer period.

[6] For example, years 1–5   Influx of foreign funds and construction starts;
           year 6   Speculative excesses, crisis, end of loans;
           years 4–8   Completion of investment projects;
           years 7–11   Output builds up and absorbs capacity;
           year 9   Profits start to improve;
           years 10–14   Continued revival of profits convinces lenders that prospects are attractive enough again.

[7] The underlying capital stock-adjustment view bears some resemblances to that suggested and tested for the 'adolescent' and 'maturity' phases of investment in American railroads. See J. Kmenta and J. G. Williamson, 'Determinants of Investment Behaviour: U.S. Railroads, 1872–1941', *Rev. Econ. and Stat.*, 48 (1966), 172–81.

[8] No estimates of export prices are available for the whole period to deflate export values, but because of the method of compilation of export values with fixed valuations for certain commodities, they present more of a fixed price picture than might be thought of at first. Export values also were relevant for import purchases which also had to be carried by rail.

[9] See Allen C. Kelley, 'International Migration and Economic Growth: Australia, 1865–1935', *Jour. Econ. Hist.*, 25 (Sept. 1965), 334–5.

Some Aspects of Postwar Growth in the British Economy in Relation to Historical Experience

R. C. O. MATTHEWS

Editor's note. This article was first published in the *Transactions of the Manchester Statistical Society* (1964–5), 1–25.
   Rates of growth and their calculation are mentioned above, p. 29. For further reading see Floud (1973), ch. 6; growth rates are normally calculated with the help of published tables. Correlation and regression analysis are discussed above, pp. 15–25, and numerous references to further reading are given in the footnotes to those pages. The calculation of weighted and un-weighted indices is further discussed in Allen (1966), ch. 6.

THE purpose of this paper is to present and discuss certain data on movements in output and input in the British economy in the postwar period, viewed in relation to trends over the past 100 years. This work is part of a research project sponsored by the Social Science Research Council of New York on the growth of advanced economies in the postwar period in relation to their historical experience. The part of this project that is concerned with Great Britain is being carried out in Cambridge by C. H. Feinstein, J. Odling-Smee and myself. Our work is still at a relatively early stage, and all the statistics to be quoted in this paper should be regarded as preliminary and subject to revision. Any conclusions to be drawn are still more provisional.

Section I deals with trends in aggregates of output and inputs since 1855. Sections II and III compare the interwar and postwar periods in more detail, with sectoral breakdowns.

The statistics are derived partly from published sources and partly from our own estimates. Dr. Feinstein has done the lion's share of the work in preparing these basic data, while most of the detailed work on the present paper has been done by Mr. Odling-Smee.

I

Annual data on G.D.P., employment in man-years, G.D.P. per man-year, capital, and output per unit of input are displayed in Chart I. Shaded periods are recessions.[1] We shall discuss each of the series in turn. Growth rates over four peace-time subperiods are summarized in Table 1.

TABLE 1. *Annual Percentage Rates of Growth*
of Output and Inputs in United Kingdom

	Real G.D.P.	Employ- ment in man-years	Capital	G.D.P. per man-year	Growth due to:	
					Residual	Change in capital per man
1856–1899	2·0	0·9	1·3	1·1	0·9	0·2
1899–1913	1·1	1·0	1·8	0·1	−0·2	0·3
1924–1937	2·3	1·2	1·7	1·1	0·9	0·2
1948–1962	2·5	0·6	2·7	1·9	1·3	0·6

Income and Income Per Man-Year

The peace-time rate of growth of G.D.P. at constant prices,[2] as shown in Table 1, has been relatively stable over the past 100 years, with the exception of the period 1899–1913, when it was conspicuously lower. There is a slight acceleration of growth between the three periods 1856–99, 1924–37 and 1948–62, but not too much should be made of this, because of the margin of error in the statistics, especially for the earlier years. As is well known, the rate of growth has not in any period come near to the 4 per cent level currently accepted as a target. As may be seen from the chart, the rate of growth has suffered a conspicuous set-back in both war periods (here defined as 1914–24 and 1938–48 to include postwar readjustment).[3]

In some respect more illuminating is the movement over time of G.D.P. per man-year. This shows some of the same features as G.D.P., such as retardation 1899–1913, but there are also certain differences: the downward shift over World War I is less pronounced (because the downward shift in G.D.P. was largely due to the increase in unemployment), and the acceleration in the period since World War II is a good deal more pronounced. The picture is much confused by the two wars, both of which led to a fall in productivity that was not quickly made up. Only very recently has G.D.P. per man-year regained the level to be obtained by extrapolating the interwar rate of growth over the interval comprised by World War II.

Whereas in modern times G.D.P. per man-year has generally fluctuated with the trade cycle, before 1914 the cyclical movement of G.D.P. per man-year was irregular. This irregularity, together with the unusually high level of production and productivity around 1900, makes it possible to read different interpretations into the record of the earlier period. On the one hand, one can say that there was a period of stagnation 1900–13, which was prolonged by the effects of World War I and by the relatively slow growth of the 1920s. Alternatively, one can argue, as Mr. Coppock has done,[4] that there was retardation already from the 1870s, culminating in actual cessation of growth 1900–13, but interrupted by an unrepresentative flash in the pan from 1897 to 1902.

CHART 1. *Output and Inputs 1855–1963* (log scale)

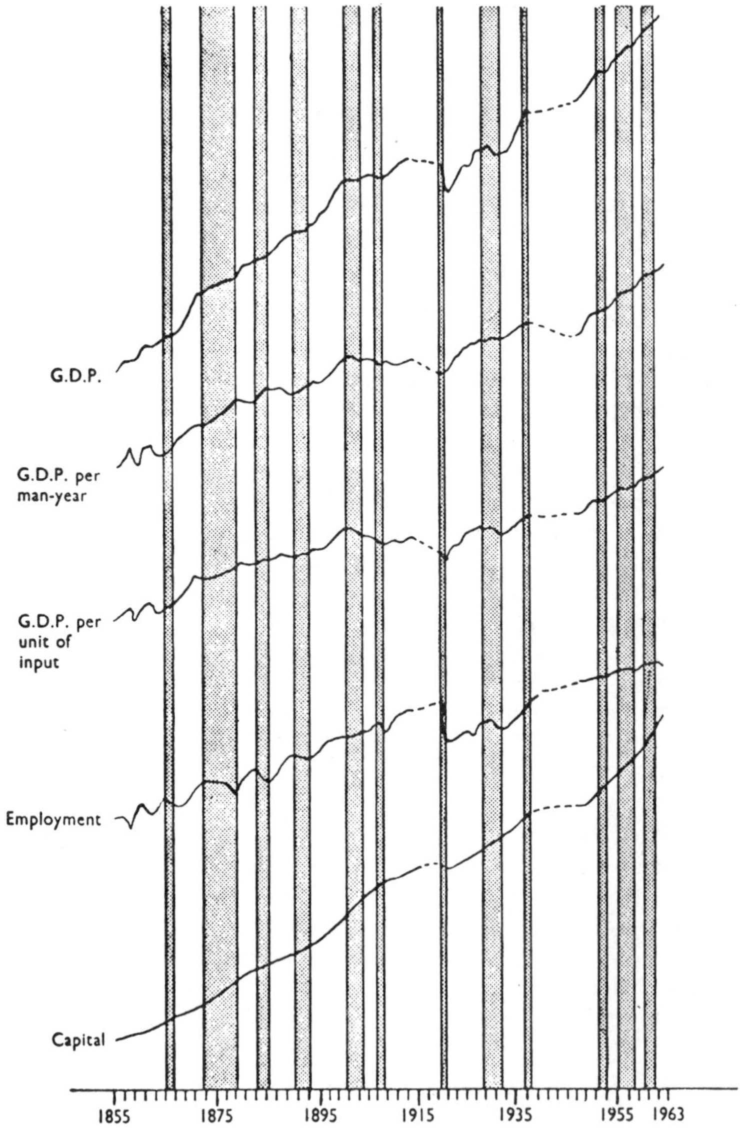

G.D.P.

G.D.P. per
man-year

G.D.P. per
unit of
input

Employment

Capital

1855   1875   1895   1915   1935   1955 1963

Both interpretations agree in identifying three broad phases in the economic history of the past hundred years: an initial phase of fairly rapid growth, terminating in the 1870s or in 1900 as the case may be; a doldrums period, running from then until the early 1930s; and a concluding period of faster growth, beginning in the 1930s, interrupted by World War II, and carrying on up to the present time.

Employment

As may be seen from Table 1, the rate of growth of labour input measured in man-years has been low in the postwar period by the standards of earlier peace-time phases. This has been due mainly to demographic causes; but the pattern of growth shown by the labour force is not identical to that shown by the population.

The level of unemployment did not alter much between the opening and closing years of each of the four peace-time phases we have distinguished, so the rate of growth of employment within them was closely similar to that of the labour force. Decennial data on the labour force are shown in Table 2.[5] It may be seen that the rate of growth of population since World War I has been about half of what it was previously. Before World War I, the rate of growth of the labour force did not differ much from that of population. Since then there has been more divergence between the two. In the interwar period, although the

TABLE 2. *Labour Force in United Kingdom*

	Annual rate of growth since last date			*Crude participation rates*			*15–64 year-olds as % of total population*	*Participation rates relative to population aged 15–64*		
	Popu-lation	*Labour Force Total*	*Male*	*Female*	*Total*	*Male*	*Female*		*Total*	*Male*	*Female*
1861	0·6	0·8	0·7	1·0	45·1	63·6	27·6	60·2	75·0	107·5	45·1
1871	0·9	0·8	0·7	0·9	44·6	62·4	27·8	59·0	75·7	107·7	46·5
1881	1·0	0·8	0·9	0·4	43·3	61·5	26·2	58·9	73·6	105·8	44·0
1891	0·8	1·0	1·0	0·8	44·1	63·0	26·3	60·2	73·3	105·8	43·2
1901	0·9	0·9	1·2	0·4	44·1	64·5	24·9	62·8	70·2	103·7	39·3
1911	0·9	1·0	1·0	1·0	44·6	65·2	25·2	63·6	70·2	103·3	39·3
1921[1]	0·4	0·5	0·5	0·4	44·8	66·3	24·9	65·9			
1921[2]					44·9	66·6	25·0		68·1	102·3	37·4
1931	0·4	0·6	0·5	0·8	45·4	66·4	26·2	68·2	66·6	98·0	34·9
1938	0·4	1·3	1·2	1·4	48·1	69·7	28·2	69·4	69·4	100·8	40·5
1951	0·4	0·3	0·1	0·7	47·3	66·8	29·2	66·5	71·1	100·5	43·9
1961	0·5	0·6	0·3	1·1	47·8	65·5	31·2	64·9	73·6	99·3	48·9

[1] Including Southern Ireland.
[2] Excluding Southern Ireland.

rate of population growth declined, the rate of growth of the labour force for a while increased. This was due mainly to an increase in the proportion of those of working age in total population. Because of this change in age composition, the full effect of the long-run decline in population growth on the labour supply was not felt until after World War II. There was also some increase in the interwar period in the proportion of women of the 15–64 age group who took employment. The continued increase in the participation rate of females is the main reason why in the postwar period the rate of growth of the labour force has been rather higher than that of population.

The slow rate of increase of the labour supply is something which differentiates the postwar period from earlier phases. The change is still more marked if one looks at the supply of male labour. Until World War II the rate of growth of supply of male labour was slightly greater than that of female labour. Between 1948 and 1962, on the other hand, the male working population rose by only 0·4 per cent per annum while the female working population rose by 1·3 per cent per annum. As a result, although females comprise only about a third of the total working population, they have contributed nearly two-thirds of the increase in the working population. The release of men from the Armed Forces, which may be regarded as a once-for-all decline in the importance of an industry requiring male labour, has meant that the relative contribution of women to the increase in civil employment has been less than this, but even so the increase in the number of females in civil employment has been absolutely larger than that of males. The increase in the female participation ratio that has brought about these results reverses the trend of 1871–1931 and has raised the rate to the highest level ever recorded. As is well known, it is mainly due to the increase in the participation rate of married women over 35.[6]

Capital

The concept of capital here used is the gross stock of reproducible fixed assets at constant prices. Capital is thus calculated before deduction of depreciation but after deduction of estimates of retirements. Inventories, land and mineral wealth, and overseas assets are excluded. The estimates for 1938–63 are taken from the work of G. A. Dean of the Central Statistical Office[7] and correspond to those in the 1964 National Income Blue Book. The estimates for earlier years are from unpublished work by Dr. Feinstein.

The growth of the capital stock is, as might be expected, subject to much less short-period fluctuation than the growth of output. Three main points stand out.

(1) The growth of the capital stock in the postwar period has been much faster than ever before. Since the labour force has been growing more slowly than before in the postwar period, the rate of growth of capital per man has outstripped that of previous periods by a still greater extent: capital per man has grown at a rate of 2 per cent a year, as compared with a rate of about ½ per cent in earlier periods. It is likely that some forms of capital accumulation are

insufficiently reflected in the data for the earlier years, so that the change may be somewhat overstated, and it must also be remembered that these figures take no account of accumulation of overseas assets, which in some years before 1914 was of the same order of magnitude as gross domestic fixed capital formation. But there can be no doubt that the rate at which domestic assets per man have accumulated in the postwar period is without parallel in the last 100 years.

(2) Net capital formation was brought to a standstill by both wars.

(3) Before 1914 a clear long cycle in the rate of growth of the capital stock is to be observed. This is to be compared with the long cycle found in many statistics of the United States economy but not found in any such clear form in series relating to output in the United Kingdom. Especial interest attaches to the long wave running from 1895 to 1914. From about 1898 to about 1903 the rate of growth of capital was conspicuously above trend. This is associated with the boom in home investment that developed in the late 1890s. It is tempting to relate it to the marked increase in the rate of growth of output per man that occurred in much the same years and which has already been referred to. But the slackening in the rate of growth of the capital stock in the ensuing period, 1904–14, is not sufficient to explain the stagnation of productivity during those years. As will be seen presently, the usual way of taking account of changes in capital input, by the output per unit of input method, does not smooth out the peak around 1900 and the subsequent stagnation. There is scope for further study and more sophisticated hypotheses relating to this peculiar period.

Capital-Output Ratio

Chart 2 shows the capital-output ratio at constant prices.[8] The largest movements shown are the fall from 1866–1871 and the rise across World War I, reversed across World War II. The first of these is perhaps too ancient and too dubious statistically to be worth very close study. The high capital-output ratio shown for the interwar period is influenced by the general unemployment and below-capacity working of that time (the capital figures are, of course, not corrected to allow for the degree of utilization); this consideration is of about the right order of magnitude to account for the higher level of the ratio in the interwar period compared with the periods before and after.

Excluding the interwar period and the years before 1870, the capital output ratio has varied only within a fairly narrow range—roughly from $3\frac{1}{2}$ to $4\frac{1}{4}$, which is hardly larger than the margin of error in the capital stock statistics. The decline across the period of World War II is a good deal less pronounced than it has been in the United States, where the capital-output ratio postwar has been about only two-thirds of its 1929 value. And this notwithstanding that there has been a greater change in the level of activity in this country since 1929 than in the United States. The *long-run* downward tendency in the capital-output ratio appears to have been both less continuous and of smaller

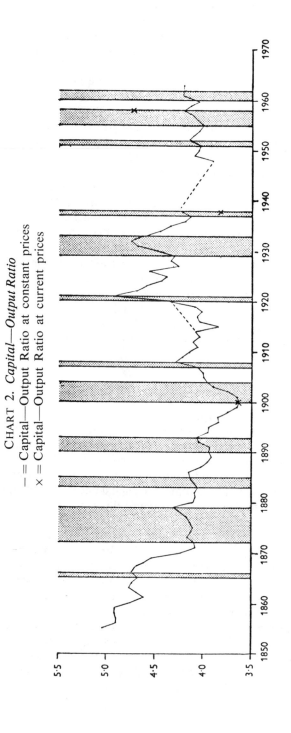

CHART 2. *Capital—Output Ratio*
— = Capital—Output Ratio at constant prices
× = Capital—Output Ratio at current prices

amplitude in this country. Indeed, at least as far as the period since 1870 is concerned, it cannot be taken as established that there has been such a long-run downward tendency.

If the movements in the capital-output ratio at constant prices are thought to be not large enough to warrant any firm conclusions, still more doubts are engendered by comparing them with data on the capital-output ratio at current prices. These are available only for the three years 1900, 1938, and 1958, which are shown by crosses on Chart 2. It will be seen that whereas the capital-output ratio fell in constant prices between 1938 and 1958, it rose considerably in current prices. This is because capital-goods prices rose relatively to prices in general. The measurement of price changes across the war is inevitably untrustworthy, especially in view of the conceptual and practical difficulties involved in making allowance for improvements in quality of capital goods. But the change recorded is such a large one that it is difficult to attribute it wholly to defects in the statistics.[9]

One way of analysing this type of data is in terms of the tautologies suggested by the Harrod growth model. The rate of growth of the capital stock, K, is equal to the average propensity to save, s, divided by value-capital-output ratio; the rate of growth of total output, Y, is equal to s divided by the incremental capital–output ratio ($ICOR$). Economists in the OECD and others who have written comparing the postwar growth experience of different European economies have made much use of this approach. The relevant figures are shown in Table 3. Because of the importance of changes in relative prices of capital goods, this price has been included as a separate item. The figures for s are therefore at current prices and those for the capital-output ratio at constant prices. s is measured net of replacement.

Looking first at the data for capital we note that the rise in the rate of growth of capital in the postwar period compared with earlier is wholly due to the rise in s. The value-capital-output-ratio (measured in Table 3 by the reciprocal of the product of the last two columns) has risen, on account of the large rise in capital-goods prices. The rise in $\Delta K/K$ has therefore been rather less than the rise in s. The same applies still more strongly in the case of Y; the value-incremental-capital-output ratio has risen substantially and the rise in $\Delta Y/Y$ compared with prewar has come about because the rise in s has been even larger.

All this of course is just a tautological way of arranging the data and no causal significance is necessarily to be inferred. In particular the $ICOR$ seems to me to be a concept with little economic significance. But perhaps it is of some interest to note the contrast between these findings and the findings that have come out from comparison of different countries in the postwar period. These have usually shown that although the faster-growing countries have had higher s than slow-growing ones, this difference has been smaller and has contributed less to differences in growth rates than the difference in $ICOR$s.[10] In the historical comparison, on the other hand, as has just been seen, the higher growth is entirely due to s, and the movement in the $ICOR$ actually works in

TABLE 3. *Growth Rates, Savings Ratios and
Capital-Output Ratios*

$$\frac{\Delta K}{K} = \frac{\Delta K p_k}{Y p_y} \times \frac{Y}{K} \times \frac{p_y}{p_k} = s \times \frac{1}{K/Y} \times p$$

$$\frac{\Delta K}{K}(\%) = s(\%) \times \frac{1}{K/Y} \times p \ (1900 = 100)$$

1856–1899	1·3	5·5	0·22	108
1899–1913	1·8	6·6	0·25	111
1924–1937	1·7	6·7	0·20	124
1948–1962	2·7	13·0	0·25	82

$$\frac{\Delta Y}{Y} = \frac{\Delta K p_k}{Y p_y} \times \frac{\Delta Y}{\Delta K} \times \frac{p_y}{p_k} = s \times \frac{1}{ICOR} \times p$$

$$\frac{\Delta Y}{Y}(\%) = s(\%) \times \frac{1}{ICOR} \times p \ (1900 = 100)$$

1856–1899	2·0	5·5	0·34	108
1899–1913	1·1	6·6	0·15	111
1924–1937	2·3	6·7	0·28	124
1948–1962	2·5	13·0	0·24	82

the wrong direction. It may be conjectured, therefore, that the reasons why the British economy has grown faster in the postwar period than earlier are unlikely to turn out to be the same as the reasons why other countries have grown faster than Britain in the postwar period—not perhaps a very surprising conclusion.

The uniqueness of the postwar period does stand out from these comparisons. If we look at the last period when $\Delta K/K$ for a while was at a level close to the postwar level, namely in the late 1890s and early 1900s, we find that although s was relatively high, a temporarily low K/Y did also contribute significantly to achieving the high $\Delta K/K$ then recorded.

Output Per Unit of Input

This has been calculated by a method that is broadly speaking that of Kendrick.[11] An index for total factor input is derived within each subperiod by weighting labour and capital according to their shares in total income in a base year. The indices for the subperiods are then spliced together, and the resulting series is divided into G.D.P. at constant prices to give output per unit of input.[12] The rate of growth of output per unit of input is the so-called Residual factor in economic growth, measuring that part of the growth in output that is due to causes other than growth in the labour force or capital accumulation.

The limitations of this approach to the analysis of economic growth are well known and need not be repeated here. Not only does its validity depend on certain assumptions implicit in weighting capital and labour according to their shares in income, but also, at best, the 'Residual' is no more than a measure of unknown forces and is not necessarily to be identified with 'technical progress' in the usual sense. My own opinion is that the approach *does* have usefulness, but as a starting-point of research rather than as its conclusion. Inspection of trends in the Residual helps to call attention to the questions most needing examination. Unfortunately in the present paper it is not possible to go much beyond the starting-point.

In general outline, the movement of output per unit of input is similar to that of output per man-year. We find a period of retardation running from about 1900 (or perhaps earlier) until about 1930, followed by more rapid growth. The rate of growth since World War II is higher than in any earlier phase, but the difference is rather less marked than in the case of output per man-year because part of the high postwar rate of growth is accounted for by the high rate of capital accumulation. Table 1 shows the parts of the growth in output per man-year attributable in each period to the Residual and to the rise in capital per man respectively. Apart from the anomalous period 1899–1913, the Residual is always responsible for much the greater part of the growth. However the increase in capital per man makes a larger contribution to growth, both absolutely and relatively, in the postwar period than either before 1900 or in the interwar period.

II

We now compare the two periods 1924–37 and 1948–62 in more detail.

Year-to-year movements in output per unit of input have been calculated for these two periods; but for present purposes we are interested in long-term movements rather than annual fluctuations, so we confine our attention to the rates of growth between the terminal years of the periods. For the interwar period this does not raise any great problems, since 1924 and 1937 were years with roughly similar levels of activity. (The unemployment percentage was 10·3 in 1924 and 10·8 in 1937.) The years 1948 and 1962 are not quite so similar, for 1962 was a recession year and 1948 can be regarded as still falling within the period of postwar reconstruction. But they are similar in both falling below the trend-line of productivity, and rates of growth between 1948 and 1962 are not very different from those that would be obtained by fitting a trend-line or else by taking a peak-to-peak comparison 1951–60.

Growth rates for G.D.P. and its chief subdivisions are shown in Table 4. 'Production and distribution' is a term used to describe those sectors that are represented in the index of industrial production (manufacturing, mining, construction and utilities), together with agriculture, transport and communications, and distribution.

The most striking conclusion that appears is that the higher Residual (rate of growth of output per unit of input) in the postwar period in G.D.P. as compared with interwar owes nothing to manufacturing or the other items included in industrial production but derives entirely from the better performance

TABLE 4. *Annual Growth Rates of Output and Input by Sector*

	Output		Employment		Capital		Total input		Residual	
	1924–37	1948–62	1924–37	1948–62	1924–37	1948–62	1924–37	1948–62	1924–37	1948–62
G.D.P.	2·3	2·5	1·2	0·6	1·7	2·7	1·4	1·2	0·9	1·3
Manufacturing	3·3	3·4	1·1	1·1	0·9	3·1	0·9	1·7	2·4	1·7
Industrial production	3·2	3·2	0·9	0·9	1·4	3·4	1·0	1·6	2·2	1·6
Services and distribution	1·6	2·0	2·2	0·7	2·6	2·7	2·3	1·3	−0·7	0·7
Production and distribution	2·6	2·9	1·0	0·7	0·9	2·9	1·0	1·3	1·6	1·6

in services and distribution. This point had already been noted[13] in statistics of the rate of growth of output per man, and it stands out still more prominently when account is taken, as here, of capital input. As far as industrial production is concerned, the position is simply stated: output grew at much about the same rate in the two periods, and so did employment, and hence output per man (the rise in employment in the industrial sector being less rapid than in the economy as a whole interwar and more rapid postwar). But the rise in the capital stock was much more rapid in the postwar period, especially in manufacturing.[14] Hence there was a faster rate of growth of total input, and the Residual was lower.

Before jumping to the conclusion that this represents a failure in industrial performance postwar, it should be emphasized that these calculations have important limitations. No allowance is made for the degree of utilization of capital. It is notorious that certain industries, notably the steel industry, were operating well below capacity in 1962. However the contrast between industrial production on the one hand and distribution and services on the other is beyond doubt. Output in distribution and services in the interwar period rose less rapidly than either employment or capital input, and the result was a substantial negative Residual. In the postwar period the Residual in distribution and services is substantially positive, though still less than in industrial production.

The hypothesis that naturally suggests itself is that in the interwar period the pressure of unemployment led to a concentration of under-employed labour in services and distribution. The question that then poses itself for the future is whether the gain in productivity in services and distribution since the war is likely to prove a once-for-all gain, due to adaptation to a tighter labour market, or whether this change in the labour market has unleashed forces of progress that will lead to continued advance.

So far the rates of increase in labour and in capital in each of the broad groups, manufacturing, etc., have been computed simply on the basis of the increase in the number of persons employed and in the value (essentially the cost at constant prices) of the capital employed. An alternative procedure is to weight different parts of the labour force and of the capital stock according to differences in their remuneration, on the grounds that higher remuneration reflects higher productivity. Table 5 shows the result of such a calculation, set against the unweighted figures already given. The weighted figures in this Table

TABLE 5. *Growth Rates of Weighted Factor Inputs*

	Labour		Capital		Factor input	
	1924–37	1948–62	1924–37	1948–62	1924–37	1948–62
G.D.P.	1·6	0·9	1·8	3·6	1·7	1·6
Manufacturing	1·5	1·3	1·1	4·0	1·4	2·1
Industrial production	1·5	1·1	1·4	4·4	1·5	2·0
Services and distribution	2·1	1·2	2·5	3·2	2·2	1·8
Production and distribution	1·5	0·9	1·2	4·0	1·4	1·8

Excess of Weighted over Unweighted Growth Rates

	Labour		Capital		Factor input	
G.D.P.	0·4	0·3	0·1	0·9	0·3	0·4
Manufacturing	0·4	0·2	0·5	0·9	0·5	0·4
Industrial production	0·6	0·2	0·0	1·0	0·5	0·4
Services and distribution	−0·1	0·5	−0·1	0·5	−0·1	0·5
Production and distribution	0·5	0·2	0·3	1·1	0·4	0·5

are derived by taking separately the data for each industry specified in section III below and weighting the increase in labour and capital in those industries by their base-year rate of remuneration.[15] The lower part of the table shows the difference between the weighted growth rates and the corresponding unweighted growth rates given in Table 4.

Where, as in most cases, the weighted index is higher than the unweighted index, it means that there has been a rapider-than-average rise in employment (or capital) in industries where the wage (or the rate of profit) is above average. This can be due to a number of causes, corresponding to different possible causes of the differences in rates of remuneration. Inter-industry differences in wages may reflect differences in the quality of the labour force employed, or else they may reflect imperfect mobility of labour of given quality between different industries. In the former case, an excess of the weighted over the unweighted measure of the growth of labour input implies an improvement in the average quality of the labour force; in the latter case it implies a move towards greater efficiency in the allocation of labour between industries. Similarly differences in the rate of profit may reflect imperfect allowance for quality in the measures used for capital, or they may reflect a failure of the system to achieve equimarginal returns; and corresponding alternatives follow in the interpretation of a difference in weighted and unweighted measures of the rate of growth of the capital stock. This difference we shall refer to as the quality-shift change. It is, of course, a statistical measure that has to be understood in the light of the way it is constructed, and it does not claim to be a comprehensive measure of all the benefit derived from changes in the allocation or quality of factor inputs throughout the economy.

Looking first at the figures for labour, we find that in both periods the aggregative figures (G.D.P.) show a sizeable quality-shift change, indicating an improvement in the quality and/or allocation of the labour force. This change is slightly smaller postwar than interwar. The increasing proportion of females in the labour force in the postwar period has tended to produce a negative quality-shift change, because females earn less than males; the magnitude of the negative quality-shift change due to the change in sex-composition in the economy as a whole is −0·1. This is the same as the reduction in the overall quality-shift change in labour between the two periods, and it follows that the magnitude of the quality-shift change due to forces other than changing sex-composition has been the same in the two periods. But this upshot is the net result of opposite movements in services and distribution and in the rest of the economy. The inter-war quality-shift change was actually negative within services and distribution, indicating an above-average rate of increase in the worse-paid sectors. This again is consistent with the notion of labour surplus forcing people into low productivity employment—not merely into services and distribution generally, but into the worse-paid parts of the services and distribution sector. Outside services and distribution the postwar quality-shift change has been less than interwar.[16] To that extent some support is given to the commonly held notion that shifts in industrial structure made a more important contribution to productivity growth interwar than postwar.

In the case of capital, the picture is rather different. Again we find a negative quality-shift change in services and distribution interwar but in all sectors the quality-shift change was (algebraically) larger postwar than interwar. This has to be viewed in relation to the much more rapid overall rate of capital accumulation postwar. The faster the rate of capital accumulation, the more scope there is for increasing the proportion of the capital stock in the sectors with an above-average rate of return. This is evidently what has happened. Relatively to the rate of capital accumulation the quality-shift change in capital interwar was somewhat higher than postwar, although, as has been stated, it was lower absolutely.[17]

The net result of the opposite trends in quality-shift change for labour and capital in manufacturing has been that the overall quality-shift change has been fractionally lower postwar than interwar. It appears that the interwar period saw a more effective redistribution of labour within manufacturing than the postwar period, but the higher postwar rate of capital accumulation has made possible a larger reallocation of capital within manufacturing. In services and distribution there has been a strong increase in the benefit derived from the quality-shift change, on the side of both capital and labour. The upshot has been that for G.D.P. as a whole, the overall quality-shift has increased slightly.

III

In this section we carry further the comparison of the interwar and postwar trends by examining individual industries.

The data on rates of growth of output and input are shown in Table 6. As noted above, for the economy as a whole and for broad groups of industries, the movements between the years 1924 and 1937 on the one hand and 1948 and 1962 on the other provide a fair measure of trends within the two periods, despite the imperfect comparability of 1948 and 1962; but for a small number of individual industries, the choice of these terminal years produces an obviously misleading result, mainly because of contractions in output 1960–2. We have dealt with this by using rates of growth between the peak years 1951 and 1960 instead of between 1948 and 1962 in the case of these industries.

We find that each of the four main groups outside industrial production (agriculture, transport, distribution, and services) show a higher Residual postwar than prewar, and so contribute to the higher Residual found for G.D.P. In the case of services, the capital stock cannot be allocated accurately between sectors, and the output figures are subject to the usual difficulties experienced in measuring this part of G.D.P. The results must therefore be treated with reserve. However the same conventions are adopted for measuring output in both periods, and moreover the higher postwar Residual in services comes about mainly from the lower rate of growth of labour input, which is reasonably free from statistical ambiguity. Therefore there is no reason to doubt the broad conclusion.

Comparison of the behaviour of other industries produces a confusing picture, and more work is needed to unravel the relationships that may be involved.

We note first that the conclusions to be drawn about the relative performance of different industries on the basis of the Residual conform quite closely, but not perfectly, to the conclusions that would be drawn on the basis of the more familiar concept, rate of growth of productivity per man. This is as to be expected. Discrepancies arise chiefly in the case of industries where there has been exceptionally rapid capital accumulation, such as chemicals and bricks, pottery and glass. In agriculture the rate of capital accumulation has not been above the average absolutely, but it has taken place at the same time as a rapid reduction in the labour force. Textiles are an exceptional case where a sharp fall in capital stock is recorded because of abnormal scrapping so that total factor input has fallen more rapidly than employment.

Although the two industries with the highest Residual postwar (vehicles and utilities) are both what would popularly be regarded as 'growth' industries, by no means all the industries that are known to have undergone large-scale

TABLE 6. *Rates of Growth by Industry*

	Output		Employment		Capital		Factor input		Residual	
	24–37	48–62	24–37	48–62	24–37	48–62	24–37	48–62	24–37	48–62
Agriculture	1·3	2·6	−1·2	−1·8	−0·1	2·5	−1·0	−0·2	2·3	2·8
Food, drink, and tobacco	2·8	2·5	1·4	1·8	0·5	3·9	1·0	2·8	1·8	−0·3
Chemicals	3·1	5·7	1·4	1·5	1·6	6·5	1·5	4·0	1·6	1·7
Iron and steel[1]	3·0	3·1	0·7	0·7	0·7	4·6	0·7	2·2	2·3	0·9
Electrical engineering[1]	6·2	6·2	5·1	4·0	2·0	3·8	3·9	3·9	2·3	2·3
Non-electrical engineering[1]	1·8	2·0	1·0	1·1	0·2	4·0	0·8	1·8	1·0	0·2
Vehicles	6·3	5·6	3·0	1·9	3·0	3·8	3·0	2·2	3·3	3·4
Other metal manufacture[1]	4·5	2·1	1·8	1·1	1·6	3·2	1·7	1·7	2·8	0·4
Textiles	1·6	0·5	−0·8	−1·1	−1·1	−3·1	−0·9	−1·6	2·5	2·1
Clothing	2·1	2·2	0·1	0·2	1·9	1·1	0·3	0·4	1·8	1·8
Bricks, pottery, glass	4·6	3·2	2·3	0·8	−0·1	5·4	1·5	2·1	3·1	1·1
Timber and furniture	4·8	2·8	1·5	0·2	2·2	2·8	1·6	0·5	3·2	2·3
Paper and printing	2·8	5·3	1·7	2·3	2·0	2·7	1·8	2·4	1·0	2·9
Other manufactures	4·3	3·1	1·2	1·2	1·6	2·9	1·3	1·6	3·0	1·5
Mining	−0·4	−0·1	−2·7	−1·5	0·4	2·9	−2·0	−1·0	1·6	0·9
Construction	4·6	2·7	3·1	0·9	1·9	9·4	2·9	2·0	1·7	0·7
Gas, electricity, water	5·8	5·5	3·0	1·4	3·6	3·6	3·3	2·5	2·5	3·0
Transport and communications	1·5	2·1	0·6	−0·4	0·2	1·0	0·5	−0·1	1·0	2·2
Distribution	2·0	2·8	2·6	1·7	1·3	4·2	2·0	2·4	0·0	0·4
Total Services	1·5	1·7	1·9	0·3	3·0	2·4	2·2	0·9	−0·7	0·8
Insurance, banking, finance	1·7	3·5	1·9	2·2					−0·2[2]	1·3[2]
Professional services	1·4	3·3	1·7	3·0					−0·3[2]	0·3[2]
Miscellaneous services	1·6	0·9	2·2	−0·6					−0·6[2]	1·5[2]
Government	1·3	−0·8	1·6	−1·8					−0·3[2]	1·0[2]

[1] 1951–60, not 1948–62. [2] Rate of growth of output per man.

technical transformations within the postwar period show a high rate of technical progress, as measured by the Residual. The poor showing of iron and steel is notable in this regard.

Previous investigations, notably that of Salter,[18] have shown certain relationships between growth of rates of output and input in different industries. The best-known of these findings is that there tends to be a positive correlation between the rate of growth of an industry's output and the rate of growth of its productivity per man—sometimes known as 'Verdoorn's Law'.[19] This can be attributed partly to economies of scale, which permit increases in productivity when production rises, and partly to the lowering of price brought about by productivity increases, which stimulate demand and hence output. Table 7 shows the correlation found in our present data between the two variables mentioned above and also between certain other pairs of variables. The service industries are excluded in calculating these correlations, because of the statistical difficulties noted above.

TABLE 7. *Correlation Coefficients (r)*

Between	1924–37	1948–62
$\Delta Q/Q$ and $\Delta L/L$	0·85	0·76
$(\Delta Q/Q-\Delta L/L)$ and $\Delta Q/Q$	0·36[1]	0·61
R and $\Delta Q/Q$	0·59	0·51
R and $\Delta K/K$	0·19[1]	−0·33[1]
R, 1924–37 and R, 1948–62	0·33[1]	

[1] Regression coefficient not significantly different from zero at 5 per cent level.

Some positive correlation is found between $\Delta Q/Q$ and $(\Delta Q/Q-\Delta L/L)$ in both periods, but in the interwar period the regression coefficient is not significantly different from zero at the 5 per cent level. This result is in some contrast with that of Salter, who for a similar period (1924–35) found a value of r of 0·67.[20] Salter took a much finer breakdown of manufacturing than ours and included only two non-manufacturing industries (coalmining and electricity generation) in his sample of twenty-eight industries. It may be conjectured, therefore, that the Verdoorn relationship holds mainly within manufacturing. On *a priori* grounds this is not altogether surprising—certainly neither of the two possible explanations (scale economies and elastic demand) for the relationship cited above would apply with much force to industries such as construction and distribution.

A natural modification of the Verdoorn hypothesis would be to postulate a relationship between $\Delta Q/Q$ and R. Here again, as shown in Table 7, some relationship is found. This time the regression coefficient is significantly different from zero in both periods.

It is sometimes suggested that the share of the product going to capital (which is the weight used in our calculation of total factor input and hence of the Residual) understates capital's importance as the vehicle of technical progress. In so far as this hypothesis would lead one to expect that industries with a high $\Delta K/K$ would show a high R, it is not supported by our data. The correlation found between R and $\Delta K/K$ is of opposite sign in the two periods and statistically significant in neither. We hope at a later stage to test more sophisticated versions of the hypothesis which are based on the 'vintage' principle and require separate valuation of each year's addition to the capital stock, with higher weight being given to the more recent and hence presumably more productive additions.

The correlation between the interwar and the postwar residuals is low and not statistically significant. Support is therefore lacking for the view that certain industries have a persistently high rate of technical progress and certain other industries a persistently slow one.

The popular concept of a 'progressive' industry is perhaps at least as much concerned with the absolute level of productivity in an industry as with the rate of growth of productivity. In conclusion, therefore, we offer certain measures of comparative productivity between industries in an absolute sense.

Straightforward inter-industry comparisons of the value of output per man are vitiated by the differing capital intensity of different industries. In order to arrive at figures of value of output per unit of input we therefore define total factor input in an industry (F_i) by the expression

$$F_i = L_i + \frac{r}{w} K_i,$$

where L_i and K_i are inputs of labour and capital, measured in man-years and in value respectively, and r and w are the national average rate of profit on capital and wage-rate respectively. In the economy as a whole w/r units of K earn the same amount as one man; the above expression therefore gives a measure of total input in equivalent man-years. This may be divided into Q_i, the value of output in the industry, to give the value of output per unit of input. Column 1 of Table 8 gives figures of output per unit of input so calculated for 1948. These figures are subject to some serious statistical imperfections, in addition to possible conceptual objections, and should be regarded as extremely tentative and subject to revision (to an even greater extent than the other figures given in this paper).[21] What they measure is essentially a weighted average of the extent to which the wage and the profit rate in any industry depart from the national average.

Different wage-levels between industries may be the result of differences in the quality of the labour used. If all differences in wages were due to this cause, it would be appropriate to amend the above formula by multiplying L_i by w_i/w, the ratio of the wage in the industry to the national average wage, thus:

$$F_i = \frac{w_i}{w} L_i + \frac{r}{w} K_i.$$

Measures of output per unit of input calculated on this alternative basis are shown in column 2 of Table 8. The result provides measures of differences in the rate of return on capital between industries, weighted by the importance of capital in the industry.[22]

In comparing the absolute level of output per unit of input in an industry with its rate of growth over time (the Residual) two opposite hypotheses suggest themselves. Industries that are efficient in an absolute sense at the beginning of

TABLE 8. *Value of Output per Unit of Input in 1948 (G.D.P. = 1·00)*

	(1) *Labour unweighted*	(2) *Labour weighted*
Manufacturing	1·09	1·15
Food, drink, and tobacco	1·63	1·95
Chemicals	1·14	1·14
Iron and steel	1·13	1·00
Electrical engineering	1·17	1·19
Non-electrical engineering	1·00	1·02
Vehicles	1·04	0·92
Other metals	1·13	1·19
Textiles	0·88	1·11
Clothing	0·87	1·19
Bricks, pottery, glass	1·09	1·15
Timber and furniture	1·05	1·12
Paper and printing	1·11	1·07
Other manufacturing	1·12	1·30
Mining and quarrying	1·1	1·0
Construction	1·2	1·1
Gas, Electricity, and Water	0·7	0·6
Transport and Communications	1·0	0·9
Distribution	1·1	1·2
Production and distribution	1·1	1·1

a period may be industries that are go-ahead in all respects and therefore have a high Residual. Alternatively, industries may regress towards the mean: those with a low level of output per unit of input at the beginning of the period may have the greatest scope and inducement to improve and hence have the highest Residual. Calculation of the correlation between the absolute level of output per unit of input in 1948 and the Residual 1948–62 gives fairly firm support to the second of these hypotheses. With labour input unweighted by w_i/w the regression equation is $R = 5·04 - 3·25 q$, where q is the output per unit of input; r^2 is 0·324. With labour input weighted by w_i/w, the equation is $R = 4·16 - 2·35q$, with $r^2 = 0·334$. In both cases the coefficient of q is significantly different from zero at the 5 per cent level.

It would be premature to draw any resounding conclusions from the calculations that have been presented. Enough has been said to make clear that the postwar performance of the British economy in general compares favourably with that achieved in any previous period within the past 100 years. But it is also apparent that the improvement has not been uniform, and that in certain important areas the rate of growth achieved in the interwar period was higher.

NOTES

[1] For this purpose the dates of recessions are defined according to conventional cycle chronology, rather than according to the behaviour of any one of our series.

[2] The series used here for G.D.P. at constant prices, and also for the capital stock at constant prices, are derived by splicing together separate series for 1855–1900 at 1900 prices, 1900–48 at 1938 prices, and 1948–63 at 1958 prices.

[3] The drop over World War I is also partly due to Southern Ireland, which is included up till 1919 and excluded thereafter. This is responsible for a fall of about 5 per cent in G.D.P., but for a rise of about 1¼ per cent in G.D.P. per man-year.

[4] D. J. Coppock, 'The Climacteric of the 1890's: a critical note', *Manchester School*, 24 (Jan. 1956).

[5] 'Labour force' is here used in the same sense as 'working population' in British official statistics and includes employers and self-employed and also members of the Armed Forces.

[6] The data quoted in the text relate to employment measured in man-years, and take no account of changes in hours. Preliminary estimates of the annual rates of growth of labour input measured in man-hours over our four peace-time periods are as follows: 1856–99, 0·7; 1899–1913, 1·0; 1929–37, 1·4; 1948–62, 0·6. These are not used in the text, partly because more work needs to be done on the data, and partly because of certain doubts about matters of principle, notably about the propriety of adjusting labour input for changes in number of hours worked when a similar adjustment is not made for capital input.

[7] G. A. Dean, 'The Stock of Fixed Capital in the United Kingdom in 1961', *Jour. Roy. Stat. Soc.*, series A, vol. 127, part 3 (1964).

[8] The original series were computed at 1900 prices for 1855–1900, at 1938 prices for 1900–38, and at 1958 prices for 1938–63. The figures for the latter two subperiods were then spliced on to those for the first subperiod in order to give a continuous series.

[9] It may be noted that the primary data from which the capital stock figures are derived relate in some cases to quantities and in some cases to values, so it is not a clear-cut issue whether the current price measures or the constant price measures should be regarded as more reliable.

[10] See for example, United Nations Department of Social and Economic Affairs, *World Economic Survey 1959*, (New York, 1960), chap. 1.

[11] J. W. Kendrick, *Productivity Trends in the United States* (Princeton, for the National Bureau of Economic Research, 1961).

[12] Write F for total factor input, a and $(1 - a)$ for the shares of capital and labour respectively in the base year b, L for labour input, K for capital input, and subscripts for time. Then total factor input in any year t is given by

$$\frac{F_t}{F_b} = (1 - a)\frac{L_t}{L_b} + a\frac{K_t}{K_b}$$

This gives measures of F_t for the years within any subperiod. Different base years and different a's are used for each subperiod, and the results are spliced to give a single series for total factor input. The superiods, base years and a's used are as follows:

Period	Base year	a
1855–1894	1875	0·40
1894–1914	1906	0·40
1919–1938	1929	0·30
1938–1963	1956	0·26

[13] C. H. Feinstein, 'Productivity and Production, 1920–62', *London and Cambridge Economic Bulletin*, (Dec. 1963).

[14] The data on Capital in Table 4 relate to fixed assets. The inclusion of stocks and work-in-progress does not alter any of the conclusions in the text. The figures for Capital and the Residual for G.D.P. and Manufacturing are then as follows:

	Capital		Residual	
	1924–37	1948–62	1924–37	1948–62
G.D.P.	1·7	2·6	0·9	1·4
Manufacturing	0·9	3·3	2·3	1·6

[15] Writing L for labour, K for capital, F for total factor input, w for wage, r for the profit rate, denoting individual-industry figures by symbols with the subscript i and aggregative figures by symbols without subscripts, the definitions of the weighted rates of growth are

$$\frac{\Delta L}{L} = \sum \frac{\Delta L_i}{L_i} \frac{w_i}{w} \cdot \frac{L_i}{L}$$

$$\frac{\Delta K}{K} = \sum \frac{\Delta K_i}{K_i} \frac{r_i}{r} \cdot \frac{K_i}{K}$$

$$\frac{\Delta F}{F} = \frac{wL}{wL + rK} \cdot \frac{\Delta L}{L} + \frac{rK}{wL + rK} \cdot \frac{\Delta K}{K}$$

For discussion of this approach see B. F. Massell, 'A Disaggregated View of Technical Change', *Jour. Pol. Econ.*, (Dec. 1961). Weighted measures of inputs were also used in Kendrick's pioneering study referred to above.

[16] Changing sex-composition does *not* help to explain this, at least in the case of manufacturing, because in manufacturing, unlike the economy as a whole, the male labour force has increased faster than the female labour force in the postwar period. Changing sex-composition made a *positive* contribution of nearly 0·1 to the postwar quality-shift change within manufacturing. Changing sex-composition does not appear to have made any significant contribution in either direction to the interwar quality-shift change in manufacturing, though the calculations here are necessarily rough.

[17] The lower rate of growth of the labour force in the postwar period may likewise be held to be partly responsible for the lower quality-shift change in labour. But as far as the industrial sector is concerned, the rate of growth of employment was the same in the two periods, so the fall from 0·6 to 0·2 in the labour quality-shift change under this heading cannot be explained in this way.

[18] W. E. G. Salter, *Productivity and Technical Change* (Cambridge, 1960).

[19] P. J. Verdoorn, 'Fattori che regolano lo sviluppo della produttività del lavoro', *L'Industria* (1947).

[20] Salter, op. cit., p.·126.

[21] The capital data used do not include stocks and work in progress and rK_i/w is calculated from data at 1958 prices instead of at 1948 prices. Land is not included in the measure of capital; for this reason it seemed best not to give a figure for agriculture. A conceptual difficulty is that the present method makes no allowance for the fact that differences in (gross) rates of return on capital may be due partly to differences in the durability of capital. This consideration helps to explain the low level shown for output per unit of input in Gas, Electricity, and Water.

[22] It would of course not do to apply the same procedure as that just described to capital and multiply the second term in the above expression by r_i/r, because then everything cancels out and the value of output per unit of input comes out as equal by definition in all industries.

Bibliography

This is a select bibliography, consisting primarily of works referred to in the Introduction, together with some important works on quantitative history and related topics.

ALLEN, R. G. D., *Statistics for Economists*, London, 1966.

AMES, E., 'Trends, Cycles and Stagnation in U.S. Manufacturing since 1860', *Oxford Economic Papers*, n.s. 11 (1959).

ANDREANO, R. L. (ed.), *The New Economic History* (New York, 1970).

AYDELOTTE, W. O., *Quantification in History* (Reading, Mass., 1971).

BLALOCK, H. M., *Social Statistics* (New York, 1960).

BRADLEY, L., *A Glossary for Local Population Studies*, Supplement to *Local Population Studies*, Jan. 1971.

CONRAD, A. H., and MEYER, J. R. *Studies in Econometric History* (London, 1965).

DAVIS, L. E., EASTERLIN, R. A., and PARKER, W. N. (eds.) *American Economic Growth: An Economist's History of the United States* (New York, 1972).

DEANE, P. and COLE, W. A. *British Economic Growth, 1688–1959* (Cambridge, 1962).

DOLLAR, C. M. and JENSEN, R. J. *Historian's Guide to Statistics* (New York, 1971).

DURBIN, J. and WATSON, G. S., 'Testing for serial correlation in least squares regression', *Biometrika*, 37, 38 (1950, 1951).

FISHLOW, A., *American Railroads and the Transformation of the Ante-bellum Economy* Cambridge, Mass., 1965).

FLOUD, R. C., *An Introduction to Quantitative Methods for Historians* (London, 1973).

FOGEL, R. W., *Railroads and American Economic Growth: Essays in Econometric History* (Baltimore, 1964).

FOGEL, R. W. and ENGERMAN, S. L. (eds.) *The Reinterpretation of American Economic History* (New York, 1971).

HAWKE, G. R., *Railways and Economic Growth in England and Wales, 1840–1870* (Oxford, 1970).

HUGHES, J. R. T., 'Wicksell on the Facts: Prices and Interest Rates, 1844–1914', in Wolfe, J. N. (ed.), *Value, Capital and Growth: Papers in Honour of Sir John Hicks* (Edinburgh, 1968).

JOHNSTON, J., *Econometric Methods* (New York, 1963).

LASLETT, P. (ed.) *Household and Family in Past Time* (Cambridge, 1972).

LORWIN, V. R., and PRICE, J. M. (eds.) *The Dimensions of the Past: Materials, Problems and Opportunities for Quantitative Work in History* (New Haven, Conn., and London, 1972).

RABB, T. K., *Enterprise and Empire* (Cambridge, Mass., 1967).

RABB, T. K., 'On Nominalism and Idealism, Historical and Statistical: a Response to Roger Schofield', *Historical Journal*, 15 (1972).

ROWNEY, D. K. and GRAHAM, J. Q. (eds.) *Quantitative History* (Homewood, Ill., 1969).

SCHOFIELD, R. S. 'Sampling in Historical Research', in Wrigley, E. A. (ed.), *Nineteenth-century Society. Essays on the use of Quantitative Methods for the study of social data* (Cambridge, 1972).

SCHOFIELD, R. S., 'Computing, Statistics and History', *Historical Journal*, 15 (1972).

SIEGEL, S., *Non-parametric statistics for the Behavioural Sciences* (New York, 1963).

SHORTER, E., *The Historian and the Computer* (Englewood Cliffs, N.J., 1971).

TEMIN, P., *The New Economic History* (Harmondsworth, 1973).

WALTERS, A. A., *An Introduction to Econometrics* (London, 1968).

WRIGLEY, E. A. (ed.) *An Introduction to English Historical Demography* (London, 1966).

YEOMANS, K. A., *Applied Statistics: Statistics for the Social Scientist* (Harmondsworth, 1968).

INDEX TO STATISTICAL METHODS